797,885 Books
are available to read at

www.ForgottenBooks.com

Forgotten Books' App
Available for mobile, tablet & eReader

ISBN 978-1-330-70289-5
PIBN 10094464

This book is a reproduction of an important historical work. Forgotten Books uses
state-of-the-art technology to digitally reconstruct the work, preserving the original format
whilst repairing imperfections present in the aged copy. In rare cases, an imperfection in
the original, such as a blemish or missing page, may be replicated in our edition. We do,
however, repair the vast majority of imperfections successfully; any imperfections that
remain are intentionally left to preserve the state of such historical works.

Forgotten Books is a registered trademark of FB &c Ltd.
Copyright © 2015 FB &c Ltd.
FB &c Ltd, Dalton House, 60 Windsor Avenue, London, SW19 2RR.
Company number 08720141. Registered in England and Wales.

For support please visit www.forgottenbooks.com

1 MONTH OF FREE READING

at
www.ForgottenBooks.com

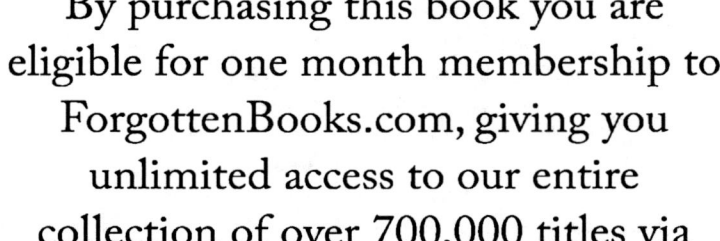

By purchasing this book you are eligible for one month membership to ForgottenBooks.com, giving you unlimited access to our entire collection of over 700,000 titles via our web site and mobile apps.

To claim your free month visit:
www.forgottenbooks.com/free94464

* Offer is valid for 45 days from date of purchase. Terms and conditions apply.

Similar Books Are Available from
www.forgottenbooks.com

Philosophy of Mind
An Essay in the Metaphysics of Psychology, by George Trumbull Ladd

Introduction to the Study of Philosophy
by J. H. W. Stuckenberg

Chance, Love, and Logic
Philosophical Essays, by Charles S. Peirce

The Philosophy of Common Sense
by Frederic Harrison

Elements of the Philosophy of the Human Mind, Vol. 1
by Dugald Stewart

Comte, Mill, and Spencer
An Outline of Philosophy, by John Watson

Light on the Path and Karma
by Mabel Collins

Methods of Knowledge
An Essay in Epistemology, by Walter Smith

Mysticism and Logic
And Other Essays, by Bertrand Russell

Auguste Comte and Positivism
by John Stuart Mill

Brahmadarsanam, or Intuition of the Absolute
Being an Introduction to the Study of Hindu Philosophy, by Sri Ananda Acharya

A Discourse on Method
Meditations on the First Philosophy; Principles of Philosophy, by René Descartes

Free Will and Human Responsibility
A Philosophical Argument, by Herman Harrell Horne

Ideal and Progress
by Sri Aurobindo Ghose

The Influence of Darwin on Philosophy, and Other Essays in Contemporary Thought
by John Dewey

The Art of Thinking
by Thomas Sharper Knowlson

Idealism and Theology
A Study of Presuppositions, by Charles F. d'Arcy

The Philosophy of the Future
by S. S. Hebberd

Philosophy of the Great Unconscious
by Samuel Eugene Stevens

What Is Philosophy
by Edmond Holmes

MAIN CURRENTS OF MODERN THOUGHT

A STUDY OF THE SPIRITUAL AND INTELLECTUAL MOVEMENTS OF THE PRESENT DAY

BY

RUDOLF EUCKEN

PROFESSOR OF PHILOSOPHY AT THE
UNIVERSITY OF JENA; AWARDED THE
NOBEL PRIZE FOR LITERATURE, 1908

TRANSLATED BY

MEYRICK BOOTH, B.Sc., Ph.D. (Jena)

NEW YORK: CHARLES SCRIBNER'S SONS
LONDON: T. FISHER UNWIN

(All rights reserved)

CONTENTS

	PAGE
TRANSLATOR'S INTRODUCTORY NOTE	9
AUTHOR'S PREFACE TO THE ENGLISH EDITION	15
PREFACE TO THE THIRD EDITION . . .	17
PREFACE TO THE FOURTH EDITION	21

INTRODUCTION:
    THE PRESENT STATE OF AFFAIRS AND THE TASK WITH WHICH IT
    PRESENTS US 23

A. THE FUNDAMENTAL CONCEPT OF SPIRITUAL LIFE

1. SUBJECTIVE—OBJECTIVE.
  (a) HISTORICAL 35
  (b) THE NINETEENTH CENTURY 44
  (c) THE POSITIVE POSITION . . 53
    1. Introduction 53
    2. The Fundamental Concept of the Spiritual Life 57
    3. The Relationship between Man and the Spiritual Life 60
    4. The Results as they affect the Concept of Truth 62

2. THEORETICAL — PRACTICAL (INTELLECTUALISM VOLUNTARISM).
  (a) HISTORICAL 64
  (b) VOLUNTARISM 70
  (c) PRAGMATISM . 75
  (d) OUR OWN POSITION: ACTIVISM 79
  (e) INTELLECT AND INTELLECTUALISM . . 81
    1. The Invasion of Modern Life by Intellectualism 82
    2. The Life-Process as the Foundation of Knowledge . 85
    3. The Quest for Truth and its Motive Power . 89
    4. Consequences in the Sphere of Knowledge . 93
    5. Consequences with regard to the History of Philosophy 96

3. IDEALISM—REALISM.
  (a) THE TERMS 99
  (b) THE CONFLICT OF PRACTICAL IDEALS 101
    1. Nineteenth-century Realism . 103
    2. The Limitations of the New Realism 105

CONTENTS

	PAGE
3. Criticism of the Traditional Forms of Idealism	107
4. The Problem of Reality	110
5. The Necessity for a New Idealism	113

B. THE PROBLEM OF KNOWLEDGE

1. THOUGHT AND EXPERIENCE (METAPHYSICS).
   - (a) HISTORICAL 119
   - (b) THE RIGHT OF AN INDEPENDENT PHILOSOPHY . . 129
   - (c) THE TENDENCY TOWARDS METAPHYSICS . . 141
   - (d) THE PURSUIT AFTER KNOWLEDGE: A GENERAL SURVEY . 149
   - (e) ESTIMATION OF RATIONALISM AND EMPIRICISM . . 155

2. MECHANICAL—ORGANIC (TELEOLOGY).
   - (a) ON THE HISTORY OF THE TERMS AND CONCEPTS . 165
   - (b) ON THE HISTORY OF THE PROBLEM . . . 169
   - (c) THE PRESENT-DAY CONFLICT 182
     1. The Philosophical Aspect of the Problem . . 182
     2. The Scientific Aspect of the Problem . . . 185
     3. The Problem in the Social Sphere . 189

3. LAW.
   - (a) HISTORICAL 195
   - (b) THE PROBLEM OF LAW IN THE MODERN WORLD . 201

C. THE WORLD-PROBLEM.

1. MONISM AND DUALISM.
   - (a) THE CONCEPTS: HISTORICAL AND CRITICAL REMARKS . 215
   - (b) THE MONISM OF TO-DAY 230

2. EVOLUTION.
   - (a) ON THE HISTORY OF THE TERM 240
   - (b) ON THE HISTORY OF THE CONCEPT AND PROBLEM OF EVOLUTION 242
   - (c) THE COMPLICATIONS AND LIMITATIONS OF THE MERELY EVOLUTIONARY DOCTRINE 255
   - (d) THE REQUIREMENTS OF A NEW TYPE OF LIFE . . 272

D. THE PROBLEMS OF HUMAN LIFE.

1. CIVILISATION (OR HUMAN CULTURE).
   - (a) ON THE HISTORY OF THE TERM AND CONCEPT . . 281
   - (b) CRITICAL 288
     1. The Nature and Value of Civilisation . . . 288
     2. The Problem of the Content of Civilisation . . 291
     3. The Uncertainty in the Relationship of Man to Civilisation . 294

CONTENTS

	PAGE
(c) THE REQUIREMENTS OF A TRUE CIVILISATION	298
1. The Necessity of a *D*eeper Foundation	298
2. The Necessity of an Inner Development of Civilisation	302

2. HISTORY.
(a) TOWARDS THE DEVELOPMENT OF THE PROBLEM . . . 308
(b) DEMANDS AND PROSPECTS 318
    APPENDIX: THE CONCEPT "MODERN" 330

3. SOCIETY AND THE INDIVIDUAL (SOCIALISM).
(a) THE RELATIONSHIP BETWEEN SOCIETY AND THE INDIVIDUAL   341
    1. Historical 341
    2. The Problems of To-Day:
        α. The Inadequacy of a merely Social Civilisation . 351
        β. The Inadequacy of a merely Individual Civilisation . 363
        γ. The Necessity for an Inner Overcoming of the Antithesis 373
(b) THE SOCIAL-DEMOCRATIC MOVEMENT . 374

4. THE PROBLEMS OF MORALITY.
(a) THE PRESENT INSECURE POSITION OF MORALITY . 385
(b) MORALITY AND METAPHYSICS 388
(c) MORALITY AND ART 393
    1. On the History of the Problem . . . 393
    2. The Problems of the Present Day:
        α. Modern Æstheticism . . 400
        β. The Position of Art in Modern Life 404

5. PERSONALITY AND CHARACTER.
(a) PERSONALITY 409
    1. On the History of the Term 409
    2. On the History of the Concept 412
    3. Investigation of the Problem 414
(b) CHARACTER 422
    1. On the History of the Term and Concept . . 422
    2. The Present Position 425

6. THE FREEDOM OF THE WILL.
(a) INTRODUCTION 431
(b) REMARKS ON THE DETERMINIST POSITION . . 434

E. ULTIMATE PROBLEMS.

1. THE VALUE OF LIFE.
    (a) INTRODUCTION: ON THE HISTORY OF THE TERMS . 447
    (b) THE PERPLEXITIES OF THE PRESENT SITUATION . 449

2. THE RELIGIOUS PROBLEM (IMMANENCE TRANSCENDENCE).
    (a) ON THE HISTORY OF THE TERMS 462
    (b) THE TREND OF THE MODERN WORLD TOWARDS IMMANENCE . 464
    (c) THE COMPLICATIONS IN THE CONCEPT OF IMMANENCE 467
    (d) THE REVIVAL OF THE RELIGIOUS PROBLEM . . . 469
    (e) THE DEMANDS MADE BY THE PRESENT POSITION OF RELIGION . 471

CONCLUSION 479

INDEX 481

TRANSLATOR'S INTRODUCTORY NOTE

THE present work is a translation of the 4th edition of the *Geistige Strömungen der Gegenwart* (Veit & Co., 1909).

I have endeavoured throughout to render the sense of the original in the simplest English I could command, but I have not attempted to secure exact literal accuracy. Considerable care has been taken to bring the terminology as far as possible into line with that employed in the other English translations of Eucken's works.

Eucken's earlier writings were historical, his constructive works being of comparatively recent date. *The Main Currents of Modern Thought* forms a link between the two periods; it starts from a broad historical basis and presses forward to positive construction. Here we may follow the growth of Eucken's philosophy, from its roots, lying far back in the historical work, to its full flower, as seen in the positive philosophy itself. While the Jena professor's other recent works concern themselves in the main with the general exposition of his convictions, the present study reveals in detail the extensive groundwork upon which these convictions have been built up, and in particular it illustrates the various steps by which the author has been led to adopt the concept of *the spiritual life* as the basis of his whole philosophy.

Eucken's method is one of elimination. One by one he examines the various attempts at a synthesis of life with which the thought of the day provides us. One by one they are found to be incomplete or to be involved in inner contradictions, while in each case it is seen that a recognition of *an independent spiritual life* would remedy the incompleteness or remove the contradiction. Far from being a mere assumption (as will certainly be supposed by those who are suspicious of the term "spiritual"), the spiritual life is thus seen to be nothing less than a necessity. Through its recognition alone can we explain the *known content of the universe*.

For those who are commencing a study of Eucken's thought a few words with regard to the exact meaning of the concept "spiritual life" may not be out of place. As this concept is the key to Eucken's whole philosophy, it is of the utmost importance that it should be clearly understood. The matter is perhaps best approached through a consideration of the most popular philosophy of the present day, namely, that general view of life which (whether it be called agnosticism, positivism, empiricism, materialism, or naturalism) declares that we know only that which is revealed to us through the senses, that man is not essentially anything more than a higher animal, and that there is no *spirit* (man's entire psychic life being regarded as no more than a mere product of natural forces); the higher is thus made entirely dependent upon the lower. Far different is the aspect of affairs when looked at from Eucken's point of view: the living spirit (or the spiritual life) now stands at the very centre of the universe, and is itself the most central and positive reality of which humanity can have any knowledge: "a spiritual life transcending all human life forms the ultimate basis of reality." This life is more primary than matter itself (the concept of matter being, in reality, one of the vaguest and most uncertain in the whole realm of thought). The recognition of an independent spiritual life is the first step towards all further knowledge and the first necessity of any adequate view of life as a whole. The spiritual life is not derived from any natural basis. It is not a product of evolution. It is superior to all time and to all change: "change (and with it evolution) is absolutely out of the question as far as the substance of spiritual life is concerned." It is entirely distinct from the whole realm of natural phenomena, and, as Eucken himself says, in spiritual life we have to do "with something essentially different from any process following natural laws." The spiritual life works within the natural sphere, but it works as an independent reality; it is itself superior to the whole mechanism of nature.

This life must be conceived of as something quite distinct from the human intellect and from every kind of merely human psychic life. The spiritual life is itself the foundation of truth and knowledge. It is cosmic, absolute and eternal.

It will at once be asked, If the spiritual life be thus independent and absolute, how can man have any part in it, how can it affect him? Why, in short, should we bother about it at all? In reply to this Eucken would maintain that man's relationship to the spiritual life is the most immediate and vital of all human interests, for this life is itself the *very centre of man's own being*. The spiritual life does not depend upon man, but man depends upon the spiritual life. In an external sense man may be natural, but in an internal sense he is spiritual, he belongs to the spiritual reality which is behind the whole universe. It is the spiritual life within him which distinguishes man from the animals and forms the root of his unique unifying capacity, as well as of his ethical and religious nature. Spiritual reality thus works *within* man, but it is not *of* man. Man attains to his spiritual self by rising above his human self; and only by thus rising does he become independent, for the merely human self is involved in a network of natural processes from which the spiritual life alone is free. The spiritual life is " a cosmic force operative in man"; here man finds a strength greater than his own. The ethical value of Eucken's philosophy lies in its recognition of a spiritual world of cosmic power and absolute and eternal values, a world set above the relativity of human affairs and yet present to man as an ethical imperative. Nor is the ethical point of view lightly to be ignored. A satisfactory philosophy of life must make room for man's ethical nature; as Balfour says (*The Foundations of Belief*, p. 356): "No unification of beliefs can be practically adequate which does not include ethical beliefs as well as scientific ones; nor which refuses to count among ethical beliefs, not merely those which have immediate reference to moral commands, but those also which make possible moral sentiments, ideals, and aspirations, and which satisfy our ethical needs. Any system which, when worked out to its legitimate issues, fails to effect this object can afford no permanent habitation for the spirit of man."

There can be no doubt that our inner life demands an authority which shall be objective and *absolute* (that is, truly authoritative), and at the same time present *within* man in such a way that its commands are felt to be inwardly compelling and not forced upon man by some external power. I should like to quote an extremely significant passage from Principal P. T. Forsyth's very valuable work *Positive Preaching and the Modern Mind* (p. 61); speaking of what he calls the "inmost authority" he says: "It emerges and wells up under psychological conditions, but it is not a psychological product . . it is not ourselves, it is objective. . . . The thing most immanent in us is a transcendent thing. . . ." In order to attain to this inner spiritual world man must fight a battle; he must overcome the resistance of his non-spiritual nature, which is in perpetual conflict with his spiritual self. The spiritual life is not immanent in man in such a fashion that he can possess it without effort; it is present "as a possibility"—it rests with us to lay hold of it. Man cannot participate in the spiritual life without continual and *active* effort; hence the name—*Activism*—which Eucken has assigned to his own type of thought. Eucken's philosophy is therefore marked by a strong dualism. There is a sharp division within man's own nature, a conflict of forces, a struggle for supremacy, a slow and laborious ascent to a world of new and permanent values, to "a new stage of reality." We read that "man stands at once *in time* and *above time*," that he lives "on the boundary of time and eternity, on the horizon where the two run together," and again that "man is the meeting place of different stages of reality, nay, of opposed worlds."

It is not, however, Eucken's intention that reality should finally be looked upon as falling apart into two separate worlds; on the contrary he regards spiritual life and nature as being, ultimately, stages of a single reality. Man, however, occupies a position at which a transition from the lower to the higher stage has to be effected. He must not therefore allow the distinction between nature and spirit to be obliterated. At the same time Eucken's ultimate goal is a *monism*—not naturalistic, as it is hardly necessary to point out, but spiritualistic in character.

"We have become insecure with regard to all our ideals, nay, with regard to our own being; we no longer draw upon a common groundwork of convictions, of uniting, directing, elevating forces. In spite of all subjective activity, an inner decline of life is unavoidable if this uncertainty should continue to spread." This brief quotation will suffice to indicate Eucken's attitude towards the life of to-day. He is profoundly convinced that the peoples of to-day, absorbed in the pursuit of material things, intent upon bettering their environment and intoxicated by the surprising triumphs of technical science, have increasingly lost touch with those central spiritual realities without which life can have no meaning or value. In a single phrase, the interests of the modern world are in the main *peripheral* rather than *central*. Eucken is not only a philosopher; he is a prophet. His aim is to lead humanity back to central realities, to act as a centripetal force in a world of centrifugal tendencies. He seeks to call attention to the great truth that the whole fabric of human civilisation rests ultimately upon a spiritual basis. It is his belief that the supreme need of the age is a comprehensive, positive philosophy of life to serve as a rallying point for the scattered and divided forces of humanity. The old syntheses of life, which were satisfactory in their day and generation, are now breaking up and there is need for a new and wider synthesis. Eucken is convinced that only through the recognition of an *independent spiritual life* can the chaos of modern opinions be made to give way to a broad and satisfying philosophy of life.

In conclusion I should like to express my warmest gratitude to Professor Boyce Gibson (now of Melbourne University), the author of *Rudolf Eucken's Philosophy of Life*, who looked through the greater part of the MS., making a large number of invaluable suggestions and clearing up many obscure points. As it is, my task has been a hard one, but without his kind help it would have been much more difficult.

MEYRICK BOOTH.

LETCHWORTH,
June, 1912.

AUTHOR'S PREFACE TO THE ENGLISH EDITION

The Main Currents of Modern Thought has met with a most friendly reception in Germany and in France, and it would give me very great pleasure should it win friends for itself within the English-speaking world. This work aims in the first place at counteracting the spiritual and intellectual confusion of the present day. I have sought to grasp the specific character of the age through a study of its more central problems; and with the object of liberating these problems from all that is accidental and momentary I have endeavoured to illuminate them from the standpoint of the historical development of humanity. At the same time, this historical treatment shows that spiritual evolution is a matter common to all civilised peoples; they have all actively participated in this evolution, and all are to-day called to the performance of great common tasks, by which they are raised above and beyond every national and political difference. Nothing is more certain to counteract the lamentable and dangerous hostility of great nations to one another than a better understanding of the complete solidarity of the various nations with regard to those great questions which concern humanity as a whole.

RUDOLF EUCKEN.

JENA,
June, 1912.

PREFACE TO THE THIRD EDITION

THE third edition differs even more from the second than did the second from the first. In the first edition the historical review formed the foundation of the work, while the discussion of the problems themselves was quite a secondary matter; in the second edition the discussion became far more independent, and in the third it obtained the full primacy. The book is above all an expression of a specific philosophical conviction as a whole, and claims to be considered in this light. This claim has had the effect of essentially altering the mode in which the material had to be presented; in particular, it demanded a more precise arrangement and division of the subject matter, extending even to the separate sections.

While carrying out these alterations, I believed myself able, at the same time, to retain the fundamental ideas of the earlier editions; the correlation of historical fact with spiritual reality on the one hand, and treatment under separate headings on the other. Both as a whole and in certain special discussions (which cannot now be anticipated) the book contends that the content of history is more than an object of scholarly research, and that, subject to definite assumptions, it may powerfully contribute to the uplifting of our own work. To start from special problems secures the advantage of tangible points of attack, from which it is possible to progress rapidly to some sort of conclusion. This method is certainly open to an objection; the general conviction underlying the whole does not as such receive adequate attention, nor is it set forth in continuous and connected argument. This defect is freely admitted. It is, however, so closely connected with the mode of treatment here adopted that it cannot be remedied. In this respect my earlier books will be found to a certain extent supplementary. The chief lack consists in the failure to provide an adequate epistemological groundwork, and my next book will be devoted to a thorough discussion of the theory of knowledge.

The different editions are held together, however, even more by a thoroughgoing fundamental conviction than by the method of treatment; by the conviction, namely, that the ground upon which our whole civilised life and scientific work stands is insecure; that this life not only contains an immense variety of individual problems, but that as a whole it needs a drastic revision and a thorough renewal. It is my belief that philosophy must participate in this endeavour; nay, that philosophy above all is here summoned to energetic co-operation. This has brought me into opposition to the main tendency of contemporary German philosophy, which believes itself able peacefully to continue its scientific work undisturbed by these questions and doubts. We thankfully and gladly recognise the valuable character of this work, more especially in the detailed development of the separate departments of knowledge; it has accomplished and is accomplishing much. But at the same time the right and the necessity of the more general problem must be insisted upon with all possible emphasis. In working in this direction we shall not allow ourselves to be in any way affected by the attitude which others may adopt towards this problem; we shall rely solely upon the inner necessity of the matter.

Recently, however, there have been a multitude of signs bearing witness to the fact that increasingly wide circles are becoming interested in the problems which we have taken up. The inner complications of our civilisation, nay, of our whole spiritual situation, are growing more and more obvious; we are becoming more and more conscious of serious lapses from truth, of a substitution of phrases for realities and stones for bread. Nothing less than the happiness and meaning of our own existence is at stake. Thus the desire for classification and consolidation makes itself felt with ever-increasing urgency and philosophy is being more and more imperatively called to lend its aid in the solution of these problems of life. New life-movements are ascending and men's minds are being swayed by new interests which bid them pursue new aims.

These inner changes have procured for my books an increasing number of friends and given me the consciousness of a close spiritual contact with the age, such as I was not previously able to enjoy. It is with peculiar pleasure that I welcome the interest of the young and growing generation, an interest which has grown with unexpected and increasing speed. I hope that this interest may also be extended to this book, and, in particular, I hope that it may assist in a further development of the problems which have here been treated in mere outline, and frequently, there is no doubt, very incompletely. For what we all see more or less clearly before us is ultimately nothing less than the idea of a new man and a new culture. A linking up of forces, an overcoming of all that is merely individual, the inception of a comprehensive movement, can alone enable us to make any progress in dealing with so gigantic a problem.

RUDOLF EUCKEN.

JENA,
February, 1904.

PREFACE TO THE FOURTH EDITION

THE fourth edition has not been so much altered in comparison with the third as was the third in comparison with the second. At the same time some important changes have been made. Several sections have been completely revised and one (that dealing with the Value of Life) has been newly added. All through there has been an effort to make the presentation more easy, the content more complete, the main theses more precise in form, and to grapple more directly with the problems of the age, thus giving the whole a more convincing and forcible form. Far more attention, too, has been given to foreign movements. I hope, therefore, that the new edition as a whole marks a distinct step forward.

RUDOLF EUCKEN.

JENA,
End of August, 1908.

INTRODUCTION

THE PRESENT STATE OF AFFAIRS AND THE TASK WITH WHICH IT PRESENTS US

IN examining the life and thought of to-day it is impossible not to be struck in the first place by the extreme confusion which prevails and the accompanying painful insecurity as to the real aim of life. On every side we perceive not only a division of humanity into factions, but often a division within the individual himself. This state of confusion and uncertainty may at first sight appear to be the result of historical traditions working themselves out. We are surrounded to-day by various tendencies which have come down to us from the past, and these are not infrequently hostile to one another; they constitute the heritage and burden that the labour of thousands of years has bequeathed to us. It is the fact of thus being torn by contradictions which more than anything else distinguishes modern culture from the simpler conditions of the Ancient World. The Middle Ages handed down a whole philosophy of life containing within itself modes of thought so fundamentally different as the Grecian and the early Christian, the artistic and the religious, the tendency to embrace life and the tendency to reject it; these were, however, rather pieced together than harmoniously combined. In opposition to this structural solution the Modern World brought forth a new life energy, the desire for the unhindered expansion of force and for complete dominion over the material world. The detailed development of this, however, led at once to a division within the Modern World itself. On the one hand, there was the soul, with its capacity for thought, demanding to rule the world and human life (intellectualism);

on the other was nature and its mechanism (naturalism). The nineteenth century, being an age of historical knowledge and close speculative reflection, threw such a painfully bright light on all these contradictions that it became impossible to ignore them any longer.

And what a wealth of experience is contained within the nineteenth century itself! Consider the profound changes it passed through, the separate phases of which, in spite of having outwardly dropped into the background, still remain inwardly near to us and incline us in opposite directions: the artistic spiritual culture of the German classical period, a powerful and self-conscious realism and a reaction against this realism in the form of a subjectivism characterised by spiritual self-sufficiency and the development of unchartered feeling. How many contrasts derived from old and new contents do we carry within ourselves, and what a great task lies before us if we are inwardly to master them!

In order to elaborate and harmonise these various tendencies a superior spiritual force is needful, but since this force is lacking we are subject to all the misfortunes that are the necessary consequences of man being overmastered by his own experiences, of his being dominated by the distracting influences of existence. No steady aims guide our endeavour, no simple ideas stand out above the chaos and liberate us from its doubt and confusion. On the contrary, we are overwhelmed by immediate impressions, and our life is disintegrated by their contradictions. So we are tossed about by every passing wave, the helpless victims of every bold assertion and pronounced conviction, as well as of our own whims and passions, the playthings of shifting moods and situations.

A peculiar tension is imparted to this state of affairs by the fact that the changes which we experience are ultimately reducible to a *single question* and bring us face to face with a solitary alternative, an alternative which permits of no obscuration and demands a decision on the part of the whole man. The quiet but continual and irresistible development of modern work has not only altered the traditional way of life in all its details, it has undermined it as a whole and made it untenable. Openly or tacitly, broadly or finely, sensuously or spiritually, the older type of thought treated man as the measure and central point of all, turned reality into a kingdom of human-like agencies and made the welfare of man the object of all activity. Modern work as a whole has fundamentally destroyed this anthropomorphism. The immeasurable enlargement of the outer world, the discovery of inner necessities and objective relationships within man's own sphere, and a wide expansion of creative spiritual effort beyond the mere subject combine to make this absorption in the human unbearably narrow; they awaken at the same time a burning desire for a wider, richer, freer being, a great thirst for a life in relation with the infinity and truth of the whole. These changes force themselves more and more upon the attention of humanity and imperatively demand a just recognition.

But this negation does not by any means lead directly to an affirmation. The breaking down is not accompanied by a building up. The new position opens up two possibilities which are directly opposed to one another and admit of no reconciliation.

Does this historical world-movement against absorption in the merely human mean that man must conceive of himself as a mere natural being and place all his thoughts and activities within the limits of nature? In that case everything that is distinctively and peculiarly human must be got rid of as a pernicious illusion, and all that gives meaning and value to our life must receive its laws and forms from nature. Or does this movement affirm that a new world, a spiritual world, arises within man himself, raising him above himself as well as above nature? Does man initiate a new stage of reality and can his spiritual life inwardly enlarge itself to form a world? Our main task would then be to seize, appropriate and develop this world. In this case man must above everything else firmly establish himself in this position and direct his whole attention and effort not so much backwards as forwards. Thus man is either *less or more* than he is at the present day apt to conceive himself to be. A decision in this respect one way or the other will have the effect of transforming the whole of life from the smallest things to the greatest. But although this decision cannot be evaded, the lack of centralising force already referred to allows us to hesitate and vacillate, we tend now in this direction and now in that, according as the influences vary. While in general approving of the one we cannot make up our minds to abandon the other. We affirm in one direction what we deny in another. We are not whole-heartedly devoted to any one position. The situation has been often enough described; its rapid shifting of tendencies and moods, its lack of logic (as revealed by an insensibility to the sharpest contradictions and the jumbling up together of quite different ranges of thought), together with its weakness in systematic thinking, in following up assertions, either in their preliminary assumptions or their consequences. In all these respects we perceive a serious lowering of the level of inner life, nay, an inner impoverishment of life in the midst of amazing peripheral progress, of undreamt-of technical accomplishments, of an overwhelming wealth of outward successes.

It is obvious that we are in the midst of a spiritual crisis which threatens to overwhelm us. But this situation has not arisen owing to the perversity or sceptical bias of individuals; it is a result of the historical position as a whole. Have we not the right to hope that the necessity which produced such a crisis also vouchsafes us some sort of means capable of leading us beyond it?

As a matter of fact there is no lack of opposition to this chaotic state of affairs. There are plenty of counter-movements, plenty of attempts to build up a uniform construction of life, a uniform conception of reality. But unfortunately these attempts remain for the most part under the influence of that which they would like to overcome. The age of self-conscious specialism which forgot to take any account of the whole through its absorption in endless detail has now passed its high-water mark. But the movement towards unity consisted at first mainly in this, that particular spheres of life and knowledge took over the whole and made of it a picture, each according to its particular impressions, experiences, and aims. More than ever before, each of these separate spheres produced within its own particular circle a compact system of knowledge and then, boldly pressing beyond the boundaries of this circle, endeavoured to capture the whole of reality. Each sphere put its own special tasks before all others and assigned universal validity to its concepts, standards, and methods. Thus each particular department became the dominating central point of the whole of reality: religion, and often art as well, constructed its own world, the social movement produced its own particular view of life, and in the intellectual sphere, the natural sciences, in particular, frequently expanded into all-embracing philosophies. The first to do so was zoology under the influence of Darwinism. Now we perceive the same attempt being undertaken by physics, physiology, &c. The tendency towards bold speculative thought has deserted the philosophers to find a home with the natural scientists; in their case there is no lack of bold raids into the land of truth, and the commingling of philosophical assertion with capable research work prevents many people from realising the outrageous character of the speculative attempt.

Thus special points of view, partial conceptions of life, result, and their sensuous immediacy and easy comprehensibility gain them many adherents and enable each to attain a certain degree of influence. But never more than a certain degree. For the truth of things must eventually oppose and break through all narrow and arbitrary limitations. This will happen all the more readily in that the different claims involved in the various movements soon come into conflict, and dispute among themselves concerning their respective rights. It now becomes apparent that the whole cannot well be built upon a part, and that truths which are valid as partial truths become erroneous when exaggerated into the whole truth. In so far as these part movements become influential and obstruct and counteract one another, they must increase the confusion which they are trying to remove. Perhaps nothing contributes so much towards division at the present time as these inefficient efforts towards unity. Never has monism been so talked of as it is to-day, and never has there been so much division!

But in spite of the inadequacy of these attempts they are valuable for what they teach us. In particular, we clearly perceive from their failure that nothing can be accomplished by starting from this or that particular basis; it is necessary to seek a unity beyond the dispersion of particulars. There is no hope of properly meeting the crisis unless we rise above the present situation as a whole and make a new beginning. But why should this be impossible? History, in so far as it affects the inner life, does not exhibit a continual ascent. It shows us not only the rise and growth of true spiritual movements, but ensuing periods of exhaustion, so that we find recurring periods when the spiritual life must needs leave its active manifestation in human existence and retire into itself to take deeper and stronger root. In this fashion alone can it transcend the age and prove effective in liberating the truth present in the age from all the uncertainties which confuse and divide us. We are again face to face with such a period. Through self-recollection we must ascertain the foundations of our existence, our fundamental relationship to the world. We must appeal from the mere age to the eternal in the age, from the mere man to the superior forces and laws which make man something more than a mere natural being.

Under these circumstances every one who is alive to the necessities of the age must work, according to his capacity, towards this goal, namely, the deepening of life and the renewal of human culture. The path which we propose to strike out in this work will be more particularly distinguished by three characteristics.

1. We shall in the first place turn our attention to the chief movements characteristic of the age, the leading spiritual and intellectual tendencies, as we may shortly describe them. We speak of movements or tendencies, rather than of concepts or ideas, in order to make it clear from the very beginning that it is not, in the first place, a matter of merely intellectual processes and that these are not the deciding factors. Although outwardly the conflict may rage chiefly in the intellectual sphere, yet behind this are great movements springing from life as a whole, with characteristic contents of reality and specific constructions of

life; in the midst of manifold conflict and through a variety of different problems it is possible that under the influence of these deeper movements a common pulsation may stir the age; so that in emphasising these vital pre-suppositions of thought we are peculiarly likely to assist in forming a conception of the age as a whole, and winning clear recognition of its specific character. Moreover, accepting as we do a multiplicity of starting-points, we gain at least this advantage, that we make the assertions and problems of the age more demonstrable and more easily comprehensible. This plan has the further advantage of leading the discussion quickly to a definite point at which intrinsic necessities become apparent and are able to show our thought its paths of advance. The enquiry will show that at every point we come to the same questions, and indeed that *one and the same central problem* manifests itself through all the varieties of circumstance. It will also show that as the battle for the whole is being fought at each point, so the decision as to the whole is effective throughout all its ramifications. Furthermore, we shall be the better able to feel confidence in our own position the more the experiences and demands of the individual points of attack press towards it and point it out as the sole possibility of a happy solution.

2. On a closer examination we discover that each separate tendency asserts (or at any rate contains) a life-process, and this it is which we propose more especially to examine. Further, we shall be occupied in particular with the question whether this life-process permits of an *independent spiritual life*. The various tendencies usually recognise (if often unwillingly) that spiritual life possesses a certain actuality. But we are generally left in complete darkness as to what this involves and what it demands beyond the immediate phenomenon, to what preliminary suppositions and to what conditions it is attached. We shall devote our attention in the first place to finding out how the movements of the age are related to the problem of the possibility of spiritual life and to seeing what these tendencies contribute towards this problem. We shall endeavour not to lose ourselves in detail, but shall push forward rapidly to the life which flows through each movement, since this is the last

point attainable and the point from which our thought-world must build itself up. Such a study of the life-process will bring us most surely to the point where the various problems in question become the personal experience of the individual, where he can most easily insert his personal experiences and can least easily escape personal decision.

3. When the content of the age forms the point of departure as well as the end in view, it is well to bring in a historical survey in support of the philosophical work. This has the effect, in the first place, of throwing light upon and more clearly defining the spiritual nature of the present by disclosing its growth and its relationships. In attempting to understand and value the dominating movements of the age it cannot be a matter of indifference whether we recognise in them merely temporary waves or enduring life-tendencies, whether the present experience has frequently been experienced before and has a recurring and rhythmic character, or whether it reveals something completely new, something unique, whether it is more an action or a reaction, more a pushing forward or a sliding back. The historical review will be more or less retrospective according to the exigencies of the case. It will frequently be necessary to follow the chief phases of a movement throughout the whole development of European civilisation, but sometimes a study of the immediately preceding stage will suffice to throw light upon the present.

A brighter illumination of existing conditions in the light of history may prepare the way for independent investigation if it enables us better to perceive the specific nature of things, to become more clearly aware of their limits and to recognise them as problems. Not only the present-day position but the historical relationships themselves and history as a whole are converted into a problem through the discovery of the life-process operating in them. The life-process and its development cannot well be thrown into relief amidst the chaos of appearances until we transcend the historical outlook and take up a position from which a timeless and direct view is possible, when the question of the truth and justification of the process must be forced upon our attention. It is impossible to throw

INTRODUCTION 31

a clear light upon the whole unless original, personally-experienced, ultimate facts are distinguished from facts traditionally accepted. In this manner we may effect a revolution and turn towards a direct contemplation and analysis of the matter. This reversal, with its conversion of history into the development of a timeless life, alone makes it possible clearly to see through the content of our existence from the inside, to proceed from appearance to fact, from mere data to fundamental truth and to recognise inner necessities and persistent tendencies in the movement of history: nay more, to wrest any sort of meaning from the whole. It is only when thus viewed from the standpoint of permanent truth that the significance of the individual epochs can be measured and that an immanent criticism of the present day achievement can be made. The assertion of the age will be tested with reference to that stage in the world's spiritual evolution which it historically occupies. If history has already revealed more content and depth than this position can contain, then progress will necessarily be forced beyond it and at the same time it may receive guidance as to the direction in which it is to continue its quest. When philosophical work and the world's historical experience are thus brought into close contact, criticism does not need to remain retrospective and reflective, it can become productive and progressive, it can itself further the forward movement which it demands.

Such an investigation must try, in the first place, to destroy the matter-of-course character which is wont to attach to the movements of a given age and at the same time must aim at doing away with the dogmatism of which they are usually guilty. The first condition is to see more precisely what it is that the age undertakes and achieves. To see precisely, means in this case to see at the same time the extent of what has been accomplished, and this alone makes it possible to attain to a judgment which is independent and effective, without being guilty of injustice or of substituting paradox for independence. Our chief aim is, then, to discover leading tendencies, simple fundamental lines of development amidst the multiplicity and apparent confusion of the various movements. And it is from this point of view that we may hope most readily to free the truth content of the age, its inner necessities, from the misleading addition of human error and passion, while at the same time gaining nuclei for our own efforts. Only those who are capable of inwardly experiencing the age can accurately judge it. No value whatever attaches to the opinions of those whose attitude towards the age is throughout merely captious and critical.

Finally, we may add that in this, as in the earlier editions of the book, the definitions of the chief concepts will receive careful consideration. The confusion of the present day is due in no small degree to the indefinite use of terms. When the same expression is used now in a strict sense, now in a loose one, it is easy for statements to acquire illicitly more solidity and content than is really due to them, and when the same word frequently possesses essentially different meanings the aspect of things easily becomes chaotic and the central decisive point tends to be obscured. In every age the agreement between terms and concepts is no more than approximate, but to-day it is exceptionally loose. With the object of remedying this unfortunate state of affairs it is necessary briefly to review the history of the terms employed, so that we shall devote a little time to this topic.

FUNDAMENTAL CONCEPT OF SPIRITUAL LIFE

1. SUBJECTIVE—OBJECTIVE

(a) Historical

THE relation of subject to object is a problem which to-day stands in the very centre of philosophical work and controversy. Our views of life, our concepts of reality, our ideas of truth, nay, the main currents of life itself, vary according as it is the subject or the object which preponderates. In the one case the main trend of life's movement is from man to world, in the other it is from world to man. All other problems lead back to this main issue, which as it confronts us to-day bears the impress of influences derived from every stage of the whole history of philosophy. The chief phases in this historical development must therefore be recalled, and as we study them we shall see that they embody the main alternative solutions of which the problem in question is susceptible. And we shall at the same time become aware of a continuous impulse constraining the world's work to develop in a certain definite direction.

That the matter itself contains peculiar complications is sufficiently indicated by the remarkable history of the expressions subjective and objective. As the centuries have passed by their meaning has been completely reversed. Duns Scotus (d. 1308) first employed them as technical terms and in opposing senses: "The word subjective was applied to whatever concerned the subject-matter of the judgment, that is, the concrete objects of thought; on the other hand the term objective referred to that which is contained in the mere *obicere* (*i.e.*, in the presenting of ideas) and hence qualifies the presenting subject" (see Prantl, *Geschichte der Logik im Abendlande*, iii. 208). Philosophers employed the expressions in these senses until the seventeenth and eighteenth centuries; but the counter-term to objective (which was more commonly used than subjective) was more often *formaliter* or *realiter*.* The systems which carried on the scholastic philosophy show, at this period, a change in the use of *objectivus* which paved the way for the more modern terminology.†

The complete reversal of meaning did not take place, however, until the words were assimilated into the German language (through the Wolffian school of philosophy; for example in A. F. Müller's *Einleitung in die philosophische Wissenschaft*, 1733; Baumgarten and Gottsched). At first the terms *subjektivisch* and *objektivisch* (as they were then written) were not used outside this school, and in the conflict between Lessing and Goetze they were still employed only as highly technical words. It was Kantian philosophy which first brought them into common use, and at the beginning of the nineteenth century they were widely employed. It was entirely owing to German influence that their new meanings became general, and at first they were frequently regarded as strange.

The exact significance of these terms in modern terminology, though distinct enough from that they bore in the Middle Ages, is in itself most uncertain, being swayed now by one influence, now by another. The first meaning of subjective is that which pertains to the mere individual act of presentation; but it frequently means (especially when employed by scientists) anything and everything which a feeling and a thinking creature experiences in itself; also all convictions extending beyond the immediate evidence of the facts are called subjective and are regarded as a species of mere trimming. Thus what is deepest

---

* In the discussions between *Descartes* and *Gassendi* there occur subjective (= *formaliter in se ipsis*) and objective (= *idealiter in intellectu*). Bayle distinguishes (*œuv. div.* 1727, iii. 334a) *objectivement dans notre esprit* and *réellement hors de notre esprit*, and even so late as Berkeley we find (Fraser's edition, ii. 477): "Natural phænomena are only natural appearances. They are, therefore, such as we see and perceive them. Their real and objective natures are, therefore, the same."

† Thus it occurs for example in Chauvins's *lexicon rationale* (1692) under *certitudo: objectiva nonnullis est ipsa necessitas objecti, seu propositio necessaria objectiva. Aliis autem nihil aliud est quam denominatio quæ sumitur ab actu intellectus per quem objectum repræsentatur.* Goclen (*lex. philos.*, 1613) makes *ratio objectiva = res ipsa quatenus definitioni respondet.*

and what is shallowest are treated as of equal value. The term objective is also ambiguous. Sometimes it refers to objects as contrasted with mental activity, sometimes as constitutive of mind itself. Goethe aimed at objectivity; so does modern naturalism.

The problem itself is obviously concerned with the relationship between man and his thought-world, on the one hand, and the world in which he lives, on the other. In so far as thought is independent it stands apart from the world, but at the same time it can never forget that it belongs to the world and is always occupying itself with the world; hence no sooner has a gap been made than there arises an imperative desire to bridge it over, to bring thought and the world together again and bind them to one another. But the more we occupy ourselves with this task the more complicated it appears. The ancient Greek world was keenly conscious of this complication, but was more able to master it than we moderns are in a position to do. The solution of this problem as attempted by the Greeks at the height of the classical period has had the profoundest effect upon the history of philosophy. The position developed by such leading thinkers as Plato and Aristotle derived its power of conviction chiefly on account of having behind it a complete scheme of life and conduct. The peculiar strength and distinguishing characteristic of the old Greek philosophy of life lay in its capacity for raising the primitive relationship between man and nature to a spiritual level. It ennobled the relationship, while at the same time it avoided any sharp separation. It assigned man a place in the world while retaining for him the purity of spiritual independence. Man and the world, the inner and the outer, had then reached the stage above the primitive one of identification, and yet they were not so sharply divided but that a spiritual connection between them could easily be demonstrated. For they both seemed of the same order of being and inwardly attached to one another; each needed the other as a complement in order to attain to its own perfection. Nature, filled with inner life, attained its greatest height when appropriated by man. The forces latent in the latter, on the other hand, could not be fully developed except by first coming into contact with the world. In such a unification as was brought about by contemplation and love, life reached the height and blessedness of spiritual creation. From such a point of view as this it is possible, without misgiving, to conceive of truth as the conformity of thought with its object (*adequatio intellectus et rei*). But this view of the matter could only suffice for a stage of life when nature appeared more spiritual and humanity more natural than they subsequently did, when the one had not reached complete independence in virtue of its own distinctive laws and forces and the inner life of the other had not so deepened as to constitute a world of its own. There can be no doubt that this intimate connection between man and the world, and the accompanying fruitful reaction of each upon the other, helped to build up a joyous, high-minded, artistic type of human culture. But it is equally certain that this close union of spiritual life with a naïve conception of the world could not be permanently maintained.

Even before the end of the classical period, the Stoics and the Neo-Platonists had attempted solutions on different lines, though these did not exert so great an influence over the Modern World as did the earlier type of thought. The latter experienced an important revival in the shape of mediæval scholasticism, through which it directly influenced the Modern World (the characteristic features of which arose more particularly from its conflict with scholastic philosophy).

The new tendency first shows its influence in a powerful development of the *subject*, in a defiant breaking away from environment, and in a bold attempt to build up a new world and reshape life by the sole agency of man and his thought, instead of seeking union with the world and adopting a receptive attitude towards it. Science altered the aspect of things in a more drastic manner than had ever before occurred. By rejecting everything which did not answer to its test, while illuminating and linking up that which remained, it brought the whole of human existence within the sphere of systematic thought, and raised it to the level of the thinkable, the conceptual, the ideal. The inner became conscious of its unity and entrenched itself within its own territory, while the outer world receded to occupy an inferior position, and lost all inner life, since its function of movement in space did not seem to need any spiritual principle. It also lost in colour and variety, because the whole range of sense properties was regarded, not as belonging to the objects themselves, but as a mere garment with which the spirit invested them. Thus nature came to be conceived of as a domain of lifeless matter and movement devoid of any inner connection with the soul; while the latter, in its turn, was looked upon as entirely self-dependent, as standing by itself, master of a thought-force dominating eternity. The soul was thus placed upon an incomparably higher plane.

That is a great achievement—perhaps the greatest which the Modern World can boast of. But it does not constitute the whole of the activity of the period. The new period was unmistakably characterised by another tendency, besides that making for a glorification of the subject; one that laid chief emphasis upon the vastness and grandeur of the external world and contrasted it with the pettiness of man; a movement which aimed at replacing the hollowness, confusion, and narrowness of human existence by a wider, richer, and purer life, derived from contact with the immeasurable universe. It was a movement towards the object; an endeavour to sink humanity in the outer world, to assimilate the latter's whole content without criticism. Salvation is thus awaited from experience, from a better acquaintance with the things of the external world. Man must not seek in any way to shape the world according to his own ideals. To base his life on truth he has simply to take his place in the cosmic scheme. Even the strengthening of the subject itself indirectly supports this movement, for the closer concentration of the subject in its own sphere and its consequent absorption of all those characteristics which it had, as it were, lent to the objects of the external world, paves the way to making an end of the ancient anthropomorphic view of life. Thus the object is left free to develop its own nature in complete purity and to link itself closer together in its multiplicity until it is firmly welded into a complete whole. Now for the first time, the concealing veil being withdrawn, nature attains to full autonomy and is seen as a domain of faultless sequences and inviolable law. In the first instance, all this works itself out as appertaining to an objective world, apart from man. But it is bound finally to come back to man, to surround him, to try to make an absolute slave of him. From this point of view it increasingly appears as if all independence on the part of the subject must be a hollow delusion; it is claimed that life should willingly adapt itself to external things and place itself entirely under their direction. Hence humanity becomes very closely dependent upon environment; there ensues a new type of life, completely dominated by the object.

We thus perceive that the modern period is permeated by two distinct movements, each claiming the field for itself; it is hence inwardly divided, and a fundamental unrest and tension is brought into our life. This twofold character of the modern world reveals itself in most of the problems we are about to deal with, and presenting as it does a difficult but imperative task, summons us to spiritual action. Neither a unity transcending this division nor an assured truth can be hoped for from the present situation, hence the latter must be developed further and a new groundwork of reality must be disclosed.

It was therefore no merely whimsical speculation, it was an inner necessity, which drove great thinkers to seek new paths and bade them oppose to the primitive view of life and the world a reality based upon thought.

Two of these attempts to express a new type of life are of particular importance. With the object of overcoming the opposition (between subject and object) Spinoza laid emphasis upon the object and Kant upon the subject. The former recognised and emphasised what is objective in the subject, the latter what is subjective in the object. Spinoza aimed at binding man and the world together by discovering a cosmic force in man and separating it from the merely human element: this force is thought, based upon nothing outside itself, governed by its own necessities, free from all connection with a sense environment (as we see it, for example, in the region of mathematics). The petty human element, on the other hand, is a purely subjective experience limited to its own private aims and moods.

The transition from such prejudice and narrowness to the clarity and breadth of *thought* opens up to man the possibility of a cosmic life: for since thought itself is conceived of as grounded within a universal life (which is also the basis of the external world), its processes correspond with the truth in all things, and are capable of directly sharing their eternal and infinite character. Knowledge thus becomes the soul of life and fulfils all our needs. In its perfected form it takes the shape of religion and artistic contemplation. It was thus, for the most part, artistic and contemplative minds that were attracted by the calm and arid greatness of this type of life. The effect of this tendency of thought made itself felt far beyond the circle of actual discipleship. It was seen in the cleavage of human nature into the cosmic and the merely human, and in an energetic resistance to the anthropomorphism both of thought and of feeling which had become so firmly established during the Middle Ages. Men came to realise more clearly the petty nature of the happiness they had coveted and the narrowness of the prevailing field of ideas, and once their insufficiency had been felt and brought home they could never again be accepted in the old uncritical way.

There still remains, however, the question, Does our whole spiritual life begin and end with thought? It is possible that the transition from the deceptive appearances of the senses to the truth of thought itself demands an act on the part of the whole man, an act lying outside the region of mere thought. Moreover, the assumption which underlies this solution (the harmony of our thought with the world about us, the comprehension of both within a single cosmic life) is by no means free from doubt; and when the cosmic character of our thought becomes uncertain the truth of the life it offers us is at once shaken.

This consideration also actuated Kant when he decided to follow an exactly opposite path. In his case the world of external things retires to an unattainable remoteness, and every possibility of verifying a correspondence with it disappears. Hence, if we are to retain any sort of truth at all, truth must be looked for within the subject itself, and not in a relationship to the object. This amounts to a decisive negation. But Kant discovers a way from this negative to a positive; he draws our attention to the great collective achievements within the sphere of human life, more particularly to the formation of a body of scientific experience and of a domain of moral action. The spiritual element in these achievements must be put to the credit of the subject, so that the latter, by itself, must outgrow its traditional form. It is now not so much a separate point, an individual existence, as a spiritual structure, a spiritual fabric. Its comprehension of itself and of its own activity thereby becomes valid for every individual, and there results a new kind of objectivity,* a new concept of truth. The precise content depends upon the nature and significance of the activity, and is hence entirely different in the spheres of theoretical and practical reason. According to Kant, all human knowledge must remain confined to a world beyond which we cannot reach; the thought-world that we develop (in response to the stimulus of the external world) is valid only for ourselves and our form of presentation; our view of life does not range beyond ourselves; the forms of thought, as well as those of sense perception, are and must remain merely human. But in the sphere of practical life the position is entirely different. Human action attains to complete originality and is held capable of evolving a world of its own. In this case truth ceases to be merely human and becomes absolute; the characteristic feature is the subordination of all human particularity to universal norms. Man now comes into direct contact with the true essence of reality; in its capacity of a moral being the subject itself becomes the upholder of a world. Morality thus becomes an independent sphere in the very centre of life.

* This new concept of objectivity is undoubtedly full of complications, and was sharply attacked by Kant's opponents. Thus Plattner, for example, says (*Philosophische Aphorismen I.* § 699, *Anmerkung*) : "If, however, it is intended to be thereby demonstrated that our knowledge has objective validity, then one is certainly doing great violence to the term objective and employing it in a sense hitherto unheard of in philosophical terminology. It is being used to denote the precisely opposite concept, subjective. No wonder that Herr Schmid, who is never remiss in his devotion to truth, found it necessary to describe Kantian objectivity as *subjective objectivity* (*Wörterbuch*, article *Objectiv*)."

Knowledge, on the other hand, withdraws to the periphery, its chief task being to guard the moral world from disturbance. The result is a new organisation of life in direct contrast to that propounded by Spinoza. Kant stands for activity, for the creation of a new world; Spinoza for restful contemplation, for searching out the foundations of the world as it already exists. The former divides reality and intensifies every contrast, the latter smooths away contrasts within a comprehensive unity. The two are at one, however, in their desire to impart, in some way, a cosmic character to life, to lift man above himself and lead him on to deeper things.

Recent years have seen a revival of Kantian modes of thought, and the discussion of this topic will be left over to the study of the present day. The immediate followers of Kant were the sons of an age which abounded in a strong and joyous sense of life, and they took strong exception to the retention of the *Ding-an-sich* (the thing-in-itself, stripped of all that is subjective), and the consequent limitation of human capacity. Along with the *Ding-an-sich* disappeared the division between theoretical and practical reason, and there now remained no obstacle to the conception of life as a single connected whole. A spirited attempt was made to evolve all reality from the workings of the human spirit (more especially from thought conceived of as provided with inner movement). Plotinus had already shown that it is possible for thought to overcome the contrast between subject and object in its own sphere, by turning round upon itself, by making thought itself the subject of thought. This only needed to be developed in all its consequences, to be freed from all reference to the mere individual and extended to the whole sphere of the world's history, to give as a result the Hegelian system; a system which transformed the whole of reality into a self-development of thought, conceived of truth as the spirit's awakening to self-consciousness, and gave man the right of complete participation in this absolute truth; he must, however, abandon all narrow subjectivity of opinion and follow the necessities of the thought-process alone.

This bold attempt not only took its own age by storm, but the manner in which it made every factor plastic and welded together all the manifold elements of our experience made a deep impression upon the content of spiritual life. As soon as the first impetus lost force, however, a reaction was inevitable. The free development of the philosophy served to reveal its limitations. Certain serious questions soon became unavoidable. In the first place it was asked if the process did not involve a demand for something outside itself, since (as a spiritual process) it requires to be re-experienced, and for this purpose a fulcrum is needed lying outside the process itself. In the second place the question arose whether the exclusive transformation of life into thought would not deprive reality of all content and leave it a mere tissue of logical forms and formulæ. Finally, it was asked whether the absolute character of human spirituality had not been too hastily conceded. Whatever may be the truth with regard to these points, the fact remains that this system was not so much defeated by philosophical opposition as forced into the background by the actual direction taken by life itself.

This brings us to the nineteenth century.

(b) The Nineteenth Century

No previous age had ever been so conscious of the problem of subject and object and of the contrast it involved as was the nineteenth century; never before had the difficulty been felt so directly and over so wide a range of life. At the same time, scarcely anything new was attempted in the way of overcoming the antithesis. The constant recurrence to Kant sufficiently indicates this.

A very important movement, and the first with which we have to deal, is that which led humanity away from inner development and turned its attention towards the conquest of the visible world by the aid of natural and technical science and social and political work. Pursuing this path, man becomes closely riveted to the external world; he looks for reality and truth solely from the concentration of his powers upon the world, and all life apart from external things comes to be regarded as a mere shadow and a vain show; thus the centre of gravity of life shifts towards the objective and life finds its meaning in work occupied with, and conditioned by, external things. This work completely emancipates itself from the mere individual; it develops an independent and very extensive network of relationships, and swells in volume so unceasingly that man becomes more and more a mere servant and tool. This tendency was first illustrated in the case of factory work, and then it spread rapidly into other spheres of life. The more human thought and effort were concentrated upon joint tasks of an outward and visible character, the more unimportant became all that took place in the soul of the individual, the more his condition became a matter of indifference, the more the subject came to be considered a mere cog in the vast machinery of the whole, a quantity to be set aside with impunity. A scientific expression of this tendency is to be found in the theory of Positivism (in so far as it is logically developed from its own principles and not amalgamated with thought of a different type).

The tendency we have just indicated is still predominant. But humanity is becoming increasingly aware of its limitations. A growing feeling of hollowness forces itself upon us. Does not this bear witness to the irrepressibility of the subject and to the impossibility of denying ourselves all inner satisfaction? An abrupt reaction in favour of the subject is consequently noticeable. The subject begins to regard itself and its condition as the most important factors in the situation; there grows up a tendency to throw off all outward restraint, to make individual feelings the only criterion, and finally to bring life as far as possible into conformity with this standard. This reaction still exerts a wide influence in literature, art, and social life. It is, however, far too devoid of real content to be capable of overcoming opposition or of satisfying the human soul. All its appeals to individual forces cannot produce a connected inner life or a common truth, and in the end it leads back to the very vacuity from which it wished to free us. The nearest scientific representative of this subjectivism is psychologism, which endeavours to build up a thought-world founded directly upon the individual soul; for a time, psychologism proved very influential, but it was rapidly followed by a reaction and it is now being realised with increasing clearness that it will never be possible to attain to a science, to a domain of truth, if such an unstable foundation be employed.

Outside the sphere of science, too, we are becoming increasingly conscious of the limitations of subjectivism; at the same time, we cannot possibly return to an objectivity of the kind described above. Hence we remain in a painful state of division, while the antagonism between the claims of work and the interests of the soul threatens to grow more and more pronounced. This involves a disintegration of life, and it is impossible to accept it as a final settlement. Some method of bridging the chasm must be discovered.

There is no lack of efforts in this direction. The most influential attempt is that which aims at so inwardly broadening and strengthening the subject as to enable it to win a new insight into the universe, and with it a new life: this is to take place, in the main (though by no means completely), along Kantian lines. A movement of this description is to be met with in theology as well as in philosophy, the forms it takes in the two cases being different. In theology the movement attempts to set religious truth free from the uncertainties of speculation and metaphysics and to place it upon a firm basis in the very centre of the soul's being. (We are here referring more particularly to the line of thought associated with the name of Ritschl.) Especially in the sphere of morality, in the development of moral personality, spiritual life seems to produce a kingdom of its own and to enthrone itself in a position of security and elevation above other phases of existence. According to this trend of thought, that which is necessary to spiritual self-preservation needs no outward support. Its veracity is inwardly demonstrated by the enrichment of ethical and religious life. The more exact development of the thought-world, in this case, depends chiefly upon the *Werturteile* (judgments of value), which represent this central relationship to life and are consequently

* The most effective refutation of psychologism is that contained in Husserl's *Logischen Untersuchungen*, 1900 and 1901. The profound influence which psychologism has exerted even upon investigators who are opposed to it on principle is here demonstrated in the most convincing manner and forms an important feature of Husserl's work.

superior to all forms of theoretical proof. The moral and religious life, following its own internal necessities, produces a body of convictions, which does not, however, claim to be a cosmic philosophy, and only maintains its validity by continually relating itself to the fundamental realities of the ethico-religious life.

This movement (which in its more detailed exposition takes very different forms) is undoubtedly justified in so far as it aims at providing a firmer and more direct foundation for men's ultimate convictions than intellectual argument is capable of offering, and in so far as it tends towards imparting a more practical character to life. But the manner in which this is attempted fills us with misgiving. Feeling is generally regarded as the core of life, and the attempt is made to raise a philosophical structure upon this basis: "Feeling is that spiritual function in which the ego finds its self-immediacy" (Ritschl: *Christ. Lehre von der Rechtfertigung u. Versöhnung*, iii. 142). But can it be truly said that life wins self-immediacy through feeling? Is not feeling sometimes hollow and empty? Feeling alone cannot evolve a content; it acquires one in its relationships with the rest of life. Since feeling is liable to constant alteration and is open to all sorts of different interpretations, it is impossible, with it as a basis, to impart either stability or content to life. The attempt to construct a thought-world with the feeling subject as basis would hardly be distinguishable from mere subjectivism if the feeling were not represented as being a necessity and the content which it affirms as something elevated above what is merely natural, human and particular. But how can this structure be erected upon the basis of the bare facts of the soul-life? However imperative a feeling may seem to be, it is so, primarily, only for a particular subject; however closely it may seem bound up with a particular content, the connection signifies more than is contained in the direct impression; it is the result of an interpretation—which may be a wrong one. Consequently the strength of a feeling is no guarantee whatever of the truth of any body of thought which may be developed from it. Among other things, the prevailing diversity and conflict of religious opinion illustrates this point.

Each religion is confident of the entire genuineness of the fundamental feelings associated with it; yet the various religions arrive at quite different truths. Thus a higher tribunal is necessary to decide between these conflicting claims, and feeling cannot act in this capacity. Man cannot arrive at truth at all unless there is born within him a life elevated above his natural particularity and individuality; truth bound down to such limitations as these is no truth. It follows as a corollary that man can never under any circumstances abandon, or even set aside, the problem of his fundamental relationship to reality. This problem is not one forced upon him through after-reflection; from the very beginning it forms a portion of his spiritual nature. The life of a spiritual being does not begin and end with its subjective condition; it includes the objective also, and must get into relationship with the objective; it is driven to insist that the rift between subjective and objective shall be overcome, and feels confinement to the merely subjective conditions as an intolerable restriction.

The complications which the Ritschlian tendency involves are very easily forgotten, because the excitation of feeling is usually supplemented by a thought-world that has come down to us as historical tradition, and this imparts a greater appearance of stability and content. As a matter of fact, the truth of the historical tradition has first to be demonstrated, and from this point of view that can only be done through the agency of feeling; feeling, too, must decide what portions of the content of this tradition are to be counted valuable; thus, pursuing more or less devious paths, we continually come back to feeling and find that we are confined within its sphere; the more we assign complete independence to feeling, the less content it is capable of offering us and the more it threatens to split up into a number of isolated states bereft of meaning. Hence this method serves rather to increase our perplexities than to diminish them. However far we may hold ourselves aloof from this mode of thought, we cannot avoid recognising the invigoration of moral and religious life which has sprung from its adoption. But with the theoretical formulation of these convictions we cannot pretend to be satisfied.

In the sphere of philosophy the matter takes on an essentially different complexion. The concept of value * is now placed in the centre of an important and fruitful movement. Regarding it as a whole, this movement represents the modern type of thought as opposed to the antique (more particularly in so far as the latter is Platonic). When the chief antithesis of reality is that between a permanent "being" and a transitory "becoming" (as in the latter case), it is only a short step to conceiving this essential being as at the same time the good and valuable, thereby uniting the two concepts so far as this is possible. From this point of view the good can be regarded as detached from all activity and quite independent of all that is human. Modern thought, on the other hand, maintains that there can be no question of a good apart from a living and active being, and that the good can have value only in proportion to its importance for life. Hence it seems more appropriate to speak of "values" than of "goods." This fundamental idea can and does assume different forms. If the individual subject with its

* Within the last few decades an extensive literature has sprung up dealing with the concept and significance of value. It will not be possible here to review or estimate this: we will merely mention Meinong's *Psychologisch-ethische Untersuchungen zur Wert-Theorie* (1894). It would be desirable to have a history of the problem and concept of value as a whole. At present we will quote only the following passages from Höffding's *Philosophy of Religion*: "We are indebted to Kant's philosophy for the independence of the problem of value as apart from the problem of knowledge. He taught us to distinguish between valuation and explanation." Further, "Kant more often speaks of purposes than of values. It is, however, clear (although Kant does not properly pay attention to it either in his psychology or his ethics) that the concept of purpose presupposes the concept of value, since I could not make a purpose of anything the value of which I had not already experienced. When Kant speaks of the 'domain of purposes' in contrast to the causal order of nature, he means thereby what later philosophers called the 'domain of values.' Kant's disciple Fries began with the concept of value (*System der Philosophie*, Leipzig, 1804, §§ 238, 255, 330; *Neue Kritik der Vernunft*, Heidelberg, 1807, iii. 14. It was more especially Herbart and Lotze, however, who procured recognition for the concept of value in wider circles. After Lotze, the theologian Albrecht Ritschl and his pupils took up the concept." Pöschmann has recently published a work upon Fries' concept of value. The concept and the problem associated with it, is, however, by no means exclusively modern; it appears whenever the subject attains to greater independence. Thus it first appears among the Stoics, who constructed a term for it (ἀξία). Nicholas of Cusa, the first modern thinker, called God the value of values (*valor valorum*).

sensitivity and feeling is made the sole basis of life, if all events are valued according to their contribution towards the comfort of the subject, and if it is considerations of pleasure and pain which decide in the last instance, it is impossible to see how this movement can in any way elevate or enrich life. For pleasure binds man down to his own unilluminated subjective feeling, and in spite of all outward success it narrows the inner life. It is inimical to any inner elevation of life, to any direct joy in men and things, to any vital assimilation of the objective. Such defects will be felt as peculiarly grievous by those who realise the great tasks and complications which are associated with man's spiritual condition; for this condition demands an upward effort, nay an inward conversion, and these are impossible if life remains rigidly bound down to a mere subjective condition.

There is another mode of thought, standing on an incomparably higher level, according to which Kant's critical idealistic method is transferred to a present-day basis and an attempt is made to develop it in the light of post-Kantian experience.* A start is made from the fact that our life and action does not exhaust itself in the mere blind immediacy of events; our spiritual nature compels us to make continual use of our judgment. Now we form judgments according to definite standards, which neither fancy nor failure in any way affects. In these standards are revealed values above all mere utility and above pleasure and pain. These values bring about an inner elevation of life and may justly claim to possess an absolute character.† We have here to deal with an important endeavour to provide human life with a basis and content derived from within, to raise it above natural impulses by the aid of critical self-contemplation without entangling it in the difficulties of speculative metaphysics, and at the same time to map out a specific task for philosophy. As a matter of fact, it cannot be seen how

---

* This movement is dealt with in a particularly clear and noteworthy manner in Windelband's *Präludien*, more especially in the sections *Was ist Philosophie?*, *Normen und Naturgesetze*, *Kritische oder genetische Methode*.

† Münsterberg, in particular, voices this superiority of the values in his *Philosophie der Werte* (1908), a warm and powerful exposition of the subject.

man can overcome the threatened division of life arising from the breach between subject and object save by recollecting his spiritual nature and seeking to deepen it.

There is only one point with regard to which we cherish doubts. Is it possible to regard the matter as concluded when it has reached this point? Is there not an inner necessity which will compel the movement to go further? In this connection several queries suggest themselves. Is it possible for the values to attain a sufficiently secure position while remaining separate experiences? Will not their ultimacy be open to attack so long as they remain in mere juxtaposition and do not join together to make a united whole?* Further, will the higher grade of life revealed in the values be able to rise up against and prevail over the entangling and enslaving power of natural and social self-preserving tendencies, unless it create for us a new spiritual self which unfolds and asserts itself in the values? But this is hardly possible without reversing the position of things as they now are, and thus we come back again to some sort of metaphysics, however different from the old type.

The doctrine of values hence appears to us to be a very promising and suggestive movement rather than a complete solution. For the time being this movement does not exert much influence outside the sphere of philosophy, and humanity remains painfully wavering between work and soul, between the absorption of the subject by a too powerful object and the dissipation of the object by a too self-sufficient subject.

The complications of this situation give rise to the question, Is not this whole division between the subject and object a mistake; is it not a mistake to recognise an inner domain existing parallel with the external world? May we not say that in the light of such a conception as this the aspiration towards truth involves an insoluble contradiction—for it wishes

* The necessity of such a connection is also emphatically brought forward by Münsterberg; he says in the preface to his *Philosophie der Werte*, "The values as a whole must be fundamentally tested and uniformly deduced from a basal act. Our modern philosophy lacks a self-contained system of pure values. Only when this has been obtained can philosophy again become a real life-power, a position which has too long been exclusively occupied by natural science" (vi.).

at the same time to divide and to unite, to keep apart and to draw together. Of recent years Avenarius and Mach, starting from quite opposite points of view, have come to the identical conclusion that this division should be abandoned as a useless and misleading duplication. The placing of a sensation in an inner world (introjection) seems quite as mistaken as the placing of processes in consciousness in an outer one (projection). These writers give us one world instead of two, and they forbid us to seek for objects beyond the reach of our immediate experience.* This penetrating treatment of the problem, by virtue of its simplifying tendency, has made a visible impression upon our age, but it is beyond the scope of our present task to examine it on its technical side. It is certainly to its credit that, in a sphere bordering on its own, namely, with regard to the physiologico-psychological theory of perception, it again opens up questions that seemed to be settled and exposes the problematical character of the conventional scientific conception of nature. We are prevented, however, from assenting to the main thesis by the consideration that our ego is in reality more than a current of sense impressions—our very knowledge is shaped in its attainment by our independent work. Moreover it is necessary to call particular attention to the fact that above and beyond all intellectual processes there develops an inner life, a life which exhibits, in spite of all manifoldness, a permanent character, persisting through all changes and movements.† The

* See Mach, *Die Analyse der Empfindungen*, 2nd edit., p. 206: "There is no gap between psychical and physical, no outside and inside, no sensation which corresponds to something external and different from itself. There are only elements of one kind, of which the supposed outer and inner are compounded; according to the circumstances of each particular case, these elements are found inside or outside. The sense-world belongs at the same time to the physical sphere and to the psychical." Page 33: "I see no contrast between psychical and physical, but simple identity with regard to these elements." See also Wlassak (in *Zukunft*, 1902, No. 18, p. 202): "No unsophisticated person finds a tree present in any sense as sensation in his consciousness; such a person will invariably regard it solely as a portion of his environment. This also applies when the tree is not seen, but only recollected; the less vivid image, also, stands in exactly the same relationship to the person perceiving it as did the tree itself."

† When Mach denies the independence and permanence of the ego, this is largely due to the fact that he confuses the *consciousness* of the ego with the

SUBJECTIVE—OBJECTIVE

whole course of history testifies to such an independence on the part of the inward life; right through all his work and the complexities of his development man has always drawn further and further away from the mere life of the senses; he has more and more converted outward events into inner experience, more and more resisted the mere influx of sensations. All this is no mere intellectual phenomenon, no mere attempt at explanation. It is an unfolding of rich actuality, the nearest and surest of which we have any knowledge, and this alone teaches us how mentally to shape and reshape our sense impressions. It is impossible to explain away such actuality as this as a mere illusion and set back the clock of history. It is equally impossible to escape from the necessity of this division between subject and object, between the inner world and nature.

(c) The Positive Position

1. Introduction

In which direction shall we pursue our enquiry? If this division is inevitable, and if there is no bridge from the one

---

living ego itself. Thus, for example, on p. 3: "The apparent permanence of the ego consists in the first place only in the continuity, in the slow change. The basis of the ego is made up of the various thoughts and plans of yesterday which are continued to-day and are constantly being recalled to us by our waking environment (hence, in dreaming, the ego may be very confused or doubled or totally lacking), and the little habits which long remain with us, unconsciously and involuntarily. It would hardly be possible for there to be greater differences in the egos of different men than appear in the course of a year in *one* man. When, to-day, I look back upon my early youth, if the chain of recollection were not present to my mind, I should have to believe (apart from a few special points) that the boy was another individual." And on p. 17: "One will no more set such a high value upon the ego, which is subject to many changes even during the individual life, and in sleep or during absorption in contemplation or in some thought (precisely in the happiest moments) may be partially or totally absent." But is there not a unity of a spiritual kind which persists with living force in the face of all the changes and obscurations of consciousness, does not all progressive scientific and artistic creation work through this unity of the spiritual individuality, and is not this same unity the source of all thoroughgoing achievement also in the practical and technical domain? As opposed to this dissipation of the ego, these experiences of the spiritual life corroborate Goethe's conviction:

"*Und keine Zeit und keine Macht zerstückelt
Geprägte Form, die lebend sich entwickelt.*"

side to the other, then no course remains to us but to accept the opposition as part of the life-process itself, and so to enlarge the latter, inwardly, that it need no longer be referred by a belated movement of thought to some outlying environment, but contains within itself a world. A whole world must come into effective activity within man himself; a world raised above this contrast, a world directly accessible to us and not refracted through the particularity of the individual medium. Then, and only then, can there be any truth for man.

To take up such a position as this may at first sight appear somewhat extraordinary. But in reality it is not without historical connections which only need to be correlated for the old which is contained in the apparently new to become obvious. How did humanity come to develop the ideas of the good and the true, and to separate them from mere utility and mere actuality? How is it possible for humanity to rise in any way above the opinions and inclinations of the mere man? It cannot be denied that we have here a remarkable phenomenon to deal with. We may differ as much as we like as to what is true and what is good, but it remains a fact that we do *ask after* the good and the true, however uncertain our answers may be. And this is in itself an important fact, rich in consequences. It involves breaking through the mere details of actual experience; it bears witness to an inward breadth of our being, which perceives and seeks its own in what is apparently foreign to it. For it is certain that man cannot be earnestly concerned about something that has no manner of relationship to his life and being—which does not in fact belong to him. He cannot possibly be interested, even in the slightest degree, in what is entirely external to him. Now in seeking the true and the good, man seeks a world outside his own immediate sphere. Must we not then, according to our very nature, participate in a wider sphere, must not our life contain the whole world, if we are so powerfully attracted and so excited to activity by its content? It is true that in this case we must alter the concept of ourselves. But concepts must be subordinate to facts, not facts to concepts; therefore why should we resist such an alteration?

To give a more definite shape to this idea of the world-nature of man remains a very difficult task. But in this respect, as in others, the most notable philosophical work of recent centuries has clearly enough shown us the way. One of Kant's greatest achievements was the separation of the enquiry into the possibility of spiritual contents from the mere psychological explanation. For example, he distinguished between the question, How does the individual man arrive at knowledge, morality, &c. ? and the question, Upon what inward conditions does the existence of science and morality depend? Thus, both the ethical and logical points of view become independent of the psychological. At first this may appear to be nothing more than a new method; but this method would fall to the ground in the absence of a new life beyond the detached experiences of our merely psychical existence—a life issuing from the whole of things, a cosmic life. The specialised developments of such a life possess, however, no firm and stable basis if they do not reconcentrate the whole within themselves. They must be recognised as heralding a new stage of cosmic development which supervenes not below but above the opposition between subject and object.

Modern art, as seen in its most important manifestations, moves by another path towards a similar goal. We admire the objectivity of a Goethe, and when Heinroth described his thought as objective, the master himself expressed his appreciation of the tribute. Such an objectivity does not in the least mean the suppression and absorption of the subject by the object, the mere reproduction of the outward impression made by a thing. It involves a meeting of objective and subjective upon the common ground of the inner life and the permeation of each by the other. The things themselves thus receive a soul and become capable of accurately recommunicating their own real nature, while human life receives a content in place of its original emptiness. In this case the things are not coloured, as it were, with a subjective mood; they are made to yield up their own true meaning. The poet "thereby appears as a magician bringing the otherwise dumb beings to speech; to his soul the whole infinitude of the world is revealed, and he enables all manifoldness to realise its own specific nature, at the same time perceiving all that is living, essential, and effective in the things themselves." (See *Problem of Human Life*, p. 472.) Goethe calls this a synthesis of spirit and world, "giving us a most blessed assurance of the eternal harmony of existence"; in reality this synthesis does not take place between the soul and the external world, but within a soul enlarged to the dimensions of an inner world, between sides and poles of its life. Hence there are not merely two kinds of artistic creation, but three; in addition to the contrasting subjective and objective treatments, there is a superior method which we have called a "sovereign" or supreme method. (See *The Truth of Religion*, trans. by Dr. Tudor Jones, published by Williams and Norgate.) This sovereign treatment alone rises above both soulless objectivity and formless subjectivity. It occupies a position of its own, according to which the life-process does not seek a world which has evolved independently of it, but evolves one out of itself. Only thus can it obtain a content—by means of the creative synthesis of a new world, not by copying an already present existence. Should not that which possesses such indisputable reality in the sphere of art be valid also for spiritual life as a whole? Could art concern itself about this matter at all if some spiritual totality did not stand behind it? Hence we should confidently follow the path thus indicated to us, and bravely persevere in it to the end, however far it may lead us away from the usual conception of life and the cosmos. For there is no doubt whatever that it is only by opposing the customary conception that it is possible to build up a world from within and to impart a distinctive form to our life and work.

Let us consider the following three problems from this point of view, and see to what results we are led:—

1. The fundamental concept of the spiritual life.
2. The relationship between man and the spiritual life (with a historical review).
3. The problem of truth.

We shall thus develop the preliminary assumptions of that to which (in its results) every man must in some fashion hold fast.

2. THE FUNDAMENTAL CONCEPT OF THE SPIRITUAL LIFE

Life of a spiritual nature is considered to be a distinguishing characteristic of man. This life it is which raises him above the level of the merely animal world; it must therefore be something more than that natural life of the soul which he possesses in common with animals. As a matter of fact, even a superficial consideration immediately shows us an essential difference. In the animal world mental life is nothing more than a derivative phenomenon accompanying the nature-process and serving its ends; skill and intelligence, however highly developed, are nothing more than mere tools employed in the preservation of the individual or the race. Being a mere tool, intelligence cannot attain to inner continuity, secure self-dependence, or any content of its own. But it is just these things which are characteristic of the spiritual stage of life. A new life-process now appears; the inner, formerly occupying a modest position on the outskirts of a strange world, now claims to stand alone and to construct a reality of its own. From this point of view, spiritual life, united together to form a whole, may be looked upon as *inner life* which has become independent and acquired a content. Reality, otherwise split up in an immeasurable multiplicity and ensnared in countless dependent relationships, here attains an inner continuity and a life which alone can really be called a self-life.

A statement of this sort at once gives rise to a question. Is this self-life directed towards forming a separate domain of its own, apart from external reality, in isolated security and contentment, or does it still retain a connection with the world as a whole? Only the latter view corresponds with the conditions of life. For in working to realise itself, spiritual life is still occupied with the world. It cannot find itself without drawing the world to itself. It can have no rest until it has completely overcome the world and assimilated it. Therefore its whole content is at the same time a positive assertion; it claims to be the last, the whole, the all-containing, the core of the whole of reality. But this cannot be true unless the further development which it brings about in things, through assimilating them, leads these things to the height of their own being, unless the content of spiritual life signifies the reality of the things themselves. Spiritual life becomes in itself an intolerable contradiction if it stands apart from and confronting the world and not within it, and if reality does not perfect itself in turning to spiritual life.

The recognition of this renders our world fluid and transforms it into a region of upward movement. The lower stages are formed by nature, from which the natural soul-life springs. This natural life exhibits a thoroughgoing contradiction; it develops a certain inner life which is at the same time stultified through complete dependence on an outward life, through the denial of any self-life. Every thoughtful observer must see overwhelming evidence of this contradiction in the great cycle of animal life, so senseless, so devoid of meaning in spite of its wealth of life and feeling. Spiritual life marks the commencement of the solution of this contradiction, since life is now directed inwards towards itself and not merely outwards.

Since it thus forms a stage in the life of the whole, spiritual life cannot be a mere property of separate points, an aggregate produced by subsequent combination on the part of separate manifestations; it must rather be a whole from the very commencement, an independent and self-contained life. Such a whole possesses a unity which transcends all manifoldness, and hence the contrast between subject and object. This whole develops itself through the agency of the antithesis of subject and object, of power and resistance, but it remains superior to it, and holds both sides together even while they are divided; in the spiritual sphere, neither side can develop itself and find its own highest level without the assistance of the other. It is not really so much a question of opposition between the two sides as between the position of unity, of complete activity, on the one hand, and the position of division, of one-sided and empty life, on the other. From the point of view of spiritual life, the mere subject is just as much an outward thing as is the object. It is not the relationship of the one side to the other, but the *creative synthesis* alone, that produces an inwardness and at the same time a complete and self-contained reality. Such a reality can never come from without.

It will not be possible to overcome the contradiction between subject and object in this manner if we begin with a given state of being. It is an indispensable condition that we should start with the life-process itself. If the former course be followed, then either the world or the subject is fixed upon as self-existing and self-contained; it then becomes impossible to pass from the one to the other, and we remain under the dominion of an everlasting antithesis. Within the life-process, however, each can, from the very beginning, be related to the other, and the condition of each side can be measured by comparison with what takes place and is accomplished in the whole; then the stubborn contrast disappears and the division is replaced by a superior connection.

A word of historical explanation may serve to elucidate and define this conception of spiritual life. The Enlightenment recognised, side by side with the mechanism of nature, no reality other than the juxtaposition of separate souls; there was no mention of a spiritual world—only of a world of spirits. Kant was the first to originate the tendency which dominated the spiritual work of the nineteenth century, namely, the recognition of a spiritual life as distinct from the mere workings of the soul; for according to Kant we have to deal with a common and fundamental spiritual structure, superior to all merely individual differences; this forms a network embracing every spiritual manifestation, dominating it, and giving it its characteristic shape. But the matter was not carried to completion, the new material was not welded together to form a compact and independent whole, and the spiritual was not clearly defined. Kant's speculative followers elevated the spiritual life to a position of complete independence, but at the same time they unhesitatingly treated human spiritual life as absolute, and regarded it as the parent of all reality. They could not very well do this without replacing spiritual life as a whole by some special activity, and they came to rely more and more upon thought. A conception of the world resulted which was far too narrow and too anthropomorphic, while reality threatened to practically vanish by becoming a mere restless process.

Spiritual life, on the contrary, is definitely raised above human existence. Man does not originate spiritual life, but he is capable of attaining to participation in it, and at the same time in a higher stage of reality. Spiritual life does not appear as a special manifestation, as a special aspect of life, but as self-contained life, itself giving rise to reality; a life which our human activity is far from penetrating, but towards which it strives as a great goal.

3. THE RELATIONSHIP BETWEEN MAN AND THE SPIRITUAL LIFE

When spiritual life thus becomes independent and elevates itself above what is merely human, the relationship between man and spiritual life ceases to be an apparently obvious fact and becomes a difficult problem. How can man, who at first appears to be an infinitesimal point, participate in a self-contained world, in a world as a whole, such as the spiritual life now represents? It is certain that he can only do so if the spiritual life has existed within his being, as a *possibility*, from the commencement, if it is in some way directly connected with him. It will not do for spiritual life to be communicated to him through the medium of his special nature (thus becoming alienated from itself); it must in some fashion be present to him as a whole in all its infinity; it must hence, working from within, open up to him (if at first only as a possibility) a cosmic life and a cosmic being, thus enlarging his nature. In the absence of such an indwelling spirituality humanity can have no hope of making any progress. If in laying hold of spiritual life he did not discover his own true self, the former could never be a power to him. If spiritual life did not present an unchanging pole, if it was not an arbitrating power assigning goals and standards to all human undertakings, man would be a helpless victim of ever-changing appearances and would never be able to attain to any truth; spiritual life alone, and not mere humanity, can ensure absolute constancy. This participation of man in spiritual life alters the whole aspect of his being. It only becomes possible by going beyond immediate human existence, so that man's life acquires a deeper spiritual basis. At the same time there separates itself from the empirical psychological method (which concerns itself with the immediate processes of the soul-life) a *noölogical* method which has to do with the above spiritual basis and its self-activity.

In this twofold aspect, man appears to be in himself a problem and a contradiction. In his case, a spiritual life is at the same time a fact and a task, a repose that can never be disturbed and an endeavour that cannot be satisfied, an inward core and a remote goal; man himself appears great in his relationship to spiritual life, but small as an isolated individual; his life becomes an incessant search after his own being, and in this sense alone can it give rise to true history. How could there be such a thing as genuine history if all effort was solely dependent upon external causes and was not directed and governed from within by a definite purpose?

The sphere of human history illustrates the gradual overcoming of original disintegration and helplessness by spiritual life. This occurs through a species of crystallisation, which, under exceptionally favourable circumstances, may occur within the life-process; complexes of spiritual activity join up together and endeavour to assert their supremacy through the construction of a characteristic system of life, an edifice of spiritual reality. There is no better example of this than Greek creative thought in its characteristic comprehension of life and the universe; a synthesis of this sort stands for the exclusive truth of its particular life-content and divides existence into "For" and "Against." It cannot endure anything that is strange or hostile. Thus movement and conflict are produced, and these lead to experiences which drive life forward; the way is paved for new concentrations, which in turn experience the same fate. In such fashion, through the growth and decay of the separate phases, the content of truth as a whole continues to grow. But this holds good only if all movement is comprehended within a basic and directing spiritual life; in the absence of the latter there would be no possibility of securing the prevalence of any sort of truth whatever in face of the obstinate resistance and numerous barriers which human conditions offer. From this point of view the historical process appears as a progressive development of inner life—of a substantial, not a subjective kind. This involves an ever-increasing separation from the immediate situation of humanity, dominated as it is by contradiction, and hence devoid of either complete inwardness or true reality.

There is also a place within this movement for that contradiction which is so inadequately described by the expressions "subjective" and "objective." Spiritual life is at the same time self-life and cosmic life; a self unfolds and becomes a cosmos, while the cosmos gains a self—each belongs to the other. In spite of this mutual relationship the fact remains that in the historical process life tends sometimes more towards concentration, sometimes more towards expansion; now we see an aspiration towards inner life and a deepening of the self, now a desire to attain width and sink the self in outward things. On the one hand we have the danger of an invasion of life by merely human elements, on the other of its domination by a soulless world. Perhaps there is a periodicity, now one tendency taking the lead, now the other. But right through every species of change persists the movement of spiritual life towards a unity transcending contradiction. A subjective or objective tendency within the spiritual life is fundamentally different from a subjective or objective tendency as opposed to spiritual life: the latter represents a subjectivity which aims at constructing a world from the standpoint of the mere subject and an objectivity which fancies it can attain to a truth in mere things by an elimination of the spiritual element. Both these tendencies must rapidly sink into nothingness unless they surreptitiously draw upon that superior spiritual life which they refuse to recognise.

4. THE RESULTS AS THEY AFFECT THE CONCEPT OF TRUTH

Whatever transformations are thus effected must exert an influence upon the concept of truth and impart some characteristic alteration to its form. Truth no longer signifies an agreement with an external object, but an upward movement towards a life superior to all human desire or subjectivity; a life which, through active creation, comprehends the antithesis between subject and object. We are now concerned with a transformation of existence into self-activity, which, with its reshaping capacity, is essentially different from all mere manifestation within a given existence. This striving towards truth has nothing to do with any passive state of being existing independently of all life; rather does reality lie within life, attainable only through life. This life that we are now discussing is, however, no merely human affair, for it represents the independent self-life of the whole of reality, which here alone attains to contents and values. Truth is not a mere means for the enhancement of this life: truth forms a part of its being. All intellectual truth that is such on principle, rests ultimately upon a spiritual truth as a whole, and all essential progress in the knowledge of truth upon a widening and extension of life. Truth cannot be obtained at any one moment. Man gradually penetrates into its depths as a result of the great work of universal history as it goes on from age to age with its experiments, experiences, and transformations. It would hardly be possible to conceive of anything more foolish than the claim set up by certain philosophical systems to exhaust, at a given period, the whole wealth of truth and to solve every riddle. That we remain thus in a state of quest, and at the same time, unavoidably, in error, cannot in any way disturb us if we possess the conviction that all human effort has a world of spiritual life behind it which can be ours only through freedom, but which is independent of our self-will.

2. THEORETICAL—PRACTICAL

(INTELLECTUALISM—VOLUNTARISM)

(a) Historical

THE question we have just dealt with is very closely connected with the present one of intellectualism and voluntarism. But here the discussion takes a more directly spiritual turn, while formerly it was concerned with the relationship of man to the cosmos. Here, too, we have contrasting types of life; here, too, a movement thousands of years old.

An important difference is that our own age approaches the present problem in a spirit of greater confidence. With us the tendency to lay the chief emphasis in life upon will, as that which alone can give life warmth, power, and firmness, is undoubtedly preponderant. How has it come to pass that such an ancient source of division so suddenly finds us united? Let us see if history can offer any explanation.

The terms intellectualism and voluntarism are of quite modern origin. The former is first met with in the philosophical conflicts of the early nineteenth century: for example, in Schelling's *Bruno* (*Werke*, iv. 309) it is employed as the opposite of materialism. Voluntarism is as recent as the last few decades.* The expressions practical and theoretical, on the other hand, can be traced back to the zenith of Greek philosophy.

---

* This term was constructed by Tönnies, who wrote about it as follows in the Viennese *Zeit* (March 23, 1901): " These terms (*i.e. Voluntarismus* and *voluntaristisch*) were first made use of by the author of this article in his treatise, *Zur Entwickelungsgeschichte Spinozas* (Spinoza's *History of Evolution*) in the *Vierteljahrsschrift für wissenschaftliche Philosophie*, 1883. Wundt took them from Paulsen (who soon adopted them) and brought them into use through his authority. The concept of ' voluntaristic ' psychology has become more and more widely current."

Aristotle first contrasts theoretical and practical reason (νοῦς θεωρητικός and πρακτικός): the former's task is to know the world as a whole with its eternal laws, while the latter concerns itself with merely human and transitory affairs. It is not, however, confined to knowledge of particulars (the bearing of general principles upon special cases); it has principles proper to itself. At the same time its general importance is rated decidedly below that of theoretical reason. The position is the same in the Scholastic system of thought and speech: when Thomas Aquinas talks of *cognitio practica* he means neither more nor less than knowledge bearing upon action. In recent times Ch. Wolff, more than any one else, helped to establish a division of philosophy into theoretical and practical, and gave the former unqualified first place.* Kant followed him, both in his language and in his division of philosophy, but with the very important difference that he reversed the position; practical philosophy—as that which " freedom makes possible "—now takes the lead, and is made to create an independent sphere of thought: " Practical reason, in Kant's philosophy, annexes territory which had previously belonged to theoretical reason, since it originates postulates, that is, theoretical first principles, which the critique of pure reason held to be doubtful" (Trendelenburg, *Logische Untersuchungen*, 3rd edit., ii. 457). Since reason was held by Kant to attain complete independence only in this sphere, it followed that here we drew nearest to truth itself—in fact, nowhere else could humanity find an absolute truth.† From Kant's position it is only a step to Fichte's: " Practical reason

* Thus for example in the *Logica*, § 92: *Palam igitur est, philosophiam practicam universam ex Metaphysica principia petere debere.* § 93: *Metaphysica philosophiam practicam præcedere debet.*

† The manner in which Kant deduced convictions from practical reason is not without its doubtful side, and it met with a good deal of opposition. Thus Harms, for example, says (*Gesch. der Philosophie seit Kant*, p. 247): "Kant calls ideas postulates of practical reason. They are, however, not postulates of practical reason at all; they are postulates of theoretical reason in the knowl‍ge of practical reason, of reason applied to conduct in the moral life of the spirit. In Kant's philosophy the term practical reason is itself ambiguous, for on the one hand it means reason applied to conduct, on the other, the knowledge of practical reason."

is the root of all reason." Thus one period reduces the practical to a mere application of the theoretical, while another exalts it to the position of a source of new truths.

A fundamental opposition runs through the history of these terms: namely, that between cosmic knowledge and moral conduct (which is the most usual meaning of practical reason). The question is, which should govern our lives and control our convictions? The answer decides our position with regard to reality and at the same time the form which reality takes. We have here two types of life in direct opposition to one another, the one tending more especially towards breadth and clarity, the other towards warmth and strength; order distinguishes the one, freedom the other.

The Greek thinkers, without exception, assign the first place to intellect. They differ only as to the greater or less extreme to which they carry out their fundamental idea. This high valuation of the intellect was the natural expression of the Greek conviction that man belonged to an unchangeable cosmic scheme, forming, as it were, a magnificent framework of undisputed reality to our human existence. There remained nothing to do except to create a philosophy of this cosmos, free from the littlenesses of everyday-life and all the confusion of human circumstance. We may mention Aristotle, who gave purest expression to Greek culture, as upholding the absolute superiority of the life of speculative enquiry over practical life (which latter only occupied people with transitory things and made them dependent upon their environment): true happiness can only follow in the track of philosophical research. Further, the trend towards morality, which took place under the Stoics, did not mean so much a separation of life from thought as an absorption of practical energy by thought, a raising of thought to the status of reasoned action. The last flash of the Greek spirit, the philosophy of Plotinus, reveals an elevation of thought to complete sovereignty and world-creative power. In its very decline the ancient Greek world emphasised more than ever its belief in that intellectual power which gave to its cultural work an immeasurable breadth and a marvellous clearness.

It lay in the very nature of Christianity to reject this valuation. When the chief problem of life is the relationship of man to God; when, along with the appearance of new depths, men become conscious of difficult complications and even dark abysses in the human soul, and when, in consequence, the chief task becomes that of spiritual ascent and renewal, then the attention of humanity will not be directed towards cosmic knowledge but towards the condition of the soul, and beyond that to the building up of a new scheme of human relationships. This means the complete rooting up of intellectualism.

But this inner transformation did not express itself to any great extent as a shaping force determining the general conditions of life. Moreover, that which filled men's hearts did not supply the strength to create a corresponding thought-world. Augustine alone made serious progress in this direction. Consider, for example, his reference of all reality to the will (*nihil aliud quam voluntates*) and the leading position which he gives to the will in his psychology (as the uniting force in the soul). But even Augustine did not develop the Christian view of life into a complete system with a corresponding thought-world.

It has thus come to pass that the development of Christianity has been powerfully and enduringly influenced by a system of thought which it had intended to replace. Christianity suffers to this day from a division between inner feeling and outward form. Christian dogma stands under the influence of Greek intellectualism. Assuming that divine doctrine replaced secular doctrine, we still have to face the fact that right knowledge was regarded as the standard for testing the truth and value of life. At the height of the scholastic period we see Greek intellectualism more powerful than ever; logical reasoning advances into the remotest depths of the Christian thought-world.* There was no lack of opposing tendencies laying stress on the will, such as Duns Scotus' † nominalism (mysticism with a practical

---

* It was only in an outward sense that mediæval philosophy was the handmaid of theology. In an inward sense it would be much nearer the mark to say that philosophy moulded theology.

† He says, for example (see Stockl, *Phil. d. Mittelalt.*, ii. 788): *Fides non est habitus speculativus, nec credere est actus speculativus, nec visio sequens credere est visio speculativa, sed practica. Nata est enim ista visio conformis fruitioni.*

tendency), and the Reformation enabled this trend of thought to achieve a great victory. Luther tried with all his might to liberate Christianity from the power of Greek intellectualism, whether Aristotelian or Neo-Platonic; he believed that Greek thought had volatilised or obscured the real substance of Christianity. Melancthon calls the "heart and its emotions" "the most essential and chief part of man."

But notwithstanding the development of will, Protestantism did not find the power to convert its innermost sources of strength into a system of life; it, too, ended in again paying homage to the power of intellectualism. If speculation was permanently dispensed with, knowledge of another kind—a knowledge of historical data—but all the same *knowledge*, appeared to be indispensable to the rescue of souls. The conception of belief, too, took a strongly intellectualistic turn; the new church became first and foremost a congregation based upon doctrine, a school of the pure word. A new orthodoxy came into existence, at least equal to that of the Greeks in self-righteousness and intolerance.

The Modern World from the very outset unreservedly and joyously took up the task of thought. It looked to thought in hope of breaking away from the yoke of historical tradition. Thought promised to bring clarity into a chaos that had become intolerable. Men believed that thought could break through the tissue of trivial human interests and open up the prospect of an infinite cosmos. As compared with the Greek method, thought has now passed from quiet contemplation to something more akin to restless work, belligerent advance; from assimilating a given world it has come to building up a new one; thought of this kind dominates the Enlightenment down to its every detail —not only the speculative school with its bold cosmic philosophy, but also the empirical with its tendency towards practical life. Here, also, salvation is expected entirely from definite and clearly defined knowledge. The type of knowledge is no longer what it was—nevertheless it is still knowledge.* Like all great movements, the Enlightenment carried within itself its own

* See for example Locke (at the commencement of the *Essay*): "Our business here is not to know all things, but those which concern our conduct."

antidote. The enhanced and excessive emphasis laid upon knowledge necessarily gave rise to doubts as to the extent to which knowledge of the world is possible and as to the power of knowledge over mankind.* But a mere reaction has never yet been able to dominate men's minds, and a positive turn had to be given to this tendency before it was capable of directing humanity into a fresh path.

Such a change was effected in the philosophical sphere by Kant. His influence in this matter, both in a positive and negative sense, was incomparably the greatest which had yet attached to any scientific work. Never before had the capacity for more knowledge been so keenly and thoroughly tested, and the conditions of its successful attainment so accurately ascertained. The result was a violent upheaval, the destructive effect of which was more than compensated for by the raising of moral action to the status of a moral world and the recognition of this world as the core of all reality. This upheaval brought intellectualism, for the first time, face to face with an opposing movement of equal force; a movement which had been in existence for thousands of years, but had not previously been scientifically classified and systematised. Intellectualism, nevertheless, raised its head again in the shape of Hegel's Panlogism —raised it as boldly as ever; but this was only rendered possible by lightly passing over the true significance of Kant's work, and soon there came the reaction with gathered force. Since then the prevailing tendency of the age has been against intellectualism. This may be noticed in the influence of Schopenhauer, with his doctrine of the will; also in the religious and theological tendency which aims at laying chief emphasis upon the claims and tasks of practical life. We see it in the preference of humanity in general for attacking practical social

* This is to be seen, for example, in the case of Pascal, and even better in that of Bayle, the most important sceptic of the Enlightenment. The latter says, for example (œuv. div. 1727, iii. 89b): *Ce ne sont pas les opinions générales de l'esprit qui nous déterminent d agir, mais les passions présentes du cœur.* Bayle's faithful disciple, Frederick the Great, agreed with him in believing that life derived its strength and fixity solely from morality: *Les sciences doivent être considerées comme des moyens qui nous donnent plus de capacité pour remplir nos devoirs* (see Zeller. *Friedrich d. G. als Philosoph,* p. 183).

questions rather than pondering over cosmic problems—the former, indeed, force themselves upon our attention with increasing persistency. Within the special sphere of science, psychology in particular tends to strengthen the new tendency, because it reveals the extent to which the world of ideas is dominated by the power of instincts and interests, and would even like to demonstrate that the will directs the movements of this world.

This high valuation of the will is accompanied by a desire to attribute every possible evil in modern life to the predominance of reason. We are uncertain as to the main direction which our effort should take and our spiritual life rests upon no sure foundation : it is stated that the intellect is responsible for this state of affairs ; in its desire to have proof for everything, it will allow us to possess only what comes to us indirectly, and the certainty of direct life is thus rendered impossible. We live in a chaos of different opinions and different values, and this, we are told, is due to the dominion of the reasoning activity, which causes individuals to rely solely on their own powers of reflection and hence inevitably drives them farther apart from one another. It is complained that things holy and divine no longer command reverence, and the explanation is sought in the undue development of human self-consciousness, itself chiefly brought about by the intellect, with its sense of power and its overweening pride of knowledge. If the intellect is thus mainly responsible for all our errors, release from its tyranny should result in a general increment of health throughout the whole of life. Has modern voluntarism the power to procure such a release?

(b) Voluntarism

Voluntarism is not a simple phenomenon; each important historical epoch has had its own special voluntarism, which has taken a form determined by the leading tendency of the age.

In the sphere of religious thought, this tendency was represented by the view that not only God's revelation but man's acceptance of it was a self-originated act of will. This view emphasised the independence, spontaneity, and pure actuality of religious life. It rejected all attempts to make religion intelligible by reference to its broader context. The opposition between intellectualism and voluntarism is clearly shown in the well-known comparison of Thomas Aquinas with Duns Scotus; the former said that God ordained good because it was good, the latter that good was good because God ordained it. Voluntarism did full justice to the specific qualities of religion, its independence and its uniqueness. At the same time a danger arose—namely, that of a separation of religion from the rest of life, an absence of all points of connection. Since a complete spiritual penetration and assimilation of the content of truth was not achieved, it was easy for the immediacy of religious experience to turn to shallow and obstinate certainty of conviction, the spontaneity and freedom to blind self-will. One cannot help thinking of Plotinus' saying, that he who strives to rise above reason is in no little danger of becoming unreasonable.

In the sphere of philosophy, voluntarism takes on a different complexion. It is now a question of shifting the centre of gravity of life from knowing to willing (more especially to willing in its connection with the moral life). A lack of confidence in our capacity for obtaining knowledge supplied the chief impetus in this direction; since our knowledge did not appear capable of penetrating to real fundamentals, it did not seem in a position to furnish a sure foundation for life. Unless truth, in the fullest sense of the word, was to be completely abandoned, another source of truth had to be found, and after the disturbance of religious faith there seemed to be no other save man's moral conduct. Kant interpreted the moral life in such a deep sense that it became the revelation of a new world; a world forming the last depth of reality. This world, however, could not be theoretically made plain to everyone, any more than could moral conduct itself. It could not be exhibited as a present possession, and was capable of carrying conviction only to those who recognised the fundamentally moral nature of life and took up their human responsibilities. Deeds thus precede knowledge, and what results from them in the shape of decisive conviction is not of the nature of theoretical knowledge, but is a practical postulate. We all know that the consequences of this teaching were deep, revolutionary, and intensely stimulating.

It is difficult to pass judgment upon this phase of the problem, because fruitful and necessary truths are here so closely combined with questionable interpretations. A clearly expressed and outstanding truth is the dependence of our ultimate convictions upon the operations of the inward life and the reality manifested in and through these, and not upon conditioning factors situated in the external world. This view puts an end to all attempts at penetrating to an inner nature of things by means of speculation and then interpreting reality from this new standpoint. Closely connected with this, truth is another; that the content of inner life is not ready-made property, acquired without effort, but must germinate within us and gradually unfold itself. The way in which a given person sees the world will depend upon the degree of this inner development. We thus see why it is that humanity in its struggle after truth becomes inwardly divided against itself, and why it is that the personal factor is so important.

As soon as we pass from considering this position in a general way to examining its results when systematically worked out, we find ourselves in a region filled with doubt. It is one thing to attach a central importance to the fundamental facts of the inward life, and to rely upon them as determining data in our quest for knowledge: it is another to exalt them to the position of a direct source of knowledge. The one is as necessary as the other is impossible. The facts of the inward life, just as they are, cannot be immediately made use of as a secure foundation. They must first of all be clarified and illuminated by the methods of philosophy. What is subsequently found to be fundamental and established as true has universal validity and its accompanying inner compulsory force; it is impossible for it to be dependent upon a personal assent.

Some mathematical truths are so difficult to understand that only very few people are capable of fathoming them. Does this interfere in the slightest degree with their universal validity? Following the same line of argument, if the truths of life do not carry complete conviction until a corresponding life has been developed, and if a decision of the whole man is necessary in order to approach them, this does not mean that they are in any sense reduced to mere possibilities, which one may accept or not as one pleases. They continue fully to retain their character as necessary truths possessing universal validity. The subjectivity does not lie in truth itself, but in the relationship of humanity to it. Nothing can be completely true that is inwardly connected with any subjective factor. Looking at the matter from this point of view, we are compelled, on principle, to reject the conception of practical reason as one-sided and misleading. There are not two reasons, one theoretical and the other practical, existing side by side. There is one reason and one alone, concerned with the whole of life. The conception of self-activity is, however, to be included in that of reason, as one of its essential attributes. Reason must not be conceived of as a thing utterly detached; it is the representative of a completely independent life—of reality self-poised and self-contained. In the absence of such a life there could be no truth at all.

Moreover, Kant's conception of practical reason is a much more exalted one than that usually in vogue. It is a conception which revolutionises the whole of life, brings about a shifting of the centre of gravity towards original creative work, and (in a particular direction) gives life a cosmic character possessing strict universal validity. If this is anything it is metaphysics, although not of the kind we deal with in ontological speculation. But in proportion as this metaphysical character becomes obliterated, the sphere of practical reason ceases to be the whole reality with all its depth, and becomes one of a number of separate spheres, thus less and less fulfilling the function of universally valid truth. Hence life based upon such practical reason tends to narrow practical and moral life and to isolate it from the rest of human culture, with the result that the former becomes subjective and impressionable, the latter superficial and merely utilitarian in its aims—life as a whole deteriorating through this division. The work of human culture should never become separated from men's ultimate convictions, for the wider the gap between them, the more impossible is it for our life to be spiritually controlled and permeated and for any real greatness to be achieved.

In the life of to-day, voluntarism presents itself in yet another aspect; namely, as a scientific theory, which comes to the front, in the first place, in psychology as a movement which aims at demonstrating the dependence of the life of ideas upon the instincts and desires, and the conditioning of its entire course by a voluntary phase—as is seen more particularly in Wundt's theory of apperception. Much new and valuable knowledge has been won along these lines and our general insight into the whole matter has been deepened. It is, however, distinctly questionable whether, in this case, we have not often to do less with an opposition between intellect and will than with one between a central and a peripheral activity of the soul, extending through the whole of life.

The shape which voluntarism (with the accompanying undue preponderance of practical activity) takes in the life of to-day must be considered from the broadest standpoint. Speaking in a general way, it may be said that it reveals itself in the prevailing view that the practical satisfaction of man (of man in relation to his immediate environment) is the one and only true goal—the pursuit of knowledge being looked upon as a mere means to this end and indeed a foolish waste of time unless devoted to the promotion of human well-being. That such is the general tendency of modern life has been already pointed out in the historical sketch. Humanity has become weary of struggling over cosmic problems. Questions of inner development, of the development of the whole man to a world-embracing personality, are pushed far into the background by the unceasing growth of political, economical, and technical problems. The struggle for economical self-preservation, in particular, more and more absorbs all our powers and increasingly causes life and conduct to be looked upon as mere matters of utility. Such a state of affairs leaves no sort of room for knowledge to retain any self-value. The pragmatic movement in particular (which, starting in America and England, has more and more occupied the attention of the civilised world) attempts to develop a specific theory of knowledge with this practical point of view as centre. Let us examine this subject a little more in detail.

(c) Pragmatism

Pragmatism is, as yet, so little known in Germany that before proceeding further it will be well to make a few explanatory remarks. We will take as our main basis a series of lectures by William James, delivered with the object of elucidating pragmatism.* The expression pragmatism was first used as a philosophical concept in its present sense by Charles Pierce in the American magazine *The Popular Science Monthly* (1878). Twenty years later James took the matter up and developed it in brilliant fashion. Among other exponents may be mentioned Dewey (Chicago) and Schiller (Oxford), the latter being the originator of the expression "humanism." It is interesting, from a social and historical point of view, to notice that now for the first time we see America taking the lead in a philosophical movement; it is in America, too, for the most part, that pragmatism has become a widespread tendency. In Europe this movement has been more influential in England and in Italy than elsewhere.

Speaking of the relationship between pragmatism and other tendencies of thought, James says (p. 51): "Pragmatism represents a perfectly familiar attitude in philosophy, the empiricist attitude, but it represents it, as it seems to me, both in a more radical and in a less objectionable form than it has ever yet assumed"; and further (p. 53): "It agrees with nominalism, for instance, in always appealing to particulars; with utilitarianism in emphasising practical aspects; with positivism in its disdain for verbal solutions, useless questions, and metaphysical abstractions." Pragmatism claims credit for being a method, and not a system. This method consists in bringing the pursuit of knowledge into close relationship with human existence and its development. Nothing is to be reckoned true that cannot be justified from this point of view. The true thus becomes a portion of the good (p. 76): "The true is the name

---

* *Pragmatism* (translated into German by Wilhelm Jerusalem (1908).) Jerusalem's article called *Der Pragmatismus: eine neue philosophische Methode* (*Deutsche Literaturzeitung*, January 25, 1908) is also worthy of notice.—*Tr. note*: The references given in this chapter are to the English original of *Pragmatism* (1907).

of whatever proves itself to be good in the way of belief, and good, too, for definite assignable reasons." Again (p. 194) · "All our theories are *instrumental*, are mental modes of *adaptation* to reality, rather than revelations or gnostic answers to some divinely-instituted world-enigma." In pursuance of this line of thought "humanism" looks upon truths as products of the human race: "Truth makes no other kind of claim and imposes no other kind of ought than health and wealth do. All these claims are conditional" (p. 230).

Such a conception as this must give a thoroughly peculiar turn to scientific enquiry in so far as the latter is now directed not so much towards establishing principles as towards following up the consequences involved in their development. We no longer consider things as they are in themselves, apart from mankind, but refer everything to humanity and estimate it according to its value for humanity.

What does this signify, and what kind of a transformation does it bring about? These questions are best answered by a consideration of the examples brought forward by James himself.

The conflict between materialism and spiritualism appears in quite a new light, and is brought to a decision by estimating the services rendered by each to the cause of humanity, and not by dwelling upon the correctness or otherwise of the principles involved in the two tendencies. By materialism is understood (in this connection) that species of thought which explains the higher phenomena by means of the lower and represents the destinies of the world as being controlled by its blind components and unconscious forces: by spiritualism, that which assigns the controlling power to the higher elements, thereby making spirit something more than a mere witness and reporter of the course of events and recognising it as capable of active participation in the same. Let the question now be asked, Which of these two conceptions best promotes human life? There can be no doubt as to the answer. The final practical conclusions of materialism are completely cheerless, while spiritualism, with its affirmation of a moral order throughout the universe, gives full liberty to our hopes (p. 108): "Spiritualistic faith in all its forms deals with a world of *promise*, while materialism's sun sets in a sea of disappointment." The religions problem is discussed along the same lines: instead of dealing with speculative principles, the matter is approached from the point of view of human needs (p. 299): "On pragmatistic principles, if the hypothesis of God works satisfactorily in the widest sense of the word, it is true. Now, whatever its residual difficulties may be, experience shows that it certainly does work, and that the problem is to build it out and determine it so that it will combine satisfactorily with all the other working truths."

He who has made himself at home within the movement will readily understand that it is quite capable of gaining wide influence in contemporary circles. By assigning first place to what had formerly been regarded as only of occasional and secondary importance, things are seen in a manner which seems to make them peculiarly simple and easy of comprehension. It is obvious that a great simplification must ensue, because all problems not related to the maintenance of human life are dropped as unprofitable; at the same time this relationship seems to provide an entirely impartial standard of valuation for the various assertions, thus enabling the matter, in each case, to be raised above mere party strife. Truth becomes more direct and fruitful, more plastic and adaptable, by being thus thrown into the centre of the stream of life and called upon to take an active share in the forward movement. Such a solution seems to be particularly suitable for a time like our own, so divided in its convictions.* The positive side of the work, moreover, receives essential support from an incisive criticism of the traditional concept of truth.

Notwithstanding the stimulating power of such a movement, supported as it is by brilliant and distinguished thinkers, we are compelled to regard it, when we consider it as a whole and in its ultimate bearings, as an error. The powerful impression

---

* James remarks in this connection (p. 194): "Certainly the restlessness of the actual theoretic situation, the value for some purposes of each thought-level, and the inability of either to expel the others decisively, suggest this pragmatistic view."

produced by pragmatism is due, in the first place, to the fact that it reverses the conventional way of looking at things. But what if, in the process, the idea of truth itself is reversed and ends by standing on its head? And this is what actually happens. The essence of the conception of truth, and the life and soul of our search after truth, is to be found in the idea that in truth man attains to something superior to all his own opinions and inclinations, something that possesses a validity completely independent of any human consent; the hope of an essentially new life is thus held out to man, a vision of a wider and richer being, an inner communion with reality, a liberation from all that is merely human. On the other hand, when the good of the individual and of humanity becomes the highest aim and the guiding principle, truth sinks to the level of a merely utilitarian opinion. This is destructive of inner life. All the power of conviction that truth can possess must disappear the moment it is seen to be a mere means. Truth can only exist as an end in itself. "Instrumental" truth is no truth at all.

We must not be understood to assert that the influence of different doctrines upon human conditions is an unimportant theme. It is certain that much stimulus and illumination may be derived from a more careful study of this influence and an examination of its causes. But what we are here concerned with is, in the first instance, something merely phenomenal; what is essential, or non-essential, right or wrong, has still to be made clear.

Pragmatism disintegrates truth by reducing it to a crowd of separate truths, and even claims credit for doing so. But can we be sure that these separate truths will dwell peacefully and harmoniously side by side, that there will be no conflict between them? In the case of conflict how is arbitration to take place?

Finally, the chief aim and end of pragmatism—the success and enrichment of human life—is, as an end, by no means free from objection. By human life is here meant civilised life on the broad scale; but in order to regard this life as so surely good, one must be inspired by the optimistic enthusiasm for human culture which was more characteristic of earlier ages than it is of our own. Is this life, when taken as in itself the final thing, really worth all the trouble and excitement, all the work and effort, all the sufferings and sacrifices that it costs? When we examine this life, with its vanity and show and its inner emptiness, when we consider how it is penetrated through and through by impurity and pretence, does it not seem a fearful contradiction? Shall the quest after truth be made a means for the preservation of this exceedingly dubious life? We cannot conceive of any belief more hazardous than a faith in life so baseless as this.

(d) Our own Position: Activism

In the introduction to the German edition of William James's *Pragmatism*, Jerusalem refers to the approximation of my own position towards that of the pragmatists, and remarks: "Eucken's activism rests upon definite metaphysical assumptions, while pragmatism is purely empirical" (p. vii). It is true that I sympathetically welcome an effort which aims at bringing truth into closer relationship with life and regarding it as more than a merely intellectual matter; at the same time I am fully in agreement with the rejection of that conception of truth which makes it consist in conformity with an entity existing side by side with ourselves. The question remains, What is meant by life? Here we must recognise a wide gap between the tendencies indicated by the above two concepts, "empirical" and "metaphysical." In the former case life stands for the actual condition of man, for the human state (whether it be the individual or the race that is referred to, does not make any ultimate difference). On the other hand, when we speak of seeking a closer connection between truth and life, we mean the life of the spirit as a self-sufficient life (*Beisichselbstsein des Lebens*), which forms, with its own contents and values, something essentially new over against all merely human conditions, and requires, moreover, a complete reversal of the immediate state of affairs. Pragmatism and activism attach very different meanings to the union of truth with life. The former regards truth as merely the means towards a higher end (which seems to us subversive of inner life), while the latter makes it an essential and integral portion of life itself, and hence can never consent to it becoming a mere means.

If we measure the achievements of various tendencies of thought in the struggle for truth by the fruitfulness of their contributions to the development of life, we arrive at essentially different results, according as we take up the one standpoint or the other. In the one case the standard is usefulness to humanity, with all the relativity which this implies; in the other, it is the preservation and content of spiritual life, and the various tendencies of thought must here be valued by the measure of their success in substantially deepening and broadening this life. The difference between these two positions may become so marked as to amount to complete opposition. A tendency of thought may call upon men to make sacrifices which their human nature will find hard; it may make their lives difficult rather than easy—indeed, all truly great thought has this effect—but at the same time it can enlarge and enrich intellectual and spiritual life. On the other hand, what tends to promote comfortable human existence may be extremely oppressive to the life of the spirit. Modern life clearly shows us that an age full of pleasure and rich in achievement may be empty enough spiritually. [For a further discussion of the concept of truth the reader is referred to my *Grundlinien einer neuen Lebensanschauung* (1907); (*Life's Basis and Life's Ideal*, trans. A. Widgery, pub. A. & C. Black).]

In company with the pragmatists we wish for a conversion of life into activity, but we think this cannot be realised so long as we start from life as we find it with all its rigid limitations; it can only take place through a reversal of this existence, through going back to a new starting-point and developing a new life. That this is a species of metaphysics we do not deny; in fact we emphatically demand metaphysics, since it is only by a reversal of the immediate condition of things that an original and self-active life is made possible, and hence spiritual life cannot maintain itself without some sort of metaphysics. In this way we again come back to the necessity of an independent spiritual life as a new stage of reality, as the unfolding of the depths which reality contains within its own nature.

Taking into account all the above considerations, it does not appear as if the contrast between intellectualism and voluntarism really went to the root of the matter. It is not sufficient to transfer the chief emphasis in life from one activity of the soul to another. This brings about no really essential change in life, no enhancement of life; it does not raise us above the old fixed limits. The real contrast is that between a free, self-active life on the one hand, and, on the other, one which, however eager or diligent, is inwardly enslaved. But once this is recognised, the whole matter takes on an essentially new complexion.

(e) Intellect and Intellectualism

The distinctive character of the activistic position is perhaps most easily explained by a consideration of its attitude towards intellectualism and intellectual work. It is under no inducement whatever to diminish in any way the importance of intellectual work. It cannot look upon the latter as an accessory to the central things of life, as something that could be quite well dispensed with. The desired reconstruction of life, the direction of life towards self-activity, will never by any chance be accomplished and maintained without energetic intellectual work. In this connection we may refer to history, which witnesses that whenever the quest of knowledge has been held in high honour it has always figured as an essential portion of life, a portion which, if undeveloped, would prevent life itself reaching its full stature; it has never appeared in the character of a mere accompaniment of life or of an explanation following upon a "given" and finished state of affairs. We see this exemplified in Plato, in the Fathers of the Church (such as Clement and Origen), and in Spinoza and Leibniz. It was universally believed that knowledge first made it possible for the spiritual content of life to reach its fullest development and to become the complete property of humanity. Even if the claims of knowledge to be the whole of life were pressed to the point of error, it was at any rate recognised that knowledge was no mere copy of reality: it did not exist side by side with life, but within life. However decisively, in consequence, we must reject the idea of making the intellect a scapegoat for everything we dislike in modern life, he who desires an independent and self-sufficing spiritual life and believes that if human life is to possess a true content it must be derived from this source, is thereby saved from any tendency to impart an intellectualistic form to life; he is much more likely to be extremely sensitive to the way in which the Modern World in particular (including our own age) has been swamped by intellectualistic movements. His regard for spiritual life as a whole will prevent him, however, from agreeing with the verdict passed by the voluntarists upon this inundation. But let us first examine this development of the power of intellectualism. We shall then be able to judge whether or no the attempted counter-movement is really strong enough to cope with it.

1. The Invasion of Modern Life by Intellectualism

In the first place we are influenced by the various forms of intellectualism which have come down to us from the past. There is the intellectualism of the classical epoch, when spirit and intellect were usually regarded as interchangeable terms. Another form manifested itself in the life of the Christian Church, which in spite of opposing tendencies, persisted for the most part in giving its belief the character of an intellectual activity. The Modern World, too, looked more especially to intellectual activity to bring about that up-levelling of life towards which it worked. This tendency has been maintained right down to the present day, and is shown not only in tendencies originating in the inner life, such as speculation, enlightenment, and so forth, but even more clearly in that type of thought which is shaped by the study of nature. For natural scientists are still accustomed to identify spirit and consciousness and to interpret spiritual life as a mere reflection of an external world. Hence, from their point of view, all moral elevation, and indeed our whole salvation, is to be expected, in the first place, from a rectification of concepts.*

Nothing could bear clearer witness to the power of intellectualism than the fact that the counter-movements have often become intellectualistic themselves and ended by contributing to its influence. A new content was desired; but it was presented in the old form, and therefore fell at once into the power of the enemy. So it was throughout the whole history of Christianity; and so it has continued to be right into the nineteenth century. Schelling, towards the latter end of his career, struggled with all his might to tear up the deeply rooted rationalism of his time and replace it by a positive and irrational mode of thought. But his new thought was expressed as a mere doctrine. To accept this doctrine and to be converted to these principles was to place one's life upon a basis of truth. If this is not rationalism and intellectualism, what is it? Very likely many present-day opponents of intellectualism are doing exactly what Schelling did!

Intellectualism has firmly rooted itself in habits of thought both old and new, and the influence which it thus exerts is even more dangerous than any we have referred to above, because it is more subtle and penetrates more deeply. From the earliest times the essential task of knowledge has been taken to be the abstracting of universals from the limitless multiplicity of appearances: in the ancient world this was in complete accordance with the prevailing view of reality as a whole, since simple and unchangeable forms seemed to constitute its fundamental structure; but now that this latter view is no longer held, the corresponding conception of the task of knowledge is discredited.

* This is seen with especial clearness in the greatest realistic system of the nineteenth century, the philosophy of Comte. We can only mention a few characteristic passages from the *Cours de Philosophie Positive* (4th ed. 1877): in i. 40–41, we read: *Le mécanisme social repose finalement sur des opinions;* according to iv. 113, the unsatisfying position of present-day affairs is mainly due to intellectual anarchy, so that our first necessity is a *philosophie convenable;* the deepest root of political corruption is declared to be *l'impuissance et le discrédit des idées générales.* Comte in fact regarded the epochs of history as corresponding to stages of knowledge. Modern monism, too, believes itself capable of raising the whole level of life by means of a rectification of concepts (see chapter on "Monism and Dualism").

In order to pick out the main characteristics of experience and unite manifoldness into a whole, far more is involved and far more is demanded than any mere abstracting of points of resemblance.*

Along with this intellectualistic over-valuation of the search for universals there goes a remarkable cult of the abstract concept—a cult which became particularly prominent during the nineteenth century. What a power is exercised to-day by such excessively vague concepts as reason, civilisation, law, value, progress, humanitarianism ! Their chief recommendation seems to lie in their indefinite character, which relieves us from making disagreeable decisions. Frequently they serve as blank cheques for each individual to fill in at pleasure. At the same time we criticise Hegel, whose concepts at any rate imparted a definite content to a connected thought-world.

The influence of intellectualistic thought is to be seen also in the popular inclination to conceive of our conduct after the fashion of a logical conclusion, as the subsumption of a particular case under a general law. As a matter of fact, scientific work itself would not be able to go very far, and in particular it would not achieve anything new, if the logical forms were not mere vessels, filled and made vital by the thought-process. Outside the scientific world the perversion becomes even more obvious; when, for example, political life and legal proceedings,

* The term abstraction itself manifests this alteration; in accordance with it the term has passed through two chief phases, a logical-metaphysical and a psychological, the former going back to Aristotle, the latter to Locke. Abstract (ἐξ ἀφαιρέσεως λεγόμενα) is the name given by Aristotle to forms existing apart from matter—more particularly the mathematical quantities. This meaning was retained during the Middle Ages (*abstrahere formam a materia intellectu*). It was not until the Modern World that abstraction was looked upon as involving a gradual selection of common properties from the multiplicity of appearances. The older meaning survived the sway of the ancient doctrine of forms; thus, for example, in Baumeister's *definitiones philosophicæ ex systemate Wolfii collectæ* (def. DCCXXXV) it runs: *abstrahere ea dicimur, si ea, quæ in perceptione distinguuntur, tanquam a re percepta sejuncta intuemur*. In Kant's *Logik* (viii. 92, Hartenst.) abstraction means "the separation of all the distinctive elements from the given ideas, so as to leave only what is common." Hence he will not say "to abstract something" (*abstrahere aliquid*), but "to abstract from something," and gives it as his opinion that "one should really call abstract concepts, abstracting concepts (*conceptus abstrahentes*)." The uncertainty in modern terminology is largely due to the confusion of these two meanings.

and indeed all human actions, are interpreted as the application of general principles to particular cases. To do this is to force everything into a rigid pattern and destroy originality and individuality. It is also one of the roots of the much attacked bureaucracy of to-day (which seems to grow unceasingly, however, in spite of all attacks).

Finally, we must not forget that intellectualism, with its tendency to identify thought and spirit and to treat the world mainly as a subject of contemplation, has sunk very deeply into our speech (more particularly in the sphere of science). Although it might appear that the mere terms did not commit us very far, as a matter of fact they may very easily lead us under the yoke of intellectualism.

Intellectualism thus surrounds us on every side; it holds us captive within the close meshes of its encircling net. No subjective feeling can free us from it; even the assertion of a directly opposite view may very easily lead us, as we have seen, more or less directly back into the old path. There is only one way of giving the matter a new turn. It is by recognising that intellectual work itself does not become positive and productive until it becomes an integral portion of *an inclusive spiritual life*, both receiving from that life and contributing to its advancement, until it is guided by the resultant drift of great spiritual organisations and impelled by the energies which originate from these sources. That this really is so can be proved both directly and indirectly: all genuine intellectual accomplishment has stood in close relationship with movements of *spiritual life as a whole*; on the other hand, whenever the work has allowed such relationships to lapse it has rapidly sunk to empty formalism or uncertain reflection. Such a maintenance of the dependence of the intellect upon the whole is perfectly compatible with the recognition of its importance and significance within the whole.

2. The Life-Process as the Foundation of Knowledge

Those who assign but small importance to knowledge, and see in it nothing more than a mere registration of appearances, will not be inclined to waste time in the investigation of its exact nature and its relationship to spiritual life as a whole. But those who seek in knowledge an illumination and an inner assimilation of reality will realise that this is a very difficult problem. How is it possible for us to master and appropriate an unfamiliar reality if we do not possess a capacity suitable to such a task, a force with which to meet the resistance of things? How can an experience become of value to us if it does not link itself to a movement coming from within and carry it forward, and how can it provide us with an answer if no question has first of all been put to it? But where can the power necessary to carry out this achievement be found if the whole life-process does not complete an inner concentration, combine its several activities together into a whole, and draw upon this whole for assistance in its struggle against the environment? Such a movement as this would impart a specific character and direction to knowledge as to every other manifestation. When life is thus linked together to form a characteristic whole, a sphere of existence peculiar to this whole is marked off from the rest of life, a specific form being imparted to experience and to the fundamental relationship between man and reality and man and his sphere of work. The aims and methods of knowledge will follow these lines. It would be impossible for any one to understand the special and distinctive greatness of Greek philosophy without perceiving it to be a scientific application of the same synthesis of life which lay behind the whole of Greek culture. This synthesis was not obtained independently of intellectual work—on the contrary, it stood in incessant need of its assistance; but it was not a work of knowledge alone, of a knowledge trusting entirely in its own power. As a matter of fact, it is only a knowledge grounded in a synthesis of life, and drawing upon its rich resources, which can possess settled tendencies and develop along inevitable lines; only such a knowledge is capable of grasping its object and penetrating to its centre; only such a knowledge can make reality into a living whole. Why does scholasticism, in spite of all the diligence and ingenuity that went to its construction, make such an impression of poverty? Why has it been comparatively unfruitful, in a spiritual sense, in spite of its extensive opportunities? It is because it has lacked the shaping force of a characteristic life, and has hence been unable to impart to its concepts an inner warmth and a power of imperative conviction. The newer philosophy was predestined to secure the victory over scholasticism, if only because a new life worked in it and through it. The same reason explains the distinction between creative thinkers like Leibniz and Kant and capable schoolmen like Wolff and Herbart; the former bring to light new syntheses of life, and their work produces an enrichment of reality. They do not merely take to pieces and rearrange given material; they do not merely speculate about reality. They are producers of new reality, parents in the spiritual world. There is no stronger corroboration of this connection between knowledge and spiritual life as a whole than the experiences within the sphere of logic itself, which, on account of the unchangeability and universal validity of its laws, is apt to look upon itself as superior to any dependence or relationship. The inviolability of these laws is clear and indisputable. But laws and forms cannot as such engender living thought. Real human thinking is by no means a mere uniform application of these laws of thought; over and beyond such application it preserves a characteristic quality which penetrates and dominates every detail, and can come only from the whole of a life-process. From this point of view, thought, in its finer structure, differs with the vital synthesis it expresses. Thus Greek science down to the very details of logical method received a characteristic formation from the general artistic tendency of Greek life, the close relationship between thought and contemplation, the desire for direct and rapid synthesis combined with an aversion to anything indefinite, the acceptance of the elements of life as given and unchangeable. Consider, too, how strongly the intellectual cast of the later classical period and of the Middle Ages shows the influence of a new life dominated by religion; the whole of our visible existence has now become the mere symbol of an invisible order, the concepts have lost their hard and fast character, the statements their rigid exclusiveness. This allegorical rendering feels and sees a higher world beyond the present condition of sense-existence, but without degrading the latter to the position of an indifferent phenomenon. Thus one and the same object is image and substance—sensual and spiritual in one. This almost visionary tendency of thought, dominated as it is by moods and intuitions, is not conscious of the untenable contradictions into which it lapses, at once binding and loosing, affirming and denying. The mediæval conception of the Church, the doctrine of the sacraments, &c., rest however on this type of thought. Scholasticism at its height became clearer and more restrained, but since, in spite of its energetic development of syllogistic method, it lacked an independent synthesis and a corresponding vigour of thought-energy, it also lacked the decisiveness of disjunctive procedure, the power to keep incompatible alternatives apart: totally different worlds (such as the Aristotelian, with its welcome, and the ancient Christian, with its repudiation, of the world, or—within Christianity itself—the ecclesiastical order and the mysticism which put itself above all order) are here found existing side by side in the most peaceable fashion. The system is so cleverly arranged and graded that so long as a direct collision is avoided the several components seem to be in complete harmony; elements which vigorous thought would at once perceive to be incompatible appear compatible. We may mention, as a further example, that the logical method of modern science, with its keener analysis and more clear-cut divisions, its breaking up even of elements, and its endeavour to penetrate the infinite, shows, clearly enough, a close connection with the modern ideal of power and movement. If, in research of the modern kind, we see the type of all research we are simply identifying a particular species of spiritual life with the spiritual life itself. Just as each clearly defined epoch has its own particular kind of logic, so has every independent thinker; without a characteristic logic there can be no characteristic mode of thought and no characteristic construction of life. The more powerful this construction the deeper will its influence penetrate, until it reaches the simplest elements and activities of thought.

Thus the work of thought will become richer, more individual and more concrete by being associated with life as a whole. At the same time new problems and tasks arise. It must be shown what knowledge accomplishes for life as a whole; it must be more closely demonstrated how, in the development of knowledge, the separation of the accidental from the essential, the linking up of particulars, the emergence of universal validity, are brought about. At first sight it might seem as if the universal validity of knowledge was particularly threatened through the intimate connection subsisting between knowledge, on the one hand, and the diverse organisations of life on the other. It may be asked, Will not this result in the disintegration of truth (which will become a multiplicity of truths) and in the complete triumph of a destructive relativism? That would only be the case if all syntheses of life stood side by side, as of equal value, and their several achievements did not work towards a single comprehensive synthesis by reference to which everything was to measure itself. Could not such a synthesis be ever present, as the first object of effort, and at the same time serve, from the very beginning, for the specific shaping and directing of life and consequently of thought also? It is no objection to an idea that its formulation should stir up new problems. If the problems are real they will tend to strengthen the fundamental point of view rather than militate in any way against it.

3. The Quest for Truth and its Motive Power

In the struggle for truth, what are really the most powerful and decisive factors? Every consideration must help to convince us that here we find ourselves face to face with genuine problems. An examination of disputes between persons of opposing convictions makes it very clear that mere reasons and proofs are not decisive. How should it be otherwise in that larger arena where mind clashes with mind in the great struggles of human thought? Each disputant translates the arguments of the other into his own language and his own methods of thought, and puts a completely different complexion upon them. The result is two monologues carried on side by side. The controversy seldom reaches the level of real dialogue. In reality arguments owe their power of conviction not to their logical or dialectical value, but to the content and force of the spiritual life, the spiritual concentrations, the life-energies, which they have to draw upon. In the discussion of questions of principle, each disputant is, at the bottom, defending himself and his own inherent character. It is from such spiritual self-preservation that power, warmth, and passion first stream into the intellectual movement. Fruitful expression and the possibility of a mutual understanding do not become possible until spiritual kinship has prepared a common ground. Aristotle, Augustine, Thomas Aquinas, and Voltaire were all first-rate logicians, but does anybody suppose that they would have convinced one another had they argued together for an eternity? Only a shallow and unstable man can change his spiritual character in response to mere argument. Standing upon the basis of merely intellectual considerations a man could never possess his own being in joy and security; he would be in perpetual fear of the advent of some more powerful controversialist who would overcome him and force him into a contrary position.

The study of history shows us that it has not been isolated figures of thought, or mere ideas as such, which have dominated men's minds and aroused their passion; it has been the specific concentrations of life, the spiritual energies. We are often told by conscious and unconscious adherents of Hegelian thought that ideas produce their consequences with overwhelming necessity, and that nothing stirs us up so profoundly, nothing drives us forward so irresistibly, as a logical contradiction. Consequences and contradictions can certainly acquire an irresistible power over men, but this is not due to purely logical causes. Consequences may lie very near and yet not be fulfilled, contradictions may be close at hand and never be felt. It is all a question, in this case, whether the problems do or do not become associated with the task of spiritual self-preservation, and whether or not vital energies unfold themselves through the problems to form a region of spiritual existence. It is only when intellectual life is thus assimilated and enters integrally into the life it expresses that its consequences are imperative and its contradictions unbearable. The power of logic is derived in the first place from the degree of unification, the power of gathering life together into a whole, with which it is associated, rather than (as is often wrongly imagined) from its own resources.

The patient endurance of a condition of mental contradiction is always an indication of a feeble concentration of life; it is characteristic of the mental life of children, of primitive historical epochs, and of the condition of average humanity, and contrasts with the demands which issue from our spiritual freedom. This weakness is only indicated, not caused, by the defect in the logic.

In the spiritual condition of to-day there is nothing more paralysing and vexatious than the prevailing insensibility to contradictions in thought. It reveals a great lack of centralising energy, of genuine personal life, and of that self-activity which maintains itself amid the busiest employment. Life, as it stands to-day, is full of fundamental contradictions. These are often softened down by superficial compromises, and (if only the harshness of direct conflict can be to some extent avoided) they may appear to be altogether cancelled. Or again, in spite of real contradictions, different types of thought may be unhesitatingly forced together and mixed up with one another. For example, the two fundamentally different points of view represented by the old ethical-religious idealism, on the one hand, and the development of human culture on modern lines, on the other, have frequently had to submit to such treatment. An extraordinary mixture of the most fundamentally different attitudes towards life is to be seen in the works of the more advanced modern writers. Any one with an ear for harmony of thought must be keenly conscious of the dissonance in the works of Nietzsche, which exhibit a mixture of modern and antique, romantic and classic, artistic and dynamic thought. However, the mass of so-called educated people, who are without really vigorous personal life, do not in the least object to spiritual dissonances; they look upon them as providing variety and mental entertainment; the more contradictions, the more "original" and "interesting" is the writer!

Nothing shows the dependence of thought upon the energy of spiritual life more palpably than the developments of religion. Effective religious movements have always come about owing to unbearable contradictions making the position at the time being intolerable; and owing, more especially, to the demand for an increased inwardness coming into sharp conflict with the outward institutions, customs, and formulas which the course of time and the attempt to suit human conditions had brought forth. But to what a small extent has the perceiving, enduring, and overcoming of such contradictions been prompted by mere logical considerations! At the time of the Reformation, for example, the contrast between the outward character of the religion offered by the Church and the desire of earnest souls for something more inward, was obvious to every one; the greatest scholar of the age, Erasmus, was not less aware of it (as we see from his works) than was Luther. Why, then, did Luther and not Erasmus become the great leader of the Reformation? Certainly not because he was the greater logician, for in this respect he was much inferior to Erasmus. It was because the existing situation, with the contradictions it involved, could not remain, for him, a mere matter of calm contemplation and intellectual reflection; it became a personal affair, causing him acute pain, a state of things which he felt to be simply unendurable. The matter touched him so nearly, that he felt a solution of the conflict to be an imperative necessity, to affect the very centre of his life. His spiritual self-preservation demanded it, with an elemental passion which swept aside every other consideration. The power of the instinct of self-preservation imparted to this simple man the capacity and the right to attack a great traditional order which had become sacred to the hearts of men and to venture upon the construction of a new one. This fundamental spiritual necessity drove Luther forward at all costs, and made him a hero, beside whom Erasmus, with all his superior knowledge, refinement, and intellectual acuteness, seems insignificant.

In spiritual conflicts it is not isolated intellectual considerations that carry the day, but basic life-processes and the content of the spiritual reality which they comprehend. Thus the different thought-systems are to be referred back to these processes and all real progress depends upon a broadening of this spiritual reality. Antiquated mental syntheses are not overcome through the sudden advent of a superior set of reasons, but by a perception of the limitations of the life which they express.

Then new concentrations, or at any rate new movements, will appear and a fresh active life will make the old, in spite of its apparent security, seem hollow and obsolete; even if it continues to preserve its outward appearance the old will lose its spiritual authority; even where it believes its rule to be safe, it is already defeated. That the decisive point thus shifts itself from the ideas to the energies, from intellectual considerations to creative developments of life, must contribute to the deepening of work and the consolidation of effort. We arrive at an incomparably larger conception of history when we regard it as a conflict of life-power with life-power, rather than of doctrine with doctrine; the problem becomes altogether more difficult and more fundamental, since it becomes a question of unearthing the roots of the doctrines, discovering the innermost sources of power, and getting at the decisive crux of the conflict. But we shall be supported and inspired in our work by the conviction that human life is enriched by more primitive forces and more fundamental necessities than any which mere intellectual work has of itself the capacity to produce.

4. Consequences in the Sphere of Knowledge

Such relationship between the work of knowledge on the one hand and spiritual life as a whole with the construction of a spiritual reality, on the other, must have deep-reaching consequences for the development of knowledge. Within the necessarily limited scope of this section, we can only deal with these consequences in so far as their result is to facilitate the solution of certain important problems which would otherwise remain beyond the reach of any successful treatment.

There is still much uncertainty as to how philosophy can find an independent task as compared with the separate sciences. The solution so often given, that philosophy has to unify the results of the various separate sciences, is inadequate. For such a unification is either a mere juxtaposition (in which case the word science is being very loosely employed to describe such an encyclopædia) or else it implies construction and transformation, and this cannot be achieved in the absence of a new principle. Now this new principle can neither be obtained from outside nor can it arise from mere intellectual processes; it must lie in the life-process as a whole. Now, at last, we come to the farthest point accessible to us. The fundamental relationship between man and reality, together with the significance of his life and being, must be determined by the nature and experiences of this vital process. From this point of view only can we link the separate sciences together, appraise them rightly, and develop their results. This fundamental process is not found upon the surface of things; it must be extricated and brought to expression, and it is the task of that central philosophical discipline which bears the ancient name of metaphysics to do this; the other disciplines have then to spread the new light in their several separate departments. Such a conception also explains the close connection between philosophy and human personality, without degrading the former to the position of a mere expression of individual character. Moreover, in order to penetrate to this fundamental progress a deep, broad, powerful life is necessary; to this extent, the measure of life is ultimately the measure of thought.

This way of looking at the matter brings us essentially nearer to a solution of the problem of truth. There can, to-day, be no manner of doubt that if truth be conceived of as a correspondence of our thought with an external world, then we must finally abandon all hope of truth. But the more confident this denial, the more doubtful the affirmation which is to meet and replace it. Now by connecting this problem with the life-process, a new light is thrown upon it. There is no intellectual truth apart from a spiritual truth as a whole, but this means nothing less than the transformation of the world into cosmic life, an apprehension of reality from within. And the assumption underlying this is that a spiritual life transcending the human forms the ultimate basis of reality. Man's own task is a continuous strife and upward endeavour, a pushing-on and climbing-up, an increasing struggle against unspiritual and half-spiritual resistances. In this struggle, as we have seen, there is no fruitful knowledge whatever that is not rooted in life-syntheses. But in spite of their actuality, these syntheses are in the first place nothing more than attempts, and it is only in conflict with the inner and outer world that they can prove their capacity. In this work of adjustment, knowledge plays a leading part; it is essential to clarification and examination, indispensable to the establishing of universal validity, to the rejection of all that is human in the petty sense of the word and to the development of the cosmic character of spiritual life. But it cannot exert this critical function without separating itself to a certain extent from that which is merely specific in these syntheses; on the other hand, the critique cannot lead us any further if it does not assist in the development of a new and a higher synthesis.

In this connection there arises the further problem of a sound starting-point for the development of knowledge. Ever since the direct connection between man and the sensuous world was lost this question has been unavoidable. Knowledge has sought in vain for a firm basis within itself. Again and again dogmatic assumptions have been detected in what was looked upon as primary and unquestionable. There is only one way in which this firm basis can be obtained. The whole of life must be linked up into a unity, and at the same time it must be transformed into personal action. In this way alone can axiomatic certainty be attained and shared by knowledge. For man, who is engaged in the struggle, this unity remains a perpetual challenge; it is only at the end of the journey (an end which lies immeasurably far away) that this unity can be fully realised. But the effort after unity would itself be impossible if the challenge which to man appears so unrealisable were not the fundamental reality of the spiritual life.

It is an old objection to philosophy that through all its long history it has done nothing more than heap opinion upon opinion until it becomes impossible even to become acquainted with them all; at the same time there is no certainty that the later opinions are more reliable than the earlier ones. Philosophy certainly retains an element of freedom and personal decision; along with religion, morality, art, and all noble things, it always demands the active participation of the individual, and cannot be imposed upon any one from without. But it is not on this account a mere accumulation of human opinions. The knowledge of its close connection with man's endeavour to reach

96 MAIN CURRENTS OF MODERN THOUGHT

spiritual reality securely protects it from this aspersion. Its historical development is thus brought into the closest relationship with the evolution of spiritual life in humanity, and as the critical developments of this evolution disclose fundamental facts, they also drive philosophical work along new paths. It is no longer possible for us to regard the great problems of life from the Greek point of view, for Christianity has brought about profound transformations in the life-process; it has discovered in it such difficult conflicts and such fruitful profundities that a return to the older standpoint would be unthinkable. We have outgrown the Middle Ages also, since the Modern World created a sharper line of separation between the world and man and aroused the inner life to greater independence. Do not these and similar experiences show the thinker in closest relationship with history and with humanity as a whole? This does not, however, involve the loss of his independence. Environment can do no more for humanity than provide possibilities and incentives; to produce therefrom a reality possessing a well-defined character demands forceful progressive action, and this is always a matter of individual initiative. Thus the two factors mutually interact, while the whole, which includes both, grows unmistakably richer and stronger.

5. Consequences with regard to the History of Philosophy

The recognition of such relationship between philosophy and life as a whole must also exert a powerful influence upon our treatment of the history of philosophy. It can no longer be considered adequate to describe and catalogue the various philosophical systems just as they are; it is now our duty to unearth the fundamental life-contents, and thus set the words of the thinker in a more comprehensive context. The main problem is not so much to determine what a philosopher did say as how he came to say it. We must fix the type of spiritual life that he expresses. It thus becomes necessary to elucidate the relationship between the thinker and his historical and human environment (though not according to the current sociologico-historical method, which puts the cart before the horse and derives the inner from the outer, the great things from a summation of small ones, the eternal from the temporal). Henceforth the significance of individual achievements will be measured according to their success in opening up new depths, in broadening spiritual reality. In this sense all great thought is a pressing forward, a reformation, and a creation.

Although this relation of philosophical tendencies to their deeper origins makes the treatment of philosophical history in some respects more complicated, in others it is conducive to simplification. Measured according to the above standards, only quite a few manifestations can really be regarded as creative, and as really adding to the content of life. Only quite a few types stand out from amidst the apparently chaotic mass of material, and these occur, in their essentials, again and again through all the variations of context and expression. The real core can thus be more sharply divided from what is merely accessory. That which is revealed by a first examination is for the most part the mere fringe of things: subtle definitions and explanations, scholarship of one kind and another, more or less intelligent reasoning—material which may provide occupation for the human mind, but which cannot actually enrich spiritual life. We are both richer and poorer than we generally think; poorer in the *extent*, richer in the *content*, of our possessions.

Finally, the process of searching for the ultimate and radical may serve to prevent the over-valuation of the mere systematic form, a practice which easily leads us away from what is more essential. At the same time we do not wish to undervalue systematic form. A systematic correlation binds the several principles closer together and makes contradictions less possible; it tends towards the organisation and uniform development of the thought-world. But all this can occur only if a living and inspiring content is presupposed, and this can result only from syntheses and energies of life as a whole: if such a content be lacking, no amount of logical power or of ingenuity in construction and arrangement can prevent the system from degenerating into a meaningless framework. Wolff's system was much more fully developed than Leibniz's, but was the former the greater philosopher? Augustine never worked out his thoughts systematically, owing to the contradictory nature of his personality, but he so enriched and enlarged the spiritual world as to influence human thought as few beside him have done. Let us fix our attention in the first place upon essentials, upon creative power, upon the centre of motive force, and not assign undue importance to mere form.

Further discussion would have little value; more detailed explanations would remain no more than fragments from a larger sphere of thought. We have devoted some attention to this subject, because it seemed important to point out that in the very interests of knowledge itself we are driven to seek something more than mere knowledge. At the same time it is obvious that we are not being driven towards voluntarism. It is possible that many of those who call themselves voluntarists aim at something not far from our own goal. We are glad to welcome this agreement. But however the matter may stand with regard to individuals, we must not allow ourselves to lose sight of the essential difference between a mere shifting of the interest within the soul-life itself and an elevation above all empirical soul-life whatsoever.

3. IDEALISM—REALISM

(a) The Terms

THE terms idealism and realism have now become so hackneyed that they have almost lost all definite meaning and scientific value. Nevertheless, they still stand for an ancient and permanent contrast and present a vital issue for modern thought. This being the case, it will be useful for us to commence with a brief discussion of the terms themselves.

The term "idealist" first appears in philosophy towards the end of the seventeenth century.* When Leibniz uses the word in the sense in which he has previously used the term "formalist," *i.e.*, in opposition to materialist (see 186*a*, Erdm.), he has in mind philosophers like Plato and Aristotle, who saw the essence of a thing in its form. At the same time the modern meaning of the word "idea" began to make itself felt. From meaning a typical form it began (at first in the French language) to mean a mere presentation existing only in the mind. Descartes and Locke, though not without contradictions, helped to introduce this meaning into philosophy, when idealism came to signify a system which allowed reality only to the realm of ideas and hence denied the reality of the external world. The term was applied more especially to Berkeley's doctrine—usually in a depreciatory sense, as implying a dissipation of reality. For example, Wolff called the idealists, the materialists, and the sceptics the "three pernicious sects" (see Wolff, *von seinen Schriften*, p. 583). Until about the close of the eighteenth

---

* For further particulars see Vaihinger in the *Strassburger Abhandlungen zur Philosophie*, p. 94 ff. In the theory of art the use of the term seems to reach further back. At any rate, I have received a friendly intimation to the effect that so far back as Pacheco's *Arte de la Pintura* (Seville, 1649) idealist was used to describe an artistic tendency; but I am not at present able to corroborate this.

century philosophers were as universally determined to defend themselves against idealism as they were later to call themselves idealists.* As opposed to this conception of idealism, realism was looked upon in the eighteenth century as standing for the existence of a world outside thought.† Herbart and his followers have preserved this use of the terms through the nineteenth century down to the present day.

Idealism and realism, like so many other terms, were essentially affected by the Kantian philosophy.‡ Kant himself at first employed the traditional terminology and hence classifies idealism with scepticism (for example, in the preface to the 2nd ed. of the *Critique of Pure Reason*). The term transcendental (also formal or critical) idealism was coined, not with reference to Plato, but to Berkeley; to the latter's "empirical," "material," or "psychological" idealism, Kant opposes a new idealism which does not in any way deny or even doubt the existence of things outside the mind, but explains the forms of perception and thought to be merely subjective. Hence all objects which can possibly be experienced by us become mere phenomena, "which have no ground of existence outside our thought." This modification of meaning contains the germ of a fruitful development, in so far as the bearer of the forms, the subject of knowledge, is not so much the individual man in his own particularity as the common structure of our being, the spiritual organisation of humanity. Since the problem thus detached itself from psychology to be taken up by a philosophy of mind, it soon became possible for all those to call themselves idealists (in the widest sense) who maintained the superiority of spiritual activity over the forces of the external world. Thus Schiller writes to W. von Humboldt (*Briefwechsel*, p. 485):

* Wolff (see *De differentia nexus rerum sapientis et fatalis necessitatis*, p. 75) will on no account hear of Plato being called an idealist. Plato certainly called the material world a mere appearance, but by that he did not mean to imply (as do the idealists) that it existed only as an idea.

† In the Middle Ages, as is well known, realism meant the opposite of nominalism; its adherents were usually called *reales*. *Realista* is first mentioned by Prantl (*Geschichte der Logik*, iv. 221) as occurring in Petrus Nigri (*ca.* 1475).

‡ For particulars see Trendelenburg, *Logische Untersuchungen*, 3rd ed., ii. 512 ff.

"After all, we are both idealists and would be ashamed to have it said of us that things shaped us and not we the things." *
No one exerted more influence than Fichte towards establishing this meaning of the term.

The German Revival of Humanism (this newest phase of the Renaissance) employed the term in a manner clearly related to the above, though giving it at the same time a characteristic complexion. Thus the thoughtful article with which F. A. Wolf commenced the *Museum der Altertumswissenschaft* (1807) explains that "the direction of the spirit towards the ideal" is the "first condition of all higher development"; by this he understands, according to his favourite saying, "it is not suitable for free and magnanimous souls to be always seeking after the useful" (Aristotle, *Politics*, 1338, b. 2), that the tendency of life should be towards the beautiful, not the useful, towards the harmonious development of all spiritual powers for their own sakes, not for the sake of any result. No one did more than Goethe towards furthering this conception of idealism, which he supported by his personality as well as his life-work, although in other connections he very justly called himself a realist. In the speech of the nineteenth century the philosophical and artistic meanings became merged into one. Idealism came to mean the recognition of self-activity and of the intrinsic value of the spiritual life, and hence, in place of the academic discussion of idealism and realism in connection with the theory of knowledge which prevailed during the eighteenth century, we have an ancient and permanent human question.

(b) The Conflict of Practical Ideals

The contrast between idealism and realism may be formulated in various ways, but in essentials the problem remains unchanged.

---

* Schiller examines these terms in a particularly detailed manner in his treatise *Ueber naive u. sentimentalischer Dichtung*. He regards a realist as one who is governed by the necessity of nature, an idealist as one governed by the necessity of reason. This change of meaning was objected to by the systematic philosophers. Thus Plattner says (*Phil. Aphorismen*, i. 412): "The concept idealism is beginning to be used altogether too broadly. It has usually been defined in the past as that system which denies the reality of everything except spirit." . . . "As idealism is now understood, every one is an idealist who looks upon the external world as an appearance; in other words, all philosophers, without exception, are idealists."

Is the real centre of gravity of our life to be sought in the visible or in an invisible world? Are the chief ends of our existence to be realised in the former or in the latter sphere? Is the life which develops in humanity a continuation of nature, or can it only be comprehended as an essentially new and higher stage of reality? Is all spiritual manifestation a mere accompaniment or tool of a life which is essentially natural? Has man no other goal than the cultivation and preservation of worldly interests, or does human life acquire a meaning and a value only through participation in an order superior to all merely human conditions? If we divide reality into higher and lower stages (according to the common view), is the higher derived from the lower or does the higher furnish the key to the understanding of the lower? The contrast which underlies and pervades all these different formulations divides life so fundamentally, from the largest things down to the smallest, in thought and in action, in value and in content, that its effects make themselves felt throughout every branch of life. This applies to the concept of reality itself. The idealist is bound to protest with all his might against the measurement of this concept in terms of the realistic standard. This is, however, what takes place when the idealistic world is treated as a mere accessory, as a sort of embroidery to a world already given and well-established. The idealist contends that without his thought-world the bare concept of a world and a reality at all would be impossible, and that the sense-world derives its content and value entirely from the thought-world.

The fate of idealism is often similar to that of religion. So long as the latter dominated life its world was regarded on all sides as the nearest and most incontestable. Augustine overcame every doubt by appealing to the idea of a Supreme Being. St. Thomas Aquinas called the supernatural world the fatherland (*patria*). The idea of a life beyond and with it that of transcendence did not come to the front in the religious world until after the commanding position of religion had been shaken and its content had lost its real force. When religion is looked upon from the outset as transcendent it is already virtually abandoned. In the same way idealism is already a lost cause when men think of its world as something strange and remote, something which cannot be attained to without laborious mental effort.

But if we set the contrast thus sharply before us we entirely abandon the possibility of mediation, even that of the so-called realistic idealism, in so far as it stands for such a compromise. The idealist should and must master the facts which constitute the basis of realism, and it is equally the realist's duty to understand idealism. What really happens, however, when they do thus study one another, is that each colours the situation according to his own convictions, thus increasing the contrast rather than bridging it over.

1. NINETEENTH-CENTURY REALISM

During the nineteenth century the old conflict entered upon a new phase, into the meaning of which it is essential to enquire. Up to the period of which we are speaking the course of human culture had run strongly in an idealistic direction. This is true more particularly of traditional religious life, but the new culture, too, had, until then, attacked the problems of life for the most part from *within* and had tried to make outward circumstances subordinate to the requirements of thought. It is true that an opposing tendency of a realistic nature was never absent, but this was not so much a definite attempt to deal with the problem as a whole as an obstinate resistance on the part of individuals who were too much interested in the joys and sorrows of the sense-world to be able to raise themselves to the level demanded by the idealists. An opposition thus consisting of a number of petty individual forces had correspondingly narrow limits. It may have exerted a depressing and disintegrating influence, but it was quite incapable of setting up a new system of life and thereby shaking idealism to the foundations. Now this was the task undertaken by nineteenth-century realism. This realism maintained that the immediate world is sufficient for man, that it can furnish him with all his aims and satisfy all his desires, and do this without putting life upon a lower level. Such an undertaking was something more than a new arrangement or new interpretation of the traditional situation; it recruited its strength chiefly from the fact that the world of immediate human existence had come to mean more to us than it had ever done before. It is only because it offers a new reality, opposed to that of the idealists, that the new realism can hope to win over humanity. It is more a battle between rival realities than between rival doctrines. This is a corroboration of the contention contained in the foregoing section, that philosophical conflict is not so much concerned with the interpretation of an existing situation as with its formation.

A great many different movements combined together in the nineteenth century to produce an enrichment of immediate reality. Man acquired a new and infinitely deeper knowledge of nature's workings, and nature became more and more a subject of human occupation and interest. The ensuing increase in knowledge was quickly converted by technical skill into improvements directly affecting human life, which became immensely enriched, accelerated, and strengthened. An amazing growth of human capacity tended more and more to remove the inflexible character of fate. Difficulties themselves, being regarded as challenges, as impulses to new activity, lost their bitterness. At the same time, human society gave rise to more and more difficult tasks. Men became increasingly convinced of the importance of the form in which society is moulded and of the possibility of effecting a real improvement of existing conditions, so as to place society upon a higher level and secure a more universal happiness. A ready recognition of the characteristic and distinguishing qualities of different nations arose, and the development of national character encouraged the growth of corresponding feelings and forces. Within the State, individual forces secured a larger sphere for their expansion and manifestation. In the economical world the tendency towards a more equal distribution of wealth coincided with difficult problems in connection with the technical organisation of labour, thereby stirring up an immeasurable depth of feeling: the power of material conditions was now for the first time clearly perceived and fully appreciated; the inner condition and happiness of human life seemed to depend upon the answers given these problems. These different movements complemented and accelerated one another, both the results and the problems of this new life binding humanity ever more firmly to the immediate world surrounding it.

Moreover man himself, the doer of the work, develops his own nature through the work that he does; and by "man" we mean man as he lives in the flesh, not as he stands transfigured in a philosophical system. History and society, as they now appear, both contribute towards this result. Their forces come more intimately together, space and time no longer separating them so effectively; they unite in a common work and become conscious of a pervasive complete solidarity. Humanity stands before us as a great whole. It unites forces that were formerly scattered, forming enduring relationships which bind individuals together and immeasurably enrich the capacity of life as a whole. Humanity thus presents itself as an object of reverence and faith, an object which seems capable of absorbing the whole ethical and practical activity of man.

This new method of thought must reshape every department of life (such as art and science) in characteristic fashion. In every direction it must produce the same effect, it must make every form of activity closely dependent upon the external world. From this point of view, only contact with *things* can lead human forces to living reality and away from mere ghostly possibilities; on the other hand, a separation from concrete things, an entrenchment of the soul in its own inner life, must make all our efforts lifeless, shadowy, and unreal. The basis and motive power of this tendency is the desire for genuine reality, and to its supporters all the older, idealistic views of life seem like wreaths of early morning mist, doomed to vanish before the victorious light of the on-coming day.

2. The Limitations of the New Realism

Is the light of this day free from shadow? Shall we undoubtingly accept the new tendency? The actual fate of the realistic movement shows us that the matter is not free from complications. Realism, it is true, has not only carried the opinion of humanity with it, with overwhelming force; it has also given an immense impetus to work, accelerated our whole existence, aroused us to a more manly overcoming of difficulties and to a more victorious attack upon all that is irrational. At the same time the growth of the movement has produced problems which take us beyond the boundaries marked out by realism and endanger the independence of the realistic sphere. The realistic system could justly pose as the one all-sufficing reality only if the simple progress of the world's work itself solved every difficulty; only if all independent inner life more and more completely disappeared and man became transformed into a mere instrument for doing work. But no such transformations have taken place. On the contrary, the actual course of events has clearly shown us that mere work by no means absorbs the whole man. To begin with, work has come more and more to mean a bitter struggle for existence, a struggle between individuals, classes, and peoples; the contrasts have become sharper and sharper and the field of conflict larger and larger. The passions which this struggle has aroused show clearly enough that standing behind the work are sensitive beings, craving for happiness and demanding from their work some personal compensation, even though the work itself lose by giving it. Is there any way of meeting the perils arising out of this demand, save by drawing upon the inner life—that is, upon a quantity which strict realism cannot logically recognise?

The complications, moreover, go beyond the conflict of the forces which work disengages and seem to be inseparably bound up with the very nature of work. Work never develops more than a portion of human faculty, and the more specialised the work the smaller the portion: the field which a given individual can cover becomes continually narrower and more limited. From the point of view of realism this neglect of all but a few special capacities, this stultification of the man as a whole, must be a matter of indifference, since from this standpoint life is no more than contact with environment. But it cannot be a matter of indifference to the actual man, who suffers loss and pain. There is obviously more in him than the realist recognises—or logically can recognise. Moreover, work indissolubly connects man with his achievement, with some result; from this point of view all effort is wasted which produces no tangible result. This has the effect of turning the mind entirely towards what is outward and making the soul indifferent to its own welfare ; indeed, realism cannot even allow the existence of inner states of soul. This continual striving after result, success, and recognition must more and more absorb men and repress all independent psychical life (it has in reality thrust it far into the background). We cannot welcome such a situation. We are conscious of a painful vacuity, and having this consciousness our work no longer satisfies us ; in spite of all its successes it leaves the soul homeless. For humanity as a whole this complete absorption of existence in work means an impoverishment of the spiritual content of life. The absence of common ideas and convictions to inwardly unite humanity results in the disappearance of a common thought-world and the infliction of a severe injury upon the whole of mankind, for without such a thought-world our life can have no independent value, no true greatness, and no soul.

These are no mere abstract philosophical considerations. They are the undeniable experiences of modern humanity. Can any one possibly deny that, in spite of the brilliant triumphs of modern labour and ingenuity, there has arisen amongst us a profound and growing discontent not unmixed with pessimism ?

The nineteenth century, more than any other epoch, enlarged the whole aspect of life and improved human conditions. One would have expected it to close with a proud and joyful consciousness of strength. The fact that it did not do so points to an error in the type of life which dominated the period. This error is to be found in the desire of realism to eliminate the soul. *And the soul will not allow itself to be eliminated.* The very attempt to deny the soul only arouses it to greater activity.

3. CRITICISM OF THE TRADITIONAL FORMS OF IDEALISM

Experience of this sort compels a revision of the whole question. It is incumbent upon us to determine, as far as is possible, in what respects each view is right or wrong. The desire for complete reality in life could hardly have manifested itself in such a powerful tendency as realism has shown itself to be if the traditional forms of idealism had not been lacking in such reality. There is no doubt they did suffer from this lack and were no longer firmly rooted in the real inner life of humanity. There were two main forms of idealism: a religious form which still makes itself felt through the various types of Christianity, and an artistic form which, originating in ancient Greece, constitutes a tendency that has often been repressed but never quite crushed.

The religious interpretation of life bases human existence upon a deeper order of reality; it raises humanity above time to eternity, above a life absorbed in external things to a life of pure inwardness. In spite of all weakening this tendency still constitutes an immense power. Even where it is denied it still works on in secret. But this form of life no longer positively convinces the modern man; it does not speak directly to his soul. This state of affairs has come about through the formation of a broad gap between the traditional form of religion and the modern thought-world. Even those who hope to be able to bridge this gap can no longer possess the directness and complete certainty of the old faith. When religion is not the most certain thing it is very apt to be the most uncertain.

Religion has suffered an even greater loss of power through the alienation of the modern man from the personal religious experience of the early Christians. In the early days men were driven to religion by an acute consciousness of human weakness and an experience of immovable limitations and clashing contradictions: men felt that their spiritual selves could not be saved without recourse to another world. Hence deep natures like Augustine felt this other world to be their nearest and most secure possession, the absolutely solid foundation of life; the world of our present existence only retained any value at all in so far as it symbolised or reflected the other world.

The modern period, on the other hand, originated in and received its characteristic impress from a youthful feeling of strength, a mighty impulse towards life. From this point of view man began to regard life as an immeasurable task, in attacking which he develops himself, inwardly and outwardly. Rigid limits and final renunciations seem to be things of the past, and the world appears to be moving, through its own development, towards a state of the highest perfection. Perhaps the matter is not quite so simple as the disciples of modern thought are apt to imagine ; perhaps the development of the future will make us conscious of our limitations, aye, of our incapacity ! But at present the consciousness of strength holds the field, nor is there any direct, spontaneous, overwhelming impulse towards religion. Religion therefore loses its imperative force and secure truth.

Idealism of the artistic type is in even greater danger of becoming unreal. It seeks to perfect the world, not from any superior standpoint, but by means of an activity inherent in the world itself. The meeting of inner and outer, of soul and world, gives rise to a conformation which appears to unite together all the manifoldness of life, assigning proper limits to each separate element and cementing the parts together into one harmonious and homogeneous whole. Every merely natural force is thereby ennobled, and the spiritual, from being an obscure and indefinite possibility, becomes a reality as clear as the day. By such an achievement as this, the artistic synthesis creates a life at once active and noble. It raises the level of human existence and refines the texture of the soul ; it proves itself to be indispensable to the complete shaping of spiritual life. But has it the body and strength to provide life with a complete content ? Is it not probable that only those with a special natural gift, with a marked creative capacity, will find the centre of life in such a movement as this ? Is there not the danger of producing an aristocracy which is not only exclusive but rejoices in being exclusive ? Moreover, must not a man, a people, or an age have already attained to a very rich life in order to experience and achieve great things in the work of artistic construction ? Must not depth of soul be possessed before it can be expressed ? In the absence of such depth the artistic life remains confined to the surface and readily degenerates to mere dilettantism, losing all real content. And when the difficult complications, bitter contradictions and appalling abysses of human existence come at last to be fully recognised (and the experience of the nineteenth century drives us in this direction), can art, in its own strength, really claim to remove every difficulty, light up every dark place, and replace all sorrow by joy ? If it cannot do this, however, it will be severely tempted to minimise what is irrational and discordant, and to represent human existence as being more harmonious than it really is. The sense of truth is thus roused to opposition and the realists feel that they are championing the cause of truth.

Even more obvious is the right of realism to oppose that type of popular idealism which, despite all attacks on its foundation and all criticisms of detail, clings to the general tendency of idealism without giving it any clear form or definite basis. This sort of idealism works up enthusiasm about the "higher" without in the least knowing what this "higher" is.* It exalts the "good," "true," and "beautiful" without deigning to provide any sort of explanation of their contents. It is hence easily understood that the traditional idealistic forms of life could not satisfy the newly awakened impulse towards truth. Although realism energetically represents this impulse, it is another question whether it, either, can fully satisfy it.

4. THE PROBLEM OF REALITY

From the point of view of realism a reality in life is only attainable by a continual linking-up of action with our visible environment; if such a linking-up does in truth produce reality for man is open to the gravest doubt. For it can only be a question of a reality experienced, or capable of being experienced, by man; any other reality lies outside his sphere and cannot

---

* "Higher" seems to have been first employed more particularly during the *Sturm- und Drangzeit* of German literature as the favourite expression for a new and presumably higher trend of thought. The romantic school frequently used "higher" to distinguish their own aims and conceptions from those of the average person. Schleiermacher's youthful works may be cited as an example. It was customary to speak of the "higher" life, "higher" feelings, "higher" education, "higher" morality, &c., until the term fell into ridicule ("higher nonsense"). Kant's clear and thorough methods of thought were fundamentally opposed to the use of such a term. When Feder credited him with a "higher" idealism he retorted (iv. 121, Hart): "In Heaven's name not higher. High towers and the metaphysically great men who resemble them (much wind blows about both) are not for me. My place is the fruitful bathos of experience."

possess any interest for him. This connection of action with environment gives rise to a wealth of deeds and accomplishments, but these are not *personal experiences*; something accomplished does not become an *experience* until it has been referred to a unity and comprised within the soul-life as a whole. Realism has not the means of explaining such a soul-life as this, although it is compelled to draw upon it for its own purposes. Realism does not develop its characteristic world with its own resources; if compelled to rely upon its own means alone, it would destroy every inner relationship and every system of life, and hence itself as a whole. It rests upon the tacit assumption of a soul-life comprehending manifoldness, and with it overcoming the opposition between subject and object. The statement that the surrounding world means far more for man than idealism of the usual type admitted, and that he can obtain far more from it, cannot be substantiated in the absence of such an assumption. And what does this really mean if not that realism is encompassed by an idealistic thought-world? Realism cannot constitute a system of life at all without the assistance of idealism. When, under these circumstances, the soul is deprived of all independence and derived as far as possible from outside, a crying contradiction results, and even if this is concealed after a fashion it is soon revealed by the incessant appearance in the concept and doctrine of elements which have no proper place in realism.

Let us consider the system of the greatest realistic thinker—Comte. In laying his foundations he took every possible care to remove from his concepts everything that was in any way derived from idealism. But as soon as the stage of design and criticism was passed and the work of execution and positive construction began, the matter assumed a different aspect. The more the constructive work progresses, the more the original quantities alter and become idealistic in conception. In particular, the critical transition from knowledge to action is brought about solely by such an alteration, physical compulsion being converted into moral obligation. A whole system of life is the final result, but this is only built up by continually calling in the assistance of that very opponent whose destruction was regarded as essential to the preservation of truth.

Does any one maintain that a divided world like this can satisfy the needs of spiritual life, and more particularly the demands of ethics? In this connection we may again refer to Comte, and again we find him suddenly changing his position—but this time in a reverse sense. The point of departure is now idealistic—the conclusion realistic. The man's deep nature was sensitive to the dark side of his age, which he regarded from a thoroughly idealistic point of view; he took the matter so seriously that nothing short of energetic, original, creative effort, nothing less than the possibility of a complete renewal, seemed capable of meeting the situation. But the realistic material with which he approaches this task is inadequate; his recommendations resolve themselves into interpretations of nature, together with suggested alterations in social organisation; by such means humanity is to accomplish the desired upheaval, the victory of good over evil. Nothing but a crassly optimistic view of humanity could conceal the glaring contrast between the greatness of the task and the inadequacy of the means. However, this is typical of realism: it either takes a shallow view of life or it involves itself in contradictions which, logically thought out, lead to its own destruction. Can our desire for truth and our thirst for reality be satisfied by a system of life which becomes more self-contradictory the more it endeavours to do justice to the whole content of human life?

These abstract considerations are supported by the actual experience of humanity. The movement towards realism took place in a spiritual atmosphere completely saturated with idealism. For however much the various special forms of idealism may have suffered disintegration, the general development of civilisation, as the result of many centuries of labour, has given rise to a type of thought, feeling, and valuation which bears the general impress of idealism though no longer definitely associated with any of its special forms. Idealism has thus penetrated the whole of our life and passed into our innermost souls. The realistic order of life has not escaped its influence, and continually draws upon it for rectification, mitigation, or complementary matter. But the further realism progresses towards independence and the more it becomes conscious of its own true character, the more completely must it endeavour to rid itself of these idealistic elements : it cannot do this, however, without narrowing and destroying itself, and hence outward victory carries with it inner defeat. Were the whole affair a mere theatrical performance it would be possible to contemplate this dialectical development of the movements of history with the completest equanimity and even to derive pure pleasure from the gigantic conflict of rival systems of thought. But the issue at stake is the destiny of man, the reasonableness or otherwise of his existence, the gaining or losing of a soul. And that is no matter for disinterested contemplation.

5. The Necessity for a New Idealism

Although realism, with its surface-culture, cannot satisfy us, the content of life has now undergone far too great an alteration for a mere return to the old idealism to be possible. The irrational element in life (within and without) is far more obvious to us than it was to the idealists of the old school ; the enormous accumulation of rigid facts and the blind indifference of the natural world to the aims of spiritual life are so closely present to our minds that we cannot pass over them so lightly as could the older idealists. Idealism must be deepened and more firmly rooted if it is to meet these increased perplexities and overcome these new obstacles. This will only be possible if it be realised that the question at issue is not the accomplishment of any special tasks or the development of life in special directions. What is at stake is the attainment of any true and essential life at all. For if there is no depth of reality in which our everyday life can take root and find sustenance there can be no true personal life, and hence no real life whatever. At the same time spiritual life must be more sharply separated from, and elevated above, what is merely human : the world of nature, the sphere of visible existence, surrounds us with almost overwhelming pressure ; our spiritual activity would be powerless to resist it, did it not represent a new stage of reality, the life of the spiritual world as a whole, and have its resources to draw upon. Otherwise idealism has no firm basis and no definite right. Only if an absolutely independent spiritual world (*eine* *bei sich selbst befindliche Geisteswelt*) works in us and has the power to fill our life does the demand essential to idealism become comprehensible and possible; the demand, namely, that the characteristics and goods of the new world should be held immeasurably superior to all human aims and independent of all human desires and opinions, and the everyday concerns of human life; only then is it possible for the spiritual world not to receive its truth from humanity but for humanity on the contrary to measure the amount of truth its life contains by comparison with the truth of the spiritual world. To make humanity the measure of goodness and truth is to inwardly destroy both. But how are we to get beyond humanity if our immediate existence is regarded as the whole of reality? * In spite of all confusing and weakening influences there is one question that will always make itself heard and demand an answer: Must our effort be devoted solely to the furtherance of human welfare, to the betterment of things within a given existence, or do we not rather, in directing ourselves towards the life of the spirit, enter into a *new kind of reality*—a reality which is at the same time a realm of true values? If the spiritual life has no intrinsic superiority to merely human affairs, no idealism can exist, and along with it disappears the whole meaning and value of our life, leaving us an existence entirely devoid of content.

If, on the other hand, the supremacy of the spiritual life be recognised, no deficiency on the side of humanity can in any way endanger spiritual things. The fundamental fact of all development then remains secure and remote from all disturbing influences. Spiritual life (as it develops within our sphere) may be invariably mixed with what is merely human; ideas may not usually exert influence unless assisted by interest; further, spiritual life, upon human ground, may have developed from obsolete beginnings and have moved slowly forwards, suffering many reactions—all this (from the point of view we

---

* In this connection we may recall the words of Kant (iii. 260, Hart.): "With regard to moral laws, experience is (unfortunately!) the mother of pretence and it is in the highest degree reprehensible to allow laws relating to what I ought to do to be determined or limited by what is done."

have described) does not in the least endanger the fundamental facts of spiritual life. It may even be said that the resistance on the part of humanity, the reluctant recognition of spiritual necessities and the appearance of spirituality with which human conduct loves to veil itself, can only strengthen the conviction that more is working within humanity than is derived from man as he actually exists.

If the best intellectual and spiritual work of to-day is again tending towards idealism, it is only to be hoped that the movement will not be satisfied with weak compromise: it must be clearly pointed out that it is a question of "*either-or*," and the indispensable reversal must be demanded in no uncertain voice. Idealism must not merely stand on the defensive; it must press forward. It must be positive and not merely critical. Only in this way can a true spiritual culture be successfully opposed to the increasing superficiality, shallowness, and pretentiousness of a merely human culture. Only in this way can a victorious resistance be offered to the crushing force with which nature, history, and society now threaten to oppress and overwhelm humanity. Without faith in the greatness and value of humanity there can be no progress—but this faith must have a firm foundation.

B. THE PROBLEM OF KNOWLEDGE

1. THOUGHT AND EXPERIENCE
(METAPHYSICS)

(a) Historical

A FEW preliminary remarks on terminology will be necessary. The term "experience" has grown increasingly ambiguous with the lapse of time. Different thinkers use it in so many different senses that it can hardly be regarded as a definite term. In spite of all the work which has been done in connection with the subject, no verbal distinction is made between everyday, pre-scientific experience and scientific experience. The conception of scientific experience (ἐμπειρία μεθοδική) is as old as the Stoics. The modern philosophers of the school of experience showed a tendency to create a distinction by using the Greek expression "empiricism," "empirical," and "empiricist" for the lower type of experience. The German scholastic philosophy of the eighteenth century also endeavoured to distinguish between "empirical" or "common" experience and "learned" experience. Kant, too, often used "empirical" in this sense. Comte, the most important representative of the school of experience during the nineteenth century, protested energetically against "empiricism." This distinction did not, however, attain universal recognition, and the only one that was generally accepted was that between *Empiriker* ("empiricist") for the lower type, and *Empirist* (no historical English equivalent) for the higher, a distinction probably derived from Kant's philosophy.

Of greater importance is the history of the kindred expressions *a priori* and *a posteriori*. The chief phases of the struggle for knowledge are to be seen reflected in the changes of meaning undergone by these expressions. The influence of these changes is to be felt even to-day. The expressions are derived from the Aristotelian method of describing the general as the (conceptually) earlier and the particular as the later, although they found no definite place in speech until the height of the Middle Ages. According to Albertus Magnus, to prove a thing *ex prioribus* was to prove it from principle; *ex posterioribus*, from consequences: Prantl (*Geschichte der Logik im Abendlande*, iv. 78) mentions Albert of Saxony (a fourteenth-century scholar) as employing *a priori* and *a posteriori* in the same sense. The terms retained these meanings until the modern period,* and they are not yet extinct.

Towards the end of the seventeenth century the question of the origin of knowledge became very pressing, and the theory of method began to give way to the theory of knowledge. This is more particularly to be seen in the case of Leibniz. With Leibniz *a priori* means originating in reason; *a posteriori*, derived from experience. This distinction could be interpreted relatively or absolutely, in a superficial or a deeper sense. At first, *a priori* knowledge meant nothing more than knowledge deduced from accepted premises, prior to an actual examination of the matter in question, that is, knowledge based on a mere process of inference; † in this case the ultimate origin of knowledge remains unexplained.

But in Leibniz's works (and afterwards in those of his followers) *a priori* has already come to mean, in addition, that which is independent of all experience, belonging to reason alone.‡

* They are thus used in the so-called Port Royal Logic (*L'art de penser*): *Soit en prouvant les effets par les causes, ce qui s'appelle démontrer a priori, soit en démontrant au contraire les causes par les effets, ce qui s'appelle prouver a posteriori.*

† Thus B. Wolff says (*Psychologia Empirica*, § 434): *Quod experiundo addiscimus, a posteriori cognoscere dicimur: quod vero ratiocinando nobis innotescit, a priori cognoscere dicimur.* And § 435: *Quicquid ex iis colligimus, quæ nobis jam innotuere, cum ante ignotum esset, id ratiocinando nobis innotescit, adeoque idem a priori cognoscimus.*

‡ Leibniz contrasts the knowledge acquired by *la pure raison ou a priori* with experimental philosophy *qui procède a posteriori* (see Erdm. 778 *b*). Lambert says in the *Neuen Organon*, § 639: "It should accordingly be understood that in absolute strictness the term *a priori* can be applied only to that which is entirely independent of experience."

THOUGHT AND EXPERIENCE 121

This whole line of development culminated in Kant's philosophy. For Kant regarded experience itself as possible only through the agency of a system of *a priori* concepts and principles. But Kant, too, not infrequently uses the word in the looser sense. At about this period these terms began to be used outside the sphere of systematic philosophy, and *a priori* acquired a perfectly definite German meaning.*

It is a clear case of the looser use of the word when modern empiricism (with the help, more particularly, of the theory of evolution) tries to derive the *a priori* element from experience. *A priori* then comes to mean that which the individual does not himself acquire; it stands for that which has been handed down to him as a product of the experience of humanity as a whole prescribing definite paths for his thought to follow. Hence humanity as a whole (but not each separate individual) draws solely upon experience. This is a totally different problem from that of Kant's absolute *a priori*, and it is a gross misunderstanding to believe that Darwin and Spencer

* In earlier times *a priori* was translated by *von vornen her* (from aforetime). This is already found in Luther's *Tischreden* (see Förstemann's edition, iv. 399), and it was in use as recently as the eighteenth century. Campe refers to Lessing's *Ernst u. Falk* as the original source of *von vornherein* (from aforetime), and I do not myself know of its occurrence in any earlier work. This, however, defines the term only in the looser and merely relative sense. Understood in the absolute sense, *a priori* is equivalent to *rein* (pure), which also has a lengthy history. Since the time of Anaxagoras's νοῦς καθαρός (see Aristotle, *De anima*, 405 a, 16: μόνον γοῦν φησὶν αὐτὸν (i.e., τὸν νοῦν) τῶν ὄντων ἁπλοῦν εἶναι καὶ ἀμιγῆ τε καὶ καθαρόν) "pure" was employed by the ancients in the sense of the simple, unsullied, unmixed nature of the spiritual as contrasted with the mixed nature of the sense world. The Neo-Platonists (and, following their example, the Middle Ages), carried the concept over into the sphere of knowledge and described as pure a knowledge free from all sense imagery (cp. for example Scotus Erigena, *De div. nat.*, 657 D, 658 B). Descartes, too, describes the *intellectio pura* as one *quæ circa nullas imagines corporeas versatur*. In this sense the Wolffian school understood *reinen Verstand* (pure understanding), while their *reine Vernunft* (pure reason) stood for what is opposed to experience and hence corresponded to the *a priori* (see Wolff, *Psych. Emp.*, § 495: *ratio pura est, si in ratiocinando non admittimus nisi definitiones ac propositiones a priori cognitas*). Gottsched also follows this terminology (see for example *Erste Gründe der gesamten Weltweisheit*, 1739, p. 485; *reiner Verstand* = without sense images; p. 486, *reine Vernunft* = reasoning unmixed with principles derived from experience. Thus Kant's use of *reine Vernunft* corresponds with the academic usage of his time.

can be employed to refute Kant, a misunderstanding which reveals an inability to think accurately about such problems.

Such a change and such an uncertainty in the use of expressions would naturally lead us to suspect the existence of complicated problems. The history of philosophy corroborates such an opinion; it reveals a struggle lasting thousands of years and continually growing in importance. But in spite of its passionate nature this struggle was not fruitful because it did not centre round the true core of the problem. People disputed as to whether knowledge was derived from external things or from the self-activity of thought; but this cannot be decided unless the actual subject and matter of our knowledge be already placed beyond the reach of doubt. It must not be continually necessary to refer the question *whence?* back to the question *what?* Yet this is what really takes place. We are by no means united as to the actual nature of our knowledge. The conflicting parties base their proofs upon fundamentally different conceptions, hence the proofs are valid only for those who already stand upon the same basis. The historical development thus becomes a series of monologues, and the opponents, instead of getting into fruitful contact, simply confirm one another in their previous opinions. The subject and matter of knowledge cannot be ascertained without going back to ultimate questions, and in particular to that fundamental problem with which our investigation is so perpetually coming into contact; the problem whether the life and activity of man is solely a continuation of a natural process, or whether it introduces a new stage of reality. Within the sphere of knowledge itself the dispute as to the origin of knowledge gives rise to another question; is it possible or necessary to have an independent philosophy along with the separate sciences? Hence this problem also enters into the discussion.

Although the question as to the origin of knowledge has been connected with philosophy since the days of Plato, it did not take a leading place until the Modern Period. Then, for the first time, spiritual life and external environment became distinctly separated, and each was thus compelled to clearly define itself and definitely reveal its own capacity. They did not become more widely separated on account of any increase of philosophical penetration, but because the fundamental content of life itself became divided, forming two opposite tendencies. On the one hand the self-contained inner life, the outcome of the labour of centuries and of multifarious experience, acquired such a powerful self-consciousness as to declare itself the centre of all things, and thereupon to venture the reconstruction of the universe through the labour of the intellect and in terms of thought; on the other hand, the sense-world, throwing off the veil which had obscured it during the Middle Ages, asserted itself as a force independent of humanity, and revealed such a powerful and solid structure and such a depth and richness of life that it appeared to completely dominate human existence and provide the content both for life and knowledge.

This contrast is too sharp for any friendly mediation to be possible. The real heart of the matter must lie either on the one side or the other, and our conception of knowledge will fundamentally differ according as we adopt the one position or the other. In this way the systems of rationalism and empiricism, with their opposing views of reality, come into existence.

Empiricism takes up a position based upon the consciousness of the individual. It shows with convincing clearness that the content of this consciousness is not ready-made, but is slowly built up from separate impressions under the guidance of environment. From this point of view the only function of philosophy is to refer knowledge back to consciousness. Only as empirical psychology has it, under these circumstances, any *raison d'être* at all. In the end, knowledge becomes a mere association of sensations and ideas devoid of any inner connection: no attempt whatever is made to throw any light upon reality itself. It remains questionable whether this can really be called science at all. Is it possible, in such a way as this, to get beyond the mere individual and attain to anything which shall be the common property of humanity? The question is a legitimate one, and much good reason has been given for answering it in the negative.

The rationalist position is entirely different. It is based upon the fact of science. Rationalism regards the true nature of science, properly understood, as affording evidence for the conviction that it is not given to humanity from without, but must proceed from thought itself as the outcome of its self-activity. The formal properties of scientific knowledge, in particular, seem to be incapable of being derived from outside. What source can we assign to the eternal and universally valid truths which support the fabric of science other than the intrinsic nature of the spirit? On these lines, knowledge reduces itself essentially to the complete working out of what is inherent in the rational nature of man, and the procedure of science and of philosophy in particular becomes at root analytic. To Leibniz philosophy appeared to be a kind of universal mathematic which kept forcing the preliminary assumptions of knowledge further and further back and converting the whole of reality more and more into rational equations. But when a systematic structure of science is built up in this way, the world tends more and more to become a domain of mere forms and relations. Reality threatens to become utterly thin and bloodless. Thus empiricism seems unable to give to its limitless material any dominating form, while rationalism fails to provide the form with a satisfying content.

Kant strove with all his might to overcome this contrast, both sides of which were represented in his own nature. He belonged to the rationalistic side in so far as he energetically sought to raise knowledge beyond the mere association of ideas and make it into a connected whole; but his rationalism received an empirical impress in this sense, that he did not represent thought as giving rise to knowledge through its own pure self-activity; knowledge must always depend upon matter being presented to the mind. Thus thought cannot attain to a world of things, but only to a domain of appearances. Related to empiricism, too, was a strong sense for facts, insisting as he always did upon an exact conception of what is individual and characteristic: rationalism was always inclined to round things off in order to make them fit neatly into its systems of thought. Kant's thought was as pronouncedly qualitative as that of Leibniz was quantitative. The former thought in contrasts, the latter in stages. Kant's judicial method of procedure possessed not only the advantage of treating the problem more systematically than it had ever been treated before, but it made a peculiarly penetrating attempt to define man's characteristic capacity for knowledge. But in spite of the greatness of the treatment, which initiated a new epoch in the study of the whole problem, the new answer at once raised new questions and doubts. Can thought be bound to a strange world and at the same time retain its independence? The extreme complication of the problem is revealed by the fact that Kant's investigation is less direct and more artificial in dealing with the connection between the function of thought and the impressions of the senses than it is in any other portion of his work. Moreover, the verdict is one that is not satisfactory to either party. Kant's exaltation of the work of thought unavoidably points beyond bondage to the "thing-in-itself" and limitation to a domain of appearances, and thus cannot be accepted by the rationalists; the empiricists, on the other hand, may enquire (nay, they must enquire) if this fabric of forms, which, according to Kant, first makes experience possible, has not been gradually evolved through experience (which would put an essentially different complexion upon his explanation). The uncertain situation in which such conflict places knowledge would be much more acutely felt if Kant's practical philosophy did not strengthen and complement the world of thought. But we must not imagine that the basis of the practical philosophy is beyond the reach of doubt.

Hence it cannot surprise us that the further developments of philosophy tended to lead beyond the Kantian solution of the problem of knowledge, and that the opposition between thought and experience became more acute than ever. This state of affairs was partly brought about by the growth of a social and historical conception of reality, such as Kant had no idea of, but which, more than any other movement, was responsible for the character of the nineteenth century.*

* The following reference to the preface of the *Critique of Pure Reason* shows (among others) how Kant denied that the doctrine of principles could undergo historical modification (thus following the example of the older rational-

Both parties seized hold of this new method of thought, and with its assistance tried to accomplish that which had not hitherto been successfully achieved. History assumed fundamentally different aspects when regarded from the two contrasting points of view. The rationalists viewed it as a single movement driven forward by inner necessity. The empiricists saw in it nothing more than the accumulation of an endless series of events. Through its association with history, rationalism developed into a speculative construction which represented the thought-process as producing the whole of reality in the course of its unfolding. More and more it attempted to convert the whole of fact into a product of reason. It had no place for experience, simply as experience. The analytical procedure of the more old-fashioned type of rationalism gave way to a synthetical method. Philosophy took the form of a world-embracing logic, and was held to have shaped the whole course of history; it appropriated all real knowledge to itself, allowing the individual sciences no shred of independence. The historical tendency affected empiricism in an exactly opposite manner; seizing upon the scientific conception of evolution, it made use of it to deduce all the supposed real possessions of the spirit from experience. From this point of view knowledge took the form of an increasing adaptation to environment, which adaptation was looked upon as becoming ever more and more serviceable and economical under the influence of the struggle for existence: all the fundamental tendencies and forms which our thought exhibits (which in the case of a single individual seem *a priori*) are believed to have thus resulted. The whole inward and logical structure of knowledge is replaced by a mere array of facts. Explanation becomes simply description. There is no room here for an independent philosophy; natural science has become the only true knowledge; the selection and arrangement of the more important results of science is the only work left for philosophy to do.

ism): "Now metaphysics, according to the conception of it that we are about to elaborate, is the sole science which may promise such a completion (and that in a short while with but a little united effort) that nothing shall remain for posterity except a mere didactic arrangement according to its aims; it will be impossible for it to add in any way to the content."

The real work of the nineteenth century followed a path between these two opposite tendencies. During the early part of the century, the highly strung self-consciousness of humanity and its occupation with problems of inner culture tended in favour of rationalism. Later on, the immense increase of interest in the external world and the boundless wealth of information — scientific, historical, political and practical — which now poured in upon mankind, promoted the cause of empiricism. During the former period man felt himself to be the centre of reality and believed his spiritual activity to be fully capable of illuminating any initial obscurities. During the latter period he was overwhelmed by the consciousness of his own insignificance; driven from the centre to the periphery, he can no longer hope to produce reality himself; he can only humbly await its revelation. Not only necessity of this kind, but also an inner desire, drives men to depend upon experience: it is the desire for more directness, more actuality, and a greater richness of life than is offered by the world of rationalistic thought, with its confinement of reality within a framework of isolated concepts and forms. The rationalistic procedure is felt to be an impoverishment and dissipation of life. As a reaction against this, in Dilthey's words, "an insatiable desire for reality has become the strong soul of present-day science."*

There was naturally no lack of attempts at reconciliation and adjustment. A resumption of Kantian methods of thought demonstrated that experience, however useful it may be, can never, of its own power, produce scientific knowledge—this requires the constant assistance of thought. In the same way, it may be shown that the individual sciences contain preliminary suppositions which go beyond the sciences themselves and cannot be justified by their methods. A counter-movement of this kind was, however, negative rather than positive. It could point to unsolved problems beyond the world of experience, but it could

* James justly remarks (*Pragmatism*, p. 16): "For a hundred and fifty years past the progress of science has seemed to mean the enlargement of the material universe and the diminution of man's importance. The result is what one may call the growth of naturalistic or positivistic feeling." See also p. 14: "Never were as many men of a decidedly empiricist proclivity in existence as there are at the present day."

not open up a new sphere of life and thought; it supplied no impulse towards a specific philosophical method and an independent philosophy. Philosophy, in this connection, had no other function than that of supplying the individual sciences with a critical and reflective background, an interesting occupation for specialists, but one hardly contributing towards the elevation of spiritual life. Nor could such a philosophy, in the absence of a dominating principle, reach beyond the subjectivity of the merely individual standpoint. For humanity it meant the loss of a world of common ideas and convictions such as it had possessed for thousands of years. The enormously rapid extension of environment during this period produced a wave of optimism which caused mankind to overlook almost entirely the awful significance of this loss and the disintegration and inner impoverishment which threatened to follow upon it. Such happy oblivion could not last. The desire for a connected thought-world and an inner unity in life is so deeply rooted that it cannot be long suppressed. The beginning of a reaction is to be seen clearly enough to-day. The separate sciences themselves demand greater unity: their own constructive progress leads to a closer examination of underlying principles and preliminary assumptions, and this results in the discovery of connections with other spheres of knowledge, and hence stimulates a movement towards solidarity. The demand for a synthesis is again heard on every side. The synthesis is not, however, genuine if the connection established be nothing more than a juxtaposition. It does not really go to the root of the matter unless it discovers common ideas and convictions, and to do this it must take up a commanding position; in other words, there must be an independent philosophy.

In the same direction there works an even stronger force—that of our common life. The disadvantages of being completely dependent on the external world and of converting life wholly into work are becoming increasingly evident. The absence of a uniting principle to fall back upon can no longer be ignored; only a superior unity can convert life into self-life and thus enable us to make it truly our own. We cannot fail to be conscious of spiritual emptiness in the midst of an overwhelming wealth of impressions, and of uncertainty about life as a whole side by side with so much certainty in details. Under these circumstances, all spiritual life and the whole meaning and value of our existence become subject to doubt. The ground beneath our feet becomes totally insecure. It is imperatively necessary to go back to the foundations of our existence and *fight a battle for the preservation of the human soul.* When such problems press for solution we cannot remain content with mere experience. We are driven to seek new possibilities and thoroughly to revise our relationship to reality. Philosophy again enters the arena, not as a mere aid to the elaboration of experience, but bringing with it a thought-world of its own and armed with power to create and construct anew.

(b) The Right of an Independent Philosophy

At the very commencement of our investigation stands the question of the independence of philosophy, for the whole aspect of knowledge depends upon the answer given to this question. But how are we to obtain an answer? In the case of the problem of knowledge there is no direct relationship with the past; there is no evident thread of connection which merely requires to be pursued further. This has already been made clear by our general historical survey, and it is corroborated by the peculiar position of affairs at the present day. We are more conscious to-day of our departure from former achievements of humanity than of any agreement with them. Connections are broken off rather than indicated. The development of spiritual life drove nature and soul inwardly further and further apart; it thereby prevented knowledge directly comprehending both and compelled it to decide for the one or the other. It thus came to pass that fundamentally different conceptions of the world came into being, each claiming to represent truth. But neither was strong enough altogether to capture the field, so that thought continued to oscillate between the two poles.

Such an experience as this seemed to point to the need for a friendly understanding, for an adjustment of conflicting claims. This seemed most likely to be obtained by recognising different factors in knowledge and allocating some to the one sphere and some to the other. This took place in the Kantian distinction between form and matter. But this solution suffered shipwreck owing to the difficulty, nay, impossibility, of bringing together for common service such essentially different factors as sensation and logical activity—factors belonging to quite different categories. It appears impossible to retain the two together, and equally impossible to decide in favour of the one rather than the other. In addition to historical experience of this kind we must take into account the conflicting impressions and impulses of the present day. We are becoming more and more conscious of the inner emptiness of a life and thought occupied solely with the world of experience, but at the same time experience surrounds us with ever-increasing pressure. We want more independence of thought, but our dislike of speculative systems causes us to tremble at each step forward and to distrust every kind of metaphysics.

Such a perplexing position compels us to face the problem outright and boldly attempt to deal with it after our own fashion. Let us begin with the question of what it is which impels man to strive beyond the world of experience and lends power to his aspiration. Is it thought itself which by its nature leads him along this path, at the same time providing him with the ability to follow it? This explanation has been put forward from the earliest times and is still frequently heard. It is said that thought involves demands which the world of experience does not satisfy. At the same time an inner necessity of thought itself compels it to insist on satisfaction. So it is driven to transform this world, nay, even to construct a new one, for its own inner necessity means more to it than any impressions received from outside. This would be simple and convincing if only the necessities upon which thought insists did not claim validity outside the sphere of thought, and if the world it projects did not claim to represent the truth of the things themselves. These claims are, however, made, and in making them thought steps outside its own domain. It cannot justify itself in its action except by artificial suppositions, which when followed up only lead to greater difficulties. Is it possible in this case to escape the objection that thought is simply projecting human conceptions into the outer world? This supposed necessity of thought is a thing standing entirely on its own basis, since it rejects and must reject every species of external support and rest ultimately upon a feeling of imperativeness, of an absolutely irresistible compulsion. But is there really such a compulsion and does not this feeling unavoidably lead to subjectivism and individualism? As a matter of fact prominent philosophers put forward diametrically opposite claims as logically necessary. Hegel maintains that thought sets all reality in movement. Herbart would remove all movement from reality. The former welcomes contradiction as the driving and uplifting force in the world process, the latter will not tolerate any contradiction whatsoever. Which of these demands represents the genuine thought necessity? Which are we ourselves to regard as binding?

There is only one condition on which mere thought could explain the world. Thought must contain the whole of reality within itself or produce it by its activity. Thus self-knowledge on the part of thought becomes a knowledge of the world, and the life-process contains its truth in itself and needs no external corroboration. The logic of facts has driven philosophy in this direction again and again, from Plotinus down to Hegel, for to follow this path has seemed the only way of overcoming the division between thought and being. But the Modern World, through its experience of the Hegelian system, has become clearly conscious of the difficulties which beset the absorption of the whole of reality by thought and of the ensuing danger of the conversion of the world into a mere shadowland of formal concepts. This experience has made an impression that will not soon be obliterated.

If thought neither coincides with being nor provides us with any means of attaining to a being external to itself, then no knowledge at all is possible from the basis of thought alone, and in particular there is no possibility of constructing an independent thought-world side by side with the world of experience. All hope of success rests upon thought entering into wider relationships and hence winning a different relation to reality.

And this is what it really does. Thought does not constitute from the outset the whole intellectual sphere of man; the mind is at first busy with the associations of particular ideas and with the weaving of their mechanical network. Thought with its tendency towards the objective, its inner laws, its synoptical comprehension of manifoldness (in contrast to the successive unfolding, characteristic of chains of ideas), has to assert itself against these associations and establish itself on an independent basis. It can do this (and in fact is a living force at all) only as a portion and an expression of a new stage of life which first arises in man. This brings us to the concept of *spiritual life*, as we have learnt to know it, in distinction from the mere life of the soul. In spiritual life we recognise a new development of the universe in which it unfolds a depth and gathers itself together to form a world-life. To participate in spiritual life means therefore to participate in a world-life. The experiences which the movements and changes of the spiritual life give rise to do not belong to any atomic self, but are appreciated only as revelations of reality as a whole. Moreover this new life has shown itself superior to the contrast between subject and object; it is no half-being needing to be complemented from without, but as fully active life it is raised above this contrast. It carries within itself the tracings of an independent reality, and its movement is a struggle towards the complete development of this reality. This spiritual life, and not mere man or the separate individual, is the basis of thought and of all aspiration towards knowledge. Knowledge appears in a new light when it is directed neither towards itself nor towards what lies beyond itself, but essentially and from the outset is directed towards the spiritual life, by which it is itself encompassed. Knowledge cannot become world-knowledge unless the spiritual life whence it issues itself constitutes the core of reality.

Such a foundation in spiritual life with its accompanying universality is peculiar to all knowledge; but it is not difficult to see the nature of the special task which in this case falls to the lot of philosophy. All aspiration towards knowledge rests upon a relationship of whole to whole. But this relationship may remain in the background as a silent presupposition, and the work may concern itself with separate spheres or separate relationships. It is necessary to have a special science which treats the matter as a whole and above everything else fully elucidates the fundamental fact and seeks to explain its content and its relationship to the surrounding world. This science is philosophy. Spiritual life is certainly not a mere juxtaposition of separate points but an inner whole; and it is just as certainly to be expected that philosophy shall open up a new aspect of the world, and that whatever be the contribution received from the particular sciences it shall be able to meet this with an independent contribution, and thus from its own basis convert the given facts anew into problems.

Hence the corner-stone of all philosophical thought and the axiom of axioms is the fact of a world-embracing spiritual life. The very fact that a new stage of reality, above nature, is recognised at all, alters the aspect of the cosmos and sets Nature herself in a different light. But spiritual life is not only something more as compared with nature; as certainly as it signifies the movement of reality towards its own inner nature and the self-immediacy of life, it must claim to be the last and final stage; as such, however, it must insist upon judging everything and understanding everything from its own point of view and measuring everything according to its own standard. This claim necessarily leads to the question how far the spiritual life present in man is equal to such a task. The difficulties must be considered and the possibility of overcoming them examined. The specific character of man results from the combination of greatness with limitations.

All this provides philosophy with a special task and vouchsafes it an independent view of the cosmos. Its work thereby acquires certain characteristic features, and with three of these in particular we shall now proceed to deal.

1. When philosophy attempts to pass from the whole of spiritual life to the whole of reality, its work does not lie within a given sphere. It must first create this sphere. It does not find its world; it must make it. The whole that it seeks never comes to meet it from outside, but must be shaped from within. It demands a creative synthesis. This philosophical conception

of the world is impelled to achieve independence more particularly by the fact that the existence which it seeks to synthesize cannot be assimilated without undergoing a transformation. The material offered is far too miscellaneous in character to be fitted together just as it is. More especially the meeting of nature and the inner world within a *single* reality imperatively drives us to effect a transformation of first appearances. A tendency towards metaphysics is immovably rooted more particularly in modern thought, if only for the reason that the Modern World has clearly brought out the contrast between nature and the soul, a contrast which necessarily becomes intensified to an unbearable contradiction when the attempt is made to gather the whole together. At the same time philosophical activity is concerned with the question how much of the whole range of our life and thought is to be taken up in this synthesis and to contribute to its construction. For not everything that we know of is present in this philosophical synthesis. Further, the dominating central point, which gathers the rest around it and gives characteristic shape to the whole, must always be first determined, and may be sought in different directions. In this respect different periods vary greatly. After the mediæval construction of spiritual life had completely surrendered the latter's whole sphere to religion, the Enlightenment emphasised the desire for a greater breadth of reality; it found this in the juxtaposition of nature and individual souls, a juxtaposition which could not be comprised within a dominating unity without violence. The Kantian movement produced the concept of an independent spiritual life, and with its historical and social development made it the core of the whole. But it converted spiritual life more and more into mere thought, and thus its range of reality became too small and a reaction was inevitable. This reaction threatened again to draw spiritual life out of the philosophical sphere and hence to fall back upon the conception of reality which was characteristic of the Enlightenment; at the same time the lack of a dominating central point was very keenly felt, for in reality this can only be supplied by an independent spiritual life.

The amount of reality which can be brought within the

philosophical synthesis and the position of the vital centre of the synthesis are continually recurring problems, and this clearly illustrates the very great freedom of philosophical work. In spite of all relationships with the particular sciences, its tendency towards bold and original construction drives it to speculation. In this task the assistance of intellectual fancy is indispensable, but the forms which imagination constructs cannot be made real to man without borrowing from the very world of experience beyond which philosophy takes us.

All this is full of dangers, but without danger no great undertaking is possible. If philosophy aims at converting our whole existence into freedom and transferring us from a given world to a self-constructed world of our own, then it must also accept the risks of freedom. Nevertheless, according to our view, the venture of philosophy assumes quite a different complexion from that it bore in the system based upon pure conceptual construction. For in our case the effort is directed in the first place towards a *fact*, a fact upon which thought itself rests, the fact of a *world-embracing spiritual life;* what it contains must be made manifest as a fact, it must be exhibited, not deduced. How it stands with regard to the surrounding world, what resistance it finds in it, and how it must further develop itself in order to overcome this resistance—these are all questions of actuality, though it is certainly an actuality which cannot come to us from without, but has continually to be obtained anew through an integration of life, through the struggle upwards to the *vision*, which ever sees life as a whole and measures it accordingly. This involves a free act which cannot be forced upon any age or any individual, but is not therefore by any means a matter of individual liking and taste.

2. It is philosophy which first justifies the endeavour to reach beyond a mere acquaintance with things to a real knowledge of them. For knowledge is nothing other than an absorption into one's own life, a finding of oneself, a self-knowledge. Such knowledge can never be afforded us by the realm of sense-experience, which does no more than provide a juxtaposition of events; nor is it attainable through the reshaping of things within the subjective life of the soul, the self-consciousness of the

mere natural man. For a self-consciousness such as this merely projects its own subjective limitations into the external world, making it merely human, like itself; hence even in its most perfect form this subjective limitation of the world is not essentially different from that childish personification of the environment which was characteristic of the early stages of human history. It is only spiritual life, seeking and finding itself in things, which reveals an inwardness not forced upon things from without but contained in their own being; with encompassing power this life converts outer resistances into inner obstacles, and transforms the struggle with them into an inner experience.

Now, it is philosophy which makes itself responsible for this movement towards inner illumination, towards an understanding of reality. It is another question how far man can succeed in such a spiritualisation of the world, and how far it can be accomplished within given conditions, but the mere fact that the problem of knowledge is raised at all signifies a complete change of position and makes it impossible to be satisfied with any mere acquaintance with things. No obstacle and no doubt can alter the fact that with man there begins an illumination of reality. How could he think at all about the world as a whole if his thought did not spring from the world as a whole? Thus the very movement of reality drives us irresistibly beyond all mere collecting and classifying of phenomena to the winning of a soul. Even limitations could not be felt as such if human life and thought were not in some way superior to them. It is the special mission of philosophy to champion this desire for soul. It can attack the task of presenting the true inwardness of reality with peculiar effectiveness when spiritual life is clearly recognised as the vehicle of this endeavour, and the whole breadth of existence is put into relationship with it.

3. Finally, it is philosophy which exhibits in its clearest form the relationship between the struggle for knowledge and spiritual life as a whole, and this imparts more security, power, and importance to the struggle. Philosophy needs this life because only the resources and powers of this life raise it above a position of fruitless reflection and lift it from tentative seeking to secure creation; the spiritual life needs philosophy because only

through philosophy does it attain its full illumination, unification, and originative power.

In order to see how philosophy springs from life as a whole and takes on different forms according to the specific conditions of life, we need only compare different ages and types of human culture. How fundamentally different, for example, is the nature and purpose of philosophy in the Indian and in the European and adjacent Asiatic systems of human culture! This difference is in close correspondence with the different types of life. In the former case we have not so much a penetration and overcoming of the world as a separation and liberation from it, not an enhancement of life in order to maintain it even in the face of the hardest resistance, but an abatement, a softening of all hardness, a dissolution, a fading away, a profound contemplation, but one not translated into deeds; in the second case, on the other hand, we see a powerful life-impulse, a determined attachment to existence in spite of every obstacle, a continual affirmation of life in spite of every upheaval and apparent destruction, a pressing forward through all limitations to the construction of new worlds and the production of new forms of life. At the same time, philosophy becomes more a penetration of the world, a wrestling with its resistances, a progress through the overcoming of these resistances.

It is, however, unnecessary to go far afield to perceive the close connection between philosophical work and the general condition of spiritual life. The experience of the nineteenth century itself shows it with perfect clearness. How was it that purely speculative systems could exercise such an irresistible influence over our fathers while they affect us as something utterly alien, and even the most energetic attempts at resuscitation give them no real power of conviction? The answer is that since then the whole position of life and its fundamental mood have essentially changed. At that time man, with his spiritual creativeness, felt himself to be at the centre of the universe; just as this power of creation seemed to convert all reality into reason, so its concepts might hope, by a courageous advance, to open up the last depth of the universe; thus a complete possession of the truth did not seem too bold a desire. To-day, on the other hand, we are ruled by a consciousness of the extreme littleness of man as compared with the immeasurable world, and we feel ourselves to be at the periphery of things rather than at the centre; to-day, spiritual life does not gather itself together to united creation; to-day, too, we are hampered by severe complications in the human sphere itself. If a philosophical endeavour is to make itself felt at all in such a situation, we must first assemble all our forces; it seems, indeed, as if it would be impossible to do more than press slowly and cautiously forward, commencing at the margin of things.

Just as philosophy draws upon life as a whole, so, too, it influences life as a whole. Every great philosophical achievement involves a striving upward on the part of the whole spiritual life; it is no product of mere intellectual ingenuity, but a work and a strengthening of the whole spiritual nature, also a self-preservation of world-embracing personality. It is characteristic of really great philosophical achievements that in them something more is accomplished than a mere classification of concepts or an enlargement of intellectual horizon; their work results in a further development of the life-process itself, in a growth of spiritual reality. Philosophy by no means delivers mere impressions of ready-made things; it takes part itself in the work of construction; thus, according to its innermost nature, it is by no means a cool contemplation but a matter of powerful life-feeling. Only such a connection with life as a whole explains the position and importance of philosophy in human existence, which otherwise involves an enigmatic contradiction; for, seen from the outside, philosophy appears to be a medley of systems which seem mutually to contradict one another and to neutralise one another's effects; moreover, these systems have, as a rule, been rather rejected than approved of by humanity; yet at the same time we see spiritual life undergo impoverishment and decay where it renounces all relationship to philosophy—religion affords a particularly good illustration of this; how narrow, how inadequate it becomes when it rejects all philosophy! The contradiction disappears when the close connection of philosophy with life as a whole is recognised. Now, its chief accomplishment is not the deliverance of ready-made doctrines, but the inner elevation of the life-process, the gain of independence and originality, the ability to see things more as a whole, more inwardly, more in their essential nature.

This union of philosophy with life serves also to explain its divergence into different tendencies, but without setting all these tendencies on the same footing and thereby abandoning the claim to reach universally valid truth. Moreover, our philosophic preferences and decisions vary with the life-centre we adopt and with the relations in which the life we shape from that centre stands to reality as a whole. In the first place, it must be asked whether it is possible to make a synthesis of life at all or whether life must remain a mere sequence of events. In the latter event there can be no sort of philosophy whatsoever. In attempting a synthesis, however, the chief question will be, Is the main basis of thought to be found in the natural existence to which the average life of the community belongs or in a superior domain, that of life in a state of spiritual freedom, with spiritual contents and values? The former position is represented by naturalism with its empiricism, the latter by idealism with its insistence upon an *a priori*. At a further point the idealistic path itself divides into two, the problem which gives rise to this division being that of the attitude of the ascending spiritual life towards the resistances offered to it by the condition of the world. Pure idealism believes itself able, through a full development of its own power, to overcome, directly, all resistance and to effect a complete assimilation of what is apparently hostile: such a type of thought will, however, tend towards speculative construction and an undervaluation of experience. When, on the other hand, the resistance is looked upon as so excessive that it cannot be overcome by spiritual power, pessimism will result, and will give rise to a scepticism with regard to the possibilities of knowledge: the task of philosophy is here understood in an idealistic sense, so that the position must be classed as idealistic; but since the task is declared to be absolutely impossible of accomplishment, life is left to bear the painful pressure of a fundamental contradiction. When the difficulties and resistances are recognised, but at the same time a further development of life is believed to be possible—a development which shall leave life, at any rate in its innermost core, free from these paralysing influences—a position results which may be called *positive idealism*: it impels us towards a metaphysic which remains entirely distinct from any merely conceptual construction. From this point of view, pure idealism appears to be abstract, to fail in properly penetrating into actual reality and in adequately estimating its resistances. The resulting main types of philosophical thought cannot be looked upon as equivalent possibilities and go on existing peacefully side by side. One alone may be permitted to reckon as the full expression of truth. At the same time such a connection with life makes it obvious that man's decision will be dependent essentially upon his own situation and experience as well as upon the work and mood of the period in question; thus, in spite of the certainty that there is really only one truth, we shall find it hardly possible ever to unite in embracing it.

We need have no fear lest such a close linking-up of philosophy with life as a whole should abandon the former to the shifting phases of history and leave it at the mercy of a destructive relativism; for this would take place only if spiritual life were no more than a product of historical and social development, a merely human phenomenon. In reality all historical and social spirituality is only the development of a timeless spiritual life, superior to all merely human existence. Human culture has only one soul and is only genuine in as far as it participates in such a spiritual life. Something timeless assists in every great historical event, something superhuman in every spiritual ascent of man. It is the peculiar mission of philosophy to work out this timeless, superhuman element—in a word, this *absolute*. Not only has philosophy the greatest width of vision, but owing to the freedom of its thought it can most readily press forward to fundamental facts and to a contemplation of things *sub specie æterni*: by means of a thorough transformation it can lift our life above the mere stream of things and give it an independent basis; it can criticise all existing achievements by referring them to the fundamental process and the inner necessities, thus measuring them, as well as assigning them new tasks from this standpoint. In thus transforming immediate existence, philosophy does no more than give expression to a fundamental necessity of spiritual life, assisting to place the latter in a position of full independence and originality. The mere fact of striving in this direction at all involves an alteration in life's direction and brings with it a liberation; it changes the aspect of life and of the whole of reality. This movement confronts us with absolute demands and compels us to realise the inadequate nature of our possession while revealing a vision of greater depths beyond—for this reason, if for no other, it is of importance.*

(c) **The Tendency towards Metaphysics**

Philosophy, as we have seen, does not acquire a specific task except in so far as it transcends the world of sense-experience; and the task is not imposed upon it from without, but springs from its own nature. Hence, from the very commencement, its work involves considerable tension, and this becomes intensified to the point of sharp contradiction through the special experiences of the human world. The fashion in which spiritual life exhibits itself in the sphere of human interests is such as completely to contradict its own being. He who clearly recognises this contradiction cannot avoid making a decision; he must either abandon spiritual life or he must assign it a position in opposition to the immediate world and make it the vehicle of a

* We may at this point introduce a quotation from that penetrating thinker, Steffensen, although his trend of thought is not completely identical with our own. In the *Gesammelte Vorträge und Aufsätze*, p. 6, he says: "It (*i.e.*, philosophy) does not draw its fame from itself, or from its works, or from the peculiar power or purity of its passion, but from the clear and lofty atmosphere in which it places the object to which it devotes itself and the significance of which it seeks to learn. Therefore without danger it may confess its own powerlessness, be silent for awhile, and go about its work very undemonstratively; its ancient and honourable existence nevertheless bears witness before men of a complete knowledge shining in upon the changeful appearances of this world and the pettiness of our everyday thoughts. The concepts and standards of empirical science stand to the knowledge towards which philosophy endeavours to ascend, as do the distances upon our earth to the immensities of stellar space; the most powerful convictions in the realm of common knowledge, when philosophy compares them with the certainty, which, though only vaguely apprehended, forms its own starting-point, seem no more than shifting and momentary opinions. A standpoint which discloses to our view so vast a horizon will know how to assert its independence."

world of its own. Spiritual life cannot dominate reality and draw it to itself without possessing full independence; within the human sphere, however, and from the point of view of nature, it constitutes a merely derivative phenomenon, while from the point of view of historical existence it appears as a product of social life. Spiritual life proceeds from the whole to the individual, while in immediate existence all combination is a joining-up of separate elements; spiritual life is distinguished by self-activity and originality, while immediate existence shows a thoroughgoing concatenation and hence a constraint affecting all its activity; spiritual life represents its truth as superior to time, while human life runs its course in time and must follow its movement. Now spiritual life cannot possibly operate within us as a world-force without also giving rise to a specific view of the world; hence we must stand fast by this view, and if, in so doing, we meet with thoroughgoing resistance on the part of the immediate world, the matter must be carried through in spite of the opposition. When the superiority to the world thus becomes enhanced to the point of opposition, speculation becomes metaphysics. Since the latter gives the characteristic features of philosophy in general a more marked stamp and sets them forth more distinctly it will particularly strengthen the reversal of the cosmic view inherent in the former. It will at the same time make it known that the given world cannot be wholly disposed of as the mere unfolding of a spiritual form of being, but that it offers resistance to this. This resistance, however, must give rise to difficult complications and severe conflicts. Into our conception of the world as a whole there must then enter a historical element; nothing is more characteristic of metaphysics than the recognition, or at any rate the suggestion, of such an element.

Meanwhile our problems increase. The gulf between the aims of the spirit and the means at man's disposal broadens. The undertaking must appear a reckless venture unless a metaphysic of life stands behind the metaphysic of thought. As a matter of fact, all life bears in itself the problem which metaphysics brings to clear expression. For all genuine spiritual life is developed, in the human sphere, not only as transcending but also as contradicting the immediate world; morality, for example, is not only something more than natural self-preservation, but it must assert itself in direct opposition to a worldly routine of selfish interests and petty aims, and in a hard struggle against this routine it must construct its kingdom. Such a kingdom, however, must possess its own view of the world. This doubtless brings difficult complications with it, but these are forced upon us; we have not created them ourselves. It is impossible to escape these difficulties by returning to the direct moral phenomenon and fixing upon moral personality, for instance, as a secure basis. For such a personality, with the unity of life and originality in action which are necessary to it, does not only stand in sharp contradiction to the mere juxtaposition and fettered state of the immediate world, but it directly involves a cosmic standpoint, it stands for the presence of a new order of things, hence it itself possesses a cosmic character. This cosmic character, however, does not become vividly present to man if there be no vision of reality to support it; thus it is that the self's very effort to preserve itself drives us to metaphysics. We thus see that in metaphysics a conflict is waged for the maintenance of an independent philosophy. If it does not advance into metaphysics philosophy falls asunder. The rejection of metaphysics signifies either that the movement towards philosophy has not enough strength to pursue its way in defiance of the resistances of the immediate world, or that a shallow optimism has caused the resistances to be underrated.

As the task becomes magnified the resistances also increase. The obstacles which the construction of an independent philosophy has always had to overcome will in this case become even more serious. The forward march and the safeguarding of positions already won alike assume a heroic character; the demands of thought cannot here be expressed in pure conceptual form, but in all which goes beyond the mere indication of an outline will be driven to seek the help of metaphor. But if fancy in this way acquires a wider field of play, the whole will never on this account become a mere image; in spite of any inadequacy on the part of the representation, necessities may operate which, from a spiritual point of view, are the most original and certain things in our whole life. The very inadequacy of the representation may make us only the more conscious of the certainty of the fundamental fact.

All depth of spiritual life has a symbolic character. That which originally ascends within it and from this position supports the whole of reality, only fits imperfectly into the human and psychical forms. What is accomplished in the soul of man is only true in so far as it is referred to this deeper basis and illuminated from thence. It lapses into falsity as soon as it becomes separate from its source and endeavours to be more than a mere means. This is particularly evident in the case of religion, which threatens to deteriorate into mere mythology when its concepts and forms are not unceasingly referred back to the fundamental spiritual process and inspired from thence. The highest art, too, we frequently find to have been ruled by the consciousness that creative power, through all its media of representation, exhibits something deeper, something which may indeed be stimulated and vivified, but cannot be adequately expressed. "I have never regarded what I have wrought and accomplished as being more than symbolical. At bottom it has been a matter of comparative indifference to me whether I made pots or pans"—so runs the confession of Goethe (see the *Conversations with Eckermann*). On every hand there is the same contradiction; the life-process in its innermost essence is raised above what is merely human to independent spirituality and absolute truth, and yet in its development it is incapable of overcoming the limitations of the human sphere. This carries with it everywhere the demand for a firm retention of the necessary in spite of all inadequacy, for a maintenance of the fundamental fact in spite of all complications associated with its execution.

Here is an easy point of attack for all doubt and faint-hearted belief, and nowhere more than here will men's minds be divided. As long as the matter is considered coolly and critically from a detached point of view, doubt will easily have the upper hand. It will only be possible to overcome such doubt when the task is taken up as the very essence of our own life and treated as a matter of spiritual self-preservation. In the case of such a sharp alternative as here lies before us there can be no compromise.

If metaphysics thus shares the fate of all spiritual life which aims at being independent, its especial task consists in exposing the contradiction with full clearness and sharpness, so that life is stirred up out of all dull indifference and imbued with an imperative inward and forward impulse. For when what is necessary to spiritual self-preservation has been wrung from the average life of an age and developed and consolidated in opposition to this, and it is then held up to this life as a task that cannot be refused, there comes into life a discontent, an unrest, an inner movement. This probing impels it to an upward effort and at the same time, by the aid of the ideal incentive, its effort is guided along definite paths. Hence, from our point of view, taken as a whole, metaphysics cannot be regarded as something which floats vaguely above the efforts and experiences of the task of human history; it is interwoven in the most intimate manner with the movements of this problem. Every important civilisation has its own metaphysics, in which it expresses its innermost being and intention; its desire is, in and through this metaphysics, to attain an essential character and a living soul, to idealise itself therein. On the one hand, metaphysics must seize on the dominant force which permeates a culture; on the other hand, it must raise what it has apprehended above all the limitations of the existing situation into completeness of form and absolute validity, and from this standpoint undertake a conflict against everything in the established customs and social habits which is inadequate, merely human, and base, thus provoking a sharp cleavage into "for and against." For example, the Platonic doctrine of ideas elevated the Greek artistic view of the cosmos into the metaphysical realm, the idea of an unchangeable eternity taking the first place. So, again, the thought-world of the Enlightenment acquired a metaphysical form in Leibniz's system, with its hold on the infinitely little and its conversion of philosophy into a universal mathematic. On every hand we perceive an endeavour to push forward from the highest point of human accomplishment into the absolute and to obtain an independence of a spiritual character for our thought and being by a reversal of the immediate order of things. Through this relationship to history metaphysics makes no surrender to what is merely temporal; rather does it elaborate the timeless element of truth contributed by the passing generations. This element does not disappear with the age, but remains continually present, at any rate as a possibility and a challenge.

If we conceive of metaphysics in this fashion we shall have no difficulty in meeting the attacks which have been made upon it from the earliest times. The very name was calculated to arouse prejudice.* But in regard also to content, metaphysics must now pursue a different path from that which it has attempted to tread in the past. There must be a decisive break with that unfettered speculation which believes itself able to produce a new world out of mere thought: this fits rather the old-fashioned mode of thinking which conceived it possible to discover the whole spiritual content of life through knowledge, and then to communicate it to the remaining departments of

* The expression "metaphysics" has its origin in the fact that Andronicus Rhodius, a contemporary of Cicero's, in his arrangement of the Aristotelian writings placed the investigations dealing with the "first philosophy" (πρώτη φιλοσοφία) after the physics: μετὰ τὰ φυσιχά (for particulars see Bonitz' *Kommentar zur aristotelischen Metaphysik*, p. 3 ff.). Even in the first century after Christ this led to the naming of the discipline itself according to its position (τὰ μετὰ τὰ φυσικά, ἡ μετὰ τὰ φυσικὰ πραγματεία). The singular form *metaphysica* belongs to the scholastic system and was probably derived from Averroës' translation. The name was an unfortunate one, in as far as, from the very beginning, the idea which it indicates attached to the concept itself, creating the impression that metaphysics has to do with what is remote or transcendental, that it represents a more or less imaginary addition to the immediate reality. It was already referred to in this fashion by the Neo-Platonist, Herennius (see Brandis in the *Abhandlungen der Berlin. Akad.*, 1831, p. 80): "μετὰ τὰ φυσικὰ λέγονται, ἄπερ φύσεως ὑπερῆρται καὶ ὑπὲρ αἰτίαν καὶ λόγον εἰσίν." To the scholastic philosophers, too, such as Thomas Aquinas, *metaphysica* meant the same as *transphysica*. Kant, however, says (viii. 576, Hart.): "The ancient name of this science, μετα τα φυσικα, already gives an indication of the type of knowledge towards which the science was directed. It is sought, with its assistance, to transcend all the objects attainable by experience (*trans physicam*) in order, where it is possible, to know that which cannot, under any circumstances, be an object of experience." The friends of metaphysics, on the other hand, strove to obtain fresh terms. Clauberg, the most important German Cartesian, recommended "ontosophy" or "ontology," but the disfavour which had attached to the old term was soon extended to the new one; Wolff already complained (see *Philos. prima sive ontologia*, 1.): *Vix aliud hodie contemtius est nomen quam Ontologiæ*. Moreover, ontology denotes only the older type of metaphysics—now regarded as an impossibility. We may ask, in passing, is it not a remarkable fact that no thinker of the first rank has ever written a "metaphysics" under that name?

life, whereas now we set knowledge within an underlying spiritual life and permit it, along with the other departments, to struggle simultaneously for truth and for the development of this deeper life. More particularly the new metaphysics form the sharpest contrast to the ontological, and therefore, at the same time, abstract and dogmatic character of the older metaphysics. Aristotle's action in determining the task of the " first philosophy " to be the contemplation of the Being as being (τὸ ὂν ᾗ ὄν), the discovery of the most general properties of being, struck a false path from the very outset. This had the effect of making certain formal properties appear to be the real essence of things, constituting the main framework, all particularity being fitted in as mere illustrative material. Thus metaphysics became mere ontology. This resulted in a movement of the thought-world towards the abstract and formal ; a setting-aside of the specific content of human life. At the same time it gave rise to dogmatism, since these formal properties seemed to be once for all recognisable previous to any closer experience and independently of all historical movement, and were for this reason conveyed from metaphysics to the other departments of knowledge as inviolable truths. This dogmatic procedure had the double effect of depriving metaphysics of inner movement and the other sciences of their independence. No wonder that this ontological and dogmatic metaphysics met with resistance from all quarters. The development of modern scientific investigation has only become possible by throwing off the old metaphysics.

But the rejection of a special type of metaphysics is not an abandonment of all metaphysics. We are inclined to agree with Kant when he expressed the conviction that "some sort of metaphysics has always existed in the world and will doubtless continue to do so " (Hart., iii. 25). At any rate, the metaphysics which our own way of thinking necessitates is not open to the objections which destroyed the old metaphysics. For where there is a germ of developing life within knowledge itself, and where knowledge is primarily directed towards the deepening and illumination of this life, metaphysics will not entice thought and life into the abstract, but will communicate to these its own actuality and definiteness; with its integration of all multiplicity, metaphysics will for the first time render clearly visible the unique individuality of our being and our world. All life's several meanings and problems, even such connected systems as those of religion, art, and morality, will be able to overcome the wretched colourlessness of current solutions and interpretations only through being assigned a definite place and goal within an inclusive scheme of life; moreover, the content which is revealed by reality as it consolidates into a totality of this kind can alone justify the form of being assumed and provide it with a meaning. Thus our investigation is impelled towards metaphysics, not through any delight in forms and universals, but through a desire for more character, for a profounder actuality, for a more energetic renovation of our sphere of life.

A metaphysic which preserves the connection between the endeavour after knowledge and a fundamental and comprehensive spiritual life is equally secure as regards the charge of petrifying dogmatism. Such a metaphysic will keep in closest touch with the movements of universal history, and at the same time gain a history of its own; this will not, however, cause it to sink to the merely temporal level.

To-day we have no metaphysics and there are not a few who consider this to be an advantage. They would be justified in this view, however, only if our thought-world chanced to be particularly flourishing; if, despite the absence of metaphysics, firm convictions ruled our life and endeavour and high aims fortified us and liberated us from the petty human routine. But in point of fact we cannot avoid recognising a limitless disintegration, a lamentable insecurity of conviction in all matters of principle, a helplessness in the face of the trivialities of our human lot, a soullessness in the midst of an overflowing outward plenty. Those who can quietly endure such a state of affairs will not be led to metaphysics by any theoretical considerations. But those who recognise how imperative is the task of welding our civilisation into a more compact and purposive whole, and of winning for it an inner independence (thereby at once more sharply dividing and more closely uniting men's minds), will side with us in our retention of metaphysics and in the seeking of new paths along which to carry on the ancient task.

(*d*) The Pursuit after Knowledge: a General Survey

The foregoing discussions express fundamental convictions as to the nature of knowledge, and these only need developing to give rise to a characteristic view of the whole. In particular, it is the conception of spiritual life which we have here advocated which promises to overcome the antithesis bequeathed to us by history. From our point of view, spiritual life is at the same time a new stage of reality over against that of nature and a creative fount of life in contrast with the soul's life as we find it, wherein the products of both stages come together.

From this deeper standpoint it will be possible both to liberate the substance of knowledge from all dependence upon externals and fully to recognise the limitations of our human quest for knowledge: many factors which formerly played the part of enemies and necessarily injured one another may now mutually contribute to one another's advancement.

We have regarded spiritual life as fully active life which does not run its course between subject and object, but encompasses the antithesis from the very beginning. In this case our task cannot lie in the attempt to copy a transcendent world, but must be sought in the shaping and perfecting of our own existence. Spiritual life must therefore contain in itself different stages of expression, the movement from the lower stages to the higher being guided by a necessity inherent in the development as a whole. That which in any way already appertains to its activity cannot become its full property until it has been converted into self-activity. This applies also to knowledge: its movement lies within life as a whole; for in its case, too, the matter with which it is concerned must be situated within the spiritual life and not outside it; something totally external could excite nothing and set nothing in motion; it could never touch thought at all, and under no possible circumstances could it even become an intellectual problem, for this can only occur when an object is already in some fashion present to the thought-world. The manner, however, in which it is so present does not correspond to the nature of spiritual life, nay, it contradicts it. This contradiction then becomes a compelling impulse towards further construction. Thus, in the task of knowledge with its pressing forward to a higher stage, spiritual life accomplishes an act of self-assertion.

If this is the position of affairs, nothing can become an intellectual problem which is not in some way already incorporated within the life-process. Thus when knowledge is to become active, it must be preceded by an inner enlargement of life. This assertion is corroborated in the most clear and convincing manner both by a study of human history and by everyday experience. For these show us that even that which surrounds man with intrusive nearness and affects him in the most strongly sensuous manner, may remain, in an inward sense, completely alien to him and not become a problem of human knowledge at all. Things will not answer those who do not question them; realities will only reveal themselves to those who confront them with possibilities. Even the hardest resistance does not produce a spiritual effect until it has been converted into an inner obstruction. Individuals, peoples, or whole epochs may suffer from the most serious evils without being greatly aroused by them or driven to any sort of protective measures. Both great artists and great educators agree in maintaining that the spiritual organs are not brought with us ready-made, but must first be moulded into shape.* A study of human history, too, shows that much that lay quite near to man (nay, that already outwardly belonged to him) has only quite recently become part of his own life and stirred his own endeavour; at the same time it permits us to recognise the assumptions and predispositions underlying that which later on was lightly regarded as a matter of course. What a slow process was the artistic discovery of

* In this connection we may mention Herbart's well-known saying with regard to the nonagenarian village schoolmaster (*Werke*, x. 8): "We should all bear in mind that *we each experience only that which we test!* An aged village schoolmaster of ninety has the experience of his lengthy routine; he has the feeling of his great labours. But can he also criticise his achievements and his methods?" Froebel was of the opinion that man, "in order to understand nature, must himself create it afresh, within and without, by means of an artistic method peculiar to himself."

nature; how recently, for example, have the beauties of landscape been revealed to us! Consider, too, how present-day art is labouring to develop our visual sensibility so that more and more may be seen in the external world and new aspects of it opened up. Moreover, man has had to discover himself, his humanity, and the common life and feelings to which this humanity gives rise; he did not find all this ready-made; he won it for himself through inward movements and developments. Pedagogy describes apperception as the absorption of new impressions within the thought-world of the individual; but the great world of history has its apperception also, like the individual; humanity as a whole cannot assimilate anything to which it does not oppose an inner movement.

What is thus so readily accepted with regard to particular things must, when extended to the whole, result in the problem of knowledge assuming a new aspect. For it thus becomes clear that all knowledge lies within man's sphere of work, and that there is no essential progress in knowledge without a growth of this sphere. In the case of knowledge, too, every really great achievement does not fall within a ready-made sphere, but itself alters the sphere of life. Modern science would have been impossible without the modern man with his bold superiority to the world and his confidence in the might of his own soul. It is only by thus giving a deeper foundation to the process of knowledge that we are able to conceive of it as an immanent procedure, and so avoid the dilemma by which we seem compelled to view thought either as being concerned with an alien world or as spinning all existence out of itself.

But precisely this recognition of the independence of spiritual life and of the immanence* of the process of knowledge is calculated to bring the distinctively human element, and with it the importance of experience, to full recognition. For the more we conceive of spiritual life and knowledge, too, as being independent and superior, the more does the given world recede from us, and the more clearly do we perceive that only under

* We here take "immanence" in its old and original sense, according to which it signifies something which takes place within the life-process and does not go beyond it; see the chapter "Immanence—Transcendence."

certain conditions and as the result of hard work will man be able to participate in spiritual life, and that the latter is accessible to him only through some kind of experience. Man is in the first place occupied with the sub-spiritual stage of reality, which finds intellectual expression in the world of sense-perception with its mechanical connections; it would be impossible for him to proceed beyond this stage at all if the higher, too, were not in some fashion operative in his sphere. But this higher is not fully present within the life-process; it must first attain to such fullness of presence; the very impulse in this direction follows, as a rule, only from special conditions, from the perplexities and contradictions which arise in the lower stage. History clearly shows us how laboriously and slowly the quest after knowledge took shape. And the very progress of the movement compelled it to recognise something peculiar in man's nature and circumstance—a peculiarity not to be deduced conceptually, but simply accepted as a fact. To this extent human knowledge bears an experiential character. In recognising this, however, we are far from committing ourselves to empiricism. As a matter of fact we could not recognise this experiential character itself unless we occupied a position superior to mere experience. Man, limited and fettered as he is, only attains to insight in so far as he participates in an independent and superior spiritual life and is able to measure his position from this standpoint.

Experience has a twofold significance with respect to knowledge: it is an external limitation and an internal determination. It is the former when spiritual activity remains bound to external conditions and is hence unable to raise itself to full self-activity. It is the latter when, for the first time, it attains its own full and definite character in conflict with resistance, learns to know itself through trial and experience and attains to pure self-activity. In both cases alike human knowledge depends upon experience; experience is here indispensable, not only for the relating of spiritual life to its environment, but also for the constituting of this life itself, not only for determining its scope, but also for deciding its content.

The knowledge which humanity develops, finds itself, in the

first place, face to face with an alien and immeasurable world, and it can advance only through close contact with this world; it may, in fact, appear to draw solely upon the world; moreover, in the elaboration of what is thus taken up, there are large departments of life, notably that of nature as apprehended through the senses, in which knowledge can never cut itself loose from the given world; that portion which enters into man's thought-world cannot be purely converted into terms of thought, it continues to be attached to something external and to present an opaque barrier. But, however necessary, in this connection, a contact with sensible things and a relation to these things may be, this contact and relation do not produce knowledge. Knowledge develops subject to conditions and limitations, but it nevertheless remains in the first place *a product of spiritual life*. It does not develop itself *out* of experience, but only in *contact with* experience, just as impressions cannot pass into the thought-world without undergoing an essential transformation. How fundamentally different does the same natural phenomenon appear to the immediate perception of the unsophisticated man and to the thought-world of the scientist! Hegel observes with justice: " It is the nature of spirit not to assimilate anything just as it comes to us from outside, nor to permit a cause simply to carry on its previous agency within it, but it must needs break off the old threads of connection and inwardly reconstitute them " (*Wke.*, iv. 229).

Not only the extension of spiritual life but also its inner nature is, for us men, a problem and a task. Spiritual life does not directly fill our own life in firm and definite form, nor does it draw us to itself in a sure and steady advance, as the intellectual optimism of speculative philosophy supposed; on the contrary, we have to gradually push forward from small beginnings (and these not incontestable), and our endeavour abounds in obstacles and dangers; in glad confidence we undertake many things which are subsequently found to be impracticable; often we seem to be tossed to and fro and to make no progress at all. That which our labour does bring us, however, does not come as the result of reflection, but of pursuing chosen paths to the end. Both our ability and our limitation are only revealed to us through the developments and experiences of life itself. It is more especially true that it is through struggle alone that our life fathoms its full depth. Resistance alone drives it to put forth its whole strength and compels it to exercise its full originative power. At the same time the growth of spirituality does not signify a pure victory over the hostile element, nor does it bring full illumination. On the contrary, the inner advance is likely to bring forth new claims, problems, and resistances, and therefore the aspect of reality will take on a more and more positive and irrational form. Such an actuality must make knowledge into something essentially different from that which rationalism would have it to be; at every point it is now referred to the experiences of life as a whole. It was only in the early infancy of knowledge that men fancied themselves to be approaching a smooth conclusion; an increased insight has led to the recognition of more and yet more unsolved problems; the world has not grown more lucid, but more enigmatic. Thus precisely at the height of modern life the general aspect of knowledge is anything but simple. Reality looms before us, a series of gradations showing an advance from inorganic to organic, from inanimate to animate and psychical, from the soul enslaved to nature to the soul filled with the spirit. Each stage presents its own characteristic aspect of reality; and there will always be conflict of opinion as to whether the lowest or the highest stage should be taken as the starting-point for explanation. Philosophy cannot avoid treating the realities which become visible upon the highest stage of life as the deepest revelations, and from this standpoint forming its conception of the whole. But it presently discovers that the categories won from this standpoint are not adapted to the world beneath us, which opposes them with a rigid nature of its own; it also discovers that this world, throughout the whole of its active being, treats this higher stage with indifference, as something quite subsidiary. It seems as if that which we cannot help regarding as the essence of all reality cannot carry out its purpose in our world with the aid either of its own concepts or its own forces. On every side there is the same contradiction; man's spiritual nature demands from him more than his mere humanity is able to compass; spiritual self-preservation compels him to affirm truths to which his intellectual capacity is not fully equal, and energetically to maintain the fundamental ideas which these truths imply, without being able to carry these adequately into practice. Therefore if our intellectual capacity is to decide as to the whole content of life, a spiritual impoverishment will be the inevitable result.

(e) Estimation of Rationalism and Empiricism

The foregoing discussion has brought us to a point from which we may attempt to estimate impartially the two opposing movements. It will be seen that while each represents important elements of truth and successfully employs them in attacking the opposite side, each falls into error and fails to maintain its own position as soon as it attempts a final solution on its own account.

The strength of rationalism lies in its advocacy of the independence of spiritual life and its superiority to all environment, and also in its defence of the conviction that life does not primarily and essentially proceed from without inwards—that (as Plato put it) a blind man cannot simply be provided with eyes from without. In the absence of this conviction there can be no such thing as truth at all. The complete dependence of our knowledge upon outward impressions would deprive it of all stability, all connection, all inner illumination, and would leave it at the mercy of mere individual accident. It is an axiomatic necessity, when rationalism, in the face of these facts, advocates an *a priori*. But the *a priori* must be understood, not as a ready-made quantity in the soul of each individual, but as a basic law of spiritual life that man has first to appropriate. Such an *a priori* involves the assertion that spiritual life carries within itself norms which continually turn our search for knowledge towards truth and away from error; it involves, further, the assertion that spiritual life is essentially superhistorical, and is no mere historical product. Without being thus superhistorical it could never subject historical formations to a superior criticism; it would be entirely at the mercy of their changes.

Since it stands for such indispensable truth, rationalism possesses a superior justification as compared with empiricism. But it falls into error in believing it possible to attain these truths directly, in treating what is really a far-off goal as a present, or at any rate easily accessible, fact: we refer to its treatment of the spiritual life in man without qualification as spiritual life in itself, as absolute spiritual life; this has the effect of blunting our sense of the characteristically human and of the limitations of humanity. We see this effect when achievements which thought can only produce in connection with an independent spiritual life as a whole are attributed to thought itself, thus depriving ideas of their vital depth; we see it also when rationalism believes our spiritual life, just as it is, to be upon a safe path and no inner perplexities are recognised.

Taking all in all, rationalism tends towards weakening and explaining away the dark and hostile element which humanity finds in the world. It sacrifices the individual to the universal, content to form. The resulting conception of reality is smooth, attenuated, and anæmic to an extreme. Both life and thought become abstract, formal, and shadowy. This is particularly obvious in the case of the view of history which rationalism produces in its leaning towards speculative ideal constructions: the movement of history is here looked upon as taking place, from the very beginning, in a sphere of reason, whereas in reality it must first laboriously obtain its rational character and as constantly confirm it. It is believed that all antitheses and conflicts are only a means towards the advancement of reason; everything irrational appears to be ultimately resolved into a great harmony, whereas in truth the struggle does not take place simply *within* reason; it is more a struggle *for* reason, and every increase of reason in human relationships is apt to increase the irrational element as well. According to this view, each epoch appears to represent a steady advance, resting securely on the one preceding, and the historical experience which humanity acquires is looked upon as a permanent possession, though in reality the struggle over ultimate issues is being perpetually renewed, a firm foundation must be continually constructed afresh, and every spiritual experience again and again resumes its problematical character. Man now appears purely and simply as the instrument of spiritual work, in spite of the fact that his predominant inclination is far rather to subordinate spiritual life to natural and social self-preserving instincts, thus grievously perverting it and alienating it from its own purposes. When the obscure and hostile element is thus slurred over, history loses its power and depth. The more exclusively this rationalistic treatment is carried out the more it evacuates and dissipates reality. If, on the other hand, it becomes clear that historical life does not advance with a continuous and steady movement, but that the whole must continually be made the subject of fresh conflict, and that there must be a continual reaffirmation of the whole, then free action takes precedence of the idea of a historical process and all possibility of a rational construction vanishes.

Thus the unrestricted development of rationalism must give rise to a reaction in the direction of empiricism with its thirst for actuality and its ready recognition of human limitation, and history shows us that empiricism has attained to power and prestige more especially when the deficiencies of a traditional rationalism have become obvious. The antipathy to speculative conceptual construction is at the back of the most recent developments of empiricism.

But empiricism, on the other hand, entirely fails to afford any suitable expression to the experiential character of our thought-world. It conceives the process of experience as sharply contrasted with self-activity, without which, however, there can be no scientific knowledge. Since it denies all independent spiritual life, it must seek to develop spirituality and knowledge from a merely human standpoint. This is, in reality, impossible,* and

* The impossibility of attaining to a science by empirical means has recently been very emphatically pointed out by distinguished investigators. Windelband (*Präludien*, 2nd edit., p. 303) calls it a "hopeless attempt, through an empirical theory, to supply a foundation to that which is itself the assumption upon which the theory rests"; and Husserl (*Logische Untersuchungen*, 1. 110) remarks in the same connection: "The greatest objection that can be raised against a theory of logic is to say that it clashes with the evident conditions of the possibility of a theory at all."

it only achieves a faint appearance of success by secretly assuming the existence of a spiritual world and employing factors borrowed therefrom. This results in a view of reality which is distorted down to its smallest detail. In dealing with the process of knowledge, empiricism directs its whole attention to the thing done, and is oblivious of the spiritual activity that is operative in the achievement itself; it clings to the external object, and forgets that this means nothing to us except through our act of appropriation. It perceives the determination of knowledge by experience, but it does not perceive that this determination takes place within an encompassing mental space and through the movement of the spirit itself, not through a communication from without.* It is so exclusively taken up with a wealth of particulars that it looks upon their connection as a matter of course. It cannot see the wood for the trees. The empiricist regards the things themselves as producing what in reality our activity has placed within them; this is seen, for example, in the concept of the world of experience, which is anything rather than a product of mere experience.† Taking Kant's work into account, it should not be easy to obscure the fact that there is a problem of knowledge as a whole, that is to say that the ground upon which experience comes

* Our mode of speech cannot be acquitted of blame in this respect, since it places thought and experience in opposition to one another, as if experience could accomplish anything without thought. So early a writer as Robert Boyle justly protested against this (*The Christian Virtuoso*—towards the end): "When we say, experience corrects reason, 'tis an improper way of speaking, since 'tis reason itself, that upon the information of experience corrects the judgment it had made before."

† It is very remarkable how often an appeal is to-day made to experience without any previous examination of its conditions or guarantee of its possibility. This takes place most often perhaps in the educational world. New types of schools are established, and soon it is said that experience has shown them to be excellent. There is a general inclination to introduce devices copied from foreign nations on the ground that these have been justified by the experience of the nations in question. But can we assume that what is suitable to one people is equally adapted to another, perhaps under essentially different conditions of life? And if an institution has good results here and there, perhaps under exceptionally favourable circumstances, is that any demonstration of its universal advantage? Experience can be appealed to only when there are essentially equal conditions; whether or not this is the case is usually not at all adequately ascertained.

to pass must first be gained, and that in striving towards truth the conflict does not bear upon isolated data, but concerns totalities—constructions and convictions as a whole. Empiricism, however, cannot avoid obscuring this fact, because it only takes into account particular aspects of reality, aspects which by no means exhaust its scope and depth. And this holds not only on the objective, but also on the subjective side, as we may briefly express it. Since our thought and life first find play as conscious processes, empiricism is content not to go beyond this point, and omits to perceive that the content of consciousness is not itself comprehensible apart from a more deeply grounded self-consciousness of spiritual life, and apart from a reversal of first impressions, as when the view of the gradual formation of a unifying ego is supplanted by the insight that it is the ego which first makes possible all inward synthesis such as is essential to the very existence of science. Now to break up the life of the soul into a mere juxtaposition of separate processes in consciousness is to abandon all inner relationship, and therefore to make all science fundamentally impossible.

On the objective side, however, empiricism clings far too exclusively to external nature and overlooks the specific character of the other spheres of existence. That portion of its doctrine which has a certain justice as applied to nature falls into error when extended to the whole world. The sensuous effects which we experience never permit of being fully translated into spiritual activity and developed from within; thus there always remains a strangeness and constraint, and we do not advance beyond mere registration and description. But even the first view of human life and endeavour reveals a different state of affairs. Here, too, we first meet with separate processes, but we can pass beyond the mere impression: these processes permit of being traced back to the life-process that produced them, and of being linked together; since the looker-on is able to transplant himself within this process he can convert the strange element into personal life. If, however, man can thus live and feel with man, not merely contemplating him from without as an alien thing, then there is a knowledge that is more than mer description. But we take a yet further step if we recognise a spiritual life within the human sphere, if we take our stand upon this in the development of knowledge, and thence illuminate and sum up the whole social and historical life of humanity, including the experiences of individuals. In this case, we can never be content with a mere cataloguing of the observed phenomena; we must effect an inner appropriation and critically transform what we assimilate. For spiritual life as revealed in the human sphere is, in its immediate condition, so much encumbered with matter of a temporal, accidental, merely human nature, that there can be no clarification without an energetic sifting and adjustment to one's own nature. At the same time it is our task here to pick out from amidst the special connections and tendencies wherein this life finds a struggling expression, a comprehensive whole whence we may illuminate this manifoldness and render it coherent. In truth the high-water mark of the knowledge revealed to man is to be seen here, in the characteristic development of spiritual life and the construction of a spiritual world; therefore here, too, lies the decision as to our whole view of the universe; it is from this standpoint that the type of our worldview must be determined and some sort of justice, too, must be done to the limitations and contradictions of human existence. The whole task is replete with experiences, full of movements which take us deep into ourselves and could never under any circumstances proceed from mere concepts; hence it lies entirely outside the sphere of mere rationalism and just as certainly beyond the capacity of mere empiricism. Both fail clearly to distinguish spiritual life from human existence; this impels rationalism to an exaggeration of man and empiricism to a denial of spiritual life; the former is unable to provide knowledge with a living content, while the latter robs it of its scientific character. A further mistake is common to both; neither makes knowledge a portion of a greater *whole* of spiritual life and treats the problem of knowledge in connection with this whole. Left thus isolated, knowledge is either under- or overvalued. At the same time, both rationalism and empiricism represent factors indispensable to knowledge: on the one hand, originality; on the other, actuality. What is needed, however, is a new standpoint from which to combine these factors of truth into a whole, and so to cling one-sidedly no longer either to the greatness of human knowledge or to its limitation, but to recognise greatness and limitation alike. When empiricism, in spite of all its obvious weaknesses, continually raises its head afresh to exert an overpowering influence over humanity, this is due not so much to what it has actually achieved as to that defective grasp of the truth-concept which so often characterises rationalism. The service and justification of the latter is to be found in its elevation of truth above all shades and divisions of human opinion, in the fact that it makes truth fully independent of man; whenever this independence becomes in any way insecure, then science can no longer be saved from utter destruction. But so long as this separation between truth and man is not in some way overcome, and the former is not in some fashion made our own affair, truth will continue to be more or less cold and dead; its ability to move us with overpowering force and to elevate the whole of life will remain inexplicable. However firmly we must reject the pragmatic method of measuring truth according to its utility for life (or indeed according to any external standard at all), the apprehension of truth must still be understood as the development of a new life, and the truth itself conceived as existing not without life, but within it. It is ultimately a question not of grasping a reality external to life, but of gaining a life which develops a reality out of itself. By pursuing this quest we may secure a more inward relation to truth. Without such a relation we fall victims to empiricism, which would not attain to any truth whatever if it did not set out with a belief in truth.

In empiricism and rationalism, as we have seen, opposing spiritual tendencies are operative. It will depend upon the character and circumstances of any given period which of the two will, for the time being, obtain the upper hand. When the thought-world is regarded as, in essentials, complete and capable of being easily reviewed (as was the case in the Ancient World, in the Middle Ages, and in the time of the German speculative philosophy), the mind's own contribution will take the first place and there will be a tendency to undervalue experience. When, on the other hand, a consciousness of the narrowness of the previous field of vision predominates, and there arises a desire for expansion, salvation will be looked for solely from experience and the constructive, nay, transforming, spiritual activity is easily overlooked. This was what happened with Bacon, and again in the nineteenth century, and this is what often happens to-day. The immeasurable enlargement of our field of vision both in nature and in history which was effected by the work of the nineteenth century was bound to exercise a particularly powerful influence in Germany, because it was accompanied by an energetic reaction against the too rigid syntheses of the constructive systems.

But the more such an empirical movement spreads, and the more exclusively it occupies the field, the more necessary opposition becomes. We saw that empiricism was only able to attain even to an ineffectual conclusion because it operates within a ready-made thought-world, superior to (and even contradictory of) its own world of concepts; but the more independent and the more impatient of restraint this tendency becomes, the more this thought-world must be shaken and broken up. Thus, through its own progress, it undermines these indispensable complements, and therefore in its outward triumph it must suffer an inward collapse. Its inadequacy becomes transparently obvious as soon as it relies entirely upon its own means. In spite of all the favour which is still accorded to empiricism in the domain of exact sciences remote from life, we perceive that such a catastrophe is now impending. It becomes increasingly clear that no accumulation and arrangement of known facts can afford any sort of knowledge, or ideas, or convictions; yet, at the same time, man cannot exist without these if he is to remain a being with a soul and not to degenerate into a mere civilised machine. Thought is imperatively driven beyond empiricism, not only by a necessity of spiritual life but, in particular, by the peculiar position of present-day culture. No culture can exist without an independence and originality on the part of thought. But so long as life proceeds along paths which are supposed to be safe, this independence may be overlooked and forgotten unless it is threatened by severe perplexities and contradictions. To-day, however, we are completely dominated by such perplexities and contradictions; we perceive the necessity for a thorough overhauling of our whole heritage of culture, the necessity for an energetic sifting out of all that has become obsolete and untrue, for a powerful synthesis and development of all the elements of truth. Nay, we are so deeply shaken that our uncertainty extends to the last elements and compels us to struggle for spiritual life as a whole. In the face of such tasks how can we make any sort of progress without a capacity for independent and original activity, without a self-recollection and self-awakening on the part of the spiritual life, without a spiritual elevation and renewal, to indicate new possibilities and reveal new realms of fact? Empiricism, however, cannot help us in any of these respects. And as the age stands in need of an inner transformation it must necessarily leave empiricism behind it. We warmly welcome the fact that the philosophical investigation of the present day is tending towards idealism, and we thoroughly understand the accompanying dislike of again adopting anything resembling the old type of metaphysics: as certainly as we need a thorough renewal and systematic invigoration of life, we need a rousing and progressive idealism. Such an idealism, however, cannot be merely critical, it must be positive. For although the critical idealism which to-day takes a leading place on the highest level of philosophical investigation renders an important service in indicating the limits of realism and empiricism, and in particular in demonstrating that they can only succeed in creating a whole of life and knowledge by secretly borrowing from their opponents, and although, in addition, it certainly exhibits, along certain main lines of tendency, the operation and control of a new order of things, it fails in adequately gathering these main tendencies into a *whole*. A whole, however, is indispensable if man is to find his spiritual self in this movement, to place the centre of gravity of his life therein, and, at the same time, reverse the current of his life. Apart from such a reversal, apart from this uprooting from the other side into a life of elemental power, the new life will hardly be strong enough to take up an independent position over against an order of another kind, and to overcome the immense obstacles offered by the worldliness at its doors. It is therefore no mere thirst for intellectual adventure which drives us towards metaphysics, but the imperative demand for a self-preservation of spiritual life.

2. MECHANICAL—ORGANIC

(TELEOLOGY)

THE concepts of the "mechanical" and the "organic" have behind them a particularly influential history. This history not only exhibits great contrasts in cosmic speculation and in theory of method, but it reveals a hard struggle fought over the character of scientific work; moreover it is full of fine distinctions and the more delicate variations of thought, and hence gives us a characteristic insight into the movement as a whole. Oppositions which hark back thousands of years still exert their influence over the work of to-day. Hence our attention will be chiefly directed to the historical side of the subject.

(a) On the History of the Terms and Concepts

The concepts mechanical and organic (like the terms themselves) are old, but it was long before the terms became associated with the concepts. Mechanical appears in Aristotle as a well-established expression, as the technical designation of the art of invention, of the construction of machines ($ἡ\ μηχανική,\ τὰ\ μηχανικά$), and one of his later writings bears the name ($μηχανικά$).* The word continued to bear this meaning throughout the centuries, and since the time of Descartes it has served to denote a theory which explains the function of nature by analogy with human contrivances, not by reference to a driving power inherent in the structure as a whole, but as the result of

---

* In this work the expression is explained as follows: "Ὅταν δέῃ τι παρὰ φύσιν πρᾶξαι, διὰ τὸ χαλεπὸν ἀπορίαν παρέχει καὶ δεῖται τέχνης. διὸ καὶ καλοῦμεν τῆς τέχνης τὸ πρὸς τὰς τοιαύτας ἀπορίας βοηθοῦν μέρος μηχανήν (Arist. 847 a, 16). Art here appears to be a kind of outwitting of nature.

the combination of diminutive particles of matter, originally endowed with motion. The works of nature appear to differ from those of man solely in their greater refinement of structure, that is to say quantitatively not qualitatively.* Theoretical mechanics, in the form of a theory of motion, provides the means of technical explanation.† The term mechanical seems to have been brought into use more especially by the chemist and philosopher Robert Boyle, who had a peculiar partiality for it and liked to make use of it in the titles of his books: he even took objection to the expression " nature " and would have been glad to see it replaced by *mechanismus universalis*.

The natural science of the following periods gave the term meanings which were sometimes exact and sometimes loose. Discussions as to these meanings were in constant progress. As a rule, however, a mechanical explanation meant an explanation of the properties of matter by means of figure and movement. A transference to mental processes was not at first thought of, and mechanical and material were frequently reckoned as synonymous terms.‡ Hence a mechanical explanation of mental

---

* Descartes says (*Principia philosophia*, iv. § 203): *Nullum aliud inter ipsa (sc. arte facta) et corpora naturalia discrimen agnosco, nisi quod arte factorum operationes ut plurimum peraguntur instrumentis adeo magnis, ut sensu facile percipi possint: hoc enim requiritur, ut ab hominibus fabricari queant. Contra autem naturales effectus fere semper dependent ab aliquibus organis adeo minutis, ut omnem sensum effugiant.* According to this, the refinement of machines brings art continually nearer to nature.

† Descartes (*Princ. phil.*, iv. § 200): *Figuras et motus et magnitudines corporum consideravi atque secundum leges Mechanicæ, certis et quotidianis experimentis continuatas, quidnam ex istorum corporum mutuo concursu sequi debeat, examinavi.* § 203: *Et sane nullæ sunt in Mechanica rationes, quæ non etiam ad Physicam, cujus pars vel species est, pertineant, nec minus naturale est horologio ex his vel illis rotis composito, ut horas indicat, quam arbori ex hoc vel illo semine ortæ, ut tales fructus producat. Quamobrem ut ii qui in considerandis automatis sunt exercitate, cum alicujus machinæ usum sciunt et nonnullas ejus partes aspiciunt, facile ex istis, quo modo aliæ quas non vident sint factæ, coniiciunt; ita ex sensibilibus effectibus et partibus corporum naturalium, quales sint eorum causæ et particulæ insensiles, investigare conatus sum.*

‡ Thus Descartes himself places the incorporeal in opposition to the *mechanicum et corporeum* (*Briefe*, i. 67). We find the same meaning in Wolff, who maintains (*psych. rat.*, § 395) that the insight resulting from contemplative knowledge (*cognitio symbolica*) *mechanice quoque in cerebro absolvi—nihil inesse notioni, qua quid in universali repræsentatur, quod non æque mechanice repræsentatur in corpore.*

processes means, in the first place, a deduction from merely corporeal causes. As regards the facts themselves we find Spinoza already undertaking to explain the content of mental life as a resultant of the combined operation of separate ideas, and he calls the soul a spiritual machine (*automaton spirituale*). And Leibniz, notwithstanding the importance he attached to the unity of the soul,* himself refined upon this idea, whilst Wolff and the French psychologists of the eighteenth century developed it in greater detail. Finally the word itself is transferred, and "mechanical" is applied to the inner life, first figuratively, then didactically.† Kant gave the term a more universal character, for he made it serve for "all necessity of occurrences in time according to the natural law of causality, without it being necessarily understood that the things subject to it are really material machines." In natural philosophy, however, he developed clearly and sharply the contrast between a dynamical and a mechanical explanation.‡

Organic, too, was first made use of by Aristotle, the great moulder of language. But it was not employed in the modern sense. Corresponding with the root ὄργανον, instrument, organic meant "instrumental"; it was used of the living, purposefully constructed body as a whole, but more frequently of separate parts of the body, in particular of such as are composed of dissimilar parts. The concept is applied only to living beings,

---

* See, for example, Erdmann, 153 : *Il faut considérer aussi que l'âme, toute simple qu'elle est, a toujours un sentiment composé de plusieurs perceptions à la fois ; ce qui opère autant pour notre but, que si elle était composée de pièces comme une machine.*

† In the case of Lessing we see the transference still in process. In *Literaturbriefe* (7) he says : " If this alteration is the result of inner springs of action, or (to use a crude expression) of the mechanism of his soul itself." Herbart was particularly energetic in carrying out the idea of the mechanism of the psychic life : he declares it to be our task (iii. 255) " to split up the organism of reason into its single threads, the chains of ideas, whose formation can only be explained by the mechanism of the mind."

‡ See iv. 427 (Hart.) : " Mechanical natural philosophy explains the specific differences of its objects, as machines, by the nature and disposition of their smallest parts. Dynamical natural philosophy, on the other hand, deduces the specific differences of objects not as machines (that is, mere instruments of outward motive forces) but as containing elemental attractive and repulsive motive forces of their own."

but does not itself comprise the property of inner life, hence it is not employed outside this particular sphere (say in political theory) to denote a living whole : there are passages in Aristotle in which ὀργανικός can hardly be translated except by the word mechanical.* The term retained this meaning, without change, through the Middle Ages and the Modern World on into the eighteenth century.† The concept instrumental could be appropriated, also, by the new mechanical theory; in the eighteenth century, both organic (natural) and artificial machines were unhesitatingly placed under the concept machine; to speak of organic machines was not at that time regarded as at all unusual.‡

Then came the German classical period, and with it a craving to endow nature with soul and motion of its own; this first added the property of life to the term organic, and made it the main characteristic. Kant, with his precise concepts and distinctions, exerted a special influence in this direction; though Herder, Jacobi and others should not be forgotten.§ This new meaning was next transferred from natural living beings to

* See, for example, περὶ γενέσεως καὶ φθορᾶς, 336 a, 2: καὶ τὰς δυνάμεις ἀποδιδόασι τοῖς σώμασι, δι' ἃς γεννῶσι, λίαν ὀργανικῶς, ἀφαιροῦντες τὴν κατὰ τὸ εἶδος αἰτίαν. Pol. 1259 b, 23: ἀπορήσειεν ἄν τις, πότερον ἔστιν ἀρετή τις δούλου παρὰ τὰς ὀργανικὰς καὶ διακονικὰς ἄλλη τιμιωτέρα τούτων.

† Cp. the last important ramification of scholasticism, the philosophy of Suarez (1548–1617), (De anima, i. 2, 6): Dicitur corpus organicum, quod ex partibus dissimilaribus componitur. Even with regard to the usage of the Wolffian school, Baumeister observes: Corpus dicitur organicum, quod vi compositionis suæ ad peculiarem quandam actionem aptum est.

‡ Even so late as about 1813 Saint-Simon called society a véritable machine organisée (see Paul Barth, Vierteljahrsschr. für wissenschaft. Philos., XXIV. i. 72).

§ According to Kant (v. 388, Hart.) : "An organised product of nature is one in which all is purpose and, reciprocally, is also means." On p. 386 it runs: "An organised being is hence no mere machine, for that has solely motive force; such a being possesses in itself constructive force, and of such a nature, indeed, that it is communicated to the materials, although they have none themselves (that is to say, they are organised)." Jacobi has (Hume, 172): "In order to conceive of the possibility of an organic being, it will be necessary to think first of that which creates its unity, to think of the whole before the parts "; in content this is only a revival and more exact formulation of Aristotelian thoughts. Kant also speaks of a wahren Gliederbau of pure speculative reason, " in which all is organ, namely, all is for the sake of one and each particular one for the sake of all " (iii. 28, Hart.).

society* and the State, then to law, history, and so forth. Organic became a favourite term of the romantic school, though at the same time we find it spreading beyond separate schools and tendencies and passing into ordinary speech. Thus while mechanical and organic in the first place meant almost the same thing, they came ultimately to stand in the most complete contrast to one another. At present these terms denote two important and contrasting views of the world. [As, for example, in Trendelenburg (*Log. Untersuchungen* (3 edit.), ii. 142 ff.)]

(b) On the History of the Problem

The terms that we have been studying serve to indicate a contrast in the nature of things which has long been recognised as a problem. In the discussion of this problem the protagonists in the Ancient World were Democritus and Aristotle. During the classic age of Greece the organic doctrine, as we may call it for short, was decidedly uppermost. The artistic and synthetic mode of thought peculiar to the age placed the whole before the parts, the living before the lifeless, and explained the latter through the former. It was in sympathy with this tendency that the idea of the organism (though not the term organism) was adopted by Aristotle. Aristotle, too, originated

---

* The transference of the expression "organisation" to the sphere of politics seems to have first taken place in the movements connected with the French Revolution; but German thinkers and poets were, however, the first to give the word its inward meaning. Kant says (v. 387, Hart.): "To speak exactly, the organisation of nature is in no way analogous to any sort of causality we know," and adds in a note: "On the other hand, one can bring to light a certain connection (which is found, however, more in the idea than in the reality), by means of an analogy with the above-mentioned direct natural purposes. Thus, in the case of a recently undertaken thorough reconstitution of a great nation in the form of a State, very appropriate and frequent use has been made of the word 'organisation,' for the construction of a magisterial system and so forth, and even of the whole fabric of the State: for in a whole of this description each member should certainly be no mere means, but at the same time a purpose, too, and since it contributes to the capacity of the whole, each member should be determined by the idea of the whole in regard to its place and function." He says on p. 364 of the same work (*Kritik d. Urteilskraft*): "Thus a monarchical State is represented by an animated body, if it be governed according to the inner laws of the people, but by a mere machine (such as a handmill) if it be governed by a single absolute will. In both cases, however, the representation is only symbolical."

the formula that in an organic being the whole precedes the parts.* This idea at once extended itself beyond its immediate sphere of application to that of the State and the cosmos as a whole; soon, too, though not till after the time of Aristotle, it was carried over to humanity as a whole, and was more especially taken up in this sense by the later Stoics. From the Ancient World it passed to Christianity, and the religious tendency now gave it a peculiar inwardness.† Later it developed into the idea of the church, as the mystic body (*corpus mysticum*) of Christ. In the Middle Ages, with its inseparable union of spiritual and sensuous, the organic idea acquired a tangible form, and with this form it dominated mediæval social doctrines; ‡ it formed a chief portion of the system of order characteristic of the age, a system which looked upon the individual as receiving all spirituality from a whole, and that a visible whole.

This organic doctrine was very influential both in practical matters and in relation to scientific method. In the former case it demanded from the individual an unconditional subordination to the whole, a service which was considered indispensable to the development of his rational nature; but at the same time it gave the individual a consciousness that within the whole he signified something special and, in its place, irreplaceable. In its later period the Ancient World dwelt with peculiar pleasure upon the idea that the individual was not merely a fragment (μέρος) but a member (μέλος) of the cosmos. "I am a member of the whole of rational being"; this conviction consoled Marcus Aurelius amidst the dangers and perplexities of life. The ancient church, however, developed more particularly the idea that all Christians, as members of the common body dedicated to God,

* See *Pol.*, 1253 a, 20 : τὸ ὅλον πρότερον ἀναγκαῖον εἶναι τοῦ μέρους. ἀναιρουμένου γὰρ τοῦ ὅλου οὐκ ἔσται ποὺς οὐδὲ χείρ, εἰ μὴ ὁμωνύμως ὥσπερ εἴ τις λέγοι τὴν λιθίνην. διαφθαρεῖσα γὰρ ἔσται τοιαύτη. According to this, the State precedes the individual.

† Characteristic of the Greek origin of this idea is the fact that the Gospel of St. John, powerfully influenced as it was by Greek philosophical elements, is the only gospel which brings it forward (parable of the vine and the grapes).

‡ Thus we see the analogy between the State and a living body carried beyond the general idea and freely worked out in detail. John of Salisbury, for example, endeavoured to point out a bodily member corresponding to every section of the State (see Gierke, *Das deutsche Genossenschaftsrecht*, iii. 549).

are dependent upon one another in fate and deed, are linked together to form a whole.

This mode of thought was not less productive in the realm of scientific work. Here it gave rise to the teleological view, which has exerted immense influence from the Ancient World down to the present day. If the whole was the original thing and the superior thing, then it offered the key to the explanation of the single members and their respective services. But, according to the Platonic-Aristotelian idea, however, the whole was an unchangeable form, a self-existent and self-sufficing life. Hence it set all movement a fixed goal and final terminus.* Nor was this conception limited in its application to the realm of living things; it was extended to cover the whole universe. The world is here looked upon as a living and firmly consolidated whole, into which all the separate parts fit as members; the various movements do not confusedly cut across one another, but each strives towards a terminus, there to pass over into a settled activity (ἐνέργεια) that returns ever upon itself. But this mode of thought is particularly fruitful within its own native region, within the sphere of animated being. The organs and functions of all the various kinds of animals are referred to an all-embracing life in which they find their explanation; at the same time all manifoldness of organic formation appears as the unfolding of a single normal type present in all the stages. This normal type is seen in its purity in man; hence, starting from man, it is possible to throw light upon the whole of this vast domain and to bring its immense content under the control of pervading ideas. In this fashion there grew up a species of comparative anatomy and physiology, as well as an evolutionary science. An attempt was also made to explain the psychical life of animals by a similar reference to the human prototype. Such a method as this must appear to us in the highest degree

---

* See Aristotle (*Phys.* 194 a, 28): ἡ δὲ φύσις τέλος καὶ οὗ ἕνεκα. ὧν γὰρ συνεχοῦς τῆς κινήσεως οὔσης ἔστι τι τέλος τῆς κινήσεως, τοῦτο ἔσχατον καὶ τὸ οὗ ἕνεκα. See further 199 a, 30: ἐπεὶ ἡ φύσις διττή, ἡ μὲν ὡς ὕλη ἡ δ'ὡς μορφή, τέλος δ'αὕτη, τοῦ τέλους δ'ἕνεκα τἄλλα, αὕτη ἂν εἴη ἡ αἰτία ἡ οὗ ἕνεκα. According to Aristotle, chance might indeed be responsible for occasional purposeful formations, but under no circumstances for the universal purposefulness; on this question see the second book of the *Physics*.

inadequate, but it provided its own age, and many succeeding centuries, with an ordered and organised material.

There was no lack of opposition to this type of thought even in the Ancient World, but this opposition did not get beyond mere criticism, it did not pass over into leadership. This did not take place until the Modern Period, when the struggle against this organic doctrine became a chief factor in the movement toward freedom and clarity. The liberation took effect, at first, within the more general life of the time: the modern mind felt the restriction to a material organisation and the communication of spiritual life through this medium to be an unbearable oppression, and, rejecting it, aspired to enter into a direct relationship with the whole, and from this source win for itself a secure superiority to all visible order. We see this tendency first in the Renaissance and the Reformation, then in the political and economical movement of liberation which originated more particularly in England. Life thus directly based upon the individual seemed to gain immensely in power, rationality, and truth. From this new point of view all institutions appear as the work of individuals and possess no rights except such as may be granted them by the individual. According to Leibniz the individual bears within himself the whole infinity of the cosmos and evolves it out of himself: what an abyss separates this view from the organic doctrine!

At the same time there resulted a revolution in the sphere of science. The traditional explanation of nature from within and from the standpoint of the whole became unendurable; men came to look upon it as a thoroughly subjective interpretation, as a mere fanciful conception that should be energetically repudiated because it claimed to be not fancy but a serious explanation. Hence the works of this period are full of complaints about the concealed figurativeness of the scholastic doctrine, with its inner forms and forces. It was described as a "Refuge of Ignorance" (*asylum ignorantiæ*; see, for example, Oldenburg in a letter to Spinoza). In opposition to this, the expulsion from nature of everything inward and the reduction of all complex facts into their smallest elements was regarded as the fundamental condition of true knowledge.

At the same time, the discovery and further examination of these elements promised to render transparent the reality which had so far been obscured, and to give power over things that were else inaccessible. For once these elements are in our power things become mobile and malleable. There is here no feeling whatever for the greatness of the old artistic view, which had indeed suffered the severest injury at the hands of scholasticism. So much for the mechanical explanation of nature put forward by the Modern World. In direct and deliberate contrast to the more ancient mode of thought it raises the elements to the first place and bases its whole constructive effort upon them; through space, time, and movement it splits up the traditional *continuum* into discrete quantities, and in this fashion it makes possible, for the first time, an exact comprehension of the phenomena. The teleological view naturally collapses along with this denial of all inner connection. All sorts of quite different considerations combine to ensure its rejection; it appears anthropomorphic, indefinite, and sterile. The unity of nature is no longer secured through purpose but through law. Laws operate universally and consistently, and as simple basic forms they dominate all manifoldness. All this grips men's minds with elemental force. It is believed that the new type of thought renders genuine knowledge possible for the first time and inaugurates an age of science. All previous work sinks to the level of mere preparation.

Thinkers of a profound type could not fail to perceive that the new type of thought left many questions open and that it even created new problems. Descartes, the most important thinker of the Enlightenment, treated the mechanical theory merely as a principle for the exact comprehension of nature, not as a metaphysical doctrine dealing with ultimate causes; at the same time he drew a sharp distinction between himself and Democritus.* His faithful disciple, Robert Boyle, maintained

* The most important reference to this is in the *Princ. philos.*, iv. § 202: (*Democriti philosophandi ratio*) *rejecta est, primo quia illa corpuscula indivisibilia supponebat, quo nomine etiam ego illam rejicio; deinde quia vacuum circa ipsa esse fingebat, quod ego nullum dari posse demonstro, tertio quia gravitatem iisdem tribuebat, quam ego nullam in ullo corporum cum solum spectatur, sed tantum quatenus ab aliorum corporum situ et motu dependet atque ad illa refertur, intelligo ff.*

the existence of a purposeful and active cause as an indispensable complement to the mechanical causes.* Berkeley drew attention to the fact that the mechanical view only explained the laws and modes of occurrence and not the causes of events. Leibniz went very thoroughly into the matter and developed a peculiar type of cosmic philosophy, which declared the whole of nature, with its mechanism, to be the appearance of a spiritual reality; he raised the ultimate units (which from a mechanical point of view constitute a mere limiting concept) to the central position and, as monads, equipped them with an inner life. Within the sphere of nature all was to be explained mechanically; the principles of the mechanism, however, seemed themselves in need of explanation and to be able to find this explanation only in the purposeful control of a rational Providence.† Leibniz believed the purposefulness of natural laws to consist in their all serving the end of securing the greatest possible utilisation of force. He found that on every hand the shortest paths are chosen and the simplest means employed.‡ The Leibnizian school firmly believed that everything was composed of parts and that the whole material world therefore fell within the mechanical sphere, while the soul, as a simple body, did not.§ In a less definite manner, Wolff, in scholastic

* See, for example, *De ipsa natura*, sect. iv.: *Harem autem partium motum sub primordia rerum infinita sua sapientia ac potestate ita direxit, ut tandem (sive breviore tempore sive longiore, ratio definire nequit) in speciosam hanc ordinatamque mundi formam coaluerint.*

† *Omnia in corporibus fieri mechanice, ipsa vero principia mechanismi generalia ex altiore fonte profluere* (p. 161, Erdm.): see also 155 a, Foucher, ii. 253.

‡ See 147 b (Erdm.): *Semper scilicet est in rebus principium determinationis quod a maximo minimove petendum est, ut nempe maximus præstetur effectus minimo ut sic dicam sumptu.* The objection that mere natural necessity might have produced the same result is answered as follows (605 b): *Cela serait vrai, si par exemple les loix du mouvement, et tout le reste, avait sa source dans une nécessité géométrique de causes efficientes; mais il se trouve que dans la dernière analyse on est obligé de recourir à quelque chose qui dépend de causes finales ou de la convenance.*

§ Thus, for example, Baumgarten (*Metaphys.*, ed. vi., 1768, § 433): *Machina est compositum stricte dictum secundum leges motus mobile. Ergo omne corpus in mundo est machina. Machinæ natura per leges motus determinata mechanismus est. At, quidquid non est compositum, non est machina, hinc nulla monas est machina.*

fashion, put side by side explanations based upon efficient causes and explanations based upon final causes, and in this connection devised the expression "teleology."*

It was of course not to be expected that the traditional organic and teleological doctrine should at once collapse under the advent of the mechanical theory; it was far too deeply rooted in the concepts and methods of the school for such a collapse to be possible. Moreover, there was no lack of capable men who vigorously upheld the distinctive character of living things.† But the age was not disposed to listen to them. For this a new wave of life was necessary, a movement calling upon men to seek and find something new in reality. This came more especially with the rise and growth of German Humanism. This movement revealed the victorious growth of a desire for a greater directness of life, for a more intimate relationship of man to nature and the world, for a view of things based upon an understanding of the whole. At first the movement shook men's sympathies like a hurricane, but it gradually settled into an artistic construction of life: from this position a return to the ancients lay close at hand, for were they not the pattern of a pure and noble nature? It was therefore not surprising that the organic type of thought was revived and adopted by this latest Renaissance and that it held and swayed men's minds with almost magic power.

It is a remarkable fact that, in a scientific sense, it was Kant (temperamentally but little artistic) who prepared the way for this new artistic type of thought. He did so by reducing mechanism to a merely human mode of thinking, thereby

---

* See *Philos. ration. sive logica*, op. iii., § 85: *Rerum naturalium duplices dari possunt rationes, quarum aliæ petuntur a causa efficiente, aliæ a fine. Quæ a causa efficiente petuntur, in disciplinis hactenus definitis expenduntur. Datur itaque præter eas alia adhuc philosophiæ naturalis pars, quæ fines rerum explicat, nomine adhuc destituta, etsi amplissima sit et utilissima. Dici posset teleologia.* The term *causa finalis*, on the other hand, is scholastic: I find it first occurring in Abelard.

† The chief place, in this respect, is taken by Cudworth, with his hypothesis of a plastic nature; see, in particular, *The True Intellectual System of the Universe* (1678), i. 3, 19. Among German scholars, Rüdiger is more especially noteworthy; see, for example, *Institutiones eruditionis seu philosophia synthetica*, p. 109: *physica vel mechanica est vel vitalis*.

clearing a free space for a view and treatment of another kind; but for such positive construction a compelling motive was needed. This motive appeared to him to be provided by the organic realm, since it could only be comprised within our concepts by the aid of the idea of an inner whole and a guiding purpose. Thus the old doctrine was again taken up, and was applied beyond its immediate sphere to the world as a whole. In Kant's own case the application was carefully guarded and put forward as representing a human point of view. But the flood of artistic enthusiasm rose so rapidly as to sweep away all confining obstacles, and the organic type of thought acquired a proud self-consciousness and proclaimed itself, in opposition to the Enlightenment, as a view of life based upon the innermost life and being of things themselves, the mechanical doctrine being regarded as bloodless and soulless. Schelling gave particularly energetic expression to the new tendency, and ranged all natural life under the idea of the organism.*

Concept and term then came rapidly into use. Though the ancient traditions were still adhered to, modern influences were now unmistakably apparent. The idea of the organism did not so much represent a conception of *being* as of *becoming;* reality did not so much constitute a finished work of art as a living being, progressing through its own power; so that this change of attitude was at first far more fruitful in the sphere of history than in that of nature. A great fascination was exerted by the idea that all historical growth proceeds not from sudden impulses but through steady advance, not from artificial reflection but from an unconscious natural impulse; that it issues not from the mere individual, but from the power of a systematic whole. And as this idea transferred itself to politics, law, speech, &c., it seemed on every hand as if a purer and richer actuality, a larger conception of the whole, a more inward and peaceful relationship of man to things had been won. Man was no longer to master things from without, but to share their inner life; for example, he was not to make law, but to find it as

* Usually, however, he understands dynamical as constituting the exact opposite of mechanical; in the latter case he looks upon the world as a given thing, in the former as something unceasingly growing.

MECHANICAL—ORGANIC 177

a product of the spirit of the people. He was now free to recognise the riches of historical tradition, retaining throughout individual character and doing justice in its own place to each individual development. Thus a tendency towards a historical view of the world (in contrast to the rational view of the Enlightenment) was very closely connected with the organic doctrine. Historical research is now the intimate ally of artistic contemplation; it is characteristic that Schelling declares the standpoint of historical art to be the "third and absolute standpoint of history."

But the onesidedness of this historical view, and with it the limitations of the organic doctrine, could not long be overlooked. Misgivings were bound to arise, if for no other reason than that political and ecclesiastical reactionaries, such as Adam Müller and de Maistre (the father of modern Ultramontanism), took up this organic doctrine with especial enthusiasm and made use of it in a mediæval sense to repress the independence, not only of individuals, but of the living forces of the present. Apart, however, from this particular development, the problematical and onesided nature of the organic doctrine soon attracted attention. The smooth, uninterrupted growth of history had been presupposed rather than proved; the objectivity which it seemed to have discovered in the things, it had itself placed in them; hence its conception of history was seen to be strongly subjective. This movement had lent a valuable stimulus to the comprehension of nature, since it directed attention to life itself and to the inner connection of things, and it had moreover powerfully promoted the quest after the unity of natural forces; but these suggestions did not become scientifically fruitful until they were transplanted to the different soil of modern natural science. In so far as the organic mode of thought attempted, with its own resources, to come to a definite conclusion, it lost itself in audacious and often fantastic imaginations. It brought danger, moreover, to life as a whole, because it induced man to adopt a predominantly contemplative attitude towards reality; it invited him rather to complacently adopt what was at hand and fit himself in, than to proceed independently and cut his own paths. The whole tendency was, in fact, unsuitable for an age burdened with great tasks and involved in difficult complications.

Hence the lead was again taken by the other side, which had never been quite suppressed, but only intimidated. It now came to the front with a fresh lease of life. It was the Enlightenment over again; somewhat different in complexion, but not fundamentally changed. From its point of view the Humanistic Epoch, with its organic doctrine, seemed no more than a mere episode. The individualistic construction of social life attained full development, for the first time, in modern Liberalism and in the modern doctrine of Free Trade. On into the second half of the nineteenth century we see Adam Smith's elaborate and extreme theory treated, even by distinguished scholars, as a settled truth and a final conclusion. Natural science for its part, while sharply rejecting the speculation of natural philosophy, undertook to thoroughly eliminate every remnant of vitalistic theory. It now demanded that organic growth and life should be brought without remainder under the fundamental laws of physics and chemistry. Among philosophers, Lotze, in particular, maintained this universal validity of mechanism—though certainly not without giving it, as Leibniz had done, a deeper foundation in a realm of psychical life. But this supermechanical element was an affair of metaphysics, while nature was handed over to mechanism, and in time the affirmation of mechanism became more influential than the doctrine of its limitation. Thus it was that the mechanical theory, properly understood and cautiously applied, seemed to offer a sure solution of the great cosmic problems. However much might remain to be done in the way of working it out in detail, the principle seemed beyond the reach of doubt.

Then came a resistance, an unexpected resistance. It came, not as an after-effect of older modes of thought, but from the movement of modern life itself, not so much from an artistic interpretation of reality as from growing experience, new facts, and new problems. The economical and industrial development of modern life drew men closer together and multiplied their points of contact; it differentiated and complicated human work, and thereby bound one man far closer to his comrade and all together into one whole. In the face of the social connections thus initiated, the isolated individual of the mechanical theory disappeared. Just as the mechanical theory had derived all social connection from the individual, so modern sociology looked upon the individual as belonging from the very beginning to a connected social whole; the doctrine of the *milieu* took into account even the invisible elements of influence, and tended to make the individual the mere product of his environment. At the same time, the defencelessness of the individual in the presence of economic complications and opposing tendencies was keenly felt, and with it the necessity of a collective will, as embodied in the State.

All this tended towards a resuscitation of the organic idea. Among philosophers Comte, in particular, came under this influence, and constructed his ethics and politics from this standpoint. But in his case the concept of organism underwent a considerable alteration as compared with its earlier meaning; it was transferred, at any rate in Comte's discussion of general principles, from the artistic and ethical spheres into the realm of natural science. It was more especially the progress of histology (Bichat) which gave empirical support to the fundamental idea. Like the living body, society is an exceedingly fine network of numerous separate elements; these are so closely connected with one another that the action or inaction, the loss or the gain, of the one directly affects the others. This has always been true; but it now appeared more true than ever owing to the modern division of labour, which convincingly demonstrates the manner in which each is linked up with each and each with the whole. This seemed to mark the discovery of a guiding principle for ethics and politics—a principle which only needed to be developed in order to mark out definite paths for our whole conduct.

In reality, such a principle is without foundation, and has been formed by a surreptitious interweaving of ancient and modern elements; the result is then, all unconsciously, palmed off as an inner whole—the mere fact as a concept of value, the "is" as an "ought." Finally, when the whole makes demands upon the individual and imposes them as duties, we find ourselves completely on ancient ground. The obscurity which has always attached to the concept organic is increased to the point of unbearable confusion by this commingling of old and new. But the concept is firmly retained because it demands that the dependence of the individual upon the whole context in which he finds himself shall somehow be brought to definite expression. Hence the modern investigator comes under opposing influences, and it cannot cause surprise when thinkers differ even to the point of sharply opposing each other. Nor is it only between individuals that these divisions occur, but also between different departments of research. The organic doctrine has been most warmly taken up by sociologists, while political economists as such have been much less inclined to adopt it; among jurists it finds chief favour with distinguished Germanists.

Along with this movement in the social sphere there has gone a parallel movement in natural science, but since this began later it is to-day involved to an even greater extent in uncertainty and conflict. Without doubt this movement has been brought about in the first place by the modern theory of evolution. The Darwinian form, in which this theory first obtained general recognition, was, in its characteristic nature, as far removed as could be from a recognition of the organic idea, and it endeavoured to subject the whole sphere of life to mechanical concepts; but in natural science, as in other departments of life, thought movements often produce results entirely opposite to those intended. Since the domain of life now attracted greatly increased attention, and was made the object of deeper research, its distinctive nature obtained a much wider recognition, and it became evident that the tracing back of its phenomena to elementary physical and chemical laws was incomparably more difficult than had been supposed during the middle of the century. The observations on protoplasm, the new conceptions of the mechanics of evolution, the problem of the continuity of life, the theory of mutation, with its demonstration of the sudden production of new forms, &c., taken together gave rise to a new and essentially different situation. Opinion became in consequence divided. Some believed that an intellectual appropriation of the new facts would be rendered possible through a further elaboration of mechanical concepts; others believed a new principle to be essential.* In connection with these movements the teleological point of view again comes to the front, though it is now brought up not so much as a piece of metaphysics, but rather as a means of scientific explanation, as "empirical" teleology; † but even in this sense it is opposed by others as a relapse into metaphysics.

Thus, as a result of studying the realm of life the mechanical doctrine is, if not limited, at any rate forced beyond its customary form; "the too simple mechanical conception" (Roux). Moreover, its own fundamental concepts are attacked in more than one way. To begin with, the infinite refinement of detail revealed by apparently elementary inorganic processes made the older mechanical ideas seem much too coarse even for the stages below the vital level. The science of "energetics" has attacked the mechanical view of the world on grounds of principle, for it has contested the basic idea of matter as something that exists outside the sphere of sensation, and acts as the special vehicle of physical forces; moreover, it has sought to trace all natural phenomena back to the fundamental concept of energy.‡

* See, among others, Rindfleisch, *Aerztliche Philosophie*, 1888, and *Neovitalismus*, 1895. Roux (*Einleitung zum Archiv für Entwickelungsmechanik der Organismen*, 1894) protests against "describing the organic form as inexplicable and only to be teleologically deduced" (p. 22), and remarks further: "The words *Incidit in Scyllam, qui vult vitare Charybdim* are in the highest degree applicable to those who are investigating the mechanics of evolution. The all-too-simple mechanical conception and the metaphysical conception represent the Scylla and Charybdis, and to sail between them is a difficult task which a few only have up till now succeeded in performing; and it cannot be denied that the temptation to adopt the latter conception has appreciably increased with the increase of our knowledge" (p. 23). See also W. Roux: *Ueber die Selbstregulation der Lebewesen*, 1902.

† See Cossmann, *Elemente der empirischen Teleologie*, 1899; further, E. König, *Die heutige Naturwissenchaft u. die Teleologie; Beil. zur Allg. Z.*, 1900, Nos. 29 and 30; also *Ueber Naturzwecke*, 1902. These problems have given rise to an exceedingly rich and unceasingly growing literature, a clear sign of the central position they occupy in the work and interest of the modern world.

‡ See Ostwald, *Vorlesungen über die Naturphilosophie*, p. 153: "Everything that we know of the outer world can be expressed in terms of existing energy. Therefore the concept of energy is seen, on every hand, to be the most universal which science has yet formed. It comprehends not only the problem of substance but that of causality, too." With regard to the meaning of the concept energy we read on p. 158: "We would universally define energy as work or as everything which results from work and can be converted into work."

It is, however, quite impossible in a mere sketch such as this to go into all the problems here suggested. The main point is that the mechanical theory has lost the matter-of-course character which it long appeared to possess. It is seldom, however, that an old theme becomes a problem once again without undergoing a transformation.

To-day the whole air is full of conflict and unrest. But the matter is not one to be settled by general reflections, but by the main direction which work and life actually take. Thus it has been in the past, and thus in the future, too, the progress of the world's work will itself settle the form in which the oppositions declare themselves, and decide what further developments both fundamental concepts must undergo; also whether new modes of explanation may supersede the old. It falls to the philosophical speculation of to-day to survey the field of reality and note how the concepts stand in relation to it, and what tasks they urge upon us.

(c) The Present-day Conflict

1. The Philosophical Aspect of the Problem

Philosophy must insist above everything else on the fact that the mechanical theory, even if it could explain everything that is known, is never under any circumstances capable of furnishing a definite conclusion. The mechanical explanation does not carry us beyond a juxtaposition of the elements, a conclusion which from the philosophical point of view necessarily constitutes a difficult problem. If the elements existed side by side without any connection whatever, and in a state of indifference towards one another, it would be absolutely impossible to perceive how one could affect another. This holds above all in the sphere of nature; Leibniz and Lotze were compelled to thoroughly reorganise the immediate view of the world through a consideration of the fact of mutual influence. Further, we cannot very well reject Leibniz's belief that nothing can be completely absorbed solely in accomplishing something for others, but must also be something in itself, and hence that whatever is taken to be the final element must be something with an existence of its own. If this thought be followed up we are led to the conclusion that the mechanical realm is the mere appearance of quite a different kind of world. With regard to the life of the soul, too, those who would trace everything back to the mechanism of association are quite unable to give an answer to the question how all these processes come to be experienced as personal life, as *my* life and *your* life. On every hand unity and connection must somehow be accounted for, and this is a task beyond the powers of mechanical explanation.

Since the mechanical view shelves an unsolved problem, then from the point of view of actual fact it cannot be admitted that it dominates the whole of reality, even if it completely explains the whole of nature. For associated with nature is the life of the soul, and this life exhibits (more particularly in the case of human beings) a completely different kind of process. For in so far as the inner life grows to be something more than a mere accompaniment of natural processes and unfolds an independent character, in so far as spiritual life grows up within us, a mere assembling of single elements no longer provides a satisfactory explanation; each single phenomenon is now a portion of a whole, and the joining-up results not directly between the separate elements, but indirectly through their relationship to the whole. Thought, for example, certainly runs its course in separate ideas, but it does not consist in a mere accumulation and summation of these; it pursues a definite aim, and is thereby inwardly held together. It cannot endure anything which disturbs this unity. Nothing is more characteristic of the distinctive nature of thought than the fact and power of the logical contradiction. It would be impossible to perceive this contradiction if, in thought, multiplicity was not comprehended within the scope of an all-inclusive activity, and it could not be so unendurable as it is if the desire for unity were not enormously powerful. At the same time contradiction reveals a totally different sort of relationship from any which is to be seen in the mechanical realm. It is not a collision of spatial elements but an incompatibility of content. This brings us to the concept of content, which is absolutely incomprehensible from the mechanical point of view. Moreover, content involves a new principle of order—that of objective reality, meaning, and interdependency; as seen, for example, in the relationship of the characteristic marks of a logical concept to one another. Only the grossest misunderstanding can confound the inner structure of such a concept with the juxtaposition within a sense-presentation. The fundamental form of connection in the former case is that of system. Each element stands within a whole, under the influence of a whole and subject to its compelling power, while the various elements mutually determine one another. Hence the whole of reality does not fall within the mechanical sphere.

Therefore, purpose or design does not disappear from the world even if nature can no longer find room for it. For design indisputably possesses reality and power in human life, not only in the soul of the individual, but also in the life of humanity as a whole; as witness the great systems of science and art, law and morality, and in last resort the whole of human culture.*
Since purposeful action is essential to inner life, it follows that it is a portion of reality as a whole; we must therefore insist on shaping our conception of the world in such a manner as to make this fact intelligible.

Finally, looking at the matter as a whole, we find ourselves face to face with a sharp alternative. It is customary to-day to regard the world as a series of ascending stages, but there is an important divergence of opinion upon the question whether the higher is a mere product of the lower (and therefore capable of complete explanation by reference to the lower) or whether, in the higher, something new and original comes to light, something which can only be understood by enlarging our conception of the world as a whole. The opposition between these two views becomes peculiarly acute in the case of the problem of the relationship between nature and spiritual life. *Is the latter a mere product of the former, or does it form the commencement of a new stage of reality?* The validity or invalidity of the idea of design will depend upon our settlement of this question. If spiritual life, with its inwardness and wholeness, has a nature

---

* That "real categories" proceed from design has been shown by Trendelenburg in a very important chapter of the *Logischen Untersuchungen* (see chap. xi).

and origin of its own, then it belongs essentially to the whole and must from the very beginning have been operative in the movement of the whole, directing it towards itself. In this case the world-process has an aim and cosmic speculation will not be able to dispense with the idea of design.* But if spiritual life is a mere product of nature, then all aim disappears and design with it. In this case the world and humanity, too, are drifting rudderless into chaos and the void.

2. The Scientific Aspect of the Problem

In the sphere of natural science the conflict centres round the question whether the phenomena characteristic of life can be explained by the general laws of physics and chemistry or whether we are compelled to recognise in them a new kind of process. This is before everything a question of actual fact, and as such it belongs to that branch of science which deals with these phenomena, but at the same time the problem is closely associated with many considerations of a more general kind which cannot here be evaded. So much is indisputable, that the uniqueness and mystery of life has again come more to the front as a problem that must be faced, nor can we settle the matter to-day so easily as our immediate predecessors thought it possible to do. It seems to be more and more out of the question that we should conceive of life as a mere property of matter, it is becoming more and more recognised that life must be granted an independent character. In this connection (to mention some prominent names outside Germany) we may refer to Bergson (more particularly in his *L'évolution créatrice*, 1907) † and Sir

---

* Thus we are again driven to metaphysics, in accordance with Herbart's conviction (*Wke.*, ii. 461): "In thinking about nature and humanity the force of the human spirit impels it unavoidably towards metaphysics, which, like the great, primitive mountains of the earth, forms the broad, deep, invisible foundation of all human thought and activity, while at the same time in isolated, sharp, almost unattainable summits it towers above all other heights and depths."

† The following passages are characteristic of Bergson's conception of life: *L'évolut. créatrice*, p. 105: *La vie est, avant tout, une tendence à agir sur la matière brute*; further, p. 197: *La vie c'est-à-dire la conscience lancée à travers la matière.*

Oliver Lodge.* Looked at from this point of view the problem is to fix upon an essential and distinctive characteristic of life; Boutroux finds this in the capacity "of creating a system in which certain parts are subordinate to certain other parts"; this implies an "agent" and "organs," together constituting a "hierarchy" to which there is no analogue in the inorganic world.† Bergson sees a decisive proof of the working of life as a psychic force in the fact that nature frequently develops like, or similar, structures in the case of very different organisms and hence appears to pursue like aims by different paths.‡

The various civilised nations differ markedly from one another

* In *Life and Matter* (1909), p. 68, Lodge says, in summing up: "The view concerning life which I have endeavoured to express is that it is neither matter nor energy, nor even a function of matter or of energy, but is something belonging to a different category; that by some means at present unknown it is able to interact with the material world for a time, but that it can also exist in some sense independently; although in that condition of existence it is by no means apprehensible by our senses. It is dependent on matter for its phenomenal appearance—for its manifestation to us here and now, and for all its terrestrial activities; but otherwise, I conceive that it is independent of matter. I argue that its essential existence is continuous and permanent, though its interactions with matter are discontinuous and temporary." Further (p. 19): "I am using the word 'life' in quite a general sense, as is obvious, for if it be limited to certain metabolic processes in protoplasm—which is the narrowest of its legitimate meanings—what I have said about its possible existence apart from matter would be absurd. It may be convenient to employ the word 'vitality' for this limited sense."

† See Boelitz, *Die Lehre von Zufall bei E. Boutroux*, 1907, p. 91.

‡ See *L'évolut. créatrice*, 1907, p. 59: *Le pur mécanisme serait donc réfutable et la finalité, au sens spécial où nous l'entendons, démontrable par un certain côté, si l'on pouvait établir que la vie fabrique certains appareils identiques, par des moyens dissemblables, sur des lignes d'évolution divergentes. La force de la preuve serait d'ailleurs proportionnelle au degré d'écartement des lignes d'évolution choisies, et au degré de complexité des structures similaires qu'on trouverait sur elles.* W. Roux, in particular, shows how even from the standpoint of a finer mechanism (but one readily recognising deeper problems) a specific character may be attributed to life. He regards "the self-regulation in the performance of all separate functions necessary to persistence amidst the alterations of circumstance" as a universal elementary property of living beings; in this regulation he sees "that property which above all others distinguishes living beings from all other natural bodies, since it effects the direct accommodation to changing outward circumstances. We may safely conclude from the immeasurably long duration of the unicellular organisms, which has produced countless generations of the same type in spite of the alteration of outward circumstances, that even the lowest forms of life possess this self-regulating capacity, apart from inheritance." (See *Archiv für Entwicklungsmechanik der Organismen*, vol. xxiv., no. 4 (1907). p. 685.)

in their treatment of these problems. Very noteworthy is the "part played by the principle of discontinuity in the most recent French thought" (see H. Höffding, *Moderne Philosophen* (1905), p. 67). With regard to this school and its motives we cannot do better than quote Höffding's words (*ibid.* p. 82 ff.) :—

"In French philosophical literature the philosophy of discontinuity has come to the front in a peculiarly interesting and energetic fashion. There are three different factors which are of decisive importance for the philosophy of discontinuity. In the first place, experience exhibits differences of quality which neither speculation nor the theory of evolution has succeeded in reducing. We may here note that Comte's positivism expressly recognised the gap which separated the different departments of nature from one another: for Comte each new science signified a special, irreducible group of phenomena. In the second place, even in each particular group of phenomena, the law of causality is not able to find more than a partial corroboration. Hence Hume is again appealed to, and his empiricism is set up against the attempt of Kant and the evolutionists to overcome it. Finally, attention is drawn to the consciousness of initiative, the capacity, through thought and action, to place something new in the world, and great emphasis is laid upon the moral importance of this capacity." *

In the case of such a mode of thought as this there can be no inclination to refer the characteristic phenomena of life back to sub-vital forces; on the contrary, any such attempt at mechanical explanation will be severely criticised. The mechanical theory seems to make the mistake of treating the world as a given and final system, not as something in process of development. Hence it denies all movement derived from within as well as all possibility of essential progress,† refuses to attribute to combinations of elements anything beyond what is due to each indivi-

---

* The most prominent protagonists of this philosophy of discontinuity are Renouvier (d. 1903) and E. Boutroux, whose work *De l'idée de la loi naturelle dans la science et dans la philosophie contemporaine* (1895) was published in Germany in 1907; trans. by Benrubi.

† See Bergson, *L'évolut. créatrice* (p. 40): *L'essence des explications mécaniques est en effet de considérer l'avenir et le passé comme calculables en fonction du présent, et de prétendre ainsi que tout est donné.*

dually,* credits the separate elements, as a rule, with everything which they exhibit when associated together,† and does not pay sufficient attention to the manner in which a more exact knowledge of vital processes increasingly does away with the supposed isolation of the elements.‡

This direction of attention towards life and its progressive movement causes the idea of design also to appear in a new light. The complete rejection of design in nature was rooted in the tendency, so long dominant, not to regard life as an original and fundamental phenomenon, but to deduce it from the lifeless —in direct opposition to the older mode of thought, which explained the whole content of nature by reference to the living. In a certain reaction towards the latter position, or rather towards a less crude variety of it, emphasis is again laid upon certain facts which seem to indicate a direction of the life-movement towards a goal which has yet to be attained, a *Zielstrebigkeit* (directivity) (K. E. von Baer), together with an endeavour on the part of separate elements to join together to form a whole. The difficulty of making this in any way comprehensible without introducing into the sphere of nature the human propensity to weigh and deliberate was already keenly felt by Aristotle:§ to us moderns the difficulty must appear

---

* See Lodge, *Life and Matter*: "One frequently hears it said that whatever properties are to be found in the whole are also to be found in the parts. This is incorrect. An aggregate of atoms may possess properties which are not attributes of the separate atom, even in the slightest degree."

† See Lodge, *Life and Matter*: "In this case that which has to be explained is simply accepted as it stands and straightway attributed to the atoms, in the hope of thus bringing the matter to an end." Bergson, *L'évolut. créatrice*, vi., finds the error of Spencer's evolutionism in that it endeavours *à decouper la réalité actuelle, déjà évoluée, en petits morceaux non moins évolués, puis à la recomposer avec ces fragments, et à se donner ainsi, var avance, tout ce qu'il s'agit d'expliquer.*

‡ See Bergson, *L'évolut. créatrice* (p. 205): *Plus la physique avance, plus elle efface d'ailleurs l'individualité des corps et même des particules en lesquelles l'imagination scientifique commençait par les décomposer; corps et corpuscules tendent à se fondre dans une interaction universelle.*

§ See, for example, Phys. 199 a, 17: εἰ οὖν τὰ κατὰ τὴν τέχνην ἕνεκά του, δῆλον ὅτι καὶ τὰ κατὰ τὴν φύσιν. ὁμοίως γὰρ ἔχει πρὸς ἄλληλα ἐν τοῖς κατὰ τέχνην καὶ ἐν τοῖς κατὰ φύσιν τὰ ὕστερα πρὸς τὰ πρότερα. μάλιστα δὲ φανερὸν ἐπὶ τῶν ζῴων τῶν ἄλλων, ἃ οὔτε τέχνῃ οὔτε ζητήσαντα οὔτε βουλευσάμενα ποιεῖ. ὅθεν διαποροῦσί τινες πότερον νῷ ἤ τινι ἄλλῳ ἐργάζονται οἵ τ'ἀράχναι καὶ οἱ μύρμηκες καὶ τὰ τοιαῦτα.

still greater. But no difficulties, however great, should induce us to neglect or set aside definite groups of fact because they do not chance to fit into the mechanical system. After all, theories must be made to fit facts and not facts to fit theories!

The main objection that is raised against vitalism and teleology, even in its more recent forms, is that the formative principle which is here put forward explains "simply everything, and that in the same way," without enabling us to find out anything about the necessarily different determining factors and their modes of producing the various purposive structures. (See W. Roux in the *Archiv für Entwicklungsmechanik der Organismen*, vol. xxvi., no. 4 (1907), p. 687). Following up this line of argument Roux (who by no means denies "everpresent ultimate problems") says: "Nothing could be easier than to deduce purposive phenomena from a real purposeful agent. This last supposition will still remain open to us when the other has been proved to be really inadequate: but at the present time, only just after the commencement of exact causal investigation, this inadequacy may very well appear to be present, and that in many directions, and yet we may be quite unable to prove that it is so. On the other hand, it is very difficult to deduce such 'apparently purposive phenomena' from non-purposeful agents. The first solution, however, leaves unknown all the different types of determination which characterise the different cases, transferring them all, as it does, to a principle whose modes of operation remain wholly obscure. And yet we would investigate these 'determining factors' also, together with their modes of operation. Common to us both is the investigation of the physico-chemical factors involved in the carrying out of determined processes, for our opponents, too, admit that that which is 'determined' through psychical action is carried out by means of physical factors" (p. 688). Thus the matter remains in a state of flux; but through the unrest of conflict we may safely hope for the progress of knowledge.

8. The Problem in the Social Sphere

It is not difficult to show that the mechanical theory does not suffice for the understanding of social life; as in the case of nature, however, it is difficult to formulate the counter-theory in definite terms. If we start from mere isolated statements it is quite impossible to make comprehensible any sort of interest in the whole, any sort of immanence of the whole within the parts; any elevation, nobility, and independence displayed by the whole (as, for example, by the State), or any kind of spiritual character which we may ascribe to the whole.* The mechanical theory is bound to convert the community into a soulless maze of wheelwork, in which each unit goes its own exclusive round. On such terms a common thought-world would be impossible. The idea of justice, to which the upholders of the mechanical theory are especially wont to appeal, is not to be explained from this point of view, from which it can be regarded only as a mystical product. For the conception of justice never develops from the basis of natural individuality; but only from that of rational being, and such is not possible without a foundation in a world of reason. Justice can appear to be derived from the mere individual only when in the process the rational spiritual being is surreptitiously substituted for the isolated natural being. So it was more particularly in the case of the English Enlightenment. The political and economical systems of Locke and Adam Smith contain a thoroughgoing contradiction: they work with natural units and treat them like rational units. To recognise this confusion is to become aware of the inadequacy of this whole philosophical movement.

But this negation does not bring an affirmation with it. To reject the mechanical doctrine does not mean to accept the organic. The concept of the organic has come to us from an older culture of a different type; it bears the stamp of the ancient social doctrine and view of the world in general. The champions of the organic doctrine would like to free it from these associations; they can point to the fact that we often employ concepts which have been developed, in the course of history, far beyond the narrowness of their original significance. But in such questions everything depends on the special nature of the case. Now, it seems to us that, in the case referred to,

* This has recently been set forth in brilliant fashion by Gierke; see *Das Wesen der Verbände*, Rektoratsrede; Berlin, 1902.

the original meaning is so firmly attached to the concept that it cannot but draw the thought back to the older interpretation. The application of the concept organism to the social sphere is in the first instance a mere analogy: although certain resemblances exist between an organic being and a social order, it is very well open to doubt whether these touch their really essential and characteristically spiritual qualities. In the first place this mode of explanation makes an appeal to the structure of the living being, and this itself is a difficult problem, one which, as we have seen, has now again become an object of the severest conflict. With regard to its philosophical definitions as given by Aristotle, and, we may add, by Kant and his successors, Lotze observed with justice that they do not so much contain an explanation as reproduce the enigmatic character of the impression. In the case of the concept of the organic, nature does not, as we might imagine, offer us the subject matter, in a certain and fixed form, but we project a characteristic method of viewing the matter from ourselves into nature, and this, decked out now in intuitive bodily form, is once more transmitted to the mind. Why this *détour?* Does it not involve the danger of an influx of natural elements into the spiritual life, or at any rate the substitution of a mere metaphor for an explanation?

The chief objection, however, is the tenacious continuance of the Græco-mediæval mode of thought in this concept; it threatens to confine the indispensable element in the idea to a stage which has been inwardly overcome. The ancient organic theory regarded the individual as being in every respect a member of the whole; in its more precise form it caused him to be completely absorbed in his relationship to the whole; it knew no kind of independence, no sort of individual right as against the whole. From the very beginning this depression of the individual was possible only as the result of a confusion of the State with human society in general; whatever social life might mean to man, that was claimed by the State. Thus ethics and politics, the ends of the individual and of the social life, were held to be completely similar.

In truth, this organic doctrine was not even the true expression of the life of the State during the golden age of Greek civilisation; it was a creation of the philosophers, an endeavour to resist the commencing dissolution of life into innumerable individual centres; it was an attempt to effect a restoration—futile, like all such attempts. Nay, the philosophers themselves did more than any one else to make their demand impossible, since they made a special point of raising man above the merely social sphere by opening up a new ideal of life, that of scientific research. The very same Aristotle who explained the State to be prior (that is conceptually prior) to man saw true happiness and blessedness only in the theoretical life, with its concentration upon the great universe. And in so doing he merely formulated the thoroughgoing conviction of the whole Greek philosophy, one of the chief achievements of which was the liberation of the individual from his social environment. The organic doctrine reached its zenith during the Middle Ages. In the shape of the Church the social whole became absolutely superior to the individual; it set up the claim to communicate all spirituality to man; the importance of the individual was measured entirely according to his position in the whole; the whole became the conscience of humanity. The economic arrangement of the Middle Ages, too, constituted an ordered system which from a position of secure superiority assigned the individual his place. The whole thought-world was indeed hierarchical in form, since the separate spheres had their guiding lines prescribed according to certain central truths of religion and metaphysics, and these lines were merely to be pursued, but neither examined nor altered. For this condition the idea and expression "organic" may seem appropriate.

Nothing is more characteristic of the Modern World than the liberation of life from such attachment to a visible central point and its uniform distribution over the whole surface of existence. The individual now became spiritually and socially independent, and each separate sphere of life set out to deal independently with its own problems: each desired, too, to fight for the whole from its own individual standpoint. To those who are accustomed to the mediæval mode of thought this must seem an audacious departure from principle, a self-willed dissolution of every relationship, just as it is usually very difficult even for free Catholics, with universal sympathies, to recognise the specific nature and rights of Protestantism. In reality this departure from the mediæval ideal does not mean the abandonment of all, but only of *visible* relationships; the greatness of the Modern World lies in the development and defence of the conviction that the spiritual life as a whole is present at each separate point and may there be brought to full activity; thus man does not need to receive his relationships first from without, they spring from within and spiritually encircle his life; it is precisely through the inner union which follows upon their complete appropriation by the individual that the latter wins a sure superiority over every visible human order. Since such union can never be enforced from without, but demands a personal decision and inward welcome, it is not in any sense opposed to freedom, but is the twin-sister of freedom. Moreover, only through such a personal welcome can life acquire a purely inward character; it unavoidably retains an element of outwardness and superficiality so long as the individual belongs, in the first instance, to a visible order. Personalities like Luther and Kant illustrate clearly enough to what an extent this revolution, this transition from a visible to an invisible whole, this chance and this call to awaken at every point an absolute and infinite life transforms for man the aspect of reality.

This transformation, however, involves a breach with the organic doctrine. The latter must now be felt as too narrow and confining. Man is not absorbed in his relation to his social environment, still less in his relation to the political community. Moreover, the spiritual character of the whole which surrounds us is not that of a fixed possession secure from all danger, a possession which the individual can draw upon without trouble; the truth is rather that that whole body of common ideas, institutions, &c., which has been developed in the course of our social and historical life loses its spiritual character at once if it be not continually filled with new life through the work of individuals, more particularly of great personalities. In the social whole, as elsewhere, spirituality does not maintain itself by virtue of its mere existence, but only through a continual renewal, an unceasing creation. The chief danger of the organic doctrine appears to us to be that it regards as once for all present what must be continually produced afresh by free action. In contrast to naturalism, it aims at giving social life an ethical character, but at the same time it does not avoid the danger of conceiving the ethical itself as a thing at rest, thereby treating it as though it had a natural origin. This is the same danger to which Romanticism has so often succumbed: the reaction against mere reflection leads men into the power of natural categories. But why should we link the indispensable truth to such a problematical form? Why not seek for the characteristic nature of spiritual relationships forms which answer to the requirements of our modern life?

3. LAW

(a) Historical

TO-DAY, the concept of law holds a central place in science; its extent and content are alike matters of dispute: now one definition finds favour and now another. The settlement, in this connection, of the rival claims of natural and mental science gives rise to particularly vehement discussion. The struggle is concerned with nothing less than the characteristic nature of the individual sciences and the character of scientific work as a whole. We thus find ourselves face to face with a simply immeasurable wealth of problems. Within the limits of the present study it will hardly be possible to contribute towards the solution of these problems, but we will endeavour to indicate their nature.

The concept of law has passed from the domain of man to that of nature, and here receiving a new form, has returned with it to man, thereby throwing a new light upon his life and conduct. This is a striking example of the manner in which man projects his own image into the cosmos and receives it back again, enlarged and transformed. From one point of view this appears a mere circle, an anthropomorphic process. From another there seems a prospect of an inner enlargement of man as a result of this self-projection and re-assimilation.

The concept of law did not become central for science until the Modern Period, but noteworthy commencements are to be found so far back as the Classical Age. At first, the expression natural law had nothing to do with the outer world but referred to man's own nature; it stood for the unwritten law in contrast to the written.* Plato and Aristotle only very occasionally use the term for nature in the sense of the outer world, and even then they do not use it in a definite technical sense;† it is more customary for them to use other expressions for the concept.‡ The Stoics were the first to make frequent use of the term natural law, to which they were led through the medium of religious ideas; "It was the concept of divine law that first led to that of natural law" (Zeller). It was easy for the Stoics to look upon the law

* For the historical origin of the term natural law see E. Zeller, *Ueber Begriff u. Begründung der sittlichen Gesetze*, 1883 (*Abh. der K. Pr. Akad. d. W.*). The subject has been treated with peculiar care and thoroughness by R. Hirzel; ἄγραφος νόμος (*Abh. der philologisch-histor. Klasse der K. Sächs. Gesellschaft der Wissenschaften*, vol. 20). According to Hirzel, ἄγραφος νόμος first meant traditional manners and customs, and this meaning was retained throughout the whole of Antiquity. Along with this there grew up (dating from Thucydides) the other meaning of the divine law written in the heart. The following quotation may be taken from p. 40 (referring to the revision and reform of the laws of Solon as carried out by Kleisthenes): "Since this reform was achieved by the power of the people it served their aims and purposes, and we can understand how it came about that from this time on the democracy of Athens regarded their laws as the bulwark of the young Athenian State. This was the beginning of the cult of the law and its name. The great deeds and victorious conclusion of the Persian war served as a consecration." On p. 50: "It is more probable that the name (ἄγραφος νόμος) first arose in contrast with γεγραμμένος λόγος, and it is certain that it first derived its more definite meaning as the result of this contrast." As to the contrast between νόμος and φύσις, see *ibid.*, p. 82 ff., and further, the even more careful investigation in *Themis, Dike u. Verwandtes*, pp. 386–411.

† The only places are Plato, *Timæus*, 83 E : καὶ ταῦτα μὲν δὴ πάντα νόσων ὄργανα γέγονεν, ὅταν αἷμα μὴ ἐκ τῶν σιτίων καὶ ποτῶν πληθύσῃ κατὰ φύσιν, ἀλλ' ἐξ ἐναντίων τὸν ὄγκον παρὰ τοὺς τῆς φύσεως λαμβάνῃ νόμους. Arist., *De cælo*, 268 a, 10 ff.: καθάπερ γάρ φασι καὶ οἱ Πυθαγόρειοι, τὸ πᾶν καὶ τὰ πάντα τοῖς τρισὶν ὥρισται. τελευτὴ γὰρ καὶ μέσον καὶ ἀρχὴ τὸν ἀριθμὸν ἔχει τοῦ παντός, ταῦτα δὲ τὸν τῆς τριάδος. διὸ παρὰ τῆσ φύσεως εἰληφότες ὥσπερ νόμους ἐκείνης, καὶ πρὸς τὰς, ἁγιστείας χρώμεθα τῶν θεῶν τῷ ἀριθμῷ τούτῳ. How νόμος, with the philosophers, easily came to mean something like an artificial preparation, over against the real essence, is shown, for example, in Aristotle, *Phys.*, 193 a, 14: οὐκ ἂν γενέσθαι κλίνην ἀλλὰ ξύλον, ὡς τὸ μὲν κατὰ συμβεβηκὸς ὑπάρχον, τὴν κατὰ νόμον διάθεσιν καὶ τέχνην, τὴν δ' οὐσίαν οὖσαν ἐκείνην, ἣ καὶ διαμένει πάντα πάσχουσα συνεχῶς.

‡ More particularly ἀνάγκη (usually in the plural), which occurs not infrequently in the most ancient medical literature and in Democritus, Xenophon (for example, *Memor.*, I. i. 11), Plato (for example, *The Laws*, 967 A) and Aristotle. The concept of natural law probably arose in Greek science in connection with astronomy and medicine.

founded by God as being at the same time a specific order in the things themselves, because their conception of God was that of reason dwelling in the world rather than that of an external power. The term soon passed beyond the limits of the Stoic school. Among the Romans it was frequently employed in the same sense by their first philosopher, Lucretius (*fœdera, fœdus, leges naturæ*). The adoption of the term helped to further the then customary personification of nature as a whole, since the regularity of its operation was regarded as the expression of an ordering will. The concept of natural law did not exert a deep influence upon the scientific work of Antiquity, more especially owing to the predominance of an artistic and teleological conception of nature which did not conduce to a splitting-up into elementary processes and the discovery of their regularities. The fathers of the Church took up the term and strengthened its religious significance. Augustine's view of natural laws was that they were mere habits of divine conduct, habits which, granted an object for so doing, might be abandoned at any moment. There was therefore no conflict between miracles and natural laws. During the Middle Ages the expression sank very much into the background. *Lex naturæ* then denoted the inner moral law, not the order of the external world.* With the advent of the Modern World the concept of natural law leapt all the more quickly into prominence on account of its long neglect. Scarcely any other concept so exactly expresses the self-conscious individuality and characteristic nature of the Modern Period. The general tendency of thought at this time and the more specific movement of industry lent each other mutual support. Natural law as an order of what does and not

* The expression *leges naturæ* had become so unfamiliar that the early Enlightenment considered it necessary to defend and justify it. For example, B. Clauberg says (*op. omn.* 103): *Est qui hic nodum in scirpo quærat, quod leges sint tantum causæ morales, quæ imperant, non efficiunt, quæ materiæ, utpote rationis experti, ferri non possunt. Causa autem hujus appellationis (Naturæ legum) est in propatulo. Quæmadmodum enim rebus ratione præditis Deus leges imposuit morales, quas abservando bene agunt, transgrediendo peccant, ita voluit res omnes naturales certo semper ordine, certis legibus moveri ac quiescere, quas quidem leges ipsæ illæ res, utpote causæ necessariæ, non possunt non observare.* Here again we have a clear revelation of the important part played by religious modes of thought in forming and applying the concept.

of what should happen, as the expression of the simple modes of action of the elements, enlisted the full sympathy of the age; and this because it promised to make reality comprehensible not in the light of some other world but according to its own nature, and because it appeared to reveal this nature as it is in itself, free from all human addition or interpolation. Following upon this came the effort, so characteristic of modern science, to obtain a new and exact understanding of nature by splitting-up reality into its smallest elements, and explaining it on this basis; whence a complete reversal of our whole conception of the world, a reversal in three chief stages: analysis, law, and development. Law with its revelation of the simple modes of action of the elements constitutes the backbone of the whole; it alone makes precise knowledge possible and prepares the way for a complete subjection of reality to thought. This method of referring nature back to simple processes not only seemed to explain things but also opened up the possibility of making new combinations of elements in the service of human ends. Law is the point at which the endeavour to secure the closest possible combination of theory and practice (a tendency inherent in modern research from the beginning) becomes converted into effective work. In this case the goal of knowledge is the starting-point of action. The growth of technics from a mere collection of isolated and accidental discoveries to an independent power taking in the whole field of life has been brought about only by the aid of laws. Thus we see laws standing at the very centre of spiritual work. They form the clearest expression of the modern desire for an explanation which proceeds from the inward nature of things, for precise and analytical comprehension and for a more active relationship between man and his natural environment.

At the same time, however, law, in its new meaning, was a difficult problem and full of the most varied complications. In the search for laws, experience and reason embrace each other. Uniformities are discovered, and a great joy results when what is at first a wild confusion reveals, on closer study, an ordered disposition. But man does not remain content with the mere cataloguing of more or less intricate facts, he wants to analyse these and reduce them to simple, ultimate, universal elements, at the same time attaining to a causal connection instead of a mere sequence and juxtaposition. The aim is to proceed from the empirical to the rational, from descriptive to explanatory laws, necessary and universally valid. Only such rational laws may claim a right to exclusive authority; they can admit no exceptions, hence no miracles. They will aim at the greatest possible simplicity and will try to represent all variety as the expression of a universal mode of action. Further, these laws will require a precise form of expression, a definite formula, because this alone can ensure control over the existing facts. This precise form is given to natural law more particularly by mathematics. Thus Newton considered the supreme task of genuine natural research to consist in the tracing back of natural phenomena to mathematical laws, substantial forms and hidden qualities being ignored * and Kant maintained that "the amount of genuine science to be found in any particular natural doctrine can be measured by the mathemathics to be met with in it" (iv. 360, Hart.). This tendency sets us difficult problems and involves the risk of many errors. Mere empirical generalisations are apt to be credited with properties which belong only to strict laws. Hardly any one has spoken so emphatically of the universal validity and unchangeability of law as Comte, although he himself insisted that law was nothing more than a description of experience. Moreover, mere uniformity is easily mistaken for an adequate explanation; the problem as regarded as settled when in reality it has only been indicated. The concept of law has often had a dogmatic influence, particularly in the realm of biology, where highly complex phenomena have frequently claimed to be rigid laws and insisted upon their rights as such.

In addition to the difficulties arising from the application of the broader view of law we have to face complications resulting from the more or less concealed influence of the older concept, with its reference to a superior will. An example of such influence is the action of seventeenth and eighteenth century

* See the commencement of the *Philosophiæ naturalis principia mathematica*: *Missis formis substantialibus et qualitatibus occultis phænomena naturæ ad leges mathematicas revocare.*

thinkers in inferring the existence of a law-giving divinity from the lawfulness of nature. Another example, in a contrary sense, is the pantheistic treatment of laws as living forces and their establishment as objects of reverence in the place of the divinity.* Law is often looked upon as a power superior to the events themselves and as determining their course. Here again we perceive the influence of the older type of thought.† Finally, it may be mentioned, in the same connection, that the more audaciously any law or formula is asserted the more readily it finds acceptance. It is customary to examine facts before we accept them; but to cast doubts upon a law is regarded as a sin against the spirit of science. Hence the authority which law possesses as a practical command transfers itself to the law of natural events, where it has not the same right; we are, moreover, required to at once acquiesce in the latter and no opposition is tolerated. It was uncritical respect of this kind that enabled the notorious "iron law of wages" to play the rôle it did. Formulæ can work miracles. How much less influential Malthus would have been if he had not expressed his doctrine of the increase of population in the well-known mathematical formula! Even Pascal complained, "People love certainty." It is only too easy, however, to mistake for real certainty what is merely self-confident and audacious.

But however doubtful all this may seem, such human errors are the inevitable accompaniment of every great movement and they must not mislead us as to the laws themselves. Let us for a moment consider the intellectual movement which has been called forth (and is continually being called forth) by the conflict

* A certain cult of natural law extends from the time of G. Bruno right through the Modern Period down to the present day. Bruno sought for the highest in *inviolabili intemerabilique naturæ lege, in bene ad eandem legem instituti animi religione* (*De universo et immenso*, 653). To-day, the more sceptical people grow towards religion the more blind becomes the reverence they pay to natural law.

† Sigwart justly remarks in this connection (*Logik*, II.² 512): "To speak of natural laws as if the mere formula exerted a magical power over the phenomena and exacted something from them which did not follow of itself from their own nature is an empty rhetorical phrase. Laws can never be the causes of actual occurrences; they can only express the regular manner in which real things behave."

which, in the Modern Period, has raged round the problem of law.

(b) The Problem of Law in the Modern World

The natural laws received their characteristic impress in the domain of inorganic nature ; hence the conquering of other spheres of knowledge by the concept of law was accompanied by a conveyance into those spheres of the categories and methods which originated in inorganic research. Thus, sooner or later, some notice had to be taken of the difficulties and limitations involved in the concept itself. In the case of natural laws the whole of our attention is concentrated upon the form of an occurrence ; causes and forces remain in the background. But will it always be possible to keep them there, and will not the aspect of the whole be changed if these problems of cause and force insist on coming to the front ? In dealing with laws we split up reality into numerous separate processes and put from us the thought of any dominating whole. But is this procedure properly applicable to all branches of investigation ? From the point of view of law, each particular occurrence simply forms a special case of a general process ; all individuality is here sacrificed in the interests of science. But will the individual always be contented with such a modest place ; in spite of all attempts at reducing it to uniformity, will it not insist upon the fact of its own uniqueness ? Finally, in the light of law (more particularly when it claims to be explanatory and not merely descriptive) all occurrence seems to be completely determined and unquestionably established. There is no room for free decision, for a choice between different possibilities. Will all the various departments of life be able to accommodate themselves to this restriction ?

Problems thus crowd upon us, and running through them all we see the problem of the whole, the question how far the mechanical concepts of nature are capable of including the whole of reality. The opposition to the concept of law may take a sharper or a milder form ; either the concept of law is entirely rejected from a particular department or it is adapted to the special needs of the latter and no longer bears the interpretation put upon it by natural science. These two forms of interpretation have together produced a very active movement, which has contributed not a little to throwing a clear light upon the peculiarities of the separate departments.

As early as the seventeenth century the concept of law began to be applied outside the sphere of nature; in particular it began to be used in psychology. The eighteenth century carried the movement further, developing and establishing its influence within the various departments of knowledge,* but the movement did not reach its culmination until the second half of the nineteenth century.

Many factors worked together at this time to place law in the centre of scientific work. The most important of these was the growing independence of the separate sciences. Henceforth, the less willing a science was to borrow laws and principles from philosophy, the more determined it must be to find thoroughgoing concepts and definite relationships within its own department. Attention was accordingly directed towards natural laws; with their help it seemed possible to introduce order into the immense mass of material and to compare different classes and groups of occurrences. The relationship between the natural sciences and the mental sciences caused this movement to develop a peculiar tensity. The brilliant results obtained by the natural sciences increased their power of expansion and induced them to aim at the domination of the whole intellectual world. The doctrine of evolution (in particular) appeared to supply concepts applicable to every department of life; hence the concepts and mode of thought associated with natural science make their way further and further into other spheres. These are thereby stimulated to resistance and forced to consider their own peculiar characteristics, whence results a vigorous conflict, during the

---

* Montesquieu advocated the concept of law with peculiar energy. At the commencement of his Esprit des lois he says: *Les lois, dans la signification la plus étendue, sont les rapports nécessaires qui dérivent de la nature des choses ; et dans ce sens tous les êtres ont leurs lois ; la divinité a ses lois, les intelligences supérieures à l'homme ont leurs lois, les bêtes ont leurs lois, l'homme a ses lois.* And a little further on: *Il y a donc une raison primitive, et les lois sont les rapports qui se trouvent entre elle et les différents êtres, et les rapports de ces divers êtres entre eux.*

progress of which the differences become more and more conspicuous.* Starting from the inorganic world, natural law, as its first task, had to conquer the organic world : the resistance which was thereby encountered, and the struggle which again raged with full force round this question, have occupied us in the previous chapter. Descartes came very near the application of natural law to the soul, and Spinoza carried it out in a most impressive fashion: the whole life of the soul was now looked upon as a network of separate processes which operate exactly after the manner of mechanical nature. According to Leibniz, each monad follows its own laws : he distinguishes between the "physico-mechanical" laws of the body and the "ethico-logical" laws of the soul (736 b, Erdm.). The English were more particularly concerned in discovering psychological laws in the strict sense of the term, such as the laws of association. In Germany, the movement advanced through Wolff to Herbart, who wished to introduce the mathematical formula into the inner life of the soul. At the same time there was no lack of thinkers to empha-

---

* A very clear picture of the movement in the science of language is given by B. Delbrück in the treatise *Das Wesen der Lautgesetze* (*Annalen der Naturphilosophie*, i. 277 ff.'. After Fr. Schlegel and Bopp had already compared the science of language with natural science (without, however, reckoning the former as a natural science), Schleicher carried the matter a stage further. The following will serve to indicate his opinion (*Die Darwinische Theorie u. die Sprachwissenschaft*, p. 7): "Languages are natural organisms which take shape independently of the will of man; they grow and develop according to definite laws, and finally age and die. They, too, exhibit that series of phenomena to which we give the name 'life.' Glossology, the science of language, is accordingly a natural science. Its method, on the whole, is the same as that of the other natural sciences." On the other hand, as Delbrück explains in detail, other scholars (more especially Whitney) have demonstrated that in the case of the origin and development of languages we never find laws of life inherent in the actual material of the language—in every case only human actions. As a product of human action and will language is not a natural organism but an institution, one of those institutions which constitute human culture. Hence the law of language is something different from the law of a natural organism. In his investigation of the phonetic laws, Delbrück comes to the conclusion that, however much these are *sui generis*, no reason exists why, on this account, they should not be called laws. "In the case of other sciences we understand by laws simply those expressions of uniformity which do not exhibit themselves in a pure form in a given case, but which would always be clearly discernible (so we believe) in a given case if every external disturbing influence could be removed " (p. 308).

sise the unique nature of the soul's life—its inner unity, its mobility, its individuality, and thus to set a clear limit to the establishment of laws in this sphere.*

Of decisive importance for the treatment of the inner world and the part laws play within it is the question whether or not there is recognised in spiritual life a new stage and independent form of reality. If such a new stage be recognised there can be no doubt that we have to do with something essentially different from any process following natural laws. Natural laws are the forms of activity proper to natural processes, understood in their purity; in a plain and simple sense they belong to the given fact-world. The laws operating in the spiritual sphere must also be rooted within some kind of actuality; laws suspended, so to say, in the air, isolated from facts, and yet exerting effects, are an absurdity.† But the spiritual life, which gives the indispensable basis, is by no means fully possessed by man, but (although appertaining to his innermost being) is at the same time a lofty aim, a difficult task—at once natural and ideal. Hence laws become norms which meet with resistance and have to overcome it; ‡ they are not ineffective. As we all know, the nature of the resistance and of the life-process in general varies according as we are dealing with the intellectual, ethical, or æsthetical sphere, each having its own peculiar characteristics.

* Sigwart (whose investigations of all these problems are noteworthy for their clarity and penetration) remarks with regard to the laws of association (*Logik*, II.² 553): "The laws of association do no more than indicate particular directions in which reproductions can take place (or frequently do take place), particular tendencies in the actual arrangement of images or words, &c.; they have not the capacity to represent laws from which every actual series of ideas could be demonstrated as necessary."

† Husserl rightly draws our attention to the fact that "every normative and *a fortiori*, every practical discipline, presupposes as bases one or more theoretical disciplines, in the sense, namely, that they must possess a theoretical content capable of being separated from all 'normation,' which has its natural basis, as such, in some kind of theoretical science (whether already defined or yet to be constituted)." (*Logische Untersuchungen*, i. 47.) See also p. 164: "The opposite of natural law (as the empirically grounded rule of an actual being and occurrence) is not the normal law (as regulating authority) but the ideal law, in the sense of a regularity not founded empirically but resting upon a purely conceptual basis (of ideas, pure class-concepts)."

‡ Among modern investigations on this subject we may mention more especially Windelband's thesis, *Normen u. Naturgesetze*, in the *Präludien*.

It will be necessary, in passing, to devote a few words to the much-discussed question of the relationship between the natural law and the moral law. Kant was mainly responsible for bringing this problem to the front. He lifted morality above all mere psychical processes, with the result that the moral law and its imperative injunction, from having been looked upon as a natural law, took up a position in the sharpest contrast to natural law. Schleiermacher regarded this as a onesided interpretation of morality, an interpretation that deprived it of a firm foundation in human nature; this impelled him to champion the close relationship of natural and moral law (see *Werke zur Phil.*, ii. 397–417). Schleiermacher carried this justifiable idea to a great extreme, thereby weakening the characteristic nature of morality. To count morality as a portion of man's nature is to impart a new meaning to the concept nature; it must now be sharply distinguished from all mere existence; so in the end Kant's position is seen to be stronger than Schleiermacher's.*

It was characteristic of ancient ethics to place natural and moral law upon the same level, but this position is now obsolete; it would be impossible, now, to ignore the complications in the relationship between man and spiritual life which have been revealed during the progress of humanity. Moreover, it would be easy to show that whenever modern thinkers have conceived of moral laws as being, in principle, natural laws, the development of their investigations has invariably compelled them to recognise the existence of a difference.†

The socio-historical method of thought peculiar to the nineteenth century inevitably gave rise to the attempt to subject the realms of sociology and history to the rule of fixed laws. Modern

---

* With regard to ethics, Zeller comes to this final conclusion (*Ueber Begriff u. Begründung der sittlichen Gesetze* (1883): "Its principles are not the expression of anything existing anywhere as right or customary; they are the norms for the activity of the human will which the idea of man demands." See also Siebeck: *Ueber das Verhältnis von Naturgesetz u. Sittengesetz* (*Philos. Monatshefte*, 1884, p. 321 ff.).

† Comte furnishes a conspicuous example. Although not admitting, in principle, that laws were anything more than descriptions, the great empiricist says with regard to sociology: *Cette généralité empirique, qui en toute autre science pourrait déjà avoir une valeur suffisante, ne saurait pleinement convenir à la nature propre de la sociologie.* *Cours de phil. pos.*, iv. 466.)

social science or sociology is distinguished from all previous attempts in the same direction, in the first place by its insistence upon precision. By dealing with large numbers the accidental element attaching to individual phenomena is eliminated, averages are obtained, limits are marked out within which any observed irregularities have been found to fall, and regularities in the social life of the community are discovered.* The demonstration of uniformities within a region of life which had hitherto appeared to be under the dominion of chance at first occasioned astonishment; in time, however, this gave way to a critical attitude with regard to the concept of law. It became increasingly clear that there was a difference between mere tendencies of social life and genuine natural laws.

The concept of law has been the cause of even more active movement in the region of political economy. In no department of life is the conflict fraught with greater consequences for life and conduct.† For the problem of law is directly connected with the question of the proper attitude of the State towards economic movements; should it play an active part or remain merely passive? If the economic process is a mere network of separate self-regulating movements, then interference on the part of the State appears to be a disturbance, and *laissez faire, laissez aller* must be looked upon as constituting the sum total of political wisdom. In reality this policy of letting things alone

---

* Quetelet, as is well known, occupies a prominent position among those who have worked along these lines.

† Neumann, to whom we owe particularly valuable investigations upon this topic, remarks with regard to the history of the concept (*Jahrbücher für Nationalökonomie u. Statistik*, 3rd Series, 1899, pp. 152–3): "Search was made for social and economical laws so far back as the Classical Period, as we have attempted to show elsewhere (see the article *Wirt. Gesetze nach früherer u. etziger Auffassung*. *Jahrbuch für Nationalökonomie u. Statistik*: N.F., 1898, vol. 16). And in later times the search has been stimulated by the successes obtained by Bacon and Newton (albeit these were achieved in another department), and has been more especially active since the second half of the seventeenth century, dating from the work of Locke and Hobbes (the first of whom already made use of the term law in this very connection). The physiocrats, in particular (having this heritage behind them), cannot quite be acquitted of blame for not knowing properly how to separate the laws in question, dealing with occurrences, from laws of duty or ethical laws (being as they were under the influence of the then all-powerful ideas of natural right)."

is in itself something other than a mere natural process. For along with this policy exist other possibilities, and as a historical development it must first assert itself over other possible conditions of a different kind, and thus, when introduced, it does not continue as a matter of course, but is capable of being reversed; it must be kept up by a persistent effort.

Hence a belief in the self-regulation of economic conditions through the natural desires and forces of individuals is not possible without an optimistic faith in the rationality of social conditions. If this optimism be undermined, then belief in the universal potency of natural laws must fall with it. Now the economic complications of the nineteenth century have very severely shaken this optimism; with an ever-increasing pressure, they have compelled the State to interfere in the economic world, and in so doing have wrested this department of life free from the sway of merely natural laws and increased the importance of the ethical and historical elements.* The acceptance of these ethical and historical considerations need not in any way prevent us from recognising economic laws. But in this case they do not simply correspond to natural laws, but are, according to Neumann's definition, " the expression of a regular recurrence of economic phenomena (tendencies or processes) actuated by certain definable motives and impelled by economic forces of a systematic kind." (See *Naturgesetz u. Wirtschaftsgesetz: Zeitschrift für die gesamte Staatswissenschaft*, 1892, No. 3.)

During quite recent times the most important discussion of all has been that concerned with the problem of historical laws; this question has come more and more to form the centre of the

---

* It may be mentioned that not only individualists, but socialists, too, have shown an inclination to exaggerate the concept of law at the expense of the free act. The socialistic view has been that a general movement of world-historical life, beyond the control of the wills or actions of individuals, produces great changes and revolutions through an inevitable dialectic. Karl Marx, especially, worked out this view in close connection with Hegel's philosophy of history. But here, too, we cannot escape the contradiction that precisely that which should result from the necessity of law cannot achieve complete victory without being recognised by man, without becoming part and parcel of his own conviction. Here, too, man is called not to passive contemplation, but to energetic action.

conflict as to the interpretation of history as a whole. The more the traditional supernatural conception of history broke up (which breaking up began with the Modern Period), the more were people impelled to demonstrate the existence of general movements and fixed regularities within the historical sphere. The Enlightenment stamped this tendency with its own peculiar characteristics; its historical research "demolished the hitherto prevailing idea of history, based as it was upon the monarchies of Daniel, upon the Apocalypse, or upon Augustine; it discovered a hitherto unknown or unnoticed world, opened up immense vistas of forgotten times, banished the Fall of Man from its position at the commencement of history, and constructed a totally different primitive condition as the earliest stage. But since this explanation, leaving miracles and the idea of providence out of the question, discovered an endlessly complicated network of human forces, it was felt with redoubled force that a simple, normal historical content was necessary, and this was found in the ideas of natural right and of natural morality and religion." (See Tröltsch in the *Real-Encyklopädie für Theologie u. Kirche*, 3rd ed., article *Aufklärung*, p. 231.) If philosophy at first showed an inclination to lay stress upon history in opposition to reason, very soon a movement grew up which aimed at revealing a certain reason and regularity of movement in history. (See my account of the Philosophy of History in the *Kultur der Gegenwart*.) Leibniz, more especially, defended the idea of a general continuity of historical development, while Vico propounded the theory of a regular series of definite stages in the development of peoples and periods. The desire for a general linking up of events to form a united whole grew ever stronger. The nineteenth century carried the matter an important stage further; in the first place it stamped history as a whole with clearly defined types of thought; in the second place it revealed empirical regularities in the immeasurably broad field which historical research had opened up. Under the former head we may mention the systems of Comte and Hegel—at once so closely related and so sharply opposed; in the one case an all-embracing logic, in the other a slow accumulation of separate elements; on the one hand a movement brought about by sharp contrasts, on the other quiet, steady progress (three main stages, "*trois états*," being distinctly recognised, however); in both cases an elimination of free action, an assured progress, and a complete dependence of all individual phenomena upon the contemporary stage of the development of the whole. In this manner philosophy communicated the idea of law to history, and with it a spirit of system which easily compressed an overflowing wealth of material into too narrow a framework and was very zealous in explaining away everything irrational. Meanwhile, working from the other side, the scientific investigation of historical material had revealed a great number of empirical regularities. The great contrasts of modern life played no small part in influencing this investigation. The tendency to discover laws, especially natural laws, in history, was strengthened by the increasing insight into the dependence of human conditions and actions upon outward circumstances; also by the knowledge of the dependence of the individual upon the whole, upon the social *milieu*. There were, however, other factors which worked in an opposite direction: the individuality and positive character of history (as insisted upon in opposition to the Enlightenment),* together with the tendency to lay emphasis upon great personalities—a tendency which found particularly fertile expression in Carlyle's work. The answer to the question as to the regularity of history does not depend merely upon the valuation of nature and spirit in our conception of reality; it depends quite as much upon the content of spiritual life, and most of all it is determined by the rationality or irrationality of our existence.

These contrasts also appear in the treatment of the methodological problem, which is to-day exciting discussion and acting

* Thus B. Steffensen (*Gesammelte Aufsätze*, p. 278) contends that "in history it is the purely individual element—which here reveals itself in its highest forms, in powerful personalities and societies, and finally in humanity itself, in the great deeds and sorrows of a true process of evolution—which produces the incomparable fascination that historical knowledge possesses for the human spirit;" also that "it is not the affirmation of the validity of general empirical natural laws, but far rather the quite unmistakable conflict of the highest earthly nature, the inner man, with ideal laws, better still with ideal powers, reflecting the absolute character of God," which "stirs our soul in the dramatic, tragic course of history."

as a source of division. Windelband has recently expressed the difference between the methods of history and those of natural science with remarkable energy and clearness [see *Geschichte u. Naturwissenschaft* (*Rektoratsrede*), 1894]. Natural science seeks the universal in the form of natural laws, history the particular in the shape it has historically taken; in the former case we are contemplating an unchanging form, in the latter the unique and definite content of actual occurrence. "If one may be allowed to coin new words, scientific thought is in the one case nomothetic, and in the other idiographic" (p. 26); "this general regularity in things supplies the rigid framework of our conception of life, a regularity which expresses the eternally abiding essence of reality and is superior to all change; within this framework develops the living sequence of all those individual situations which constitute human history, and hence are of such value to man" (p. 38).* This conviction has been further developed by Rickert with great penetration and independence (see *Grenzen der naturwissenschaftlichen Begriffsbildung*, i. and ii.). It has given rise, altogether, to a great deal of literary activity. In opposition to this individualistic tendency, Lamprecht maintains that the individual is suitable for artistic comprehension only, and that scientific thought (in history, as elsewhere) must confine itself to the typical; from this point of view he develops the doctrine of socio-psychical stages of evolution, which follow one another in a definite order.†

At the present stage a more detailed discussion is hardly possible; but we shall return to the central problem in our chapter upon history. In conclusion, we may say that a full appreciation of the actuality and unique character of history need not hinder the recognition of certain uniformities. The manner, for example,

---

* Paul, in his *Prinzipien der Sprachgeschichte*, had already distinguished between "historical sciences" and "sciences dealing with laws." He says (p. 1): "As for each branch of historical science, so for the history of language, there must be a parallel science concerning itself with the general life-condition of the object whose development we are tracing and examining the nature and action of such factors as are superior to change."

† A capital guide to the discussion upon the problem of historical laws is supplied by Bernheim in his *Lehrbuch der historischen Methode u. der Geschichtsphilosophie*, 3rd and 4th ed., p. 91 ff.

in which the development of a whole people takes place and in which particular spheres of life, such as religion and art, complete their evolution by passing through a series of stages, may very well be, to a certain extent, related or even similar, since these developments are products of the permanent character of man. To this extent we need have no hesitation in recognising historical laws. But such laws would only refer to the form in which occurrences took place; the actual content would depend upon the specific character of each particular epoch, and would hence lie beyond all derivation. How far the individual processes in history are to be credited with independence, and how far the whole of history is to be conceived of as a separate process, are questions depending upon our attitude towards *the problem of the character of spiritual life and its relationship to the situation of humanity*. This attitude will determine whether we are to regard personalities or group movements as the determining factors of the historical movement. All this, however, threatens to take us beyond the bounds of the methodological problem, and we shall have to return to the subject at a later stage.

C. THE WORLD-PROBLEM

1. MONISM AND DUALISM

IN turning our attention to the problems which centre round the idea of the world we shall still find ourselves in continual touch with the problem of the life-process, and in particular with that of spiritual life. In this sphere, too, the last word does not lie with abstract conceptual considerations, but with the concrete facts of reality; in this connection nothing is more important than the question what is the content ot spiritual life, and what, consequently, is its position in the universe. This is the centre whither all the different lines of investigation must converge, and here all that experience gathers from an examination of things in detail finds its ultimate valuation. In all his struggles with the problems around him man is ultimately seeking himself, the essence of his own being. Historical research, too, corroborates this by showing that it was always the specific shaping of spiritual life which produced the theories and lent them their power.

(a) The Concepts—Historical and Critical Remarks

The terms monism and dualism have come into existence during the last few centuries. Dualism was first employed by Thomas Hyde in the *Historia religionis veterum Persarum* (1700)—see, for example, chap. ix., p. 164—where it served to designate a religious system which recognised two eternal principles, one good and the other evil. The word, still bearing the same meaning, was introduced to a wider circle of readers by Bayle (see the article Zoroaster) and Leibniz (see *Theodicée*, ii. 144, 199). It was first used in contrast with monism by Wolff, who at the same time transferred the expressions to the relationship between soul and body: Wolff also originated the word "monists" to stand for those who admit only one kind of being (corporeal or spiritual); hence the term included idealists as well as materialists—dualists, on the other hand, were those who looked upon body and soul as substances independent of one another.* Wolff himself declared for dualism. Both expressions remained confined to this school of thought, and monist in particular occurs very rarely until the nineteenth century. Hegelians first brought the term into more general use by employing it to describe their own type of thought (thus in 1832 there appeared a work by Göschel entitled *Der Monismus des Gedankens*). Then the word was dropped for a time until the Darwinian theory of evolution (Haeckel and Schleicher) took it up and adapted it to its own ends. Further, the term monism is used to denote any system which aims at subordinating and correlating body and soul, nature and spirit, not one to the other, but both to a higher third. In this sense monism and "Spinozism" are often taken as equivalent.

The study of these expressions now leads us to the problem of the relationship of body and soul or (from the cosmic point of view) to that of nature and spirit. The contrast which now faces us is aggravated in a peculiar degree by its intimate connection with the core of our own being, and by the fact that it seems to have continually increased throughout the whole course of history. The world, it seems, is revealed to us in a twofold manner: from without, through the channels of sense perceptions, from within, through self-active thought —as a world of sensuous impressions and as a world of non-sensuous ideas. Does the one series really include the other, or will it be possible, as a result of deeper knowledge, to show that the antithesis is apparent rather than real? In

---

* Wolff drew up the following scheme of philosophical parties:

Sceptics	Dogmatists
	Monists Dualists
	Idealists Materialists
	Egoists Pluralists

addition to the contrast between these two modes of viewing the world we must take into account the increasing width of the gap between the contents of the two worlds. In the interests of a more exact conception and more secure dominion, science has increasingly driven the spiritual element out of nature. At the same time, however, spiritual life, in its own sphere, has been continually raising itself further and further above mere nature, and has made increasing progress towards establishing itself as an independent kingdom. Thus historical development has tended to make the corporeal seem less and less spiritual and the spiritual less and less corporeal. This makes for dualism. Yet at the same time there is a growth of inducements to monism: in this category we may include the fact that exact research shows a connection between mental and bodily life (a connection which is becoming progressively clearer and more detailed), also a growing impulse towards unity, which makes it impossible for man to accept different worlds in juxtaposition. Hence our concepts fall wider and wider apart—although experience shows the worlds to which they refer to be increasingly connected! We have no choice but to attempt a thorough reconstruction of such a contradictory state of things. History has already shown us what are the chief directions in which such an effort might be made, and the modes of thought thus suggested have not passed away with the epochs to which they belonged; they remain with us as ever-present possibilities and are continually calling for our consideration and decision. Through the course of the ages down to the present day specific types of life and thought have continued to assert themselves in spite of the changes which their concepts have undergone.

The living history of the subject (that is, the history bearing upon our own task) does not go back further than Descartes —nothing earlier possesses serious historical interest for us. It is true that during classical and mediæval times the problem attracted a good deal of attention, but the work done upon it did not lead to a precise definition and clear distinction of concepts until the beginning of the seventeenth century. The psychical was interpreted rather as a denial of the corporeal than in any positive sense.* It was hence unavoidable that the concept of the soul should be largely influenced by this negative idea and the psychical thought of as something corporeal but finer, subtler and more ethereal. The body, however, was regarded as formed, vitalised and directed by forces of a psychical nature. The whole of nature was inwardly vitalised.† Relying upon concepts of this description, natural science frequently made use of psychical factors, a practice which precluded an exact understanding of natural processes. On the other hand, the science of the soul fell under the influence of sensuous and spatial concepts; it experienced no difficulty in conceiving of outside influences passing into the soul or impulses of the will being translated into spatial movement. It was a chaotic state of affairs and did little justice either to nature or to the soul.

Thus the matter stood until the time of the Enlightenment. Descartes, in particular, brought about a thoroughgoing distinction and clarification. Now for the first time the characteristic nature of each sphere was fully recognised. The life of the soul was understood as something intrinsically self-sufficient (*ein reines Beisichselbstsein*), the unity of whose being—*unitas essentiæ*—is quite distinct from any mere compounded unity—*unitas compositionis*—such as is seen in the outer world; consciousness precedes all special activity and first imparts a psychical character to it; the activity of the soul continually returns upon itself and links all manifoldness to a dominating ego. Nothing external can pass into such a soul-life, no external impulse can do more than excite it to produce certain results out of its own depths. Thus it remains fundamentally self-contained in spite of its apparent dependence upon the external world. This independence on the part of the soul corresponds with the independence of nature. The movements and factors which remain after the expulsion of the spiritual element form a

* Thus Descartes could justly claim to have first positively defined the soul, as a whole, as *thought* (that is, conscious activity).

† Characteristic of this is the Aristotelian definition of nature as that which "bears within itself the principle of rest and movement" (in contrast with art, to which this principle is external).

world of their own: a soul had previously appeared indispensable in the explanation of natural movements, but these are now attributed from the very beginning to minute moving (but soulless) particles, whose manifold combinations are made to account for all the immeasurable variety of nature. Nature thus loses all inner forces and tendencies. Moreover, the rich and varied sense properties (colours, sounds, &c.) with which nature, as seen by man, is invested, are no longer looked upon as belonging to the things themselves, but as lent to them by the soul, projected into them by man.

This position represented a very sharp separation of the two spheres, a separation so complete that it could not long be accepted as an adequate explanation. Hence this position gave rise to many new problems and complications, although at the same time it constituted an enormous step forward and supplied much fruitful stimulus. Now, for the first time, the two spheres could develop their characteristic principles and methods with proper distinctness, now for the first time it was possible to understand the psychical psychically, and the corporeal corporeally, and there arose an exact physics and an explanatory psychology. At last reality appeared to become clearly visible as if by the lifting of a veil. This separation brought with it something more than a mere clarification of concepts: it was the forerunner of the two contrasting tendencies of life and human culture, which from this time forward ran right through the Modern World. On the one hand we see an increased activity of thought, a conversion of reality into forms of thought, a measuring of existence by rational standards, an aspiration towards the rationalisation of conditions in general, and an intellectual culture which boldly overleapt the hitherto recognised boundaries; on the other, the establishment of the external world in a position of complete independence with regard to man, a more intimate relationship between man and his environment, a prodigious influx of new experience, an increased recognition of the importance of material factors, and an ever-swelling tide of realistic culture. Who could deny that these two tendencies are present throughout the life of the

Modern World, keeping it in a continual state of tension and introducing a sharp division into every sphere of life? This contrast within life itself is the deepest root of the dualism in concepts and doctrines, and it continually supplies this dualism with new force, however much the desire for unity may tend to drive man beyond it.

A desire for unity is in the very nature of the case unavoidable, for human thought cannot remain satisfied with such a state of division. Dualism had given us a powerful analysis, and had established a more precise terminology, but there existed a continual impulse to progress from the analysis to some sort of synthesis, from the antithesis to some sort of comprehensive unity. Moreover, there was no lack of formidable arguments against this division of reality: for example, the direct impression we have of an intimate relationship between body and soul, the increasing knowledge of the dependence of the life of the soul upon bodily conditions, the philosophical demand for the unity of reality, and finally, the fact of art with its weaving together of the visible and invisible, the outer and the inner, and its bringing of both into a relationship of fruitful reciprocal action. Taking everything into consideration, dualism appeared to be no more than a kind of half-way house on the road to unity: it was true this unity was not to be found ready-made; it was an object of spiritual effort, and in working towards it it was certainly necessary to go against first appearances. Hence the disposition towards unity became bolder in the Modern World than it had ever been before.

The tendency towards unity divided itself into three main movements—materialism, spiritualism, and monism: the all-embracing being was conceived of as matter or spirit, or both of these were regarded as aspects, phenomena, or modes of expression of an underlying reality.

In the strict sense of the word there was no such thing as materialism until the time of Descartes and his clear definition of concepts, and this tendency received no fixed name until then.*

* The term **materialist** was first employed by the chemist and philosopher Robert Boyle, who had a special predilection for clear-cut terms (see his work of 1674: *The Excellence and Grounds of the Mechanical Philosophy*). Giordano Bruno still used the ancient term " Epicurean."

Materialism ran its course through all the grea civilised nations, one after the other, taking a somewhat different form in each case. English materialism was the most efficient, French the most intellectual and ingenious, German the coarsest and most robust. Frequently refuted and crushed, it has always raised its head again and attracted large bands of followers. This clearly demonstrates that there is more in materialism than its naïver critics imagine; critics who think to dispose of it once and for all with a clever argument, and wonder how it is that the long-exposed error again and again draws adherents to itself. As a matter of fact it would not be difficult to overcome materialism if it were simply a question of theoretical considerations. The indisputable dependence of the life of the soul upon bodily conditions, and the advantage materialism possesses of being very simple and easily understood, are factors telling in its favour; yet the dependence is capable of being otherwise interpreted, while the simplicity is an illusion which vanishes upon a closer analysis of concepts. It would in reality be hardly possible to think of a more difficult and problematical concept than that of matter; it eludes us in the very act of definition. But the more exactly we try to conceive of matter, the more impossible it becomes to derive mental life from it. It is precisely the sharper modern definition of the concepts of body and soul, a precision vital to exact science, which has made materialism impossible as a cosmic philosophy. As F. A. Lange has very justly observed: "To think clearly about materialism is to refute it."

However, the strength of materialism does not lie in scientific arguments. It derives its power of attraction and conviction from conditions of life and civilisation. We find it strong and victorious in ages when the traditional forms of civilisation are no longer felt to be true, but weigh upon many with oppressive force. In such ages materialism not only appears to offer the best means of liberation from oppressive restraint, but to constitute a return to a simpler basis of life. It seems to promise a more natural and truthful construction of all our relationships. Moreover, it makes a special point of assigning full weight to the importance of material conditions for civilisation as a whole.

Hence its power of carrying men with it, as seen in the movements which preceded and accompanied the French Revolution and in modern socialism.

What life has thus brought forth only life can refute, and this it does—negatively and positively. Negatively by means of the inner contradiction to which a materialistic construction of civilisation succumbs as a result of its own development; positively through the opposition of a civilisation of another type. The root of this contradiction is that material factors are credited with having accomplished what in reality has been produced through them by a superior spiritual life. Just as the latter allows us to perceive incomparably more in the visible world than the senses can directly demonstrate, so it makes material things valuable as tools for the manifestation and development of reasonable living beings. As materialism in the one case mentally adds a spectator, so in the other it unconsciously postulates a purposive personality and treats the experience of such a personality as an external event. Since, however, the materialistic view of life dissociates human work and aspiration from the real life-bearer, it condemns the latter to become ever more wasted and empty. If at the same time the increase of external relationships has given rise to a great desire for life, the result must be an exceedingly painful disparity between what we desire and what we possess. The ensuing distress will finally and with perfect certainty drive men beyond a materialistic way of life.

This is illustrated on a large scale in the historical development of humanity, which, all through its course, shows a continual overcoming of materialism. Once awakened to an inner life through the toil of thousands of years, through fruitful experience and painful disappointments, it is impossible for man to see his whole reality in the material world, and find his satisfaction in its goods, as children and savages do. As a consequence of this movement towards an inner life, the material world itself appeals to him in an essentially new light. The variegated domain of sense-impressions has now become a great network of forces, laws, and relations. It is no longer the palpable concreteness of the sense-impression which stands guarantee for the reality of the whole, but the causal order with its concatenation of all isolated events, and its subsumption of all that happens under simple laws. The outer world, too, has become non-sensuous. Factors derived from thought, ideal factors, form its core. It is true that in this case the spiritual activity remains attached to an unspiritual subject, but, even so, it is something very different from any sentient faculty, however much developed. There is an immense gap between the world of the natural scientist and that of the uncivilised man, however practised his organs of sense.

Not less different is the relationship which exists between the civilised man and the outward things of life. What makes the latter valuable to him to-day is not so much sense-excitation and pleasure as mastery over the things, the capacity of subjecting them to his will, and hence indefinitely enhancing the significance of life. The civilised man does not so much enjoy the things themselves as himself in the things. His thought imparts value to the sensuous and shapes it into ideal constructions. Think of the gulf between the savage, enjoying the shining appearance of pieces of gold, and the self-conscious power of the great business man whose economic influence stretches to the ends of the earth and who is yet entirely emancipated from sensuous tokens of value!

Thus there are spiritual forces operative in our shaping of the material world which are beyond the comprehension of materialism. But at the same time it is clear that the development of life which is thereby produced cannot be accepted as final; what accomplishes so much with foreign material must necessarily be something in itself; no subjection of the external, and no extension of power, can save from painful vacuity if spiritual life is not given some kind of content. But no enhancement of material or economic power can possibly do this. Hence the attempt to base happiness upon external things must finally result in disappointment and upheaval. The materialistic scheme of life will come into the severest collision with the desire for happiness which it has itself fanned into flame, and hence suffer destruction. Thus materialism must practically refute itself through its own development. But a critical analysis of materialism, however destructive, does not ensure that materialism will be positively overcome. This result can be accomplished only by a powerful development of *self-active spiritual life*. When this life and its tasks fill our minds, it will seem hardly conceivable that man could (like the materialists) regard that which is inwardly nearest to him, and the source of his characteristic greatness, as something secondary and derivative—turn his own existence inside out and seek happiness from outside.

It is peculiarly easy for materialism to influence the masses, on account of its ease of presentment and apparently obvious character. Spiritualism, on the other hand, appeals rather to a few superior minds and to select circles; for immediate appearances are against it, and without spiritual energy the way which it aims at travelling cannot be pursued to the end. The Modern World exhibits two forms of spiritualism: one which conceives of reality as a kingdom of separate souls, and one which regards it as the life and being of a universal spirit; the former view is represented by Leibniz, and the latter by modern German speculation (seen at its greatest in Hegel's philosophy). In both cases the outer world is entirely converted into inner life, the relationship between spirit and nature is not understood as a contrast, but as a gradation within the spirit, the sensuous is no longer looked upon as a world grounded in itself, but as a lower form of spiritual or psychical life—a form not yet arrived at full consciousness.

It is only necessary to devote some thought to this view of life to realise that it is not so extraordinary as a first impression might lead us to suppose. Is it not true that the inner life is the most immediate and certain reality that we possess; and does not the simplest reasoning convince us that we can never wholly leave this sphere and transfer ourselves into another state of being, and that what is called the outer world signifies only a peculiar and specially limited form of the inner life?

But however justifiable and convincing the general idea may be, when the attempt is made to strictly carry it out, human capacity is apt to overstep the limit and overestimate its resources. The spiritualists cannot undertake to convert the whole of nature into spirit without treating our spiritual life as spiritual life pure and simple, as absolute spiritual life. Nature will never allow itself to be reduced to the position of a stage of *human* spiritual life; it is far too independent of the latter for such a supposition to be possible, far too much given to following its own path, and offers far too determined a resistance. Spiritualism could only feel itself equal to this independence on the part of nature, and this firm resistance, by converting spiritual life into mere thought and knowledge, while conceiving of the unspiritual as something not yet fully understood, something which had not yet got beyond the unconscious stage. But only an exaggerated intellectualism could reduce the world-life itself to the level of a mere view of the world, thus presenting reality in a form so attenuated as to be robbed of all living content.

Such an intellectualistic overestimation of human capacity can only be explained as due to the particular character of some special phase of human culture, a phase in which consciousness of spiritual power and the afflatus of spiritual creation led man to think himself the centre of reality, and lifted him in bold flight above all the inertia of the things. But the difficulties cannot long be ignored, and this type of culture must soon reveal its shallowness. This is the fate of any kind of spiritualism which claims to be a complete system.

The failure of the attempts to establish either of these types of life as exclusively true must tend in favour of monism. Monism, too, aims at unity, but does not seek to obtain it by sacrificing the one side to the other, but by the comprehension of both within a third. This seems to give each sphere the chance of fully developing its specific character without losing its connection with the whole, and it appears to do away with the difficulty of interaction between body and soul, since the process on the one side corresponds directly with that on the other. A particularly powerful factor working in favour of monism as a scheme of life is the equilibrium between nature and spirit which is here sought for and is supposed to have been obtained, a balancing, as it were, of outward and inward, sense-life and thought, realistic and idealistic culture. Such an equilibrium seems peculiarly suited to elevate and enlarge life, to lift man above the narrowness of a particular sphere, and give him a share of the whole wealth of reality. Hence monism, more particularly since Spinoza gave it, or appeared to give it, classical shape, has proved in the highest degree attractive to poets and thinkers, natural scientists and religious natures. It has seemed a magic formula with power to still every conflict.

But it only possesses this magic quality because it allows every man to think along his own lines, because each interprets the general idea from his own particular point of view. Although this idea contains an indisputable truth, yet when put into practice it soon appears that the antithesis which was to be overcome has not really disappeared at all. It becomes apparent that in the case of this problem also humanity is called upon to make a definite decision; it is a case of *either—or*. It is not possible for the contrasting positions to be peacefully united.

According to monism as expounded by Spinoza, the two spheres should be in perfect equilibrium. This is also the teaching of "psycho-physical parallelism," which has recently developed this point of view in a more exact manner. As a matter of fact, it is not possible to carry out the fundamental idea in detail without emphasising one side more than the other. Spinoza himself, closely studied, is not a true monist. He alternates between spiritualism and materialism. In the groundwork of his system he is materialistic, and in the conclusion spiritualistic, more particularly in his ethics. He begins by regarding nature as the central thing and the measure of reality, while the life of the soul is relegated to the position of a merely derivative phenomenon, a reflex of the process of nature.*

In bringing the system to a conclusion, however, this materialism becomes spiritualism. What else can we call it,

---

* Herbart very justly protests against this in his *Allgemeine Metaphysik* (*Wke.*, iii. 198): "Moreover, in the case of Spinoza everything psychological is deduced from the corporeal; one hardly notices that, according to his teaching, thought should exist independently of matter occupying space. But how could it be otherwise in any doctrine which begins by looking upon thoughts as representations of the extended? Such a view will invariably be compelled to subject spirit to mass, in virtue of the relationship between copies and their originals."

when a divine life is declared to penetrate and consolidate the whole of reality, when nature becomes a development of this life, and when man is to attain to a participation in infinity and eternity through an intellectual love for God? And this division reaches beyond the concepts and affects the core of life itself; it is not a single but a double life which is visible in Spinoza—sometimes naturalism, sometimes mysticism. Whatever judgment we may pass upon Spinoza, it is certain that he did not succeed in obtaining the desired unity. Later attempts to bring about an equilibrium of nature and spirit have not been any more successful. "Psycho-physical parallelism" has failed in this respect: it either makes the life of the soul a mere reflex of natural processes or the latter mere appearances of the spiritual reality; in neither case is it neutral—it approximates either to materialism or to spiritualism.

Still less does this supposed equilibrium result in a characteristic type of human culture. For the harmonious settlement between nature and spirit, which proved specially attractive to artistic natures, did not take place between the outer and inner world, as though these were elements with equal rights; it came about entirely within the field of the inner life. When, for example, in the creative work of Goethe, everything inward forces itself into outward expression in order thus to find itself, the outer at the same time obtains an inner life; spiritual life is in this case enriched and shaped by a more vigorous comprehension of nature, and in particular it is liberated (by a closer relationship to the world as a whole) from all that is petty, human, and narrow; but human being is not divided between spirit and nature.

The monism associated with the Darwinian theory of evolution even more definitely abandons neutrality. It is only distinguished from materialism by the fact that it looks upon the life of the soul as a primary instead of a secondary phenomenon, as an attribute of matter from the very beginning, and not as something which develops subsequently at special points. But this is practically the view which has always been held by the more subtle materialists, and, like them, the monists really make nature, as perceived by the senses, everything, and allow the whole of reality to be dominated by natural concepts, while denying all independent spiritual life. If this position is logically followed up, the resulting type of life and culture will be purely materialistic. The matter would take on a different complexion if the idea of the spiritualisation of all the elements of reality were really taken earnestly, for that would result in a conception of the world similar to that of Leibniz. But materialistic monism does not usually go so far; it merely adds soul to the elements, as a property along with other properties, without their becoming thereby essentially different. In reality a soul cannot be had, it can only be.

If we thus come to the conclusion that materialistic monism is open to all the objections which can be urged against the coarsest type of materialism, it must be admitted that spiritualistic monism is a more promising solution of the problem. Monism of this type would base itself upon the fact that inner life does not appear merely at separate points, scattered and divided, but that it unites to form a comprehensive connected whole, which reveals, at the level of human existence, a spiritual life elevated above the individual and with it an inner world rich in its own problems and powers. The critical point of reality is not in this case sought between nature and the soul, but between the unspiritual and the spiritual. The life of the soul has a share in both stages, because in the first place it is a portion of nature, and in the second, a vessel for the reception of spiritual life. The question of how is body related to soul gives way to that of the comprehension of spiritual and unspiritual together within the one world. The answer to this question from this point of view is that the unspiritual merely signifies the sub-spiritual; that the same being which exhibits nature and the natural life of the soul in a condition of dissociation and as a network of mere relationships begins in spiritual life to consolidate itself to form a whole and to develop a content. Now, for the first time, reality appears to gain an inwardness and to reach its own depth. Such an elevation from sub-spiritual to spiritual is no mere speculative demand, but a task which claims the whole of human life, for all specifically human achievement, more especially ethical progress, is an ascent from nature to spirit, an elevation of our being from the natural to the spiritual stage. Hence in this case the problem passes from the mere intellect into the centre of life.

When, however, spiritual life appears, from this point of view, to be at the same time the fundamental substance of reality and its goal, this does not in the least mean that in the form in which it is possessed by man it is in a position to command the whole world and simply to find itself again in nature (as was affirmed by pure spiritualism). For although it is certain that spiritual life must somehow be present to man as something superhuman and universally valid, its specific form is continually being influenced by much that is merely human. We do not possess spiritual life itself, but only a human spiritual life; that is a spiritual life whose superhuman core is never accessible to us except through human wrappings. Therefore, if we endeavour to explain the whole of reality from the point of view of human spiritual life, we unavoidably fall into a narrow and anthropomorphic mode of looking at things. An indispensable protection against this is found in nature, with its infinity and its superiority to all petty human ends: nature saves man from sinking into narrow ruts, and continually forces him to separate the general idea of spiritual life from its merely human form of existence. But all these influences operate within the spiritual life, and the position here outlined differs from dogmatic spiritualism only in the fact that two separate points of departure and two distinct bases are recognised within the inclusive whole. It is exactly this, however, which gives rise to a type of human culture different from that represented by spiritualism. Spiritual life now presents itself not merely as the basal fact of life, but also as a *task* which is perpetually renewing its claim upon us. Far more than before is human life set between opposing forces; it appears far less complete, far more immersed in the beginnings of an upward effort. There is a call to personal initiative and decision, a demand to pass beyond the satisfaction of the intellect into wholehearted alliance with the progressive forces of the universe. Hence the ethical rather than the intellectual, the ethical, that is, in the widest sense of the word, becomes the focus of human effort.

The particular form in which this challenge is met will no doubt vary with the man and the age, but there can be no doubt where the chief point of conflict in these struggles lies and at what point, in particular, opinions become divided. The crucial question is this: *Do we or do we not recognise an independent spiritual life, and with it a new stage of reality?* To answer in the negative, or even to hold one's judgmen back, is to surrender the situation to a coarser or finer type of materialism. With our "Yes," on the other hand, we win guidance along new paths and the secure prospect of ultimate triumph. Whether the decision falls on the one side or on the other does not depend merely on intellectual acuteness, but primarily on the power and clearness with which the spiritual life inspires the man or the age. This again brings us back to personal life and being.

(b) The Monism of To-day

In the course of a critical study of the spiritual and intellectual tendencies of the present day, it would be impossible to avoid discussing modern monism. The monism of to-day goes far beyond the special problem of the relationship between nature and spirit; it has become a powerful and exceedingly energetic movement, which it will be our duty to explain and evaluate. Let us bear in mind that the more violent the conflict with which we have to deal, the more bound we are, as philosophers, to treat it in a sober and judicial manner.

It is not possible to understand contemporary monism without some consideration of the wider basis upon which it has been built up. The progress made by the idea of nature in influencing our concepts of the cosmos and our views of life in general has provided this basis. This progress involved a necessary reaction against the older and onesidedly religious and transcendental type of thought, which was in the habit of looking upon nature as something subordinate, and of altogether secondary importance, or even as an object of suspicion. The rapid growth of natural science and the transformation of life which it effected gave this reaction tremendous weight and triumphant power. The scientific precision of the concepts used and their united influence in welding together a systematic whole of thought were silent but powerful factors. The influences proceeding from this source could not be escaped even by those whose object it was, in the main, to work in an opposite direction; this is obvious, for example, in the case of Leibniz, whose unceasing struggle against naturalism did not prevent natural concepts forcing their way into, and dominating, some of the innermost portions of his thought-world.

Was it not influence of this description which caused him to make of the idea of vital progress the all-powerful concept of value, to convert all contrasts into differences of degree, and to make the concept of logical possibility coincide with that of inhibited force? During the nineteenth century this movement continued to make progress. The mode of thought peculiar to natural science silently increased its influence over our concepts and convictions, while we ourselves remained quite unconscious of the real nature of the affirmations and negations which this process involved. The idea of evolution took upon itself the form of a natural process and through the strict causal nexus thereby introduced, destroyed the very notion of activity and (logically) the idea of a real present as well, without our being in the least disturbed. The law of persistence (the so-called "law of inertia"), which held increasing sway in the domain of nature, was, without hesitation, carried over into the spiritual and historical sphere, although in this case the conditions of life must be continually produced afresh by original creative action if they are not to sink immediately. On the natural level, happiness is identical with the pleasures of sense: this natural concept was uncritically carried over into the spiritual world, and people came to look upon spiritual happiness as a species of pleasure, though perhaps of a more refined description. When nature is perpetually forcing itself upon us from outside and inside, it cannot be regarded as remarkable if nature comes to be treated more and more as itself absolutely constituting world and reality in one, and if a "scientific view of life" unhesitatingly, and in perfect confidence of victory, claims to be not merely a particular portion of reality, but an exhaustive representation of the whole of reality.

But notwithstanding all its progress, the movement could not be completely victorious as long as man occupied a privileged and unique position. It was this very position which was now shaken in the severest possible manner by the theory of evolution, a theory which closely connected man with animal life, thereby identifying him with nature, and reducing him to the position of being merely one of a number of natural phenomena. The immense influence of this tendency was still further increased by the results of its practical application: by diligent and fruitful work it succeeded in revealing a prodigious number of facts, linking up hitherto isolated data and combining them into an effective whole. Man seemed to be at last returning to his true home after a lengthy period of delusion and vain self-glorification. His life appeared to gain a firmer basis, to become simpler, fresher, and more genuine; the old seemed new and the new old. A thoroughgoing transformation was commenced.

Modern monism appropriated and co-ordinated these tendencies and modes of thought. From the point of view of monism, natural concepts merely required a certain extension in the direction of the spiritual in order to be capable of absorbing the whole range of reality and dominating the whole of life. But all these advantages and possibilities would hardly have been able alone and of their own capacity to give to monism the power and influence over men's minds that it really possesses. There was another factor which directly tended to inflame passion and to excite great masses of people. Monism was *negative* as well as affirmative. It not only stood for a position of its own, but it represented opposition to the religion of the churches. From the beginning, a wide gap has existed between modern civilised life and traditional religion, and although a persistent attempt has been made to bridge this gap, its futility has become increasingly obvious, and the alienation has developed more and more into complete and sharp opposition.

For a long time these problems did not appear likely to affect the lower strata of society,* but more recently they have penetrated deeply into the masses and are now increasingly agitating them. If the old type of religion is officially kept up in spite of all these changes and upheavals, and, in particular, if it continues to be imposed upon the schools, a condition of serious strain is bound to result, and with it the danger of a paralysing lack of sincerity. He must be a poor psychologist and a shortsighted statesman who can escape seeing the anger and the suppressed scorn which such a state of affairs develops—emotions which will be forced finally to seek some kind of outlet. Now monism stands close at hand to provide just such an outlet. Is it surprising that it sweeps people along with the force of an irresistible whirlwind?

The monistic movement is quite comprehensible. It would not have acquired its extensive influence unless both its positive and negative sides contained elements of truth. But while understanding the historical causes which have produced the movement and justly estimating the element of truth which it contains, we must refuse to assign it the leading place in life. First, with regard to religion, there is now a growing movement in progress in all civilised nations to liberate it from antiquated elements and to shape it in accordance with the present position of the historical evolution of life; such attempts are less simple, but more fruitful and more promising for the future, than the summary rejection of religion which is usually associated with monism. The question is: Is religion (looking beyond all ecclesiastical forms) grounded in the inner necessities of our being and our relationship to the cosmos or is it not so grounded? If it is, then none of the weaknesses and difficulties of the present situation can in any way justify the abandonment of a

---

* Thus, for example, it appeared to P. Bayle to be entirely out of the question that the Enlightenment should ever win over the masses. He believed that a certain amount of superstition was indispensable to the interests and needs of society, which, in his opinion, are essentially the same in all ages: *Les besoins dont je parle ne sont point sujets aux vicissitudes de la lumière et des ténèbres, ils sont de tous les tems; ils sont les mêmes sous un siècle d'ignorance, et sous un siècle de science.* (See the article on Francis of Assisi in the *Dictionnaire*.)

life-power whose work it is to place man in a proper relationship to reality as a whole, a power which undertakes to give man's life greatness and his soul a self-value and a true inner life. The opponents of religion are in such a hurry to inflict some injury upon the Church and the clergy that they usually forget that this negation (with its abandonment of all independent inner life) injures no one so much as themselves. We are reminded of the boy whose father had refused to give him a pair of gloves, and who stood still in the bitter cold, with freezing hands, saying: "It serves my father quite right that my hands are freezing. Why didn't he give me those gloves?"

We are still left with the main question—and whether we hold monism to be right or not will depend on the answer we give to it—the question, namely, whether the natural concepts exclusively employed by monism are sufficient for the full interprotation of reality. In two directions, in particular, doubts are bound to arise—in the sphere of the theory of knowledge and in that of the content of spiritual life, as revealed in history. In the first place it must be pointed out that our conception of the world is not a thing given to us from outside; we build it up ourselves by means of psychical processes, according to the laws of our own minds. This subjective point of view usually bases itself, in the first instance, upon Kant, whose pre-eminent energy has compelled philosophical research to proceed along these lines. This compulsion is not due, however, merely to Kant, or indeed to any individual philosopher, but to the whole character of modern life and thought. For nothing is more typical of modern life and modern civilisation than the liberation of the subject from its dependence upon environment, and its establishment within a life of its own. If at the same time the possession of the world is not abandoned, but passionately sought after with all available strength, then life takes a completely new turn: instead of proceeding from the object to the subject, from the world to man, it proceeds from the subject to the object, from man to the world. Such a reversal must essentially change the content of life and hence affect each particular department. This remark applies also to knowledge. Our conception of reality will be refined, vitalised, and spiritualised when the result is understood in the light of the development which led up to it, when it is fully recognised that our conception of reality is pieced together from within, that not the outer world, but our spiritual organisation, supplies both the outline and the general form, and that elements which at first sight appear simple often embody the results of a very complicated process. At the same time it becomes clear that with all our toil we cannot get beyond a human view of reality, which in its turn becomes problematical when subjected to a more penetrating analysis and called upon to demonstrate its truth. New questions and new difficulties arise. We feel ourselves incomparably less settled in our opinions than we were before, but in spite of this we experience a deepening of reality and of our own personal life.

The materialists and monists recognise nothing of all this. The sense-world, just as it stands (or appears to stand) constitutes for them the genuine and whole reality. From the point of view of the theory of knowledge this is as if some one were to maintain the obsolete Ptolemaic astronomy and refuse to admit the discoveries of Copernicus! It reveals a naïve realism best compared with that exhibited by the mediæval scholastics— usually so despised by the naturalistic school. Thus philosophy (in opposition to naturalism) represents the rights of the subject as defended by modern thought. It represents a truth which may be obscured but cannot be abandoned.

Passing on to the second main objection, we find ourselves face to face with a problem which goes yet deeper down. It is the problem of the content of reality. Naturalism and monism agree in conceiving this content as something far less significant than it really is. They ignore what (to those of another opinion) is of primary importance—*the life of the spirit*. Their position being that all inner life is a mere adjunct of nature, they are compelled to treat the psychical life as a mere process taking place within each separate individual; in pursuance of this line of thought they lay stress upon the indefinable nature of the boundary between the animal and the human, and point out that what was formerly looked upon as a human heirloom has in reality slowly worked its way up by a historical process of evolution, and that even the civilised man remains to a very great extent under the power of natural instincts. We extend our full recognition to the foregoing and have no desire to diminish its importance. But it is not the whole. For the life of the human soul does not remain in a state of disintegration and confinement to separate points, as does that of animals : it results in an integration and the formation of a common life, which in turn develops an immeasurable wealth of concrete fact, displaying essentially new features as compared with the merely natural world. History and society, in their distinctively human sense, would be impossible without this integration. In its absence, how could speech be employed to communicate thought and how could human culture have developed at all ? Upon this basis is built up a vast and complicated system of human activities, such as law, morality, art, and science. These separate activities have (like the whole) their own laws, problems, and experiences. They bring man face to face with difficult tasks ; they exercise an increasing attraction over him, and in return make him into something immeasurably greater than he was ; from being a mere fragment of nature he becomes more and more a spiritual being, and in this capacity he inwardly experiences the infinite, while as a moral personality he is gifted with the power of converting the world into personal action. Such a profound transformation as this necessarily reveals a new aspect of reality. It is clear that man has now entered upon a *new stage* in the progress of the world, the recognition of which must essentially enlarge and deepen his general conception of the whole. This is no mere theory. In the course of the historical and social development of man as we know it, reality has actually been thus unfolded and has worked itself into the institutions of life, forming a developing force which surrounds us with a thousand influences. To bring this inner solidarity of human life to full recognition was the chief task of German speculative philosophy. It was conscious of having reached a far higher level than the Enlightenment, because it explained spiritual contents and values by reference to this solidarity and not, like the Enlightenment, by derivation from the mere individual.

Naturalism, however, overlooks this rise of the spiritual life, this development of a specific stage of civilisation, this inner growth of man through the work of millenniums, and ignores the whole wealth of reality thus revealed. From the point of view of naturalism, all this is simply non-existent, or at any rate it receives no systematic appreciation. We are given a picture of the whole which disregards everything specifically human, everything spiritual and everything which imparts a content to life. This involves a terrible restriction and impoverishment of life. It signifies a rejection of the whole inner content of history and an abandonment of everything in which humanity seeks its greatness. Naturalism constructs and rounds off its conception of the cosmos without taking man into account—and then, with his distinguishing characteristics as far as possible eliminated, he is squeezed in as well as may be! We speak of reaction when we see life being screwed back to some old stage of being already inwardly obsolete. Yet all such attempts to confine life to an outworn historical position are modest indeed compared with this attempt to chain life down to its prehistoric beginnings, and so deprive it of all chance of inner elevation and true development. When contemplated from this standpoint, the whole of human history, with all its characteristic features, is seen to be nothing but a colossal error, a complete departure from truth, since it has more and more deceived man by holding up to him an inner world which is in reality a mockery and a delusion.

At the same time we are not infrequently called upon to endure the annoyance of seeing this denial of an independent spiritual life parade itself as a thing to be taken for granted—something which only ignorance or obstinacy could avoid recognising. It is quite possible to understand this attitude. Negative tendencies have always stood in peculiar danger of engendering dogmatism and fanaticism towards other types of thought. In order to be able to criticise oneself and to justly value others, nothing is more necessary than the capacity of sympathetically entering into other modes of thought and contemplating one's own position from the new point of view. This capacity is especially endangered when a system rapidly attains completion and begins to regard everything outside its limits as non-existent. As a thinker and investigator Hume was certainly a great man, and as far as his own life was concerned he was anything but a fanatic, yet could there be a more flagrant example of intellectual fanaticism than his famous dictum which consigned to the flames all philosophical literature not conforming to his opinions?*

The equilibrium of spiritual life was long enough threatened by theology and religion, and now in the very course of its reaction from this influence it is in danger of being disturbed by the exclusive domination of the natural sciences. It is not so much the natural sciences themselves which are to blame as the philosophical systems based upon them, such as monism and naturalism. It may be remarked in addition that it is doubtful whether monism fulfils the very object which is its main aim (an object that we others, too, regard as of essential importance), namely, the establishment of unity in the thought-world. The question is, does it not, while forcibly welding its concepts together, inwardly divide life as a whole? Its concepts and doctrines are modelled on nature as seen from the mechanical point of view, hence the cosmos becomes a domain of mere blind actuality, in which there is no room for conduct, only for mechanical occurrence; no inward impulse, only juxtaposition; no real unity, only a fitting together of separate parts. To the really logical mind this means the disappearance of all contents and values. There remains no place for the concept of truth, and therefore no place for science. Any spiritual consciousness which is produced can do no more than calmly and uncritically submit to the world-process. This is the theory. But how is it carried out in practice? Monism is carrying on an active struggle for truth, and is filled with joyful faith in human progress; in its construction of human life it

---

* See the *Enquiry concerning Human Understanding*, at the end of the twelfth section: "When we run over libraries, persuaded of these principles, what havoc must we make! If we take in our hand any volume of divinity or school metaphysics, for instance; let us ask: Does it contain any abstract reasonings concerning quantity or number? No. Does it contain any experimental reasonings concerning matter of fact or existence? No. Commit it then to the flames. For it can contain nothing but sophistry and illusion." Should a speculative philosopher pronounce judgment in this fashion, people would pronounce him an imbecile or a fanatic. But when such a method is adopted against philosophy there are many who see in it the evidence of a powerful and undaunted spirit!

clings firmly to the old ideals of the good and beautiful, and it derives the chief motive for its scientific efforts from the conviction that through science it is possible to bring more truth and more reason into human existence—in a word, we find monism, in these respects, travelling along a purely idealistic path! Is it possible to imagine a crasser dualism than to hold materialistic views of life while acting according to the principles of idealism? This is but another example of the ancient experience that men often accomplish with their labour the exact opposite of what they themselves intended.

2. EVOLUTION

(a) On the History of the Term

NEITHER the terms expressing the idea of evolution nor the concept itself came into general use until the Modern Period. *Entwicklung* (evolution) appears in the German language for the first time towards the end of the seventeenth century, but did not become at all popular until the second half of the eighteenth. An older term is *Auswicklung* (also *sich auswickeln*) which was probably first used in a philosophical sense by Jakob Böhme. *Entwickeln*, according to Grimm, was first employed by the lexicographer Stieler (*Der deutschen Sprache Stammbaum*, 1691), *sich entwickeln* by Haugwitz (in *Soliman*, 1684), and by Hagedorn. The scholars of the eighteenth century frequently spoke of an *Entwickeln* and *Entwicklung* of a concept, proof and proposition; "the procedure whereby a concept is worked out in detail is called the *Entwicklung* of the concept" (Lambert). *Entwicklung* in the sense of a self-evolution (*Sichentwickeln* and *Selbstentwicklung*) came into use with the growth of the German Humanistic Movement, which, seeking as it did for a soul in reality, and for the recognition of constructive forces in nature, found for this desire characteristic expression in this term. It is sufficient to refer to Herder and Goethe. Tetens brings *Entwicklung* into the title of a book, that of his chief work, published in 1777: *Philosophische Versuche über die menschliche Natur und ihre Entwickelung* (Philosophical Investigations with regard to Human Nature and its Development). *Entwicklung* now completely replaced *Auswicklung* (which still predominated in Kant's earlier works). *Einwicklung* (involution), which was usually used in the opposite sense to *Auswicklung*, also disappeared from the philosophical vocabulary.

The German expression was a translation of the Latin term, which it partly replaced and partly tolerated as a rival. The terms *evolutio-involutio* and *explicatio-complicatio* or *implicatio*, are derived from Latin classics, but there they were used only in a methodological sense and were not applied to actual growth.* So, too, in the Middle Ages; Thomas Aquinas used only *explicitus* and *implicitus*, and these only in their formal sense. Only the mystical speculation which originated in the writings of Pseudo-Dionysius employed the words and concepts in order to give expression to an inner relation of God and the world. Thus Scotus Erigenus has *involutus, convolutus, complicatio, replicatio*. Since Nicholas of Cusa, the philosopher who stood on the threshold of the Modern World, connected himself with this mode of thought, he made continual use of the terms *explicatio* and *complicatio*. When he employed *evolutio* he thought it necessary to add an explanation.† With the growth of the Modern World the expressions became more and more usual. Together with *developpement* and *enveloppement*, *evolutio* and *involutio* were favourite terms of Leibniz's; eighteenth-century physiology, also, adopted them in the sense of the later so-called pre-formation theory (the "box theory"). In contrast to this, the theory of a new formation by development (represented with especial brilliance by C. F. Wolff in the *theoria generationis*) was called *epigenesis* ‡ in place of "evolution"—now understood as implying a merely quantitative increase, and

---

* Cicero (see, for example, *Top.*, 9) has: *Tum definitio adhibetur quæ quasi involutum evolvit id, de quo quæritur.*

† Nicholas says (Paris ed. of 1514, i. 89 *a*): *Linea est puncti evolutio.—Quomodo intelligis lineam puncti evolutionem ?—Evolutionem id est explicationem.*

‡ C. F. Wolff expressed himself very clearly with regard to these concepts, more especially in the German edition and in the second Latin edition of 1774. The following passage occurs in the latter (*Præmonenda*, § 50): *Evolutio phænomenon est, quod si essentiam ejus et attributa spectes, omni quidem tempore, at inconspicuum, exstitit, denique vero, speciem præ se ferens ac si nunc demum oriatur, quo-modo cunque conspicuum redditur.* See also Kant (*Krit. d. Urteilskraft.*, v. 436, *Hart.*): "The system of generated things as mere educts is calle` .hat of individual pre-formation or the theory of evolution; that of generated things as products is called the system of epigenesis."

so rejected. But at the same time evolution retained the larger meaning of development in general; thus (particularly with non-Teutonic peoples) it has become the most popular designation of the most recent form of the theory of descent.

(b) On the History of the Concept and Problem of Evolution

The doctrine of evolution illustrates, perhaps more clearly than any other, the gap between the old mode of thought and the new. The doctrine of permanence (*die Beharrungslehre*) is as closely connected with the ideals of the Ancient World as is the doctrine of evolution with those of the Modern World. Hence the study of this subject will again render necessary a rapid review of the whole historical movement.

It is true that important beginnings of a theory of evolution were to be found in the earliest Greek philosophy; but in the mid-classical period the doctrine of permanence was decidedly predominant, for the artistic character of the Greek people was more in sympathy with this mode of thought and much better able to form clear concepts with regard to it. Reality, in its fundamental content, was regarded as a living work of art arranged strictly according to rule, and controlled by an unchanging order. The chief aim of science was to throw this truth into clear relief and free it from the confused crowd of passing sense-impressions. This task could not be accomplished without recognising a state of being superior to time, and the truth of the concepts was derived from their correspondence with this being; through thought the concepts were communicated to action and supplied the latter with permanent aims. According to this view of life, science is in the first place a transference from a world of *becoming* into a world of *being*, and of living being. Being is consistently placed before becoming.* This type of thought takes on a more

* In illustration we will content ourselves with a single passage from Aristotle (*De part. anim.*, 640 a, 18) : ἡ γένεσις ἕνεκα τῆς οὐσίας ἐστίν, ἀλλ' οὐχ ἡ οὐσία ἕνεκα τῆς γενέσεως. b, 1 : ἐπεὶ δ' ἔστι τοιοῦτον, τὴν γένεσιν ὡ δὶ καὶ τοιαύτην συμβαίνειν ἀναγκαῖον. Even the term denoting science is brought into relationship with the idea of permanent being (see *Phys.*, 244 b, 9) : ἡ δ' ἐξ ἀρχῆς λῆψις τῆς ἐπιστήμης γένεσις οὐχ ἔστιν· τῷ γὰρ ἠρεμῆσαι καὶ στῆναι τὴν διάνοιαν ἐπίστασθαι καὶ φρονεῖν λέγομεν.

detailed character in the doctrine of forms, created by Plato and further developed by Aristotle. Independent of time, the forms serve as the prototypes and fundamental forces of the things. These unchanging forms continue right through a world-process which knows neither beginning nor end. All change comes from matter, which, at any rate in this earthly life, does not permanently adhere to form, but, although for a time seized and moulded by it, continually eludes it again and loses form · therefore form must ever anew seize and mould matter; this explains the unceasing change, the restless becoming and ceasing to become. This view was applied, in the first place, to individual living beings. But it was not denied that there was movement and alteration outside this sphere; changes in the positions of the stars, and the rising and falling of nations were readily recognised. But such changes as these were thought on closer examination to confirm the doctrine of permanence; for in spite of their great changes of position the stars revolve in their courses and come back to the starting-point in order to commence a new cycle. The change is thus only apparent. History, in the same fashion, consists of an endless succession of cycles of essentially similar content; for the ascent of a people only proceeds to a certain point and then changes into descent, until some elementary catastrophe of fire or water brings about rejuvenation and the same movement is free to begin again. Thus we have an everlasting repetition. What we are experiencing now has already taken place countless times and will take place countless times again. The world was not represented as a rigid state of being, but as full of movement—movement such as that of the days and years, strictly rhythmic and full of secure peace in the midst of all outer changes. In every direction life is confined within fixed limits; there is no real aspiration beyond these limits, no progress into the infinite, no hope of an essentially better future. In its stead we have a conviction that the present, just as it is, can comprehend the eternal and fill our life with it. Activity itself has in this case to absorb rest, and it accomplishes this by itself becoming an operation satiated and satisfied in itself ("energy" in the Aristotelian sense) instead of a mere striving. Such an activity is secured in the first place by the contemplation of the true and the beautiful, but, in its highest form, conduct, as well, becomes the representation of a constant type and character.

Such a type of thought consistently looks upon the unchangeable as good and the changeable as bad. The main characteristic of the divinity is eternity, a state of being unmoved by the course of time. An unchangeable ideal status is held up as a guide to conduct and as a standard of reference; this we see, more particularly, in the construction of ideal constitutions independent of historical changes. The conviction that our life rests upon fixed foundations and moves within fixed limits imparts a characteristic quality to the work of every sphere of life, even of logic and scientific method. The fundamental truths are supposed to exist in a completed form as concepts and judgments. All that remains for us to do is to clearly define them, to place them in their relationships to one another, and to follow up their consequences. Inference thus becomes the main portion of philosophical work, while the new age, on the other hand, has laid emphasis rather upon the concepts and judgments.

The philosophical doctrines were reinforced from the very outset by the subjective temper of the individual, who desired to obtain a constant and worthy content of life, in spite of the manifold and wearisome changes arising from the relations of the city-states to one another. The desire to leave the human sphere and turn to the universe was due at the same time to the search for an inward elevation and consolidation of existence. Towards the close of the antique *régime* this tendency gained in power and Christianity gave it fresh nourishment. The problem was now passing from the realm of art to that of religion. The most advanced Greek thought had sought for rest within movement; the problem now was to rise above the inconstant and meaningless activity of the world and find rest in God, there to seek a refuge, as in a safe harbour, from the storms of life. There was a desire not for pursuit but for possession, for firm and secure possession. This type of thought was deepened and strengthened in a peculiar degree through the influence of mysticism. Mysticism held the essence of all wisdom to consist in reducing time to a mere appearance and becoming "younger" every day through an increasing absorption in the eternal being. At the time of the passing away of the ancient world and the dawn of the Middle Ages, this idea seized hold of men's minds all the more powerfully because it corresponded with the general state of civilisation. An old type of human culture had just exhausted its influence, and as yet no fruitful beginnings of a new type were at hand. Even the greatest minds could see no task higher than the faithful preservation of man's existing possession, and its conscientious communication to future generations. Religious truth, as a divine revelation, seemed, even more than anything else, to be unchangeable. But in other departments of life, also, such as philosophy and medicine, law and politics, there seemed no hope whatever of man attaining to anything more than that which he already possessed. The dogmas of the Church were hardly more authoritative than the teachings of Aristotle and Galen.

The mighty ordered system of the Middle Ages rests upon these convictions—a system which set up throughout the whole of life unchanging standards and fixed connections, outward and inward, more particularly in economical relationships, and guided life in secure pathways while permitting no desire for alteration to find expression. Such a mode of thought is far removed from the comprehension of nature as a realm of gradual development; on the contrary, it regards nature as engaged merely in the conservation of the forms imparted to it, in the first instance, by the Creator.*

From the very beginning the Modern World was hostile to the doctrine of permanence, for it could not develop an independent character without a belief in movement and in the right to move, and in fighting for this belief it could not fail to advance its own aspirations. As a matter of fact, the position of humanity had altered very appreciably since the close of the Ancient World. New races had arisen, full of exuberant youthful energy;

* We have not space to quote more than one characteristic passage. Alanus de Insulis puts the following words into the mouth of nature (see Baumgartner, *Die Philos. des A. d. J.*, p. 79): *Me igitur tamquam sui vicarium rerum generibus sigillandis monetariam destinavit, ut ego in propriis incudibus rerum effigies commonetans ab incudi forma conformatum deviare non sinerem.*

the long centuries of the Middle Ages had served to accumulate much latent capacity, which increasingly strove to manifest itself trusting in itself to see the world with its own eyes and to shape it towards its own ends. Men grew tired of mere receptivity and acquiescence in tradition, and there arose a tendency towards the further development and renewal of life. A changed life-consciousness opened up new prospects and new tasks, while the idea of a progressive movement increasingly dominated the life and work of humanity.

It was, however, no easy task to secure a proper outlet for this vital energy. The history of the idea of evolution shows that this task was successfully accomplished only by relating the new impulse to older efforts, and it indicates various stages through which the movement passed. The impulse towards a renewal of life reaches back to Christianity itself; although in its ecclesiastical form Christianity clung firmly to the doctrine of unchangeability, its thought-world was not lacking in fruitful impulses of an opposite character. History meant far more to Christianity than it did to the Ancient World. It was the Christian conviction that the divine had appeared in the domain of time, not as a pale reflection but in the whole fullness of its glory; hence as the dominating central point of the whole it must relate the whole past to itself and unfold the whole future out of itself. The unique character of this central occurrence was beyond all doubt. Christ could not come again and yet again to be crucified; hence the countless historical cycles of the Ancient World disappeared, there was no longer the old eternal recurrence of things. History ceased to be a uniform rhythmic repetition and became a comprehensive whole, a single drama. Man was now called upon to accomplish a complete transformation, and this made his life incomparably more tense than it had been in the days when man had merely to unfold an already existing nature. Hence in Christianity, and nowhere else, lie the roots of a higher valuation of history and of temporal life in general.

But the realisation and definite expression of the principle underlying these changes was a slow process. Philosophical speculation played a chief part in this work; at that time it went hand in hand with the desire for a more genuine and inward appropriation of truth, and above everything else it sought to bring the world into a more intimate relationship with God than mere primitive credulity could do. What is this world with all its activities, and what does it signify from God's own point of view? According to Augustine's answer, the world can be nothing other than the self-manifestation of the Divine Being. According to this conception, however, all manifoldness acquires an inner relationship and the various historical events can no longer remain a mere disconnected sequence, but become parts of a general movement, nay, of a single world-embracing action; even that which subsequently comes upon the scene must have been in some way already present in the preceding events. Thus the whole world-process may be compared to the development of a tree from its seed.* The mystical speculation of Dionysius, Scotus Erigena, and others carried this line of thought still further, conceiving the whole world as an *auswickeln* (unrolling) of that which is *eingewickelt* (rolled up) in God, as a development of eternity to temporal life, of invisible unity to visible plurality. The terms and images associated with this type of thought are certainly not of such a nature as to lead us to identify it too closely with modern evolutionary doctrines. Both the fundamental being and the motive force remained of a wholly transcendental description; the chain of occurrences and the series of sequences did not spring from the realm of time itself; they were a timeless differentiation of the divine unity. As this unity, with its eternal rest, was held to be unconditionally higher than the world, life, in these latter days, did not strive to enter

---

* Augustine is the leading spirit of the above tendency. The following passage is particularly characteristic of his teaching with regard to evolution (op. iii. 148 D): *Sicut in ipso grano invisibiliter erant omnia simul quæ per tempora in arborem surgerent: ita ipse mundus cogitandus est, cum Deus simul omnia creavit, habuisse simul omnia quæ in illo et cum illo facta sunt, quando factus est dies, non solum cælum cum sole et luna cum sideribus—sed etiam illa quæ aqua et terra produxit,* POTENTIALITER ATQUE CAUSALITER, *priusquam per temporum moras ita exorirentur, quomodo nobis jam nota in eis operibus, quæ Deus usque nunc operatur.* V. 714 E shows how he conceived of the development of a tree from its seed: *In illo grano seminis exiguo, vix visibili, si consideres animo, non oculis, in illa exiguitate, illis angustiis et radix latet et robur insertum est et folia futura alligata sunt et fructus, qui apparebit in arbore, jam est præmissus in semine.*

into the fullness of the world, but rather to retire from it into the unity superior to all plurality and movement, separation and unrest. But in spite of these important differences it was the world of mystical and speculative thought which introduced the modern doctrine of evolution. The former, in describing the world as a manifestation of the Divine Being, had taught men to think more highly of it and had directed life towards the eternal and infinite. The world would not appear so imposing to the modern investigator if the idea of God, of the Absolute Being, had not lent it life and splendour.

Before secure progress in this direction was possible, an important modification had to take place in the view of the world's relationship to God. It would not do for the closer union of the world and God to have the effect of allowing the world to become completely absorbed in God; it must rather tend towards giving it a higher value as the expression of the Divine Being. Now, this alteration in point of view is to be seen in the teaching of Nicholas of Cusa (1401–64), the pioneer philosopher of the Renaissance; he saw the world as the unfolding of the infinite life (the new speculation, in dealing with the idea of God, usually placed infinity before eternity), and hence filled through and through with life; he fancied it thirsting at every point for participation in the infinite life, and for this very reason carrying in itself an impulse towards unlimited progress.* It was

* Only a progress into the infinite can provide the wealth of life contained in the Absolute Being with the means of expression; see, for example, Nicholas of Cusa (Paris ed. of 1514, ii. 188 a): *Posse semper plus et plus intelligere sine fine, est similitudo æternæ sapientiæ, et ex hoc dice, quod est viva imago, quæ se conformat creatori sine fine.* II. 187 b: *Semper vellet id quod intelligit plus intelligere et quod amat plus amare, et mundus totus non sufficit ei, quia non replet desiderium intelligendi ejus.*

In spite of the prevailing doctrine of permanence the concept of progress was by no means strange to the Ancient World; Plato and Aristotle have the expressions ἐπίδοσις and ἐπιδιδόναι for it; the Stoic προκοπή was, however, far more prominent and was used (for example by Polybius) exactly in the sense of our " progress." The idea of a progress into the infinite has its roots among the Platonists and mystics, but did not attain full development until the philosophy of the New Period came into being. Leibniz represents its highest level (see, for example, 150 a, Erdm.): *In cumulum etiam pulchritudinis perfectionisque universalis operum divinorum progressus quidam perpetuus liberrimusque totius universi est agnoscendus, ita ut ad maiorem semper cultum procedat ff.;*

the duty of created beings to approximate, by means of a gradual growth, towards those qualities which God already possessed. In this manner the function of movement was essentially ennobled and an upward aspiration was imparted to the whole world. At the same time, in exact contrast to the latter days of the Ancient World, the artistic was assigned a place by the side of the religious ; nay, it began to replace the latter. As the world more and more took on the form of a living work of art in whose harmony all apparent contrasts vanish, it seemed to produce movement (like all development) from within, through the unfolding of its own being. The absolute now meant not so much a domain of its own as a depth or background of the world. Giordano Bruno's thought represented the victory of pantheism over theism. Henceforth the immanent and artistic form of the theory of evolution predominated, and down to the present day the terms and symbols we make use of stand under its influence. The upward movement of nature, working from within outwards, was now compared to the quiet and unceasing growth of plants. The Enlightenment, since it split up nature into soulless elements, was less favourable to this type of thought ;* on the other hand, the reaction against the Enlightenment (as exemplified in German Humanism) did full justice to it. Here not the mere movement but the artistic construction was looked upon as the main work of nature : hence all change became a development from within and all

further, *Deutsche Schriften*, ii. 36 : " The perfection of all creatures, including man, consists in a strong and unhampered forward impulse towards ever new perfections." In the case of Wolff and his school, *perpetuus sive non impeditus ad majores perfectiones progressus* was reckoned the highest good. The term *Fortschritt* (progress) probably first took rank as a fixed term in the second half of the eighteenth century.

* At the same time there is no lack of stimulating ideas along these lines. See, for example, the little noticed passage in Leibniz's chief work (*Nouv. Ess.*, iii., c. vi., p. 317 a (Erdm.) : *Peut-être que dans quelque tems ou dans quelque lieu de l'univers les espèces des animaux sont ou étaient ou seront plus sujets d changer, qu'elles ne sont présentement parmi nous, et plusieurs animaux qui ont quelque chose du chat, comme le lion, le tigre, et le lynx pourraient avoir été d'une même race et pourront être maintenant comme des sousdivisions nouvelles de l'ancienne espèce des chats. Ainsi je reviens toujours à ce que j'ai dit plus d'une fois que nos déterminations des espèces physiques sont provisionelles et proportionelles à nos connaissances.*

multiplicity of form seemed to be reducible to a single fundamental type. Spreading beyond the realm of nature, the idea of evolution then mastered the life of man and the cosmos as a whole; "everything which occurs in reality" was now viewed as the "development of an absolute reason" (Schelling, i. 481). In the more detailed working out of this idea different tendencies became apparent; Romanticism laid special stress upon the quiet growth and increase, while Hegel with his cosmic logic brought a larger element of self-activity into the conception of evolution; in every case, however, the movement works from within outward, the superior force of the whole being looked upon as operative at each separate point.

It is precisely this inwardness which distinguishes the artistic view of evolution from the strictly scientific (which is peculiar to the Modern World), for the latter abandons all inner relationships and considers the problem entirely from the point of view of immediate existence; the empirical co-operation of the elements is to teach us how to understand nature as a whole, and all progress is to take place in a temporal sequence. The idea of evolution, thus interpreted, has become a corner-stone of modern science It has the effect of reducing the immediate aspect of things to a mere appearance; starting with this, it still remains for us to penetrate to the real conditions. This is accomplished by a process of analysis, which picks out the simplest elements; laws are then discovered which reveal the manner of operation of these elements, and finally, by means of the idea of evolution, the world is built up anew and the existing state of affairs is made comprehensible as the result of historical growth. Thus modern science makes use of the evolutionary doctrine as a chief synthetic principle, and it is at the same time the completion and the touchstone of the whole work of scientific enquiry: no wonder that modern thought and modern humanity feel themselves to be indebted to it.

The new doctrine of evolution came into being simultaneously with the definite uprising of the modern type of thought. Descartes already entertained the idea (if only as a possibility) that the present state of the world had been gradually brought about as the result of a temporal process (*cum tempore, suc-*

cessive).* As the centuries passed by this idea mastered each separate department of thought and engraved itself more and more deeply upon the body of our knowledge.† In cosmology, the ancient idea of the unchangeability of the astronomical world gave way to that of the gradual development of the celestial bodies and their systems (Kant and Laplace). Again, the content of the soul is no longer taken as ready-made and then described and analysed, after the old-fashioned style, modern psychology having striven, since Locke's time, to understand the growth and development of the soul genetically, through a study of the simplest phenomena of life. Human history, too, takes on the appearance of a gradual upward movement from almost imperceptible beginnings to unlimited heights of achievement. Similarly, the other departments of human culture are looked upon as being in a condition of flux and change: in fact, on every hand science has undergone a transformation as compared with the former point of view. Formerly, science selected what was permanent and immediately linked it up to form a fixed whole; it was an artistic presentment of manifoldness as a whole; but now it brought the (apparently) fixed into flux and dug its way with unceasing energy down to smaller and smaller elements, converting reality into an unfinished process. In this way it seemed to come into much closer touch with things, while formerly it had approached them from outside; hence to bring a thing within the sphere of evolution meant to throw a new and powerful light upon it.

Although the modern idea of evolution had long been influential, it did not really become predominant in life and work as a whole until Darwin set his mark upon it. To begin with,

* Clauberg described the Cartesian method after the following fashion, and his description is, in essentials, accurate: *Hanc methodum Cartesiana physica tenens considerat omnes res naturales non statim quales sunt in statu perfectionis suæ absoluto (ut vulgo fieri solet ab aliis), sed prius agit de quibusdam eurundem principiis valde simplicibus et facilibus, deinde explicat, quomodo paulatim ex illis principiis, suprema causa certis legibus opus dirigente, oriantur et fiant aut certe oriri aut fieri possint, donec tandem tales evadant, quales esse experimur dum consummatæ et absolutæ sunt (op. philos. 755).*

† An important part of this movement is dealt with in an admirable manner by H. Heussler in *Der Rationalismus des 17 Jahrhunderts in seinen Beziehungen zur Entwicklungslehre*, 1885.

his work filled up a great gap. Until then organic forms had persistently resisted genetical explanation, subsisting as an unbridged gulf between the universal concept of evolution, on the one hand, and the experiences of human development on the other, thereby preventing the thoroughgoing application of the former to the latter. It is true that important beginnings of an explanation existed (for which we are indebted for the most part to Lamarck), but these beginnings were not connected up to form a complete whole, and hence failed to compel conviction. Through his combination of the doctrine of descent with that of selection, Darwin filled up this gap and supplied the whole with the portion necessary for its completion. The peculiar strength of his teaching lies in the fact that by means of an exceedingly detailed investigation of his particular department he elaborated concepts which seemed to be capable of immeasurable application in every direction. As Helmholtz expresses it: "He elevated each separate department above that condition in which it merely contained an accumulation of enigmatical observations and connected it up with a great development, at the same time establishing definite concepts in the place of what may be called an artistic mode of viewing things" (*Pop. Wissenschaft. Vorträge*, 2nd ed., ii. 204). The service which Darwin has rendered us suffers no diminution through the ever-increasing insight into the limitations of the doctrine of selection, with its struggle for existence and survival of the fittest: for Darwin himself did not offer this theory as the sole explanation of organic forms. The fact remains that it was he who raised the problem into a new position, and that it was through his establishment of the idea of evolution in the sphere of organic life that this idea was enabled to enlarge itself to a view of life as a whole.

This development was due, in the first place, to Herbert Spencer, who, approaching the matter from a realistic point of view, was the first to employ the doctrine of evolution as the basis of a specific view of life. For him, evolution was a transition from a comparatively disconnected state of things to one that was more connected. Evolution seemed to him the most universal fact in the world; he saw it in the integration of matter and the disintegration of movement, and following upon this period, so as to form an endless cycle, he perceived another period of dissolution—an absorption of movement and a disintegration of matter. Thence follows a transition from the similar to the dissimilar, an increasing specialisation and differentiation in the world as a whole, in the various celestial bodies, in human society, in human culture, and in the individual; the period of disintegration follows in the opposite direction. There is no mistaking the relationship between this rhythmic movement and certain ideas put forward by the oldest Greek philosophers (more particularly Empedocles). If Spencer's teaching (which in general outline preceded Darwin's) supplied the latter's thought with a universal background, it gained immeasurably itself in fullness, demonstrability, and penetration, by its association with Darwinian ideas.

In spite of the great progress made by the theory of development, the doctrine of permanence is too deeply rooted in important departments of life for it to yield without offering considerable resistance. Religion, in particular, not only sees individual portions of its traditional sphere of ideas threatened, but also the (to it) indispensable idea of an eternal truth. But in this case, as in others, the view is becoming more and more established that it is not so much the doctrine of evolution *itself* which involves an irremediable opposition to religion as its (by no means necessary) amalgamation with materialistic, or at any rate naturalistic convictions.*

* In this connection we may mention, among others, a passage from the works of the eminent French theologian, Archbishop Mignot. He says in his well-known speech on the methods of theology (see *Bulletin de littérature ecclésiastique*, Nov., 1901, p. 272): *Vous savez avec quelle défiance justifiée fut reçue dans nos écoles, il y a trente ans, l'idée d'évolution, qui paraissait liée par de graves compromissions avec la philosophie panthéiste; depuis que l'analyse en a précisé le contenu, on est à peu près unanime à reconnaître qu'une certaine façon d'entendre l'évolution est conciliable avec une conception religieuse et chrétienne de l'univers; on en trouve le germe dans saint Augustin, et on découvre, avec Vincent de Lerins, qu'appliquée à l'histoire religieuse, elle peut apporter de grandes clartés dans des problèmes qui seraient restés insolubles.* Reischle, too, makes a sharp distinction between evolutionism as a view of life and the actual facts of evolution (see *Wissenschaftliche Entwicklungsforschung und evolutionistische Weltanschauung in ihrem Verhältnis zum Christentum*, in the *Zeitschrift für Theologie u. Kirche*, 12th series, 1st vol. We may also draw attention to Newman's theory of development (see *Cardinal Newman*, Lady Blennerhassett)

All these considerations combine to make evolution something far more than simply one of a number of theories; it has taken over the leadership of the whole and given rise to a new type of life—a type which very essentially alters our fundamental relationship to reality and the nature of our conduct. It is no longer a question of assimilating an already existing reality. We have now to assist in the completion of an unfinished reality. Activity thus becomes more closely associated with environment, and in this manner it is enabled to acquire its more precise form; it may be said to stand, not by the side of, but in the midst of the world, and to co-operate in its development. There is an end of the ancient flight from the stream of temporal affairs to a changeless eternity, as well as of the erection of an ideal consummation of things as the predestined goal of the universe: our task is now rather to follow wholeheartedly the movement of the age, and to adapt conduct as far as possible to the demands of the existing situation. This rouses every department of life out of its inertia and brings it into brisk movement; it sets law and education, for example, in closer relation to the age, and confronts them with the tasks of the living present. Thus there has arisen the characteristic concept "modern," the seizing of the immediate instant and the moulding of all relationships according to its needs, an elasticity of life, a readiness to take up new developments. When growth constitutes, to employ Hegel's expression, "the truth of being," then ideas, too, must share in the general mobility; our ends also become liable to change, and truth becomes a "child of the age" (*veritas temporis filia*). Obviously this places life at the mercy of a complete relativism; but since the older type of thought lost its force this has ceased to frighten us; for the appropriation of a complete truth, already existing around us, is no longer regarded as the chief end, our aim, now, being the production of as rich a life as possible within our own sphere; and for this purpose the more relative type of thought, with its unlimited mobility and adaptability, seems particularly suitable. Nor does this simply affect the inner movements of the soul. The outward developments of modern life, also, have most effectively supported this conversion of existence into a restless progressive movement. Technical science has accelerated the life-process in undreamt-of fashion, made the immediate moment more important, and immeasurably multiplied points of contact and possibilities of change: all work is now involved in unceasing variation, which extends to its very instruments.* Taking all this into account, the victory of the doctrine of change seems to be definite and final, and it appears to have brought us a freer, fresher, and more vigorous life.†

(c) The Complications and Limitations of the merely Evolutionary Doctrine

The foregoing possesses its own truth and justification. It would be folly to place oneself in opposition to such a mass of facts, and it would be petty to pick out isolated errors and emphasise these. But it by no means follows from these discoveries that life and the world are absorbed in the process of evolution, that the struggle between the doctrine of movement and that of permanence is finally settled. It would be a very extraordinary thing if the idea of development itself were quite free from difficulties, if a tendency which has carried the age

* The consequences of this as they affect social problems are dealt with more particularly by Karl Marx, whose treatment of the subject is very penetrating. He says (see *Das Kapital*, i. 479): "Modern industry always looks upon and treats the given form of a process of production as variable; its technological basis is therefore revolutionary, while that of all previous modes of production was essentially conservative."

† It is sufficiently remarkable that in the very age which is notable for the victorious progress of the theory of evolution, science is raising serious doubts as to the permanent existence of life; doubts which are based upon the fact that warmth can pass only from warm bodies to colder ones, and hence the universe is moving towards a state of equilibrium in which life must cease. It may be asked if there is no opposing movement, and in this connection we refer to the theory of pressure due to radiation, which has been applied to this problem in a very fruitful manner (more especially by Arrhenius). Thus Arrhenius comes to the conclusion (see *Das Werden der Welten*, p. 190): "Through this compensating co-operation of gravitation and pressure due to radiation, as well as of equalisation of temperature and concentration of warmth, it becomes possible for the evolution of the world to proceed in a continuous cycle of which we cannot perceive either the beginning or the end, and according to which life has the prospect of existing continuously and without reduction."

so overpoweringly with it did not contain much that was obscure, if the exclusive devotion to one particular line of thought did not neglect much that should not have been neglected, whether of a supplementary or a contradictory nature. Following the plan of our work, we will proceed to consider more particularly the following points: How do these changes and these theories affect the life-process, and how does the latter shape itself under their influence—in particular, is it capable, under these circumstances, of preserving a spiritual character? Every movement must justify itself with regard to the problem of the possibility of spiritual life.

The terms which it employs would alone reveal the fact that in the modern doctrine of evolution different tendencies are operating together. The use of the terms "development" and "evolution" really involves the assumption that the things unfold from within according to a law of the whole, and are being definitely directed towards an end. This is not, however, the accepted doctrine of the predominant modern tendency, which, on the contrary, looks for all progress from the combination of elements which are originally indifferent to one another, and from a slow summation of small movements; it rejects all inner aims and tendencies, all " working from a whole." What, then, is the object of the above expressions, which inevitably give rise to the misleading idea of a movement steadily and quietly growing from *within* ? Do they not impart far too agreeable an appearance to a view of the world which is in reality soulless and meaningless; do they not serve to conceal the upheavals and negations which are involved in this conception of life?

Meanwhile, the popular mind is not much troubled by any such doubts. Intoxicated by the idea of evolution, of endless progress, of an unlimited improvement of everything, it does not feel the lack of a more precise conception. Many of the disciples of evolution are to-day filled with an enthusiasm so vague that they forget to ask *what* or *how*, *whence* or *whither?* The greater the absence of precision, the vaguer the conception, the more confident is their assurance, the more heedless their enthusiasm.

At any rate there is no mistaking the fact that in the leading

EVOLUTION

systems of modern evolutionary thought a mechanical view predominates and is looked upon as the final solution of the problem. The older view of evolution, artistic or logical in character, has been for the most part thrust aside: Hegel (although his influence may be secretly operative to a greater extent than most people imagine) has been superseded by Darwin.

In the case of Darwin and Darwinism the two chief ideas of descent and selection must be clearly distinguished from one another. The theory of descent receives so much corroboration from so many different quarters, and has demonstrated itself to be so immeasurably fruitful, that it can hardly be said to meet with any scientific opposition. The theory of selection, on the other hand, which for a time carried the scientific world by storm, has met with increased opposition. From the very beginning the predominant philosophical tendency has been against the idea that all the forms we see around us have come into existence solely through an accumulation of accidental individual variations, by the mere blind concurrence of these variations and their actual survival,* without the operation of any inner law. Natural science, too, has more and more demonstrated its inadequacy. Within the very sphere of the theory of evolution itself this particular view has to meet increasing opposition. We cannot now go into these problems more in detail, but we may just refer to Weissmann's theories, to the mechanics of evolution, and to the doctrine of mutation. The same movement

* We may here refer more particularly to the tireless and penetrating work of E. von Hartmann, who has demonstrated the inadequacy of this doctrine in the most convincing fashion (from the point of view both of speculation and of fact). In his most recent treatment of this question, in the *Abstammungslehre seit Darwin* (see the *Annalen der Naturphilosophie*, ii. 3) he sums up (on p. 354) the results of the investigations of the last decade as follows: "Selection can accomplish no positive achievement at all; it can only operate negatively by exclusion. The production of new types through minimal alterations is possible though not proved, and since the undulating character of minimal alterations has been known it has become less probable. Sudden alteration has now come to the front. Accident gives way to a definitely directed, systematic evolutionary tendency due to inner causes; this makes itself seen just as much in the smallest as in the sudden alterations. The claim put forward by Darwinism to explain purposive results from purely mechanical causes is totally untenable."

which is again bringing the characteristic features and the problems of life more to the front is bound to resist the attempt to abide by a mechanical doctrine of evolution, and will recommend a dynamical one. This is seen in the re-acceptance and development of Lamarckian ideas, also in the accompanying sharp criticism of a merely mechanical doctrine of evolution, denying, as it must, all development from within and from the whole. Amongst other things, it is urged against the mechanical theory that its denial of all inner impulse abandons, in principle, all essential progress in life, and with it the idea of evolution; * another equally important objection is that this doctrine only reaches a plausible conclusion by assuming that the elements already possess the qualities visible on the highest levels of development.† Here are great tendencies side by side, and the conflict between them still continues, moving now in this direction, now in that. One thing at any rate is certain: the situation does not appear so simple to-day as it did to Darwin's enthusiastic disciples (Darwin himself was less dogmatic).

Singularly enough, however, this same doctrine of selection, which in its original sphere is being more and more critically handled and increasingly limited, is constantly gaining ground

* Bergson remarks (*L'évolut. créatrice*, p. 40): *L'essence des explications mécaniques est en effet de considérer l'avenir et le passé comme calculables en fonction du présent et de prétendre ainsi que tout est donné.* Bergson himself defends the idea *d'un élan originel de la vie, passant d'une génération de germes à la génération suivante de germes par l'intermédiare des organismes développés qui forment entre les germes le trait d'union. Cet élan, se conservant sur les lignes d'évolution entre lesquelles il se partage, est la cause profondes des variations, du moins de celles qui se transmittent régulièrement, qui s'additionnent, qui créent des espèces nouvelles. En général, quand des espèces ont commencé à diverger à partir d'une souche commune, elles accentuent leur divergence d mesure qu'elles progressent dans leur évolution. Pourtant, sur des points définis, elles pourront et devront même évoluer identiquement si l'on accepte l'hypothèse d'un élan commun.*

† See Lodge, *Life and Matter*: "In this case that which has to be explained is simply accepted as it stands and straightway attributed to the atoms, in the hope of thus bringing the matter to an end." Bergson, *L'évol. créat.*, vi., finds the error of Spencer's evolutionism in that it endeavours *d decouper la réalité actuelle, déjà évoluée, en petits morceaux non moins évolués, puis à la recomposer avec ces fragments, et à se donner ainsi, par avance, tout ce qu'il s'agit d'expliquer.*

outside this sphere in the general study of things human. In all quarters there is a widespread inclination to go back to the simplest possible beginnings, which exhibit man nearly related to the animal world, to trace back the upward movement not to an inner impulse, but to a gradual forward thrust produced by outward necessities, and to understand it as a mere adaptation to environment and to the conditions of life. It seems to be all a mere question of natural existence, of victory in the struggle against rivals. In the so-called "higher," then, nothing essentially new is introduced, we have nothing but combinations and variations of the elementary phenomena of life; as a necessary consequence spiritual life cannot be credited with the least independence. The change of concepts which this view involves penetrates deeply into the various departments of life. When all development of life is reducible to a maintenance in the struggle for survival, when all spiritual manifestation becomes a mere adjunct of physical existence, then the useful becomes the value of values, the concept of the good-in-itself sinks to an empty illusion, and the true, too, can continue to exist only by taking on the character of a conjunction of ideas fitted for assisting in the preservation of life. Ethics, æsthetics, and the theory of knowledge must all undergo a complete transformation; they must all look for the solution of their problems to the discovery and retention of the primitive elements.

The conception as a whole affects us with the fresh energy of a new insight. It reveals much that is new in the ancient experiences. It illuminates by bringing otherwise scattered matter into a related whole. Its backward vision is fruitful of many discoveries. The natural conditions of our existence, the continued operation of elemental instincts in the midst of all the complications and apparent refinements of civilisation, the slow and phlegmatic nature of the historical movement, now come to full recognition. All this seems to lend a more natural colour and a more vital truth to the conception of our existence, and at the same time efforts directed towards the elevation of human conditions acquire more definite opportunities for exerting their influence.

But if the foregoing is to be employed purely in the service of reason and truth it must be placed in a greater whole and estimated from the point of view of its relationships. If it endeavours, by itself, to come to a final conclusion and seeks to build up a thought-world with its own resources, serious error is unavoidable. Underlying this error is the mistake of treating the particular fashion in which spiritual life and reason are developed in man as the creating and impelling basis of spiritual life itself; if, however, the latter is thus from the very beginning reduced to a mere appurtenance of humanity and deprived of all independence, then its derivation from mere nature can give rise to no difficulty. He who stands outside the charmed circle in which this type of thought moves will at once perceive the circular nature of the argument and realise how destructive is the transformation of spiritual life which it effects. Spiritual values, and finally spiritual life itself, are not merely changed by being thus made subordinate to the useful; they are annihilated. A good (such as right, honour, love, or loyalty) which is aimed at on account of its usefulness, that is to say, as a mere means for the physical and social preservation of life, thereby undergoes an inward transformation and ceases to be a good. The same thing would happen to the concept of truth if it sank to be a mere utilitarian arrangement of our ideas; it might then be all manner of other things, but could no longer be truth. However, inward experience, than which we know nothing more certain, resists such a degradation of life. However much conflict there may be as to the more detailed conception of the good and true, however little part the individual may have in these values, as mere *life possibilities* they are facts which it is absolutely impossible to explain away, facts which make the whole of reality something more than it could be without them. Finally there arises the question, if, from the above point of view, spiritual life can be said to exist at all. When the whole life of the soul is converted into a mechanical system of elementary forces, then there is no life bound up with the whole, no thought, no experiencing subject; thus the person who is judging brings about his own disappearance and declares all spiritual work, including his own, to be an illusion! So long as he does not do this, and cannot do it, the form of his statement contradicts its content; the *denial itself* (which is put forward as a scientific and universally valid truth) corroborates the operation of a spiritual life superior to the process of nature.

Along with this contradiction (whereby spiritual work is made use of in the destruction of its own fundamental conditions) are associated complications in the more detailed carrying out of the theory. The most remarkable thing of all is that this abandonment of all independent spirituality and this state of being bound down to mere nature presents itself as a heightening of life and a liberation. As a matter of fact, when closely examined it is seen that this position destroys the whole meaning and value of our life. From this point of view the labour and struggle of man and of humanity as a whole, the vast complex of civilisation with its countless ramifications, has no other task than the preservation of physical life, of sensuous existence; it merely accomplishes, in an extraordinarily roundabout way, what animals achieve in much simpler and easier fashion.* Everything which asserts an object and value of its own, as compared with physical existence, must disappear as untenable. Such a life can offer no sort of content. But it is a fact that we *are* thinking and judging beings, we are actually in possession of a self-centre and are compelled to relate all experience to it and measure it from thence. Hence we are bound to feel this absence of content as a painful emptiness, an emptiness which is all the more intolerable because the connections of the evolutionary scheme do not permit of the slightest hope of any change; they remorselessly tie us down to the senseless routine of the nature process. Could there be a more comfortless construction of life? It demands unceasing work, unaccompanied

---

* We may here draw attention to Kant's saying (in the *Critique of Practical Reason*, v. 65, Hart.): "Man is not in the least elevated above mere animalism by the possession of reason if his reason is only employed in the same fashion as that in which animals use their instincts." Nay, from this point of view the supposed progress is in reality retrogression. For is it not retrogression when, for the attainment of the same goal, more and more complicated means are employed, more and more care and labour expended? If, however, new contents and values are recognised, then we have already abandoned the mechanical theory of evolution!

by any inner profit; it bids us put forth all our forces with feverish energy, and yet has no object other than the eking out of a bare existence.

Moreover, considered from a methodological point of view, as soon as this type of thought attempts to include spiritual life it becomes involved in serious difficulties. We then see the construction of evolutionary ethics, evolutionary æsthetics, evolutionary theories of law, &c.; all these hark back to commencements in the animal world and seek in these the key to all further development. The older view certainly made the mistake of projecting the higher stages into the commencing ones and hence falsely idealising the latter. To-day, it can hardly be doubted that the spiritual life did not drop from heaven, but commenced with little, half-animal beginnings. But is it necessary that these commencements should remain decisive for the whole movement; could not the life-process itself raise itself; could not new forces come to light in it? In reality, this tying down to the first commencements does not so much strengthen evolution as deny it. Moreover, are the first beginnings so simple and clear that they are capable of shedding light upon what would otherwise be obscure? Can we form any direct image of them; is not our conception of them necessarily dependent upon our present-day position? This path really leads us into the profoundest obscurity of all; to try to explain higher stages by going back to hypothetically constructed beginnings is not a direct way but a by-path.*

Thus far we have been engaged in opposing the mechanical and

---

* Volkelt has recently shown this to be the case in the sphere of æsthetics. See his penetrating and convincing article *Die entwickelungsgeschichtliche Betrachtungsweise in der Aesthetik* (*Zeits. für Psychologie u. Physiologie der Sinnesorgane*, Bd. 29). This has been reprinted as a separate booklet, and we read on p. 7 : "It must not be overlooked that in order to answer the question how are we to approach artistic creations, poetically, artistically, æsthetically, we must start, if we are to have any firm foundation for our reply, from the standpoint of the mature man of to-day." P. 8 : "In reality the æsthetics of primitive peoples, to employ a brief term, is not a methodical means but rather one of the most obscure and impenetrable special problems known to the whole of æsthetics." P. 11 : "'Æsthetics upon a historical and evolutionary basis' is therefore a reversal of the proper position of affairs."

naturalistic type of evolutionary teaching in so far as it aims at moulding the whole of life according to its own standards. But the whole idea of evolution, in the form in which it permeates the modern world, involves more problems than are apparent upon the surface. To begin with, it is far too readily taken for granted that all movement is progress, is development in the sense of a continual ascent. Even the ancients fully realised that the world, particularly the world of human action, was in perpetual movement; but they regarded this as a lower stage of reality, they saw mere confusion and disarrangement, no steady forward movement. A chief article of faith with moderns, on the other hand, is the belief in a consistent upward trend. Of religious origin, this idea was supported and further developed by speculative philosophy. Religion and speculation are to-day mere shadows of their former selves and for many people non-existent; but their product, the belief in progress, has remained. After the removal of these foundations, has it still a strong enough basis? Does mere experience proclaim it to be an irrefutable fact? Can experience with its limitations really demonstrate a continuous progress at all? Much subjective feeling enters into all these questions. Men are very apt to regard all change as progress; they perceive the new which their own age brings, and while accepting it, forget the old which has meanwhile been lost. In this way, every age readily conceives that it represents the highest that man has yet reached, because it values all endeavour according to its own standard: an artistic age will usually value from the point of view of art, a technical age from that of technical progress. To these permanent influences we must add temporary ones; nothing is more favourable to the belief in progress than a strong sense of power and consciousness of the present, feelings which penetrate ascending ages and in particular permeate the main tendency of the Modern World. From this point of view, everything which promises an increase of life is vigorously taken up; experiences in particular spheres which seem to point in this direction are generalised; isolated and scattered matter is linked up and supplemented; obstacles, on the other hand, are overlooked or set aside, even resistance itself is understood as an impulse to further activity:

in all the foregoing mere experience is transformed by an inward and vital impulse.

Such a view and treatment of human existence must necessarily expose itself ultimately to the danger of reaction. A calmer and more critical mode of thought will destroy much of this belief in progress, will direct attention towards retarding factors and will discover much that was raised by this belief to the position of permanent law to be mere temporary appearance. For example, during the last few centuries the doctrine of an unceasing growth of population was generally accepted; the cessation of growth in the case of particular nations was looked upon as a notable exception. Yet how recent is this doctrine! Even so modern a writer as Montesquieu believed that the population of Europe was less than it had been in ancient times, and that it was advisable to promote the increase of the race by special laws. Then the opposite assumption prevailed, and Malthus gave strong expression to the dangers of an excessive increase. For a time statistics corroborated this assumption, but recently indications have increasingly appeared that upon a certain level of civilisation the increase is retarded and comes to a standstill—nay, there may even be a decrease. This compels us to ask if the law of increase is perhaps not permanently valid but applies only to particular phases of civilisation. How greatly, however, must the pursual of this thought alter the whole aspect of history!

Moreover, the problem passes beyond the quantitative into the qualitative sphere. Does history bring a spiritual growth of humanity; does it increase the sum of spiritual capacity? In this respect the antagonism between spiritual achievement and power of reproduction so emphatically maintained by Lorenz runs directly counter to the optimism of popular opinion. Lorenz calls it " a very noteworthy fact that higher and stronger spiritual activity involves a diminished capacity of reproduction " (*Lehrbuch der Genealogie*, pp. 486-7), and holds that "in all probability, an experience that has been elsewhere observed could be also corroborated genealogically; the experience, namely, that the male germ migrates from below upwards and in the higher classes, or, as one may say according to present-day social organisation, in the higher professions, becomes extinct." Following up this line of thought, it seems that the "decay of higher civilisation and civilised peoples is not a result of their being overpowered from without, but far rather expresses the natural reduction in power of reproduction of the higher, cultivated individual"; it appears that "nature is incapable of directly propagating the spiritual (to employ this term only in the sense of causality)" (p. 487). Thus the movement of humanity would itself exhaust itself, civilisations would live their day out and grow aged, and stagnation set in, until there again came new impulses and, above all, fresh men. The whole would then no longer appear as a continuous ascent, but would become an up and down movement in different phases. Any progress which took place under these circumstances would at any rate present a different appearance from what is usually understood by progress.

In connection with the present theme it may also be pointed out that the various departments of life exhibit different types of movement, and that the predominance of one of these departments usually exalts its own method of valuation to universal validity. The technical and exact sciences show a more continuous progress than do any other departments of life, though in their case, too, there is no lack of losses and backslidings. Spiritual creation, in the sense of an inner elevation of human life, finds full embodiment only at individual special points, and then rapidly sinks; in a moral respect, humanity appears to progress alike in good and bad, both in action and reaction, the contrast thus becoming increasingly great. Religion, finally, offers its fundamental truth as superior to all temporal change; it is apt to consider this truth as having been already obtained at some earlier period, and thus it links endeavour with the past. Each of these types tends to construct, from its own point of view, an all-embracing conception of history and the world. The problem of progress is hence full of perplexities; that which presents itself as matter-of-course and universally valid is often merely the product of a special temporary situation.

Finally, there is another sense in which the idea of evolution must give rise to doubts. It easily leads to the understanding of movement as exclusively an act of necessity, thus setting man in too contemplative and passive a relationship to his environment. Progress seems rather to *happen to* man than be *achieved by* him. There seems no necessity for personal decision or initiative. This is evident, for example, in the evolutionary ideas of the German Romantics, who attributed all formation to a quiet, steady growth from within outwards, and thus paralysed man's impulse towards personal activity. The same thing can happen if the moving force be placed in sensuous natural impulses and outward necessities. In both cases the evolution endangers the ethical character of life and destroys the fundamental condition of a true history—an ever fresh insertion of original life, a conversion of all that we receive into personal action and living present. While human spiritual life acquires its tension and its character, in the first instance, through the conflict between freedom and fate, such a doctrine of evolution wholly sacrifices freedom to fate. It is the confusion of a laxer with a more strict view of the concept of evolution which allows such problems to be overlooked. It is quite a common thing for all progressive movement to be called evolution, without the least enquiry as to the cause of progress; in this case there may well remain a place for freedom. On the other hand, evolution in the stricter sense signifies a natural process driven forward by an imperative necessity — it matters not whether this operates by an integration of separate elements or by a movement of the whole—and according to this view all freedom vanishes and with it all history (in the distinctively human sense). There is then a mere *taking place* but no *action*. In this sense of the word historical evolution is an absurdity.

Nay, doubt penetrates yet deeper; it attacks the very predominance of movement and will not admit the conversion of the whole of reality into a process. At first, the Modern World saw nothing but gain in this mobilising of all connections, in this melting down of all rigid distinctions; it saw only the enhancement of life, the growth in freedom and strength. The fact that there is also a great loss cannot, however, be permauently hidden. Something indeed is lost which is indispensable to the existence of spiritual life. For down to its most elementary basic forms spiritual life demands and exhibits a permanent character, a permanence not within time but in opposition to it. A truth valid only for to-day or to-morrow is an absurdity. What is true at all is true for all time—or better still it is true irrespective of time; although the statement, under particular circumstances, may be for a period of time only, the manner in which it is expressed is always timeless; as spiritual experience all truth involves a liberation from all time. Moreover, that which we value and recognise as good derives its value not from the point of view of a particular epoch but independently of all time; it derives it from a timeless order of things. Certain as it is that the concepts of good obtaining in various ages alter with the age in question, it is none the less certain that whatever any given epoch apprehends as good is taken to be absolutely and permanently valid. No alteration of human circumstance is able to destroy this inner superiority of spiritual life to time. Further, concepts like personality, character, spiritual individuality, also proclaim this supra-temporal quality of spiritual life; for they demand the formation of a permanent type and its consistent retention in the face of all movement; conduct in all its various phases aims at bringing this type to expression and at promoting its welfare. Thus to convert spiritual life entirely into movement is to destroy its very foundations.

Nay, movement itself, regarded inwardly, bears witness to the indispensability of permanence. It cannot be reviewed, gathered together into a whole or experienced as a whole in the absence of a standpoint superior to itself and a synthesis effected from thence. Otherwise it becomes split up into numerous separate states which may indeed occupy and entertain the soul with kaleidoscopically changing impressions but cannot provide it with a whole and a content. Therefore the more a force superior to movement disappears, the more does life tend to become superficial and to lose all spiritual freedom.

This quality of spiritual life by which it is raised above time is peculiarly well illustrated by the construction of a history, in so far as it is a characteristically human and spiritual history.

For history, in the human sense, is by no means a mere succession of events, a mere floating of humanity down the stream of time ; that would never lead beyond an accumulation of outward effects, such as nature shows us in the formation of the earth's crust. All *human* history is far rather a resistance to the mere flux of phenomena, some kind of an attempt to bring the current to a standstill, a struggle against mere time. Even the most primitive attempt to preserve customs, deeds, &c., in the memory of succeeding generations, and thus retain them in the consciousness of humanity, shows such a resistance to time. The more, however, history is to mean for man, the more it is to bring him not merely an enlargement of knowledge but an elevation of life, the more self-activity must he put forth. This demands, of necessity, a standpoint superior to time. To experience the past inwardly we must liberate ourselves from the accidental character of the present, or at the least strive towards such a liberation ; otherwise in everything earlier we should see solely a projection of the present type, and in the midst of all outward enlargement remain, inwardly, just as we are ; an understanding of other epochs according to their own distinctive relationships would be totally denied to us. To gain such insight we should not merely know the past but relate it to our own life, convert its wealth into our own property, raise ourselves to the level of what is great in it. With this object it becomes necessary not only to acquire an understanding of previous ages but to sift their content, to decide what is essential and valuable and what accidental and indifferent. But how is this possible without some sort of standard superior to the movement of the ages, and without transferring the sphere of activity to a timeless standpoint ? Finally, history is valuable to us only in so far as we are able to convert it into a timeless present ; its main function is to lead us out of the narrowness and poverty of the merely momentary present into a wider present superior to, and encompassing, time. There is no more dangerous enemy of a real present than devotion to the mere moment.

Such being the outlook, it is absolutely out of the question to allow the whole of life to pass off into the flux of movement.

Even when our consciousness has been entirely filled with the idea of movement, our work has always sought a counterpoise in something permanent. Thus even the most extreme protagonists of the doctrine of movement, as understood in natural science, have recognised some kind of supplement to movement; this is seen in the doctrine of the permanence of matter or energy and in the subordination of all phenomena to unchanging laws. Without such a consolidation its work would lose the character of science, and instead of being a causal interpretation would become a mere disconnected narrative.

Philosophers, too, have not been able to make evolution the central idea of their thought-world without recognising a permanence superior to change, and indeed encompassing change. Hegel's system would have become split up into mere separate points, and the shifting nature of the separate phases would have destroyed all truth, if a point of view superior to time had not enabled him to comprise it as a whole, to convert all succession into a self-life of this whole, at the same time raising it above the temporal stream into a timeless present. Whether in Hegel's case the desired goal is completely attained is another question: but with regard to the aspiration itself there can be no doubt, and indeed the whole greatness of the Hegelian system is closely connected with it.

When we come to consider Comte, Hegel's realistic counterpart, we discover a similar situation. He succeeds in constructing a scientific system only by elaborating and emphasising certain permanent elements. It is true that he brings all previous history into a state of flux, and allows the earlier stages no more than a relative truth; but in coming to Positivism he believes himself to have attained the absolute and final truth, and although the future may see a further unfolding of this, the core seems permanently secured for all succeeding ages. Moreover, the historical retrospect takes place entirely rom this highest fixed point. In the midst of all movement a permanent truth is therefore held fast.

Social life, it is true, gained but little by such a concealed recognition of a permanent element; the progressive conversion of modern life into a mere process met with no adequate resistance from this point of view. In this respect a much greater influence was exerted by the continued effect of permanent elements and forces proceeding from the older systems of life; these were firmly incorporated in the existing state of things, making an atmosphere that all men took for granted; in these elements and forces the flux of movement had tacitly found now a support and now a supplement. Such a position as this, exhibiting opposed tendencies not yet brought into equilibrium, cannot, however, be permanently maintained, and the lead is unmistakably being taken by the principle of movement, which will thus increasingly occupy the field. This principle will produce its own consequences, namely, a dissolution of everything fixed and the conversion of the whole of life into a restless process.

At the same time, those results will become apparent which follow upon the disappearance of all permanent elements and forces; in particular we shall miss the inner synthesis, the experience that sees life whole; and in the place of these must witness a decay of all independent spirituality and an enfeeblement of the effort to raise the standard of spiritual existence. The triumph of mere movement means the complete victory, not only of relativism, but of sensualism. It signifies the abandonment of all life-content, the dissolution of existence into separate moments, the loss of any true present. Moreover, humanity must at the same time become split up into mutually exclusive associations, and lose more and more completely the elevating and consolidating influences of a common thought-world. Can it be denied that a review of the present situation already exhibits clearly enough the destructive force of this tendency, and that the problems and doubts to which this tendency gives rise reach down to the very foundations of modern life? It is indeed true that we have obtained a more varied and less rigid life; no authority or tradition confines us, we are free to follow up each impression with all our might, to seize the instant, to accelerate the speed of life. But in the midst of all this mobility and busy activity, life threatens to leave us upon the mere surface and to become emptier and emptier in its spiritual character; we lose our grasp of an inner unity of being, and with it of our sole possible support against the flux of phenomena; incapable of asserting our independence with regard to the latter, we are tossed helplessly hither and thither. At the same time we lose touch with any real present, for this requires that life should be at rest in itself, and involves an elevation above mere time.* In its place we get a succession of mere instants, whose ever-varying character converts life into a restless flight and inevitably inclines us to seek immediate effects, to gratify the senses, and secure outward advantages. As a necessary consequence we have a continual eager pursuit of the new, the dazzling, the exciting, a seeking after sensation, effect, &c., a pandering to the whims and moods of the crowd, the low average of humanity. This unworthy "actuality" has so perverted Aristotle's noble concept that it has acquired a significance exactly opposite to that which it was intended to bear! †

The more, however, the present thus slips from our grasp, the more keen becomes the yearning towards an indefinite future, the snatching and anticipating of what is there expected. "Never," said Lotze, at a time much quieter than the

---

* At the classical period of German literature this was fully and clearly realised. We need recall only Goethe's saying (from the *Conversations with Eckermann*): "Every situation, nay, every moment, is of infinite value, for it is the representative of the whole of eternity." In this connection, too, the thoughtful words of a more modern thinker (W. Gidionsen) may be brought to mind:—

> *Nicht vom Tage sollst du leben,*
> *Auf und nieder schwankt die Welle*
> *Lass dein Inn'res fröhlich weben,*
> *Stets verjüngten Daseins Quelle.*
> *Ist Ursprünglichkeit dir eigen,*
> *Darfst sie hegen, darfst sie zeigen,*
> *So nur spürst du in der Zeit*
> *Vorgefühl der Ewigkeit.*

† The term *actualis* is a product of later antiquity (Augustine, Macrobius); in the Middle Ages *actus, actualis, actualitas*, derived from Græco-Latin translations of Aristotle, became widely used (more especially after the time of Duns Scotus), and were thence carried over into the New Period. The word served to represent the Aristotelian concept of energy or entelechy—activity resting within itself and self-sufficing, in contrast with movement still striving forward and incomplete.

present (*Microkosmus*, 2nd edit., ii. 281), " has this contradiction been so prominent : men hold the whole life which they so eagerly and diligently take part in, to be, at bottom, not the true life, and dream of another and more beautiful one that they would like to live and will live, so soon as the present life gives the leisure for it and opens the way."

Thus an exaggerated and frenzied movement causes the inward life to crumble to pieces; it ceases to be a true life, and becomes more and more a mere will to live, a something that points to life but is itself no life, but an illusion. This cannot possibly be allowed to continue. Such a conversion of existence into mere movement involves a complete destruction of life, and must therefore be resisted. Humanity must and will overcome this dangerous crisis, for the desire to do so arises from an imperative necessity of man's innermost nature. But this overcoming will not be accomplished without a thoroughgoing transformation of existence, without the construction of a new type of life, without the courage and power to ascend to a new spiritual height.

(*d*) The Requirements of a New Type of Life

Although the problem into which our investigation has resolved itself cannot here be fully discussed, yet without some sort of indication of the path to be pursued our study would appear to end in nothing. Therefore we must proceed, as briefly as possible, to sketch at any rate an outline.

It is necessary above everything else to find some firm support with which to oppose this threatened volatilisation of life. This support cannot be supplied by the outer world, since we never experience the latter except through the medium of our soul, and therefore even the most fixed external thing must become movable to us if the soul-life should be given over entirely to movement. Neither does the immediate life of the soul provide any fixed principle. For in this case the most varied elements are mingled together, and the fleeting phenomena overlap in a confused medley. Hence only one hope remains; we must penetrate to some spiritual activity, which, being firmly established in itself, promises to impart firmness to the rest of life. The Modern World has seen this attempted by various great thinkers in different ways: Descartes sought the Archimedean point in pure thought, Kant in moral action; both undertakings, however, were rooted in wider movements of modern life, since, on the one hand, the work of science, and on the other a moral initiative, were bent on giving human existence a firm foundation and so preventing its dissipation into mere phenomena. Both movements have accomplished great things, and are continuing to do so; at the same time there arises an increasing doubt as to whether they penetrate to the last depth and are able from thence to embrace the whole of life. To begin with, they constrain life in a particular direction and give it a particular bias, in the one case, intellectualistic, in the other, moral. From the point of view of our problem, however, it is a still more serious objection that the adoption of a particular standpoint as central can always be doubted and contested from other standpoints; conduct can pit itself against intellect and *vice versâ*, while scepticism can attempt to reduce science to a mere tissue of images, and naturalism to convert morality into a product of mere natural instincts. No particular sphere can offer us the highest certainty to which we can attain; only a synthesis of the whole can offer us this. If a unity superior to all division is not found in spiritual life, and if an original life does not manifest itself in this unity, then our life and endeavour can never acquire any stability.

The thought of an all-embracing unity is something more than a mere fancy; this is witnessed by the movement towards personality which animates our human striving. For however much our true human personality may be commingled with what is human in the pettier sense of the word, and however much it may be subject to the most manifold conditions and limitations, a new kind of life, a greater depth of reality, here begins actively to manifest itself. In this case, spiritual life does not appear as a particular manifestation but as a new kind of reality, a new stage of being, to which the particular manifestations (including scientific thought and moral conduct) have to subordinate themselves and into which they must fit. Thus we see that a stable conclusion is reached only when the whole life, pressing forward, attains to the spirituality which is the source of all wholeness of life. In this way, also, an ideal is held up to civilisation—an ideal which transcends the antithesis between theory and practice, discriminating, within each factor, between a spiritual and a pre-spiritual stage.

Thus it is solely by means of an energetic upheaval and revolution of existence that we can press forward to a steadfast centre and take up the struggle against the time-current and the meaningless flux of mere movement. The outlook would be entirely hopeless, and even our aspiration in this direction would be incomprehensible, if man were not grounded in a spiritual world superior to immediate existence and yet directly present in the life-process.

This regress, however, involves the further requirement that spiritual life should not be looked upon as a property of our mere human nature, but rather that man should be conceived as participating in a spiritual life superior to himself. Spiritual life in its substance must be recognised as *independent* with respect to man. If spiritual life and human nature thus become more widely separated than would be warranted by the current conception, at the same time a mutual adaptation between fixity and movement, and the formation of a type of life superior to the antithesis, is now made possible. Change (and with it evolution) is absolutely out of the question as far as the substance of spiritual life is concerned. The concept of truth (and this concept, also, is superior to the antithesis of theoretical and practical) tolerates neither growth nor change. It is essential to its existence that it should belong to a timeless order. Man, on the other hand, can only obtain a life-content within time and through gradual experience. For this purpose freedom and mobility are essential. Moreover, the truth to which man attains is not won once for all, so that he can peacefully enjoy his possession; it must continually be reconquered, again and again must it become the subject of struggle. Doubt is continually at work sapping the foundations of our spiritual existence and requiring of us again and yet again strenuous reconquest.

Thus there arise three quite distinct types of life: one of these is exclusively directed towards permanence, nay, towards a state of eternal rest, and seeks as far as possible to free human being from all movement; another is wholly taken up with movement and will know of nothing that escapes its influence; the third strives to get beyond the antithesis and aims at an inward superiority which shall do justice to both sides. The first of these tendencies dominates the antique and the second the modern construction of life; the third has from the earliest times been operative in the world's spiritual work, but it has yet to be recognised in principle, and to be developed as a type of life into full power and clarity. This is the task of the future. The strength of the old type of life lay in the firmness and repose which it imparted to the spiritual life, and in its power to raise it, as an inviolable order, above all mere preference and prejudice, whether of the individual or of the crowd. The solution, however, became problematical when it treated truth not only as unchangeable in its substance but as ready to man's hand; when, in brief, it identified substance with the human form of existence. Thus, during the Classical Period and to an even greater extent during the Middle Ages, scientific truth was looked upon as a final and settled thing; nor did ecclesiastical Christianity admit any further development of the religious thought-world. The possession of a particular age is thus set up as a permanent thing, all further endeavour is inhibited and a rigid yoke laid upon humanity—a yoke which is bound to become more and more oppressive with the passage of time. Moreover, truth itself suffers injury, since it becomes incorporated with accidental matter derived from particular periods or peoples. All this brings with it an inevitable reaction. Movement insists upon the recognition of its rights, while man begins to be conscious of his limitations and of the conditional nature of his achievements. There commences that development of modern life the greatness of which, self-corrosive as it is, we have already noted. If the doctrine of permanence makes the mistake of directly fusing the substance of spiritual life with its human form of existence, the doctrine of change errs in subjecting spiritual life to the conditions of the human type. The one petrifies spiritual life, the other volatilises it.

There has been no lack of attempts at compromise. Life as

a whole has sought, and still seeks, for help more particularly by reading the new, which the passage of time brings with it, as far as possible into the old; and in respect of the formations of history a distinction is made between kernel and shell, the former being, as well as can be, retained and the latter cast off. But this is no more than a makeshift, and its success is made increasingly impossible by the historical temper of modern thought, with its demonstration of the unique and characteristic nature of the individual ages. If we do not wish to remain subject to these oppositions and to be crushed by them, we must strive to overcome them inwardly by essentially transforming the idea of reality. This will not, however, be possible until spiritual life is recognised as independent and more sharply separated from human life. For in this way alone can we retain both permanence and change. In the last depths of his being man must be grounded in an unchanging spiritual world, and from this centre outwards must proceed the influences that move and direct. At the same time his immediate existence remains in the highest degree insecure and incomplete. Change is slow, and progress toward the goal can take place only under time-conditions. But owing to its connection with this unchanging basis the movement of change does not lose itself in what is vague and strange to it; there takes place in it a realisation of its own being, and though it passes from one transition to another, it is no longer mere change. Considered from the point of view of man, such a conviction demands that life should be based upon something deeper than the psychical functions in their separate manifestations. For these reveal reality already in a state of flux; and the thought-world, in particular, figures as in ceaseless transition. But a strongly-defined and fundamental type of life can maintain its identity through all such changes as these, express itself through them, and unfold within them, a truth superior to time. Thus man stands at once *in time* and *above time:* his life possesses a two-fold character, since it has to realise a truth superior to time as a fact of experience and ground itself within this truth, and at the same time must strive, within the realm of time, for a clearer unfolding and more forceful application of this truth. Truth is therefore, here, both a possession and a problem—a possession in the innermost depth of our being, a problem in so far as we are called to transform existence into a life of full self-activity.

From this point of view we may establish a relationship with history which will absorb and overcome the opposition between permanence and change. Let us consider, for example, our attitude towards a historical religion such as Christianity. The form which it has historically acquired cannot be permanently retained. Taking into account all the immense changes which have taken place in our outward and inward existence, it would follow that not only our thought, but our emotions and convictions as well, would be in danger of unreality if they were to be forced into the mould of this older type. We may easily be unjust to our own age if our sole aim is to do full justice to other ages.

But this retreat from the immediate form of existence does not necessarily involve the least abandonment of substance. A genuine type of spiritual life may have come to light in forms of existence that have since become inadequate, and this life may have imparted, and may continue to impart, vitality to events of more than temporal significance, whose influence pervades the whole of human history. Human life can never under any circumstances afford to cut itself loose from spiritual life of this type. As far as its human form is concerned this eternal remains at the same time a perpetual task; it does not demonstrate its superiority to time by retaining a rigid self-sameness through the ages, but far rather by entering into the distinctive character of each age without losing itself, by enabling each age to discover the eternal which dwells within it and thus liberating it from mere time. But in opposition to this view of the Ancient World, that which assigns to time a reality has this immense advantage, that it is only as a time-process that progress within the eternal first becomes possible.

We have not space at our disposal to pursue the question how the aspect of the world and man's relationship to reality are transformed when "becoming" drops into the second place, without, however, being looked upon with the contempt meted out to it by Greek thought. But there is one point we should like to mention before closing this section. The fundamental conviction we have referred to, with its reconciliation of permanence and change, can never contradict the facts of evolution; but it must needs come into sharp conflict with a self-sufficient evolutionary philosophy, a merely naturalistic theory of evolution. The ultimate decision depends upon our whole conception of spiritual life and at the same time of our own being. How the evolution of reality as a whole is to be understood depends chiefly upon whether we recognise in spiritual life *a new stage of life* or whether we see in it nothing more than a mere prolongation of nature. In the former case, evolution assumes a different appearance; the process in which we ourselves are immediately involved, with which we are familiar through experience, does not itself give rise to all progress, the higher does not arise as a mere product of the lower, but new forces belonging to a greater whole enter into the movement. Thus our reality acquires background and depth; it must adjust itself to the larger whole which includes it. Change is then no longer a mere race without goal or meaning, but moves within the realm of eternal truth, and is borne on by its inspiration. If, on the other hand, spiritual life is a mere by-product of nature, there remains no possibility of providing a counterpoise for change and wresting a content from life; but humanity and the whole world with it are in headlong flight towards the nothingness which is their sole destination. Thus, in this case, as at all the other critical points of our enquiry, it is *our attitude towards spiritual life*—more particularly the recognition or rejection of an *independence* on the part of spiritual life—*which decides the direction in which our thought must move.*

MS OF HUMAN LIFE

1. CIVILISATION (OR HUMAN CULTURE)*

In dealing with man himself we shall find that the problems which confront us centre around one dominating idea, that of human culture or civilisation. This idea, as it ramifies, takes a complex shape, which, in its turn, reacts upon the parent-root and helps to determine it more closely. If we ask how civilisation has come to be the thing it is, we are led to the problems of history and social life. If we ask what civilisation is, we are met by the problems of morality, art, &c. As preliminary, then, to this whole discussion, let us first consider in outline the concept of civilisation.

(a) On the History of the Term and Concept

Following our usual practice, we will again commence with the term. *Kultur*, in its present-day sense, is of comparatively modern origin. For although the later Classical Period and the Renaissance were familiar enough with metaphors comparing the state of the soul to the cultivation (*colere*) of the field, Bacon was the first to make of the idea of culture a distinct and finite concept. The culture or Georgics of the spirit became a chief portion of his ethics.† At first, however, this attempt produced no results; it was not directly taken up and developed.

---

* It should be understood that the term "civilisation" is used as a translation of the German *Kultur*, a word very difficult to translate satisfactorily, but which would perhaps be more accurately rendered by "human culture." As the latter is a somewhat awkward expression it was, however, thought best (as a rule) to use "civilisation." *Tr. Note.*

† See *De augm. scient.*, vii. op. 1: *Partiemur igitur ethicam in doctrinas principales duas, alteram de exemplari sive imagine boni, alteram de regimine et cultura animi, quam etiam partem georgica animi appellare consuevimus. Illa naturam boni describit, hæc regulas de animo ad illas conformando præscribit;* see also op. 3. The expression Georgics shows how strongly the pictorial character of the term was felt.

Not till the advent of French civilisation in the seventeenth century did a more extensive movement take place in this direction. Then, the proud self-consciousness of a classical age favoured the distinction of its own type of civilisation from that of all lower stages of development, and the result of this distinction was to give rise to a more general reflection upon the different conditions of human existence. The eighteenth century, always eager to establish history on a natural basis, pursued this tendency still further and occupied itself more and more with the contrast between natural and civilised conditions. So far from lacking expressions for the progress of humanity, different images and ideas here exist side by side and often cut across one another; for example, to cultivate, to civilise, to polish, to enlighten.* A definite term for the whole status implied in these expressions appears to have been first supplied by Turgot with the word *civilisation*.† In Germany, the Latin of the Renaissance possessed the term *civilisatio;* ‡ *civilitas*, too, was employed in a similar sense; § but the living speech remained unaffected and down to the beginning of the Classical Epoch still relied on designations of an equivocal kind.‖ The

* We just select a few here from a simply endless number. Bayle (see *œuv. div.*, La Hague, 1727, i. 453 *a*) has *cultiver leur esprit et leur raison*; when, in the same work (407 *a*) he speaks of *toutes les sociétés où l'on cultivait l'esprit*, we should hardly translate this otherwise than by "civilised nations" (*Kulturvölker*). But at the same time he employs *civiliser* (for example, in the dictionary; 1465, *se civiliser*, and 1472 *b*, *nations civilisées* in contrast to *nations barbares*). In a similar sense, Bossuet uses *nations les plus éclairées*. Leibniz (398 *a*, Erdm.) has *le siècle qui passe pour éclairé;* where we should say "savage" and "civilised man," he says "wild man" and "European." Montesquieu, too, contrasts *peuples éclairés* with *peuples grossiers*, but more often he uses *poli* or *policé* (for example, *les peuples les polis, la Grèce seul polie au milieu des barbares, un pays policés, un royaume aussi policé comme la France, les peuples policés, peuples bien policés*). In England, too, there is no definite term; thus Adam Smith uses indiscriminately "civilised" and "polished nations" (see, for example, *The Theory of Moral Sentiments*, v., cp. 2).

† See Barth, *Die Philosophie der Geschichte als Soziologie*, p. 253.

‡ According to Paulsen (*Gesch. des gelehrten Unterrichts in Deutschland*, pp. 78 and 131) it was said of Wittenberg at the beginning of the sixteenth century that it lay in *termino civilisationis*.

§ In Kepler, for example (ii. 730), it stands for the opposite of *barbaries*.

‖ This is seen, for example, in the works of that sterling and thoughtful writer, Iselin. In his *Geschichte der Menschheit* he usually contrasts *Stand der Natur* (natural condition) with *Stand der Sitten* (well-mannered condition) and accordingly speaks of *gesitteten* (well-mannered) peoples. But not less often he employs *Polisierung* (polishing) and *polisiert*, and in this connection, antici-

decisive distinction, so far as Germany is concerned, was the outcome of this Classical Period. The then prevalent desire for a vitalising of the whole man and an artistic construction of human existence involved so original an ideal of human culture that the terms were inevitably adjusted to suit it. As a result of this adjustment the concept of human culture acquired a definite meaning and assumed the leading place; *Zivilisation* * was held distinct, as indicating a lower stage of human progress; *Aufklärung* (enlightenment) lost its more general meaning almost before it had passed into common use, and came to designate the social manner peculiar to the eighteenth century, thereby taking its place as a historical category; in its place appeared the familiar term *Bildung* (formation), but enriched now with an inward meaning (mental culture), and the word in this sense soon became fashionable. But let us look a little more closely at these alterations in terminology, for they have dominated German usage down to the present day.

Kultur, without any addition, is first met with in Herder; the new meaning still seems to be in a state of flux, but it has already solidified sufficiently to require for its expression a definite term.† *Geisteskultur* (spiritual culture) was employed

pating the subsequent distinction between culture and civilisation, he distinguishes two kinds of *Polizierung*: "one which provides society with its outward form" and "one which improves men's minds and feelings" (Book 7, Section 21). He also contrasts *Barbarei* (barbarism) and *Menschlichkeit* (humanity), and employs *Milderung* (softening and humanisation) and *Milderung der Sitten* (humanisation of manners), also *Erleuchtung* (illumination) and *Erleuchtung der Geister* (illumination of men's minds) as equivalent to our "human culture." In his youthful writings, Goethe speaks of a *polierter* man and of *polierte* nations. Kant writes of the *geschliffenen* (polished) classes.

* This must not be confused with the *English* word "civilisation," which approximates to the German *Kultur* (see p. 281). *Tr. Note.*

† With reference to this term the section ix. 1 of the *Ideen zur Philos. der Geschichte* is particularly important: "If we wish to call this second genesis of man, which runs through his whole life, culture (from the cultivation of the soil) or enlightenment (from the idea of light), we are at liberty to make use of the name. In this case, however, the chain of culture and enlightenment stretches to the ends of the earth." Culture has for its ruling aim *Humanität* (humanity in the sense of human feeling), which to Herder signified the complete development and harmony of all powers, according to a conviction which idealised the intimate union of life and beauty. The distinctive mark of man as compared with mere nature is, however, freedom; hence freedom is essential to the concept of culture. The subject is dealt with in greater detail in Genthe's *Der Kulturbegriff bei Herder.*

for a long time side by side with *Kultur* (as, for example, in Goethe), but gradually *Kultur simplicitur* prevailed. The further application of the concept took place in two directions, following the two chief tendencies of German idealism—the artistic and the ethical. With the poets and humanists the former tendency predominated; in this case, art and science in their union as literary creation appear to be the authentic vehicles of culture, the distinguishing mark of true cultivation.* On the other hand, Kant and still more decisively Fichte make freedom the soul of culture, and hence give the latter a predominantly moral character. Kant defines culture in the following terms: "Culture," he says, "is the drawing forth of a rational being's capacity for certain ends in general, which, being general, are within the scope of his freedom. Hence the ultimate purpose which one has cause to attribute to nature in respect of the human race can be no other than culture; this purpose cannot be human happiness upon earth nor even the prospect of ranking as the most distinguished instrument in the establishing of order and concord in irrational external nature" (v. 464, Hart.). Fichte developed this idea still further, expressing it forcibly after his own fashion. For him, freedom or full self-activity is at the same time the content of culture; thus the latter signifies (*Wke.*, vi. 86): "The exercising of every power towards the end of attaining complete freedom, complete independence of all that is not ourself, our own pure Self." Since this task, from his standpoint, comprised all others, "nothing in the sensuous world, nothing in our human lot, be it what we do or what we suffer, has, when regarded as a phenomenon, any value except in so far as it makes for culture." Religion, science, and virtue are expressly counted among the higher branches of rational culture (vii. 166); culture also forms the end of statecraft, and the State of which the thinker dreams is described as a culture-state.†

* See the passage from F. A. Wolf which we are shortly about to cite.

† The concept of the "culture-state" contradicts, in the first place, the conception of the State as a mere "juridical institution." To begin with, the "culture-state" stood in opposition, too, to the national State; see vii. 212: "Which is then the fatherland of the truly educated Christian European? In general, it is Europe; in particular, it is that European State which at the

These two different phases of the movement towards human culture agree, however, in distinctly separating culture, as a development from within and an elevation of the whole man, from all mere social order; the term *Zivilisation* serves to denote the latter. Thus *Zivilisation* and *Kultur* are distinguished as lower and higher, as beginning and completion.*
Closely connected with this development and enrichment of the concept of culture is the appearance of *Bildung;* during the second half of the eighteenth century this term was transferred for the first time from the outward to the inward, from the corporeal to the mental.† It was taken up with particular eagerness by the Romanticists, who seem to have been more especially responsible for bringing the expression *die Gebildeten,* "men of

period in question stands at the highest level of culture." Later, it was Fichte himself who raised the concepts nation and fatherland to honour; but it was always the spiritual content and never the sensuous existence which gave them their importance in his eyes.

* This is already quite clearly to be seen in the case of Kant; see more especially iv. 152: "We have become cultivated in a high degree through art and science. We have become civilised to the point of being overburdened in every kind of social behaviour and convention. But there is yet a great deal to be done before we can call ourselves 'moralised.' For the idea of morality is a portion of culture; though when the idea is employed only in the sense of mere uniform conventions of honour and outward propriety it does not amount to anything more than civilisation." Pestalozzi says in the same sense (xii. 154): "The collective existence of our species can only civilise the same, it cannot cultivate it." F. A. Wolf was a peculiarly energetic advocate of specifically literary culture; see more especially the famous treatise which serves as introduction to the *Museum der Altertums-Wissenschaft* (1807). He makes use of the distinction between culture and civilisation in order to elevate the Greeks and Romans above all other peoples. In this connection the chief characteristic of genuine culture is regarded as the possession of a literature common to all; culture is that position of society brought about by the development of literature and art. See p. 16: "One of the most important differences between these nations and the others is that the latter are not in the least (or only a few degrees) elevated above that kind of cultivation which should be called a condition of respectable polish or civilisation, in contrast to genuine higher spiritual culture." P. 17: "That higher culture, the spiritual or literary." P. 18: "Asiatics and Africans, as merely civilised peoples—not cultivated in a literary sense—are unquestionably shut out of our domain." During this whole period, Europe and culture were closely associated. W. v. Humboldt also adopted this distinction between culture and civilisation.

† Upon this point see Imelmann's edition of Klopstock's *Oden*, p. 86; Paulsen, article *Bildung* in Rein's *Enz. Handbuch der Pädagogik*; Biese in *d. N. Jahrb. für das Klass. Altertum*, year 1902, p. 241

culture," into general use.* In Fichte we can clearly trace how this word, so indefinite in its original meaning, acquires a fixed connotation. *Bildung* and *gebildet* undergo a characteristic development differentiating them from the other allied terms in this respect, namely, that they are used not so much of whole peoples, or of humanity in general, as of the higher intellectual section within a given nation. In *Bildung* stress is laid rather upon personal activity, independent appropriation on the part of the individual.† It is thus contrasted with culture in general as being something more inward.

The distinction between *Kultur* and *Zivilisation* has recently become very vague and shifting.‡ There is an intrinsic reason for this, in so far as that inner culture which hovered before the minds of our poets and thinkers and claimed superiority over any mere civilisation has ceased, in our own age, to possess any firm foundation. Moreover, in this respect there is no agreement between the nations; when we Germans speak of *Kultur*, the French and English say "civilisation." § We cannot, however, pursue this matter any further at present. As to the general meaning of *Kultur* there can be no doubt; its more exact meaning is, however, quite unsettled, and every powerful mind is free to impress its own mark upon it.

However indefinite the concept of *Kultur* may be to-day, it certainly points to a very old problem. The Ancient World could not avoid recognising great contrasts between the nations

---

* This expression then meant far more than it now does, after the weakening influence of centuries. This must be taken into account in Schleiermacher's *Reden über die Religion an die Gebildeten unter ihren Verächtern*. For more detailed information as to the meaning of this expression among the German Romanticists, see Haym's *Die Romantische Schule*, pp. 420, 430.

† With regard to the problems connected with the concept *Bildung*, see amongst recent literature) O. Weissenfels, *Die Bildungswirren der Gegenwart*.

‡ For a full account see Barth's *Die Philosophie der Geschichte als Soziologie*, p. 253.

§ When an article of mine, *Religion u. Kultur*, was translated in the *Liberté Chrétienne* (1907, No. 3, p. 114) it was noted with regard to *Kultur*: "*Nous n'avons guère l'habitude, en français, d'employer ce mot sans quelque déterminatif : ' la culture intellectuelle,' ' la culture des lettres.'*"

as well as different intellectual stages within individual nations; Attic life at its zenith was bound not only to increase the self-consciousness of Greek civilisation but to produce a sharper division within Greek life itself. There was much, however, to militate against a full appreciation of the problem of human culture. National isolation made it easy for the higher cultural position of a particular nation to be regarded as merely the natural gift of a special race; at the same time, the historical belief in endless cycles confined all progress within narrow limits and easily hindered an impartial examination of national origins. On the other hand there was considerable inclination to recognise an ascent from a crude natural condition. The broadening of horizon and closer connection of peoples which began with Alexander * was necessarily hindered, however, by the division of humanity into Greeks and Barbarians. The same age, too, which saw a weakening of national contrasts produced a sharpening of the distinction between educated and uneducated among the Greeks themselves, since without a scholarly education it was no longer possible fully to participate in the inherited riches of civilisation.† The later Classical Period devoted much thought to the problem of civilisation. In the early Christian world and in the Middle Ages this question sank into the background, but with the Renaissance it came to the front again with renewed vigour. Civilisation has since

* This does not impart a cosmopolitan tendency to philosophy only but transforms thought in general. What Strabo says of Eratosthenes (at the end of the first book of *Geographica*) is worthy of note: ἐπὶ τέλει δὲ τοῦ ὑπομνήματος οὐκ ἐπαινέσας τοὺς δίχα διαιροῦντας ἅπαν τὸ τῶν ἀνθρώπων πλῆθος εἴς τε Ἕλληνας καὶ βαρβάρους.—βέλτιον εἶναί φησιν ἀρετῇ καὶ κακίᾳ διαιρεῖν ταῦτα. πολλοὺς γὰρ καὶ τῶν Ἑλλήνων εἶναι κακοὺς καὶ τῶν βαρβάρων ἀστείους. Strabo, on the other hand, defends the supremacy of the Greeks by explaining that, in their case, there is a predominance of legal order and cultivation, while with other nations there is the opposite state of affairs: τοῖς μὲν ἐπικρατεῖ τὸ νόμιμον καὶ τὸ παιδείας καὶ λόγων οἰκεῖον, τοῖς δὲ τἀναντία.

† Already, in the works of Plato and Aristotle, παιδεία had the further meaning of polite culture, cultivation, in addition to its ordinary significance of education. As an indication of this we see, for example, the Aristotelian conjunction: wealth, nobility, efficiency, culture (πλοῦτος, εὐγένεια, ἀρετή, παιδεία) *Pol.* 1291 b, 28 (see similarly 1293 b, 37: παιδεία καὶ εὐγένεια, 1296 b, 18: ἐλευθερία, πλοῦτος, παιδεία, εὐγένεια, 1317 b, 39: γένος, πλοῦτος, παιδεία). In Aristotle, πεπαιδευμένος and ἀπαίδευτος correspond completely to our "cultured" and "uncultured."

remained in the centre of spiritual work, and all the opposing forces of the Modern World have shared in the struggle raging around this centre. Idealism has endeavoured to build up civilisation from within, realism to piece it together from without. Artistic, intellectual, and ethical conceptions have cut across one another and struggled for the upper hand, while there has been no lack of all kinds of compromises. During the nineteenth century a co-operation of history and natural science has caused the older speculative treatment of these subjects to give way more and more to an exact scientific treatment. At the same time the psychical conditions on which civilised life depends have been more closely examined,* and whilst facts have accumulated without limit, the need for a conception of the whole has given rise to fresh attempts at a philosophy of civilisation. From among the very numerous problems and controversies thus originated we will at present pick out only those which directly touch the problem of life and spirit.

(b) Critical

1. The Nature and Value of Civilisation

Civilisation is one of those subjects which become more complicated the more we think about it. The concept should comprise everything which raises man and humanity above mere nature. But in what does this superiority of man to nature consist? Does it simply mean that man attains to a greater independence and power within a given existence, and that he is merely able to take a wider view of his environment while adapting it more skilfully to his purposes; or do we find in him an essentially new type of life, are new depths opened up, permitting him to construct a new domain of reality? In the former case the civilisation is no more than outward; in the latter it is inward. The one is a mere drilling and polishing of society; the other is a *true spiritual culture.* There can be no doubt as to the reality of the former; but the possibility of the latter has been sharply disputed.

* Upon this point, see Vierkandt's valuable work, *Naturvölker und Kulturvölker: Ein Beitrag zur Sozialpsychologie;* 1896.

If the content of civilisation be quite uncertain, the same may be said of its extent. It certainly includes a translating of human life into greater activity, nay, a founding of it upon personal action; this is indeed indicated by the expression *Kultur*, since it calls to mind the cultivation of a field in opposition to the wild and free growth of nature; but does this activity comprise everything which is in any way characteristic of man, or is it merely one aspect of life, side by side with which other possibilities may exist? An insecurity with regard to the relationship of religion and human culture in itself intimates the existence of a problem. Sometimes the former is ranked along with the latter, and religion seems to depend upon the state of civilisation; sometimes they are presented as contrasts, which cut across and impede one another, and it not infrequently occurs that civilisation is attacked from the point of view of religion, and at the same time religion from the point of view of civilisation.

The question of the value of civilisation occupies pretty much the same position. If it denotes everything which raises man above the level of uncultivated nature to that of cultivation and education, then it must appear the highest of all values, and anything which is to be in any way of value to us must rest upon it. At the same time, however, history is full of complaints as to the evils and dangers of civilisation, and sometimes these become so alarming that we are tempted to regard the whole of civilisation as a Danaean gift. In three directions, in particular, civilisation has from the earliest times been the object of severe attack.

From the standpoint of religion it was easy for civilisation to excite serious doubts, as it involved a strengthening of human power and an increase of human self-consciousness. The pious mind saw in the bold, upward effort of humanity an exaggeration of man's capacity, an overstepping of the bounds set by his nature, a lack of religious feeling. The evils and reverses of civilised life were hence interpreted as a punishment for such folly. A belief of this description is seen in the Babylonian stories of the Fall of Man and of the tower which was to reach to Heaven, also in the legend of Prometheus; as applied to an undue desire for knowledge, it is unmistakably present in the Faust legends.

Within the human sphere itself, however, there has often been no little doubt whether civilisation really brings man the happiness it so confidently promises him. It gives rise to a great complexity of life, it develops artificial needs, it makes man increasingly dependent upon his environment, it makes work and trouble for him, it arouses unattainable wishes and wild passions; taking all this into account, it may appear to be an uprooting of man from his native soil, a process which, in spite of all outward appearance of success, produces inward unhappiness. Ideas of this description have been current since the earliest times; they are to be met with, for example, among the ancient Jews, as is seen in Hosea and Isaiah.* The later Greek period was particularly full of doubts; a dislike of the refinement of contemporary civilisation, a yearning for simple conditions and a simple mode of life, became more and more widespread: the philosophers, in particular, gave expression to this mood, the Cynics in broader, and the Stoics in more refined fashion; the Belles Lettres, too, fell under its influence, and thereby proclaimed its extension to general social life.† In the Modern World Rousseau, in particular, placed the problem before humanity in the clearest possible manner; with his sensitive, excited, and exciting style he imperatively forced it upon the attention of modern society.

This threatened loss of happiness might somehow have been endured if at the same time there had been no doubt as to the growth of man's efficiency. But such was not the case. On the contrary, complaints as to a diminution of strength and efficiency, due to the progress of civilisation, usually accompanied those with regard to declining happiness. Civilisation, we are informed, weakens man, because it makes him dependent upon others; it assigns first place to the effects of his social

* Upon this point, see Budde, *Das nomadische Ideal im altem Testament* (*Preuss. Jahrbücher*, vol. 85).

† Interesting information upon this point is to be found in E. Rohde's *Der griechische Roman und seine Vorläufer.*

conduct, thereby placing outward achievement before feeling itself and threatening to reduce life, down to the most inward feelings, to the superficial and unreal. The individual comes more and more to play a mere part assigned to him by society, and his life grows increasingly alien to himself; it becomes a mere outward possession. Under these circumstances, how can man retain his greatness of soul, how can he be a true, strong, whole man?

At the same time civilisation does not lack its defenders. These evils, it is maintained, are no more than secondary phenomena, the shadows without which there could be no light. It is only man who drags down to pettiness, and thus makes doubtful, what is in itself great and of incontestable value.

Meanwhile civilisation lies within man's sphere of life. Is it not bound up with his human status, and will it be able in any way to raise itself above the petty routine of human affairs, while clearly dividing essential content from human addition, right from wrong? For the time being these doubts remain unsettled, and it continues to be an open question whether civilisation is a curse or a blessing to man.

2. The Problem of the Content of Civilisation

There can be no doubt that civilisation makes human existence depend to a very large extent on man's own activity; but the general concept of activity does not carry us at all far. Activity cannot attract its environment to itself and, transforming itself, impart its content to this environment, without more closely determining itself, without giving life a firm nucleus, a dominating tendency, a distinctive character. Thus the answer at once gives rise to a question. The resulting problem has been solved in very varying fashion during the development of the world's history. Different types of civilisation have resulted, not one of which seems to give full and permanent satisfaction, and yet it is impossible, taking into consideration their contradictory aims and values, to combine these together.

Within the development of civilisation as a whole there stand out more especially three definite and specific forms of culture—the artistic, the ethical, and the dynamic. These we see embodied in Hellenism, Christianity, and Modern Life. The central characteristic of the Hellenistic form was the combination of the elements furnished by nature to form a harmoniously arranged whole pervaded by an inner life. This combination, order, and vivification can come to man only as the result of his own activity, which must wrest a permanent and correlated conception of the world from sensuous impressions in a state of disintegration and movement; it sets the individual within the firm structure of a closed community, it binds together the separate forces and instincts of the soul (without surrendering or weakening anything whatever thereof) to a work of life as a whole; at every point it accomplishes a transformation from chaos to cosmos. This activity places nature and spirit in close and fruitful relationship, creates a powerful, active, and joyful life, ennobles and reconstitutes the whole cycle of existence. Questions and doubts, however, still remained. The whole rested upon the conviction that life was fundamentally possessed of a certain tendency towards reason, and this conviction grew more and more unstable. The form which in this type of civilisation dominated life could retain its position only so long as it possessed a soul, and this it did not seem capable of permanently preserving. Finally, the complications and perplexities of life came so much to the front, and man appeared so severely threatened in the innermost centre of his being, that his basic relationship to the world and the salvation of his soul became the most imperative of all tasks.

Christianity took this task upon itself. While fully recognising the negation, it undertook to lead man to a superior affirmation; in the midst of an immense upheaval it preserved fixed poles for life. This demanded an absolute concentration upon the ethical task. The problem was to build up a completely new life, as compared with immediate human existence; in opposition to the hardness and soullessness of the latter there was set up a kingdom of benevolent love and childlike surrender. In the development of this ideal a tremendous deepening of life resulted, invisible relationships opened up, and a great sensitiveness of feeling went hand in hand with profound earnestness; temporal and eternal, finite and infinite, human and divine, now came into closest contact. But as regards its historical position this mode of thought remained predominantly transcendent and won no secure hold within the environing world; this world remained unaffected and unpurified, side by side with a sphere of pure inwardness; in the retreat to a world of feeling the task of grappling with the resistant elements of existence was regarded as a secondary matter, and in this way the virility of the whole was endangered.

The Modern World, on the other hand, made this task the hinge upon which its whole activity turned. The first place in men's thoughts was now occupied by the idea of a complete overcoming of resistance, of a thorough rooting out of all that was obscure. The development and unlimited increase of life itself became the goal of goals, the all-sufficing happiness. Man now appeared in a fresh light. His chief distinction seemed to be his transcendence of all rigid limits, his ability continually to increase his own strength, to perpetually strike out new paths, to make ever fresh beginnings. The movement resulting therefrom gives rise to radically new conceptions of the universe, of social life, of the soul of the individual; it creates a new kind of work, a work which wins, for the first time, the consciousness of a superiority to the world. More than ever before man becomes the master of his existence; there results in every direction a process of revivification, an awakening of all that is latent, a liberation of all that is bound; on every hand life becomes a restless forward endeavour while spirit and strength immeasurably develop.

If the beneficent results of the foregoing are present to us in a thousand forms, there are also present the countless perplexities which this vivification and liberation has brought with it: much that is irrational has allied itself to the joyously progressive reason, and with the successful growth of spiritual life is involved so much petty human error and passion that the belief in modern civilisation as the sole source of happiness has become in the highest degree uncertain. It becomes increasingly impossible, too, to suppress the question whether, even in case the dynamic ideal should be realised, man can be entirely absorbed in it. For, as a thinking being, he surveys movement from a point outside it, comprehends it as a whole, and must demand from it a permanent furthering of his being; from this standpoint a civilisation which merely pushes incessantly and recklessly forward and never grants him a possession beyond the flux of time will become meaningless and intolerable.

All this is developed in sequence, but the successive phases do not simply replace one another; that which has outwardly vanished retains an inner presence and continues to exert an influence upon human life. Now the basic tendencies and general characters of these historical movements are so different that only a shallow type of thought could entertain the idea of a direct combination. Such a combination is all the less possible because the historical consciousness of the present day causes us to perceive distinctions with peculiar clearness. Thus the different solutions remain alien and alternative, waging warfare with one another, though for the most part not openly: the artistic type of civilisation finds the ethical narrow and gloomy, the dynamical formless and restless; the ethical inevitably regards the artistic as shallowly optimistic and fettered to nature, the dynamical as self-conscious and arrogant; the dynamical will find the others deficient in movement and progressive impetus. In the midst of all these contrasts stands the man of to-day. Will he not be borne down by them and spiritually depressed? He cannot unite these different types of civilisation; nor, to secure one, can he abandon the others; in order to do justice to each and eliminate its errors he must attain to a secure superiority, but he is not only lacking in such a superiority, he does not even see in which direction it is to be sought.

3. The Uncertainty in the Relationship of Man to Civilisation

Our perplexities become increased when we consider the relationship of man to civilisation. There seem to be only two possibilities—either civilisation must serve man or man must serve civilisation. Now, we may easily perceive that neither of these alternatives is possible.

If civilisation were a mere means for the welfare and comfort of man, then its growth would make his life more and more agreeable; an increase of civilisation would be synonymous with an increase of happiness. Such, however, is not the case. For, as far as its effect upon human comfort is concerned, civilisation seems to be injurious rather than beneficial; it gives rise to unlimited desires and demands unspeakable effort and labour, it surrounds us with perplexities, cares, and excitements, it hems us in with rigid limitations, it calls for obedience and sacrifice. That all this tends to make life smoother and more pleasurable can hardly be maintained. Mere comfort is far more likely to be found, and man is far more likely to feel contented, on lower levels of civilisation; moreover, individuals of lower spiritual susceptibility will secure this comfort far sooner than those who are more sensitive. If contented and agreeable existence were the highest goal, how greatly we civilised men should envy the careless ease of the Brazilian nigger's life! In the same sense it would be easy to show that spiritual movements which have made happiness the highest goal (such as Epicureanism and Utilitarianism) have done extraordinarily little to promote and build up the inner structure of civilisation. Given a certain state of civilisation, they may soften much that is hard and they may relieve much necessity, but it is not within their capacity essentially to elevate life or to strike out new paths.

There is only one alternative: to recognise civilisation as an end in itself, and to make man a mere means for its furtherance. In favour of such a conception is the impression of inward greatness which it conveys. Civilisation grows in incomparable fashion when, in thus becoming independent, it combines to a whole, and works with the force of an inner necessity of its own; man, moreover, in spite of all outward subordination, appears inwardly to do nought else but grow when he lays aside all care with regard to his own condition and surrenders himself wholly to the stream of the world's life. Hegel's system magnificently embodies this type of thought. But spreading far beyond the limits of this system, the view we are considering exerts no small power in modern life. Amidst all that is depressing in human circumstance and amidst the growth and decay of races, many are to-day comforted and sustained by the conviction that throughout all our toil and effort civilisation pursues a steady path, and that its gain imparts a meaning, a value, and a permanent character to the life and labour of those who work for it. "Many will come and go, but knowledge shall increase."

But however attractive this thought may be, it has not the capacity to prove victorious. For there is no such self-sufficing civilisation. A civilisation which attempts to cut itself completely loose from man, reducing him to a mere means, must itself collapse into nothingness. Civilisation exists only within the life of man, and if it is to mean something for the latter, man must have a spiritual self to express in and through the civilisation; if it is to enable man to obtain his full power it must allow him, in spite of every resistance, to achieve high ends. An impersonal civilisation, completely isolated from man, would be a ghost, a thing devoid of flesh and blood; in so far as it attained any reality in our minds it would lead us into error, bid us sacrifice ourselves for unknown ends, and deprive life of its soul. How could a hope in the future sustain us and encourage us to joyful effort in the labour and conflict of the present, if this future were nobody's affair, nobody's joy, nobody's advantage?

Our own age is making it continually and increasingly obvious that this self-abandonment of man to civilisation is absolutely impossible of accomplishment. Above all the speed and racket of the machinery of civilisation there breaks out with ever-increasing loudness the call for the furtherance and development of the living man, for the building-up of the soul, for the salvation of the spiritual self. We recognise at the same time that this is indispensable for the truth and depth of civilisation itself. Such experiences teach us clearly enough that man is no mere receptacle for civilised life, that the latter does not shape him like wax this way or that according to its needs, but that he has an independent nature with which to oppose it, a nature which cannot give up its right to satisfaction. Civilisation does not progress along a definite path, propelled by an indwelling compulsion; on the contrary, it appears that its specific form is continually ageing and decaying. New beginnings are continually necessary, and new uprisings of original life; above all else, however, new men. Consider, for example, the close of the Ancient Period; the life of civilisation did not regain vigour until new races took it up and brought new forces to its rejuvenation. Will such a rejuvenation be necessary for the present day, and will it come through new races or through freshly awakened, spiritually less exhausted classes?

'Whatever may be thought of the foregoing, the living man maintains his independence in the face of every attempt to reduce him to a mere tool. But on the other hand civilisation, as we have seen, must not sink to a mere means unless it is to suffer disintegration. Thus we find ourselves in a difficult dilemma from which we must escape, and yet we do not at first see how escape is possible. On the average level of life we are to-day driven now to this side, now to that; we oscillate helplessly between empty subjectivity and soulless work.

All these perplexities combine in the life of to-day and mutually aggravate one another. The most painful effect of all is that produced by the insecurity we feel concerning the relationship of man to civilisation, by the lack of a comprehensive and guiding purpose to make the work of civilisation man's own concern, the preservation of his spiritual self an imperative necessity; a purpose which would, at the same time, lift its object above the petty human routine to which we otherwise fall helpless victims. It is this spiritual poverty alone which prevents us from striving for a new and distinctive type of human culture, capable of holding its own against the various formations which exert their influence upon us from a more or less remote past, taking possession of us yet not fully satisfying us. In all the confusion which thus results the value and essential nature of civilisation itself finally becomes uncertain. Ingenious reflection scantily enough conceals that lack of real substance from which the whole suffers, and we are put off with fine-sounding speeches and artificially elaborated " points of view." All this mere veneer of civilisation and culture, more especially as we see it in our great cities, ultimately grows intolerable; the gap between what is declared to be the goal and what is really pursued as such becomes wider and wider, and in this way the untruthfulness of life grows greater and greater. This must be resisted. The growing discontent shows clearly enough that a reaction is already in progress.

(c) The Requirements of a True Civilisation

1. THE NECESSITY OF A DEEPER FOUNDATION

In such movements and upheavals as these, philosophy may play ever so modest a rôle, but it cannot withdraw from the struggle. It will be its particular task to discover the direction in which our endeavour is to press forward in order again to convert life from a "business" to an "existence" (J. Burckhardt). For this purpose it is in the first place necessary that civilisation should proceed from ourselves, that it should become an imperative necessity of our self-preservation, and yet not succumb, in the making, to the petty allurements of mere pleasure. Now, our conception of spiritual life and its relationship to man offers a practicable path towards this end. For spiritual life, as we represent it, grows towards independence, and the civilisation which subserves its development will be liberated from the soullessness of the human treadmill and placed upon a deeper foundation, while at the same time it will not be alienated from man; for in accordance with his specific nature man will discover his true being and realise the possibility of a genuine selfhood only in spiritual life as a whole. Looked at in this way, man does not take part in the work of civilisation for any alien ends, but rather to realise his own purpose, and he is able even in the furthest extension of his activities to control these from a central point. Hence, spiritual life, in our sense, unites man and civilisation in the closest possible manner without directly fusing one into the other and thus surrendering one to the other. It should be more especially emphasised that the union does not in this case appear as a ready-made fact, conveniently occurring for our benefit, but as a high ideal awakening the whole of life and stirring it to activity. In this connection civilisation appears as our co-operation in a great movement of the universe, whereby reality advances to a higher stage, the stage of spiritual freedom. Hence the power of the whole stands behind our work and operates within it.

When civilisation is thus understood as the *development of an independent spiritual life,* something far more is signified than a slight alteration of tendency or a mere change of name. For so understood it permits of the fulfilment of demands essential to all genuine cultural aspirations, demands which the current conception entirely fails to satisfy.

Thus, for the first time, the contents and values which inspire the work of civilisation find their independence made possible. If civilisation were a process circumscribed by purely human ends, it would have no standard other than the human; there would be no splitting and dividing of the chaos which surrounds us, nor could civilisation impress our human existence with the constraining force of its ideals; it would then lack all power to rouse and propel. The matter takes on quite a different complexion, however, if in civilisation we recognise a movement which transcends the merely human and is alone capable of revealing to man the core of his own being.

Further, unless civilisation be based upon independent spiritual life it can acquire no genuine greatness. For if life remain entirely confined to the merely human, and we do not pass beyond absorption in our own immediate concerns into a life that is confluent with the whole of reality, we may wax ever so enthusiastic over greatness, may devise complex distinctions, and may in a spirit of pride and vanity raise ourselves or our class above the common herd; none the less in reality there is no elevation but only littleness, a littleness which displays itself more particularly in its illusion of greatness. Within this merely human circle there is no sublimity, no genuine greatness, nothing which can command reverence and elevate while it subdues. For this purpose there must arise in man something that is more than human, something to which he is compelled to attribute a complete superiority; yet he must be able to regard this as in some manner belonging to himself. Only from this position will a true elevation of his being be possible, and with it the greatest of all liberations—the freeing of life from the narrowness of the merely human.

This superhuman in man is the source of all true greatness, and it alone preserves civilisation from becoming a mere man worship, whether of individuals or of men in the mass. We must never forget Kant's words, "All things, even the most sublime, grow small under the hands of men when they turn the ideas thereof to their own use."

Further, with regard to the spontaneity of civilised life it is clear that the present time cannot dispense with a new stage of reality. For if civilisation is nothing more than a human addition to nature, its progress must carry it continually further and further away from its basis, and its content must grow more and more artificial and complex. Civilisation will then subject life to increasingly rigid limitations, close up more and more possibilities, and make life less and less spontaneous: in this way it will become the destroyer of all youthful freshness and all originality. Can we wonder that when humanity, at any particular period, awakens to a special consciousness of this it sets itself against it, and just as the individual would often like to recover the freshness and rich possibilities of childhood, it yearns with its whole soul for a return to nature, to the most primitive beginnings. But it is forbidden for mankind to return to nature; it is as impossible as for the individual to go back to childhood. The effect of history can never be obliterated. So we must resign ourselves to see civilisation grow progressively more senile and more lifeless, to see humanity sink into the same unprofitable Philistinism in great things, as is the fate of most individuals in small ones, unless it be possible for something original and new to reveal itself, for new forces to come into play, for new possibilities to open up. These things cannot take place, however, unless life possesses a spiritual depth, which in the midst of all that is exhausted and obsolete in mere human civilisation, provides us with new beginnings, produces simple units, and opens up a new world in simple things. When we say, however, that everything great is simple, we have in mind a simplicity very different from the mere naïveté of nature's first beginnings.

Finally, civilisation lacks the necessary motive force if it merely adds something to a given world instead of opening up a new and, to us, indispensable world. Nothing can powerfully rouse us and move us with constraining force except the consciousness and experience of contradiction in our own life and the impossibility of allowing things to remain in this condition. A civilisation which merely embroiders and decorates life can never give rise to such contradiction. That addition to life which it desires may be rejected at will, or it may pass off from us like water from a duck's back ; as a matter of fact, the common run of life is inwardly exceedingly indifferent to civilisation, and receives it more as a social compulsion than as an inward joy. That it should have been otherwise at the great epochs of creative genius, and that such creation should have been possible at all, is due to this, that at these times work was looked upon as the winning of a truly spiritual life and hence of spiritual freedom, and also to this consideration, that when once such desire made itself felt, existing conditions no longer seemed tolerable, silencing, as they did, an imperative call to self-preservation. It was this call which infused into the endeavour of the ages a passionate warmth, a warmth which knew no care for man, was ready for any sacrifice, and drew back before no obstacle.

Through all these queries there runs one and the same problem, one and the same antithesis—that of a genuine and a sham civilisation. *Civilisation is genuine only in as far as it preserves its relationship with the basic spiritual life and serves its development*, and becomes false as soon as it subordinates itself to the aims of the mere man and drags spiritual life down with it to the same low level. The conflict between these two forces, spirit and man, runs through the whole of history and forces us to perceive in it something other than a pure triumph of spirit. To-day, however, it is peculiarly needful that the ancient truth should be more clearly laid hold of, that the necessary condition of a genuine civilisation should be more definitely recognised, and that the division of forces for and against should be more decisively declared.

2. The Necessity of an Inner Development of Civilisation

It must already be sufficiently obvious that we need a further development of civilisation, and that there is a particular direction in which this is to be sought. We are affected by the great practical ideals of history, none of which we feel ourselves able to abandon, yet we have no synthesis which directly comprises these ideals. What else remains, then, but to look about us and see if there is not a life-movement at hand capable of being further strengthened, a movement which may lift us above the existing antitheses and make it possible to struggle against them, a movement at the same time universal enough to extend itself over the whole of life and divide its content into "for" and "against" and characteristic enough to impart a specific form to everything which it comprises. In this life-movement an original presence must be accessible and present to each individual consciousness, and this presence must extend an awakening and formative influence over the whole of life.

Now, such a dominating original factor is not to be found in this or that appurtenance of spiritual life, in this or that spiritual achievement, but in *spiritual life itself*, as we understand it—the movement of reality towards spiritual freedom. Only in spiritual freedom is true being reached at all; everything else is but the shadow of it. Such being cannot lie outside activity, but only within it, and it issues out of the depths of activity as it organises itself to a self-subsisting whole and passes, as a whole, into a variety of particular functions. In this way, alone, is the ascent of mere life to self-life achieved; or, better still, it is in this way, alone, that the contradiction which is otherwise involved in the very concept of life is overcome. For is it not a contradiction that a certain inwardness should come into being and yet remain continually bound down to what is alien, never attaining to independence?*
Only after taking up this position does the concept of life-

---

* For anything further I must refer the reader to my systematic works, and in the first instance to the *Grundlinien einer neuen Lebensanschauung* [*Life's Basis and Life's Ideal*, Eng. trans. by Alban Widgery; pub. A. & C. Black.]

contents become intelligible; the concept of value, too, now distinctly separates itself for the first time from the lower grade of pleasure. From this point of view all activity falls under the antithesis of real and unreal, independent and dependent, and at the same time we have to face a far-reaching task, namely, the elimination of the customary confusion which obliterates all distinction between the two types and the definite elaboration of the demands associated with the formation of an essential being, and, finally, the carrying through of these indispensable demands. Only those elements in civilisation will then reckon as genuine which further the formation of an essential being and involve an extension of spiritual reality, and with it of our own true self; everything else, however pretentiously it may assert itself, thus sinks to a merely human level, to a burlesque of civilisation. In so far, however, as this formation of essential being is successful, it must produce a thoroughgoing consolidation and deepening of existence: the chief sentiment in life then becomes the desire for truthfulness, for a liberation from all show and sham.

Hence results a specific type of life, rigid in its demands and powerful in enforcing them. Within its sphere, however, there remains room for manifold movement, for the transition towards spiritual freedom must be consummated under the conditions and restrictions of human existence; hence a plurality of points of attack becomes possible, nay, indispensable. We men are bound down to immediate sensuous existence, and remain dependent upon it for the continuance of life. We cannot simply separate ourselves from it, master the essential unity of life, and from this standpoint unravel the whole of reality; for when we have transferred ourselves to this standpoint we must still continue to occupy ourselves with the old sense immediacies and adjust ourselves to them. Thus there ensues a sharp conflict between the demand to work from the whole for the whole, the propulsion through the inner power of truth inherent in all true spiritual life and creation, on the one hand; and, on the other, the natural impulse of self-preservation, which, being blent with spiritual forces, increases to a boundless egoism: a complete transformation of feeling now becomes indispensable, and shows itself to be the fundamental condition of all really genuine spiritual life. This raises the ethical task high above all others. At the same time artistic activity, with its formative power, makes its specific value felt. That measure of spirituality which strives upward in man, exists, in the first place, side by side with crude and soulless existence; hence it easily remains in a condition of semi-reality. Artistic construction (which reaches far beyond art in the stricter sense of the word) alone enables the different sides and stages to mutually influence one another, and in thus bringing them into contact is able to give shape to the inward and to impart soul to the outward, thus effecting an integration of life. Without art there is no thorough spiritualisation of life. If we lack its formative and ennobling activity, even the most eager and rapid ethical advance will not be able to preserve life from barbarism. Finally the task of enhancing the vitality of life asserts also an incontestable right. To spiritual life belong absoluteness, infinity, complete control of reality, while man, in his immediate sense-existence, lives subject to innumerable conditions and limitations; compared with the spiritual task required of him he is miserably narrow and weak. Hence it is necessary that his power should be augmented, his existence enlarged, all his latent faculties aroused. Can we wonder that certain epochs took this to be the whole object of civilisation?

Such a juxtaposition of different lines of life must result in sharp tension and severe conflict. This is by no means due to mere error and misunderstanding on the part of man, for none of the tasks in question permits of being taken up with complete devotion and pursued with full intensity without coming to figure as an end in itself and being felt at the moment of action to be the main affair of life. It thus becomes comprehensible that human life, as a whole, is not merely affected by the operation of ethical, artistic, and dynamic impulses, but that specific types of civilisation are built up and compete for the mastery. Compromises and diluted forms are here powerless; they only too easily depress the level of life. But if it be impossible to avoid the struggle, and if its cessation is not even to be wished for, it becomes all the more desirable that something superior to the conflict should remain and wage conflict against mere conflict. This can be done, however, only by bringing into vital operation that essential being which experiences itself in and through every difference, which refers what is variously achieved back to a superior unity, and from that standpoint applies its standards and works towards a synthesis. All these movements are now oriented towards the development of a self-dependent, essential, spiritual life and spiritual reality: here a life-space is provided in which to meet and adjust their differences. Nor do we find ourselves powerless in the face of this or that conflict; we can work towards harmony, we can oppose the formation of mere partial civilisations by the development of a *whole* civilisation.

The partial civilisations, with the work they have accomplished, thus find themselves face to face with a sharp alternative: shall they establish relationship with the depth and wholeness of life (for only through moving in the direction of depth does life become a whole), or shall they detach themselves from the foundations of life and so become more and more dispersed? The two decisions imply diametrically opposite developments. In the one case we have a real, in the other an unreal type of civilisation. In the one case an adoption and assimilation of the experiences and destinies of the whole man, and with this a full-fledged development, in the other an unchartered freedom of function and therewith a great vagueness; in the former case, an elevation above everything pettily human, or at least a brave resistance to it, in the other, a spiritual defencelessness over against merely human culture. Thus, in the absence of a real spiritual world, the ethical movement of life tends to degenerate into a mere system of laws and formulas, to favour narrowness and oppression and to sink into a self-righteous Pharisaism. The artistic tendency, when left to itself, inevitably leads to sensuality, indulgence, flippancy; the dynamic to egoism, wildness, brutality. The truth of the partial civilisations themselves depends upon their having a whole and essential civilisation behind them, upon that deeper foundation of civilisation which is only possible through union with an independent spiritual life.

In the following sections we shall be considering the consequences and requirements which flow from the idea of a civilisation at once real and universal in contrast to the immediate position of civilisation. Civilisation will have to be studied through its means and vehicles as well as through its content. On the one hand we shall have to discuss the problems of history and society, on the other, those of art and morality, in their manifold relationships. Point for point we shall see that this idea of a spiritual civilisation is no mere matter of a new name, but of a new thing and of a new task.

At this juncture we will refer to one point only; the world's present state makes it in the highest degree imperative that civilisation should be based upon a more solid foundation. The situation has become critical, more particularly through a coincidence of two facts. In the first place, the foundations and traditions of civilisation, as handed down to us by history, have become very insecure, in as far, at least, as they affect man's inward life as a whole: this has occurred mainly because we now feel the older type to be too anthropomorphic, too pettily human, and we therefore become doubtful whether man can in any way overstep the confines of natural sense-existence, and whether the whole of that "more than human" which he believed himself to lay hold of be not a mere mirage, a product of human delusion. This doubt enters very deeply into life, far more deeply than those imagine who, while depriving the world of all spirituality, delude themselves into believing that they can at the same time preserve an ideality for man. For in reality the one stands or falls with the other. It is impossible to preserve here and there and subjectively what has been abandoned as concerns the whole and in its real essence. Thus we have become insecure with regard to all our ideals, nay, with regard to our own being; we no longer draw upon a common groundwork of convictions, of uniting, directing, elevating forces. In spite of all subjective activity, an inner decline of life is unavoidable if this uncertainty continues to spread. In the second place, we perceive in the very midst of this shifting and wavering age a violent surging forward of the masses towards a full participation in civilisation and happiness. This movement is accompanied by a claim on the part of the masses to form their own judgment as to what elements in civilisation possess content and value, and to form it according to the immediate impression and power of comprehension of individuals who have scarcely been in the least affected by the great historical movements and experiences of humanity. Now this inner insecurity on the part of the existing systems of civilisation, in particular the fact that they are weighted down with much that is obsolete and effete, makes them incapable of meeting this demand of the masses with an irrefragable truth and thus guiding it into safe paths. Hence this movement threatens to carry everything before it; and indeed it already operates in a vulgarising, shallowing, narrowing, and negating fashion.

There is absolutely nothing which can lead us beyond such a crisis except a new growth of life, *a deepening of spiritual life in itself*, a discovery of inner facts and inner relationships. Salvation cannot come from without. We can replace the props and helps which have thus been irreparably lost only by an inner strengthening, by ourselves attaining to a superior world, fortifying ourselves therein, and thence imparting a content to our life and building up a new civilisation. If such a deepening and strengthening is successful, then the threatening crisis may lead to a renewal and rejuvenation of life, and, in spite of all human error, provide existence with a greater content of truth. If, on the other hand, there exists no possibility of such a deepening, of an uprising of elemental, originative forces, if in human existence there is no real spiritual world to be revivified, then all hope of a happy issue vanishes. In this case reason and civilisation must remain the slaves of human selfishness and passion.

2. HISTORY

(a) Towards the Development of the Problem

OUR relationship towards history is to-day full of confusion; we depend upon history and derive nourishment from it, yet at the same time we feel our life to be severely oppressed by it, we think of it as a burden which we should like to cast off. In attempting to thus cast it off, however, we find ourselves threatened by the vacuity of the mere moment, and fleeing from this danger we return to history. Thus we waver between the two, a position which makes purposeful action and happy creation impossible of success. Let us examine a little more closely the causes which have brought us to this unfortunate pass.

In its relationship to history the nineteenth century was dominated by a reaction from the rationalistic tendency of the Enlightenment. Modern humanity had sought to escape from its perplexing circumstances by returning to universal, indwelling reason; nothing seemed capable of liberating human existence from obsolete and erroneous elements except a vigorous enlivenment of this reason; this alone promised to lift life above childish prejudice and stupid limitation and to bring it to full maturity and clarity. The past and its authority receded before this claim to place life and activity in a timeless present of thought. Undisturbed by tradition, and for the most part in conscious opposition to it, reason created a "natural" religion, a "natural" morality, a "natural" social economy, and a "natural" education. This movement exerted an irresistible influence over men's minds and played a great part in the construction of life. In this way much freshness, freedom, and independence was acquired, and in spite of all hostility and obscuration, this could not again be lost.

But from the very beginning this tendency contained problematical elements. In course of time these increased and finally brought about a reaction. The youthful sense of power with which the Enlightenment commenced gave it joyful confidence; it felt itself drawing near to an absolute truth. This confidence of victory in its opposition to the traditional position was due to a firm belief in the direct control of reason in reality and in humanity; it was thought that this reason existed in each individual and was easily attainable by a powerful self-recollection. A clarification, an elevation to full consciousness, seemed sufficient of itself to secure the mastery of the good and true. This had the effect of concentrating the work of life chiefly upon thought and knowledge, so that human culture acquired a onesidedly intellectual character. As the first rapid advance ceased, life became more and more dominated by an isolated intellectualism which placed its considerations and aims between man and things themselves and thereby increasingly endangered man's inner relations with the world and the directness of his life. The reality which thus resulted was finally felt to be too narrow and soulless: the life-impulse revolted and demanded more content as well as more manifestation of the whole man. The historical tendency formed a main feature of this new life.

The motive force behind this historical movement was supplied, in the first place, by a thirst for an increased reality, for a broader groundwork of existence, for more objectivity, for a greater fullness of life, and for a more extensive linking up of manifoldness in great relationships. How much richer in content life thereby became is seen in all its particular spheres, such as religion and art, law and science: an infinitely increased quantity of reality, which would otherwise have remained unused, is here associated with personal action. Work as a whole produces a historical mode of thought and thereby alters the character of life. Man no longer tears himself apart from his environment and places himself over against it, to master it, as if it were something quite alien, as was the case during the Enlightenment, but he yearns after an inner union with the environment so that its life may flow over into his and lift him above all pettiness. Hence his existence grows not only wider but more restful. Man finds a reason in things, to whose guidance he may confidently trust himself. This has, moreover, the further effect of bringing earlier ages close to him and allowing manifold relationships to become apparent in them, while his own age appears as the summit of a united structure comprising all ages; from this summit everything earlier appears as a gradual ascent and the lower levels become interesting, not so much on account of the differences and contrasts they afford, as on account of their significance as ascending preparatory stages. When the sharpness and hardness of an absolute valuation, such as was characteristic of the Reformation and of the Enlightenment, gives way to a more universal and harmonising mode of thought, then there is room for more understanding and more love. The Mediæval period, perhaps more than any other, has experienced a very drastic alteration in treatment.

This more relative treatment did not at first by any means signify a sinking to relativism and an abandonment of an absolute truth. For a spirit of proud self-consciousness permitted the spiritual strength of the period to feel itself equal to the assimilation of any influx of matter. According to the philosophical mode of thought, at any rate, reason, while itself undergoing an inner expansion, drew history to itself rather than subjected itself to history. This mode of thought found its most magnificent and systematic expression in the historical philosophy of Hegel. All tension between reason and history now seemed happily overcome, since the latter became totally converted into the development of reason, while in this same development reason found its own essential nature.

Whatever doubts may be suggested by this construction of history, the superiority of reason and hence of spiritual activity is most decidedly preserved. The treatment of history which was developed by the Romantic School was not so much directed towards this end. The movement of history was now looked upon as resulting from an unconscious guiding and formative force; independently of human effort, there flowed, out of the past, a stream of reason which swept man securely along.

Floating upon this stream his life and work seem to be guided into safe channels. This weakened the activity and interfered with the right of the living present: men made themselves at home in past ages, at the same time idealising these, and they were apt to shut their eyes to the tasks of their own age. Even at this stage, there appeared the danger of the power of association and appropriation not corresponding to the enlargement of the sphere of vision produced by history, and therefore of man acquiring outward gain while suffering a loss at the centre of his life.

Then came the tendency peculiar to the nineteenth century: a turning away from the problems of the inner man and of spiritual creation towards *work*, with its concern for the things themselves in their objectivity. In the case of history this brought about a victorious progress of exact research as opposed to construction in general outlines. This tendency acquired a special consciousness in Germany, since here it had first to fight for its rights against the predominance of the speculative treatment. The Hegelian construction of history, in particular, found itself opposed by a desire for more width, actuality, and individuality; even from the outward point of view this conception seemed too narrow, for its concepts, at bottom, comprised only the European world of civilisation and were more particularly concerned with the contrast between the Ancient and Modern Worlds; it suffered further from an inner narrowness, since in squeezing the individual phenomena into its dialectical framework it was bound to very seriously weaken their individuality and positivity. The new desire for pure and unlimited actuality saw, in this, a forcing and a falsification of the things. With all the greater eagerness recourse was had to historical investigation as a liberation from this state of affairs.

This historical research has exceedingly well understood how to convert the desire for breadth and actuality into work and achievement: it has elaborated new methods for its work, and through content and form it has produced a specific mode of thought which is a powerful influence in the life of the Modern World. This research does not make the slightest claim to be philosophy. Its chief desire is to free history from all philosophical tutelage and make it entirely self-reliant: yet this tendency could not possibly have made such victorious progress and won such whole-hearted devotion unless it both carried in itself and aroused definite convictions. Research cannot develop and defend the desire for pure actuality without perceiving how much there is lying between man and this actuality, without becoming aware of much subjectivity—in tradition as well as in man's own apprehension. Hence an energetic struggle was undertaken with the object of eliminating this subjectivity, its success permitting life to become calmer and clearer. This tendency towards actuality had the effect of revealing a boundless wealth of individual formations and it thus ceased to be possible to string the course of the ages on a single thread, the new insight rather revealing a vast network of confused threads, hardly to be disentangled. The incapacity of man to grasp all this from within and convert it into simple concepts now became evident, and he was thus compelled to adopt a more modest and restrained attitude; no longer could he satisfy his desire to adjust and round off the facts to suit his own point of view. But since instead of ruling he now had to serve, his life experienced an immeasurable enrichment, a thoroughgoing liberation from the ancient narrowness.

At first all this was regarded as pure profit, free from complication. But perplexities very soon became apparent. The gain in knowledge threatened to bring with it a loss of life. The objectivity demanded was seen to be a by no means simple thing: if this pure actuality applies only to the things in themselves without any reference to the subject, apart from any action of thought, then everything inward which appertains to them would have to be abandoned, for nothing of this nature can be comprehended at all without a putting forth of personal thought, without an exercise of sympathetic understanding.

Moreover, a distinction between big and little, essential and non-essential, in history is really impossible without standards, and these standards must have their origin in some conviction as a whole.* A history deprived of all inwardness and all

* In this connection see Arvid Grotenfelt's excellent works, *Die Wertschätzung in der Geschichte* (1903) and *Geschichtliche Wertmassstäbe in der Geschichtsphilosophie bei Historikern und im Volksbewusstsein* 1905). These exhibit a calm, judicial, and independent judgment.

gradation must become a mere chaotic sequence of events and would hardly be worthy of the name of science. The recent and ever-increasing conflict with regard to the main content and motive forces of history very well exhibits how little history, in spite of all attempts to reject philosophy, can dispense with certain fundamental convictions. But when all philosophy has been put aside, whence are these convictions to come? There are two ways in which the age has endeavoured to meet these difficulties or rather to evade them.

On the one hand the very speculative mode of thought which as a whole is so decisively rejected is unmistakably maintaining a certain influence, albeit in a weakened form and in a manner which is not outwardly obvious. Hegel is set aside, yet some sort of indwelling of reason in history, some sort of inner necessity of progress, some sort of domination of intelligence in the historical process is unquestioningly retained. This is but a portion of a more general phenomenon which to-day confronts us. The pantheistic mode of thought produced by the development of the Modern World was formerly backed up by a firm conviction and a joyful life-temper; to-day it still makes itself felt in various ways, although the foundation has ceased to be secure; concepts like spirit, reason, progress, humanity, remain with us, turn our thought in certain directions and provide it with certain values: the difference is that, following upon the destruction of the foundation, everything has become pale and vague; living forces have become shadowy conceptions, and fruitful ideas have degenerated into empty phrases. The whole must become more and more untrue the more we are influenced by convictions directly contradicting the fundamental conviction. The most powerful contradictory tendency is pessimism, which spread more and more during the nineteenth century; since it clearly brings to light the obscure and unreasonable element in the world and in history, pessimism pitilessly destroys the illumination and glamour with which pantheism enveloped existence; it is so energetic in bringing before our eyes new groups of facts and new aspects of the whole that the old belief in the rationality of reality cannot remain undisturbed. In this connection we notice a remarkable contradiction: the mood of humanity becomes heavier, man and fate create an impression which is on the whole gloomier, the contradictions of existence are sharply forced upon our attention; yet along with all this the work of the period retains the pantheistic mode of thought with its idealisation of things, clinging to it as to the sole possible prop which can save it from total collapse. This co-existence of pessimism, on the one hand, and optimism, on the other, affords an example of that division of soul and work, of that cleaving in two of the whole man, from which modern life suffers.

But there is yet another way in which the present-day meets this problem. It has no particular type of thought with which it confronts the ages; it endeavours to pass judgment upon them and gain a standard for them, relying solely upon the ages themselves, and through the ages themselves it strives to develop and demonstrate what has been thus obtained. Present-day research would like to sink itself so wholly in the ages it studies that they should be understood and valued solely through their own type of thought. In this direction much important work has been accomplished. No previous age has been so ready and skilful in giving other ages their full rights, in wresting from them their most inner purpose, in abstaining from the forcing of relationships upon them from without, while drawing such relationships forth from their own work and desire; no previous age has shown a greater facility in placing itself with equal sympathy in the most difficult and contradictory positions. Later ages will be able to judge better than can we ourselves as to whether, in this endeavour, we do really strip ourselves of everything that is peculiarly our own, whether in spite of every precaution our supposed objectivity is not mingled with subjectivity: it is clear enough that we ourselves, as a result of this attitude, are exposed to danger and injury through the weakening of our own purpose and being consequent upon this very facility in coming into contact with, and adapting ourselves to, strange positions. Our immeasurable enlargement of horizon permits all sorts of different elements to pour in upon us, impress themselves upon us and overmaster us. Our souls become stages upon which all sorts of characters appear and play their parts. We forget that the extension of our circle of ideas by no means carries with it an enlargement of our life. We incline to substitute scholarly knowledge for spiritual life. This life of sympathetic understanding, which, after all, is never more than a half-life, leads us into the danger of increasingly surrendering a full life of our own, a life of clear thought and firm will. We are greatly concerned to discover the spiritual syntheses occurring in former ages, but we are incapable of completing a spiritual synthesis for our own age!

Our weakness becomes apparent chiefly in the attempt to establish a connection between the past and the present, between bygone aspirations and our own. We feel ourselves safely at home in the past, we see clearly how everything has come to pass, how one thing resulted and could not but result from another, and we follow this line of thought down to the threshold of our own period; only one short step and the connection would be established, the result of all the long labour would communicate itself to us and be converted into personal life. But, remarkable though it may seem, we do not succeed in taking this short step. The gap remains, and knowledge and life are not brought together. Nay, the progress of historical knowledge actually hinders the connection of history with life. For the more clearly science exhibits the specific character of bygone periods, the more it becomes apparent that their contents have depended upon special conditions, the more definite are seen to be the boundaries which separate one age and mode of thought from another, the more impossible it is seen to be that there should be a simple flowing-over of strange life into the specific life of a given period. The fact that historical investigation dwells with peculiar zest upon remote ages, and there achieves its most brilliant triumphs, is another example of the separation between knowledge and life. In studying the remote past we are less concerned with the state of affairs in our own life; the nearer, however, we draw to the present day, the more unavoidable our own problem becomes, and the more painful our own insecurity.

This gap between knowledge and life, between the preliminary conditions of spiritual life and spiritual life itself, is at its widest in the sphere of religion. Religious investigation has to-day made immense progress; in particular it has placed the great religions and their various phases before our eyes with greatly increased clearness and has presented us with a wealth of living facts and details. Yet how defenceless we are when confronted with all this actuality, how little our own religious convictions and religious life profit by it, how great is our helplessness in this respect! And this helplessness will continue as long as we do not find the power to effect a personal construction of life. It is history, in the first place, which prevents us from finding such a power. History allows us to cling to the mere appearance of a possession. Through a perpetual occupation with bygone things it distracts us from our own thought and responsibility, giving us learning in place of life.

It is therefore no wonder if from time to time there arises a passionate anti-historical movement, and that to-day a feeling of anger against an enervating historicism, confined, as it is, to a mere half-life, is gaining ground. "Cast away from thyself the yoke of the past and set thy life wholly in the present; then it will again grow fresh and genuine, then, at last, will it become thine *own* life." But such a casting away is no simple matter, and moreover the attempted liberation involves the loss of much with which we can hardly dispense! In reality history holds us much faster than its opponents imagine; it holds us fast even against our own wills. For the opposition is itself a product of a historical situation and derives a specific colour therefrom; its negation is concerned with particular evils and its affirmation is subject also to contemporary influences. Such a historical dependence, even on the part of anti-historical movements, is clearly perceived as soon as the course of time has given us a sufficient perspective: for example, how quickly has the Enlightenment, which wished to do away with all historical relations and to build up life solely upon timeless reason, itself become a historical quantity, a past category; how much of its work now impresses us as belonging to a remote past! In reviewing history as a whole we notice a kind of cyclic movement:

now there is a period when historical relationships are sought, now one when they are rejected; this observation may well convince us that the negative attitude is just as much a historical phenomenon as is the affirmative, and that the passionate attack upon history, with its tendency to assert the opposite of what is transmitted to us, does not produce true independence so much as a different kind of dependence.

At the same time, it makes no inconsiderable difference whether the conscious aspiration of man goes with history or against it. In the latter case we are called upon to build up our lives solely upon the immediate present and to recognise as true only that which is convincing to the thought and feeling of each individual. But will not this limitation cause life to become narrow and poor? If that which is present to the mere individual is alone reckoned as the measure of all things, will not life inevitably become superficial and split up into numerous separate phenomena? In this way will not the inner independence, the spiritual character of life, suffer the severest injury? The Enlightenment provides us with a clear demonstration of this. For it did not succeed in establishing a firmly grounded spiritual world equal to nature, and those of its thinkers who most energetically maintained the superiority of spiritual life as compared with nature continually succumbed, in the construction of their thought-worlds, to the influence of natural concepts; this was certainly partly due to the fact that they thought themselves able to despise history with its rich content, its fixed relationships, and its deepening experiences. Unless the inner life can itself attain to a super-subjective integration it would seem that it cannot prevail against the unlimited world which so overpoweringly presses upon us from without. For this purpose, however, history is essential. Further, we must ask ourselves if the attempt to place life entirely in the present must not destroy itself, since the present is ever changing; to-day soon becomes yesterday, and thus the whole threatens ultimately to be reduced to nothing. We are certainly protected from this last extreme by the circumstance that, as we have seen, history holds man fast even against his own intention. But does not the matter then amount to this:

that so far as we rid ourselves of history we volatilise life, so far, however, as history retains a content for us we unwillingly affirm the very history from which a liberation appeared indispensable to the power and reality of life?

It follows that we find ourselves in a highly complicated position—nay, in an intolerable dilemma. We can neither retain history nor dispense with it. When we shake it off we fall into emptiness, when we submit to it we enter upon a shadow-life. Under these circumstances the average type of mind may have recourse to compromises and find satisfaction in a middle course between freedom and submission, but a more energetic mode of thought will thoroughly realise the impossibility of compromise and demand an overcoming of the antithesis. Is it possible, however, to effect a liberation from history which shall, at the same time, signify a reconciliation with history? *Can life attain to something beyond history and at the same time leave history a value?* Can we conceive of a type of life which does not unstably waver between the rationalism of the eighteenth century and the historicism of the nineteenth, but is able, in building up an independent type, to recognise and at the same time to limit the rights of each? This is certainly not to be attained without thoroughgoing transformations of first appearances and energetic further constructions of life. Let us see if our investigation as a whole affords points of approach for this task.*

(b) Demands and Prospects

The next question is, whether human life is in any way capable of freeing itself from history and independently confronting it. The answer will depend upon what our position is with regard to human life as a whole. It necessarily involves a

---

* The discussion will remain confined entirely to this one main point. For a further treatment, see my outline of the " Philosophy of History " in the *Kultur der Gegenwart* (volume entitled *Systematische Philosophie*). That the content of history, together with our relation to history, has again become insecure is clearly indicated by the uprising of manifold disputable points and by the passion to which their treatment gives rise. Otherwise how could the philosophy of history have again come so much to the front in the last few years, when only a short while ago it was generally regarded as a settled matter lying beyond the reach of discussion?

statement with regard to the centre of this whole. If man belongs entirely to nature (that he does to a considerable extent so belong is beyond question), then he remains inescapably subject to the stream of time and can never rise above it to a life of his own. Further, if he steps beyond nature only by virtue of isolated characteristics not rooted in the whole of a life and being, he may perhaps attain to some sort of further aspiration, but never to a real liberation from time. There is no possibility of such a liberation being realised except through the existence and recognition of an *independent spiritual world*, such as constitutes the main subject of our whole investigation. For, as we have already seen in reviewing the problem of evolution, this elevation above time, this operation by means of a timeless order, is inherent in the very nature of spiritual life and is indispensable to it. In this sphere effort is consistently directed towards that which is of timeless validity; historical effect or recognition can never establish a truth and a right, for in the realm of spiritual life truth is directly given as proceeding from an original life. Hence, in this region, the past can never replace the present and to-day can never grow out of yesterday, like fruit from its blossom. For the spiritual life produced by earlier ages does not by any means continue to exist because it once existed; in this case the law of inertia (the law by which a thing retains its existing state until some external force produces an alteration) is not valid. We here observe quite another law: that whatever is not being continually converted afresh into personal life and action sinks immediately and sinks lower and lower. This means, at the same time, that all spiritual life must proceed from the immediate present and that every obscuration of this fact tends to weaken the distinctive character of spiritual life. Within the realm of human experience, too, it is clear enough that it is not so much the past which decides as to the present as the present which decides as to the past, and that in accordance with this, our picture of the past continually changes, depending upon the spiritual nature of the present. Consider the different views and valuations of the Classical Age which have been current at various times; these have in each case been determined by the tasks and necessities peculiar to the actual time in question. Scholasticism sought in the Classical Epoch a secular culture which could serve as complement to a religious order of life; the Renaissance looked for encouragement in its strife for life and beauty; the Enlightenment, in so far as it valued the Classical Epoch at all, valued it for its clarity and utility; * German Humanism turned to the same period as a refuge from the complexity of modern life, seeing in it something more natural, pure, simple, and great. Thus this one epoch shows different sides to different ages. But there have been and are many who approach it without possessing a life of their own, and to these, in spite of much diligent research, it reveals, in a spiritual sense, absolutely nothing and never could reveal anything. Hence everything depends upon this life; the decisive thing is the possession of a present, and a present of a definite spiritual character. It is we ourselves, now living and acting, who can alone impart such a character to the present. A spiritual present is not the result of accident. We must ourselves build it up. Moreover, it is no mere moment; it is a consolidation to lift us above the moment, it is a timeless life.

It would never, under any circumstances, be possible to attain to such a life—and even the attempt to do so would be folly—if there did not exist *an eternal order as a new type of reality*, and if, moreover, this order were not in some fashion present within our own sphere of life. For how could this order help us if it did not operate within us? Hence, without this order there is no liberation from history, while with it we may obtain a secure position with regard to the past. Since we have been forced in the consideration of all our problems to thus recognise an independent spiritual world, the demand for such a world cannot surprise us in this case. But at the same time we become aware of a tremendous perplexity with regard to man; this spiritual sphere in which he must somehow be ultimately rooted, stands, in his case, in sharp contradiction to the immediate constitution of existence. Spiritual life is before everything else a whole. It places all manifoldness in

* Leibniz (see Foucher de Careil, *Lettres et opuscules*, ii., introd. xxxiii) loved the ancients on account of *la clarté dans l'expression et l'utilité dans les choses.*

comprehensive relationships, whereas human life falls into individual circles within which the separate phenomena are merely jumbled together; in the one case the inner power and joy of the thing itself is the motive power of conduct, in the other natural self-preservation is predominant, and in its contact with spiritual power this easily increases to a boundless egoism; the eternity demanded by the spiritual life contradicts the strict dependence of man upon time, the unceasing flux of all living phenomena, and the rapid disappearance of individuals; in the spiritual sphere the world attains to a content and forms itself into a kingdom of spiritual freedom, whereas man seems spiritually empty and defenceless in the face of infinity. How can such a rude contrast be overcome?

The first necessity is without doubt an inner transformation of life, an elevation above the merely human type, a transposition to the spiritual standpoint. In reality, all work which is concerned with the whole and affects the whole man produces such a transformation; it is only necessary, in this case, that that which penetrates our life in a thousand effects should be understood as a whole and be taken up in full activity. But such a transformation and such a new position do not straightway enable the new life to adequately unfold itself. Through an exaggeration of human capacity there arises a desire to directly produce all spirituality from the human standpoint, through the most energetic possible output of force; this exaggeration revenges itself by producing a much too pale and shadowy construction of the world. The limitations of man having once been sufficiently impressed upon us, we shall not so easily again attempt to construct reality out of self-dependent activity. Our endeavour to develop a spirituality superior to time needs an effective support. Such a support is offered by history. Certainly not history just as it stands; this is no more than an unsifted whole, for we have, for the time being, abandoned the idea of understanding this whole as a domain of pure reason, a pure development of spiritual life. But this does not exclude the belief that within history some kind of revelation of spiritual life is taking place, that an esoteric history separates itself from the exoteric, that a spiritual history is to be distinguished from the merely human. In the former there may be manifested an independent spiritual life speaking to us through all the mutations of the ages, a life capable of furthering our own human aspiration. The most demonstrable examples of such spiritual life occur at certain periods of exceptional elevation, called classical, because at these times there manifests itself a creation superior to the mere age and the mere man: the truly great element at such epochs has not consisted of particular thoughts and efforts; it has been a revelation of a new type of life as compared with everyday purposes and opinions. A revolution is thus accomplished, and with it comes an opening up of spiritual sources of life, of spiritual forces and necessities, a liberation of man from what is merely human. Certainly this does not take place without a relationship with the rest of life, without manifold preparation and close reference to the historical position, but never under any circumstances is this classical element, with that which makes up its essential being, a mere summation and development of existing elements: on the contrary, it always represents a breach of continuity and a reversal, a transposition to a new standpoint, the winning of a new sphere of life, the building up of a spiritual reality; it is hence usual for its manifestation to be accompanied by serious upheavals, and in so far as it becomes victorious it becomes so through struggle and pain. It makes martyrs of its pioneers, even in those cases where martyrdom is not sealed with blood. Moreover, the outward recognition which the great does as a rule ultimately find, by no means signifies a pure victory and a transformation of the human position; for this recognition involves a reduction to the level of human existence and an adaptation to petty human feeling, and in any case it is only particular effects and not the whole of its being which obtains general recognition. Thus at bottom the antithesis is not removed but only concealed, and through the whole of history true spirituality and merely human life-conduct remain in sharp conflict with one another.

Further, independent spiritual life does not merely manifest itself at isolated points, for these points seek a connection with one another, their desire being finally to unite in the construction of an all-embracing domain. This brings with it serious perplexities and severe conflicts. Under human circumstances every revelation of spiritual life has definite limits, since it attacks the problem only at a particular point, and solves it only in a particular direction. It will not be able fully to satisfy the whole of that spiritual life which operates from the deepest foundations of man's nature: a counter-movement will ultimately come forward and compel new developments. Further, this does not merely produce new opinions and new efforts; it enlarges and deepens the life-process: it is the life-process (and with it spiritual reality itself) which grows through the progress of the ages; revelations of spiritual life take place in it, and these are no mere products of reflection, but revelations which speak with the power of actuality—though this is certainly an actuality of a spiritual kind, and therefore to be appropriated only through self-activity.

Although this revelation of spiritual life by no means covers the length and breadth of human existence, it exercises power within the sphere of spiritual work and presents it with a high goal, without the attainment of which this work is not capable of giving full satisfaction or of effecting a real furtherance. That which lags behind this historical position may for a time rouse and influence humanity, but finally it will meet with a superior resistance and its inadequacy will become apparent. Such a historical position works both negatively and positively: negatively in shutting out certain solutions as inadequate, positively in setting certain tasks and providing certain incentives to progress—thus humanity as a whole cannot be satisfied with any construction of life which does not comprise in itself the spiritual deepening and the moral earnestness which Christianity gave us, nor with any that rejects that liberation of the subject and that acquirement of an inner infinity which were the gifts of the Modern World.

Thus, spiritually viewed, history contains indications, demands, and possibilities which must be appropriated and vivified in order to become full reality for us; this can occur in as far as the spiritual element, however much it may have been brought into our existence by special needs of the age, is, in its essence, timeless and therefore permanent. It is necessary to seize this timeless element in its full power and in its specific nature, when it can become a living present for us; history is then no mere sequence and the earlier no mere preparation for the later; every quantity has then not only a self-value but an imperishable truth; and it then becomes possible to strive towards a whole beyond the multiplicity. When, in this way, history, instead of being a mere sequence of events, becomes the gradual revelation of a spiritual world, the acquirement of a present superior to time, the desire for a spiritual life charged with a full content, can find in history a most powerful support. The essential thing is to penetrate from the temporal to the eternal and to separate a spiritual history from the remaining chaos.

This task is, however, subject to definite conditions. In the first place, it demands that there shall be operative a depth of life beyond the immediate form of existence, and a whole beyond the separate formations. For in this way alone can characteristic types of life, powerful life-currents, manifest themselves in the history of the world—phenomena which do not remain tied to the particularity of their visible source, but work beyond this in the whole, and work, too, in definite and distinctive fashion, not merely in a vague and general way. Thus only can an inner unity be recognised in the flux of the phenomena and be carried over to the present.

It appertains, further, to such a carrying over and appropriation that our age should itself develop an independent spiritual life. To this end, it must effect a powerful self-concentration, grasp its own task in the history of humanity, seize the vital centre of its own aspiration, and energetically sift out that independent spiritual element superior to time which it contains, at the same time securely elevating itself above the mere flux of phenomena. In order to perceive what is characteristic in others we must become conscious of our own self; in order to discover the eternal in other ages and in history as a whole we must discover the eternal in ourselves. In this case, it is peculiarly true that to him that hath shall be given. It is clearly evident that the past may well elevate the present but can never replace it

Our whole view of life must undergo an alteration in so far as a thoroughgoing task is thus discovered in the movement of history and progress towards a timeless truth is made through all the changes of the ages. We are now no longer swept helplessly down the stream of time. On the contrary, our participation in eternal truth brings us calmness and firmness. Through the experiences of history, the life-process will now continually acquire a more and more concrete form and become more and more replete with content; spiritual life itself will be revealed to us in a more definite form, while the specific nature and status of humanity will become increasingly clear: in all this a characteristic type and a permanent moulding of our spiritual being will come to development. Human life thereby attains a solidity in its deepest foundation and becomes superior to mere movement. Even in change, it will now, in the first place, experience *itself* and become strengthened in its characteristic nature. It may be that the upheavals of historical life will continually shake even the ultimate foundations and again make man regard as problematical what already appeared to be secured; it may be that the eternal which works within us must enter into the particularity of the ages and shape itself accordingly: nevertheless it signifies a revolution of the most fundamental kind, if, through the participation in a spiritual world superior to time, we can secure an eternal in the core of our life, and it becomes the task of tasks to take this up in our activity and to convert that which our spiritual life indicates to us into our full possession. Now we can endeavour to separate the transitory in history from the permanent and to win from the latter a spiritual present. History no longer appears as a whole with a self-contained purpose, but as a mere aspect of life and being. It now wins a spiritual content and some kind of meaning only when referred to a timeless order.

Regarded from this point of view, we see that it will never be possible to go back to the older type of life which thought to grasp the eternal by a single effort, and then to build it out completely: the restfulness which was thereby obtained appears to us a petrifaction, a denial of the living present in favour of the dead past. But we need on this account by no means succumb to the modern dissipation of all that is fixed and permanent, to the dissolution of life into separate moments, to the abandonment of all inner relationship and all superior unity. For when our connection with a world of timeless truth permits of the working out of a spiritual character and of the reversal of life through a development of its essential nature, then our main position may be taken in the eternal and we may press forward through time to a timeless reality, retaining a superior permanent element in the midst of all movement. The past is then no longer a mere past. It can become a portion of a present superior to time and thus remain a matter of personal life, of unceasing labour.

With such a conviction, science must develop a characteristic treatment of historical phenomena, seeing and seeking the permanent in the temporal, the whole in the particular. This took place, for example, in Ihering's great work on the spirit of Roman Law, which shows a full understanding of this method of procedure : the central matter is "not the *Roman*, but the *legal*, investigated and exemplified in the Roman" (3rd edit., introd. ix), and the task thus becomes "the separation of the temporal and purely Roman from the permanent and universal" (i. 15). It is true that such a philosophical treatment can come only as the end point of arduous scientific work, but those who would reject it through a weak fear of its dangers should bear in mind Hegel's well-known saying with regard to metaphysics. They are seeking to build a temple without a holy of holies.

The new type of life extends itself also to the life of the individual, throwing a new light upon it. From the standpoint of the individual, existence is a restless flight of phenomena only so long as it is without an independent inner life and does not in some way attain to a whole of personal being and spiritual individuality. But when this whole is attained and events are thus converted into experiences, we are able to experience a spiritual self in work and destiny, and that which in any way moves us no longer passes by like a shadow and sinks into the abyss of annihilation, but is capable of striking root in us, of developing and furthering what is permanent, of fitting itself into a present superior to time. The chief object remains always the same—to secure for life a present full of content and thus consolidate it against the mere moment; in such a present there operates a force which will always be a portion of real personal life, in love or loss, happiness or unhappiness. For this reason, men of spiritual strength have always scorned to complain of life's transitoriness, since it rests with us to rise above this transitoriness and establish our life in the eternal. "I am sorry," says Goethe, "for the men who make a great to do about the past and lose themselves in the contemplation of earthly nothingness. The truth is that we are here for the very purpose of making the temporal eternal." Hence we cannot regard as justified Dante's well-known saying, that the greatest misery consists in remembering, in unhappiness, past happiness. For if the happiness were true happiness it would be indestructible; it would persist and would still be operative, as a living presence, through all unhappiness.

Moreover, the natural phases of life, the different ages, do not appear, when thus contemplated, as a mere sequence. These phases do not play themselves completely out in themselves, neither are they absorbed in the preparation for future phases; each remains inwardly present to life and affects its position as a whole. Hence the importance of a fresh, joyful, genuine youth: this is no mere matter of sentimental recollection, for such a youth can remain a portion of a further present, an ever-flowing source of fresh life.

According to this view man is far from being a merely temporal being; profound mediæval thinkers believed with more justice that he stood on the boundary of time and eternity, on the horizon where the two run together, and that he participated in both. Time is for us rather a problem than a rigid destiny. How far, however, life overcomes time and attains to a present superior to it depends, above everything else, on the spiritual power which it is capable of putting forth. It rests with ourselves whether the centre of gravity of our being falls in the temporal or the eternal. In any case, this action of ours in thus overcoming time has for its indispensable preliminary condition *the reality and the inner presence of a spiritual world.* Even the most passionate excitation of the mere subject can never give rise to a spiritual content and with it a superiority to time, and it remains true that, for man, all creation is at the same time a reception, a drawing upon invisible relationships.

In the light of the foregoing it will be clear that our rejection of this weakening and disintegrating historicism does not mean that we fall back upon rationalism. We freely admit that if compelled to choose between the two we should prefer rationalism, for, however narrow and one-sided may be the life which it develops, it is nevertheless a true personal life and endeavour, whereas historicism is satisfied with a mere imitation of an alien life. Nevertheless, we stand far enough removed from rationalism. Its exaggerated consciousness of power misled it to underrate its task; its failure to appreciate the broad gap between immediate existence and the real depth of human being caused it to expect from a mere direct comprehension that which in reality demands a thoroughgoing deepening and transformation. It could hardly have looked to an intellectual enlightenment for our whole salvation if it had not believed that reason was already at hand in our human sphere and needed a mere liberation. Far beyond the limits of rationalism itself, it was the error of the New Period, in general, to regard the essence of spiritual life as a mere elevation of existence to consciousness; it was thought that what was operative round about us (though in a limited and obscure fashion) attained, within us, to full freedom and clarity. Such a standpoint as this reveals a thorough lack of appreciation of the great difficulties and perplexities of our view of life; it also involves a reduction of the life-process, which according to such a superficial view has no opportunity of attaining the necessary depth. The matter takes on quite a different aspect, however, if spiritual life is not regarded as a mere illumination of nature, but as an essentially new type of life, characterised by spiritual freedom. It is true that this may result in a much greater tension, but, on the other hand, history acquires a deeper significance. We can no longer attempt, however, to convert it into a domain of pure reason, but must be content to discover within it some sort of revelation of reason.

The Enlightenment, too, was unfavourable to a recognition of history, in so far as the intelligence which there took the first place in life had a far too narrow and intolerant conception of truth. A merely intellectual truth insists upon being directly reckoned as exclusive; therefore, from this standpoint, different things cannot exist side by side; to affirm the right of the present day means to place the whole of the past in error. Our earlier sections should have made it clear enough how completely the situation alters when the intellectual is carried over to the spiritual and when there come together in history not only doctrines and opinions but *life-developments* and *life-complexes*, when the historical conflict is fought, not for mere pictures of reality, but for *realities themselves*.

The decisive matter, in this case, is always the gaining of a present superior to time, with the accompanying reversal of life. For only through such a present can history become more than a matter of scholarly investigation, only in this way can the unlimited expansion of "becoming," and hence of the historical point of view, be prevented from giving rise to a destructive relativism. The victory of a historical point of view is indeed the greatest triumph of our whole modern investigation. This point of view does not only permit of all existing things associated with the formation of the world and with organic forms being understood in the light of evolution; it extends itself to the most elementary processes of lifeless nature, since even in the domain of physics events take place to a very large extent in a definite sequence and are not reversible at will. A much clearer picture of human existence has, however, been obtained since the present was understood as the last link of a long chain; in the chief directions of human aspiration not only is much recognised as changeable which formerly passed as fixed and inherent, but it is also shown how man, even down to his psychical nature, depends upon the specific character of his age (as is seen from the fact that different ages have exhibited different types of men). An immeasurable wealth of life is thus opened up, and our understanding becomes much more exact in coming into contact with such wealth.* All this may be welcomed as an essential enlargement of our field of vision, a liberation from the limitations of a particular age. But the gain in knowledge may well lead to a loss in life if it does not succeed in meeting this enlargement with a consolidation and the growth of time with a strengthening of the eternal. *History must remain in a secondary position: it must never take the first place.* It is true enough that, when thus regarded, our sphere of existence appears much less complete than it did to the rationalists and constructive historical philosophers. But why are we so sure that we ourselves round off the whole cycle of life? And is it a defect in the more modest conception if, along with the reduction of man, there takes place an enlargement of reality, and it life, in presenting itself less simply, gains in depth?

Appendix: The Concept "Modern"

The concept "modern" to-day moves and divides men's minds to such an extent that some discussion and explanation of it cannot be avoided. In the first place the history of the term demands explanation, for with respect to this point very indefinite if not erroneous opinions are extant.

* We may, in the first place, mention Dilthey's brilliant delineations of the men of different centuries; Lamprecht's investigations, too, should not be forgotten in this connection. R. Baerwald, among others, deals with the psychical position of the present day; see *Psychologische Faktoren des modernen Zeitgeistes* (published by the *Gesellschaft für psychologische Forschung*). The problem of the dependence of man upon his age has, however, occupied men's minds from the earliest times, and even so early as the seventeenth century it had become a definite point of conflict. As it is not possible for us to go into this matter more closely, we must content ourselves with taking a single passage from Walch's *Philos. Lexikon* (contained even in the 1st edit. of 1726), article *Sitten*, p. 2377: "Now because such a change (that is, of customs) takes place almost unnoticed and we do not usually become aware, until it is over, that such and such customs were in vogue at such and such times, it has become usual to attribute the customs to the ages Thus some have endeavoured to set up a *genium seculi* which guides men's minds and alters their customs according to the ages. Barclaius (Barclay) was of this opinion, and in his *Icon animor.*, p. 505 (John Barclay's *Icon animorum*, 1614) he says: *Omnia secula genium habent, qui mortalium animos in certa studia solet inflectere.* In agreement with him were the anonymous author of the *Germaniam milite destitutam* and the so-called Pater Firmianus who published a special book with the title *Seculi genius* (Paris, 1663, 12).

The actual problem connected with the term "modern" naturally reaches back far beyond the coining of the expression. Whenever it was desired to define the characteristic nature of the present, some sort of term will have been found.*

In "modern," however, there arose a permanent expression, and it will be worth our while to follow its development a little more closely. This word (derived from *modo*=just, now) has been used more especially when men have been divided by the consciousness of inner alterations: the friend of the new then calls himself "modern" to announce his superiority as compared with those who tenaciously cling to the old; while the latter, on the other hand, make use of the term in a reproachful sense, applying it to those who, lacking in constancy and reverence, follow the fleeting impressions of the moment. The history of the word shows us when the conflict reached an especial height and the point which more particularly caused dissension.

The expression appears in the transition period which divides the Ancient World from the Middle Ages, being employed by the grammarian Priscianus in the sixth century and by Theodoric's official, Cassiodorius (d. abt. 575).† It occasionally occurs in the following centuries.‡ After the end of the eleventh century "modern" was made use of in the logical conflicts of the period as a party term: it served to denote the nominalists —that is, those who refused to recognise the objective reality of intellectual concepts.§ Others, however, were also called

* Thus Aristotle, for example, repeatedly employed the term οἱ νῦν. In *Met.* 992 a, 33, he clearly denotes the Platonists of his age: γέγονεν τὰ μαθήματα τοῖς νῦν ἡ φιλοσοφία, similarly in 1069 a, 26 : οἱ μὲν νῦν τὰ καθόλου οὐσίας μᾶλλον τιθέασιν τὰ γὰρ γένη καθόλου, ἅ φασιν ἀρχὰς καὶ οὐσίας εἶναι μᾶλλον διὰ τὸ λογικῶς ζητεῖν· οἱ δὲ πάλαι τὰ καθ' ἕκαστον, οἷον πῦρ καὶ γῆν, ἀλλ' οὐ τὸ κοινὸν σῶμα.

† In *Cassiod. Variarum*, 4, 51, an architect is recommended as *antiquorum imitator, modernorum institutor.*

‡ An article in the *Historisch-politischen Blätter* (1895, year 1907) mentions a letter of the Abbot Benedictus Avianensis (written between 800 and 821) in which it says: *Unde apud modernos scholasticos, maxime apud Scotos (i)ste syllogismus delusionis, ut dicant trinitatem sicut personarum ita esse substantiarum (Mon. Germ. hist. Epist. Carol. Ævi*, vol. ii. 563).

§ Prantl (*Geschichte der Logik im Abendlande*, ii. 82) quotes the oldest passage in which the nominalists are described as *moderni: non juxta quosdam modernos in voce, sed more Boethii antiquorumque doctorum in re discipulis legebat*—namely Otto, Bishop of Cambray from 1106.

"moderns;" for example, the scholars of the period.* The term acquired a more important content and a more exact application when, after the days of John of Salisbury, the Aristotelians of the thirteenth century (in particular the great Dominicans, such as Albertus Magnus and Thomas Aquinas—the very man who is now the pillar of all that is anti-modern) drew the term to themselves in contradistinction to the Franciscan school,† which lent its support to a mode of thought more influenced by Plato and Augustine. The "modern" thought was accused by its opponents of flooding theology with dialectical considerations and petty discussions.‡ Later, both the concept of modernity and the term itself were transferred to Occam and his school; "Occam's doctrine remained the 'modern' theology down to the time of Luther,"§ and Luther himself announced his adherence to it. The word has, however, yet another meaning: the brothers of communal life stood for a *devotio moderna*, understanding by this a devotion which, along with the outward form, laid great emphasis on "inwardness"; one of Johannes Busch's works bears the title *Liber de origine devotionis modernæ*. ||

The Middle Ages then sank into decay and the Renaissance opened up a new world. But it was a long time before that which was already active in men's minds rose to the level of clear consciousness and acquired definite terms. From the point of view of the Renaissance, of course, "modern" could not mean a new type as opposed to the Ancient World, but only a new method in the treatment of the Ancient World. Since, at the same time, the mediæval terminology persisted

* It would be of no interest to go into this matter further here, but we may refer to Prantl (see, for example, ii. 116 ff., 195 and 241).

† Roger Bacon called Alexander of Hales and Albert *duo moderni gloriosi* (see the article *Scholastik* by Seeberg in Herzog's *Realenzyklopädie*).

‡ The papal legate, Simon de Brion, who played an important part in the movements which at that time excited and almost broke up the University of Paris, makes a depreciating reference to the *moderna curiositas, quæ plus solito innumeras multiplicat quæstionis* (see Mandonnet's excellent work: *Siger de Brabant et l'Averroisme latin au XIII siècle* (1899), ccviii, note 1).

§ See Seeberg, Herzog's *Realenzyklopädie*, 3rd edit., xiv. 279.

|| See Gustav Boerner's article *Die Brüder des gemeinsamen Lebens in Deutschland* in the *Deutschen Geschichtsblättern* of June, 1905, particularly pp. 244-5.

things became seriously confused. This is clearly illustrated by the *epistolæ obscurorum virorum*.* The more, however, the Modern World, with the commencement of the seventeenth century, won independence and self-consciousness, the more powerfully it compelled contemporary scholars to separate clearly what was peculiar to their own age from everything earlier, thus making an arrangement and division of human history which was quite different from anything previously attempted. It was chiefly the growth of the natural sciences and the influence of French literature at its highest level which lent that epoch the consciousness of being something new and of being superior to all previous ages. This resulted more particularly in the contrasting of "ancient" and "modern." Perrault's well-known book, *Parallèle des anciens et des modernes* (1688 ff.) treats the expressions as already established; the book is characteristic of the self-consciousness with which the second half of the seventeenth century was filled.† The contrast once having been set up, it was but a step to examine into the specific nature of the ancient and the modern; we know to what important developments this gave rise, and how Schiller, in particular, considered a more exact definition of these concepts worthy of thorough and devoted work.

On the other hand the modern had to define itself as opposed to the mediæval, and for this purpose it was first necessary to form a concept of the Middle Ages. This took place very late.

* Here *modernus* occasionally means merely "new" (*modernus episcopus, modernus imperator*). The older meaning, originating in the conflict of the different schools of logic, is also retained (*antiqui et moderni*). As a rule, however, it denotes the adherents of the new humanistic mode of thought, for example, *poetæ moderni; ex quo in Ephordia sumus moderni; artista de vic modernorum*. The term is not by any means always employed.

† We may quote, in illustration, a couple of passages from the first dialogue of this work: *Je pretens que nous avons aujourd'hui une plus parfaite connaissance de tous les arts et tous les sciences, qu'on ne l'a jamais eue*. Further, he speaks of the *progrès prodigieux des arts et des sciences, depuis cinquante ou soixante ans*. Again: *Il ne faut que lire les journaux de France et d'Angleterre et jetter les yeux sur les beaux ouvrages des académies de ces deux grandes royaumes pour être convaincu que depuis vingt ou trente ans il s'est fait plus de découvertes dans la science des choses naturelles, que dans toute l'étendue de la savante antiquité*.

In this connection Bernheim remarks (as above, p. 69): "In spite of occasional attacks the ban of tradition lasted long. Even so comparatively recent a writer as Sleidan, the well-known historian of the period of Charles V., calls his chronicle *De quattuor monarchiis*, and in spite of all the indications which he produces of the disintegration of the Holy Roman Empire he firmly retains a belief in its continuance, because, according to the prophecies of Daniel, a fifth earthly world-monarchy is impossible." The seventeenth century first saw a practical arrangement of material. It was the philologians and men of letters who first felt the need for some definite expression to denote the obvious difference between the classical and mediæval language and literature, on the one hand, and between the latter and the literary culture which followed the Renaissance on the other. As a result there arose the term *media ætas* or *medium ævum* for the literary period ranging from Augustus or from the Antonines down into the fifteenth century. It was Professor Christopher Cellarius of Halle (1634–1707) who introduced this mode of division, as applied to history in general, into his works: *Historia antiqua* was used to denote the period down to the time of Constantine the Great (it did not stop with Augustus because, as he expressly explains, the inner and outer power of the Roman Empire endured far beyond the time of Augustus); *Historia medii ævi* represented the subsequent period down to the conquest of Constantinople by the Turks, and *Historia nova* the following epoch. This method of division gradually obtained recognition, though not without vigorous opposition.* Thus

* How slowly this matter was settled and how it aroused conflict even down to the present day, is but little known. An article by George Goyau in the *Revue des Deux Mondes* of January 15, 1907, on the important Belgian historian Godefroid Kurth, contains the following remarks with respect to the attitude of the French Academy towards the term "Middle Ages": *Les cinq prémières éditions du dictionnaire de l'Académie française contiennient au mot "moyen âge" l'article suivant: "On appelle autheurs du moyen âge les autheurs qui ont écrit depuis la décadence de l'empire romain jusque vers le X siècle ou environ." C'est seulement dans la 6e édition (1835) qu'on lit: "Moyen âge, le temps qui s'est écoulé depuis la chute de l'empire romain, en 475, jusqu'à la prise de Constantinople, par Mahomet, en 1453."* Kurth himself was in very decided opposition to the concept and term "Middle Ages." In *Qu'est ce que le moyen âge* he wishes to secure the recognition of a single main division — the commencement of Christianity; accordingly, his great work *Les origines de la civilisation*

"modern" was defined with respect to the Middle Ages also. To follow the subsequent fate of the expression in the Modern World would lead us into an unlimited discussion, and is by no means essential to our task. This much we have seen: that the term "modern" is much less modern than is usually supposed, and that the concept is of a very elastic description.

So much for the history of the expression; now for a few words as to the problem itself. The ultimate source of the lively movement and conflict which centres round the concept modern is to be found in the fact that for the happy progress of civilisation there is necessary not only a bringing forth of what is new but a retention of what is old. Our progress would be slow indeed if we had always to begin afresh, if our work did not attain to a safe possession of suitable instruments and paths of least resistance, if much which at first required a full effort of conscious activity did not subsequently acquire an unconscious and habitual form, thus leaving more free time for progressive activity. For example, how useful, nay, indispensable, to philosophy is the rich store of concepts and technical terms with which the connected work of millenniums has provided us. But the matter goes yet deeper. The measure of truth and of spiritual content in general to which the race has attained can win the conviction and devotion of man only by *elevating itself above every temporal change and rejecting every alteration.* In so far as we possess genuine truth we stand above the movement of time. It was this mode of thought which gave rise to the saying:

"*Die Wahrheit war chon längst gefunden,*
Hat edle Geisterschaft verbunden:
Das alte Wahre, fass' es an!"

("The Truth has long ago been found,
Has lofty minds together bound;
The ancient Truth—Now seize it fast!")

---

moderne (3rd edit., 1898) treats the "Middle Ages" as the beginning of the modern world. In the former and smaller work he says: *Loin que le moyen âge soit intermédiaire entre la civilisation antique et la civilisation moderne, le moyen âge est lui-même le commencement de la civilisation moderne. Loin qu'il faille faire descendre le point de départ de celle-ci aussi bas que l'époque de la Renaissance, il faut constater au contraire qu'elle sort du christianisme.*

This justified a high appreciation of the old and a demand for its close connection with our own work, for an avoidance of each and every sharp breach.*

But the advocates of modernity have much to say on the other side. Spiritual things are not easily transferred from one age to another, after the manner of outward things; they continually demand to be recognised and appropriated afresh, and in this reappropriation it will be hard to avoid a certain alteration. Even if the outward state remains the same the valuation of the separate parts and their relation to one another will easily undergo change; men will see new aspects of the old and lay emphasis upon different portions of it. Moreover, new positions are found, presenting us with new problems, and humanity cannot meet these problems without a corresponding inward forward movement. Civilisations become exhausted and new races appear with fresh mental characteristics. Is it right that the position of spiritual life should remain quite unaffected by all this? Further, is it a matter of absolute certainty that the traditional life is based upon unquestionable truth and that the chosen path leads directly to the goal? Nay, is there any genuine life at all without personal decision, and can there be personal decision without doubt and struggle, without transformation and reconstruction?

The alterations which result may at first appear to take place within a world of indubitable validity; nay, for a long time they may not be felt at all. Then, however, there comes a point when the tension becomes excessive and a breaking away from the old becomes indispensable to the freshness and genuineness

---

* In the field of philosophy this gave rise to the idea of a *philosophia perennis*, which, already contained in Scholasticism, was maintained with especial vigour by Agostino Steuco, who wrote *De perenni philosophia lib. X*, Basel, 1542. Leibniz took up the expression, but owing to his idea of a continually progressive evolution he gave it a different meaning. Of recent years, Trendelenburg, in particular, and again in distinctive fashion, has defended the idea of the stability of philosophical work: "Philosophy," he says, "will not regain its ancient power until it acquires permanence, and it will not acquire permanence until it *grows* like the other sciences do, evolving in continuity, taking up its problems historically and developing them, instead of making a fresh beginning and again coming to a stop in the mind of each individual" (Preface to the 2nd. edit. of the *Logische Untersuchungen*, p. viii).

of life, a time when spiritual self-preservation imperatively demands a breach with tradition and a creation directly out of the present. Historical experience alone can inform us whether such transformations are necessary and when they become necessary; to an impartial mind they are, however, sufficiently evident. Such a transformation (and perhaps the most radical we know) is to be seen in the appearance of Christianity, with its fundamentally new standard of values; the Reformation and the new science may also claim with justice to have brought about great transformations. The religious life of the Modern World could not have developed its power and inwardness without a new and independent setting and an uprising of elemental forces, and it would have been just as impossible for the new science, with its entirely new methods and points of departure, to have gradually evolved itself out of the scholastic philosophy. In order that it may remain in fresh movement and develop its full depth, human life certainly requires continuity, but not less does it require discontinuity. In the case of these new movements the only matter of dispute must be whether they are impelled and governed by spiritual necessities, or whether it is only a human craving for change which is in question.

It is by no means to be denied that all change does not spring from such spiritual necessities. There is operative in human existence, more especially in our social life, a merely subjective fatigue on the part of man with regard to the old, a mere craving for change; this is peculiarly well illustrated by the vagaries of fashion. In this way, different periods become widely separated from one another; some ages are contented to quietly pursue the old paths, while others show a marked unrest, a discontent with everything which is found already in existence, a preference for all that is new. This difference of character on the part of different ages is closely associated with the position of spiritual life. The unrest is significant of a gap between inner necessities and outward possessions, and under these circumstances we are apt to be dominated by a merely human thirst for newness, and to develop an inclination to reject the old because it is old, and to welcome the new because it is new.

Hence we must distinguish between true and false modernity.

There is a modernity in which a spiritual necessity is operative and a modernity which is the expression of merely human whims and moods: these two are fundamentally different in their effects and prospects. If the movements are the result of a mere desire for change on the part of humanity, an instability of mood, they may violently excite the surface of life, but they cannot penetrate deeply or win any creative power; the same wind which brought them will soon blow them away again, while the rapid change, which allows men to swing so easily from one extreme to another, must ultimately give rise to severe fatigue. Sad will be the lives of the men and the ages which devote themselves to such a modernity.

It is a totally different matter, however, if a genuine modernity represents a new movement on the part of historical life and aims at securing the recognition of its content of truth: now the modernity bears within itself a spiritual necessity, to the penetrating power of which no permanent resistance can be offered. Such a modernity possesses marvellous power. Events which were apparently scattered and isolated are now seen to point in the same direction: quite different spheres of life are dominated by the new mode of thought, by the spirit of the age, which finds its way into the most remote corners, affecting even those who regard themselves as distinct opponents; in the face of such a movement, deeply rooted opinions and even selfish interests lose their power. Difficulty arises, however, from the fact that as things appear upon the surface, true and false are usually closely entangled. Some believe themselves able not only to reject the superficial modernity but the true spiritual movement of the age with it, while others, under cover of the idea of true progress, fall a prey to the most transitory situations and moods. The champions of the old usually feel that they stand for order, while the friends of the new regard themselves as the representatives of liberty; the former claim moral, the latter intellectual, superiority; the former believe themselves to be protecting the interests of society, the latter, the interests of the individual. At the same time the matter bears within itself a peculiar dialectic. What is now old was once new; even Thomas Aquinas was once reckoned as a "modern" That which is new to us will one day be old and have in its turn to defend itself against what is then new. The uprising modern movements of to-day owe no small portion of their strength to the mere fact that they are in opposition. In the hour of victory this advantage will disappear and will now be found on the side of fresh movements.

The perplexities which may result from such a conflict have made themselves felt with peculiar force in the life of to-day. On the one hand we find a most determined resistance to all that is new, a resistance which is represented in the first place by a great world-power, the Roman system—nominally catholic, but in reality as far removed from catholicism as is well possible; for it devotes its whole energy to guiding the movement of humanity into particular channels of its own, thus keeping the movement permanently confined within a mediæval form. On the other hand, a superficial modernity is spreading far and wide and is being powerfully assisted by the most recent developments of civilised life. The speed of life has become accelerated to an appalling extent; more and more people are crowding into our great cities and world-capitals; nothing is listened to that is not self-assertive, loud, nay, shrieking; attention is paid only to that which is new, exciting, unheard of, that which claims to be a novelty not to be missed by any considering themselves really cultured. Thus we have an exaggeration and overvaluation of the new. The new is valued merely because it is new, however empty or foolish it may be in itself. At the same time we perceive an endless amount of vain appearance, a dislike of all that is earnest and deep in life, a delight in mere bold negation, as a whole, a wretched pseudo-culture, an attempt on the part of the semi-educated mass to dominate the spiritual movement of humanity and to make itself the judge of good and evil, of truth and untruth.

It will be impossible for the genuine modernity to make progress unless it separates itself in the sharpest possible manner from the superficial modernity and takes up a vigorous struggle against it. The right of true modernity cannot be in the least affected by the aberrations of false modernity. The whole course of our investigation must have shown us that our age is of such a nature that it cannot quietly pursue traditional paths; it must seek new ones through an energetic self-recollection and self-deepening of life. Under these circumstances all wilful connection with the old is branded as a bare and sterile conservatism. It is our duty to maintain our independence and secure an open way for the spiritual necessities which are now striving upwards. In this way it will be possible to retain eternal truth while at the same time we eagerly and joyously seize what the present offers us; old and new will then be able to assist one another.

3. SOCIETY AND THE INDIVIDUAL

(SOCIALISM)

(a) The Relationship between Society and the Individual

1. HISTORICAL

TO-DAY the problem of society occupies a position similar to that occupied by the historical problem. The nineteenth century saw a reaction against the Enlightenment, a reaction which, although still in full operation, has already produced a counter-reaction. Thus movements and counter-movements cut across one another, giving rise to a highly complicated situation. To escape from this will be no easy task.

It will be well, at first, to devote a little space to such an explanation of terms as may seem necessary. "Individual" and "individuality" are of ancient origin, although the Modern World first saw them come into more general use. The primary meaning of "individual" was indivisible, incapable of being separated. Cicero uses the word as a translation of ἄτομον. This meaning predominated during the latter days of the Ancient World* and on into the Middle Ages—the oldest German translation is *unspaltig* (Notker). But towards the end of the Ancient World the word had also come to mean the separate thing as something unique, different from anything else, occurring only once in its particularity.† The

---

* Thus, for example, Seneca (*De provid.* 5) has: *quædam separari a quibusdam non possunt, cohærent, individua sunt.*

† In this connection, the works of the highly influential Boethius are especially noteworthy; we may quote the following passage from his Commentary upon Porphyry (edit. Bas. 1570, p. 65): *Individuum autem pluribus*

Middle Ages extended this use further and also coined (at any rate as soon as the twelfth century) the expressions *individualis* and *individualitas*. Leibniz first brought these into general use, acting in his familiar capacity as mediator between the old and the new.

The early stages of civilisation reveal the individual as a fragment of a more or less extensive society, depending in his action and inaction essentially upon his connection with the community. As life develops further, the tendency is more and more towards strengthening the individual: the latter gains in independence, begins to ask questions as to the basis of the traditional social order and to enquire into its validity, and finally reaches the point of endeavouring to throw off all restraint and make his own opinion the standard of truth, his own welfare the sole object of action. From the point of view of those who are concerned for society as a whole, this appears to be a ruinous subversion: hence they resist it with all their power, and endeavour, by granting him certain rights, to restore the individual to a connection with the whole and win him over to their purpose; it is the function of spiritual work to restore what, as a natural possession, was lost. The conception of society as an organism (with which we are already acquainted) was at first employed with the purpose of again fitting the individual into the social whole: it seems peculiarly adapted to serve as a means for reconciling the respective claims of society and the individual; in a real body, the more each limb develops its own character and strength, the more useful it is for the whole; the whole, on

---

dicitur modis. *Dicitur individuum quod omnino secari non potest, ut unitas vel mens; dicitur individuum quod de soliditatem dividi nequit, ut adamas; dicitur individuum cujus prædicatio in reliqua similia non convenit, ut Socrates: nam cum illi sunt cæteri homines similes, non convenit proprietas et prædicatio Socratis in cæteris, ergo ab iis quæ de uno tantum prædicantur genus differt, eo quod de pluribus prædicetur*. In Porphyry, the chief passage runs (see Prantl, *Geschichte der Logik*, i. 629): ἄτομα λέγεται τὰ τοιαῦτα, ὅτι ἐξ ἰδιοτήτων συνέστηκεν ἕκαστον, ὧν τὸ ἄθροισμα οὐκ ἂν ἐπ' ἄλλου τινός ποτε τὸ αὐτὸ γένοιτο τῶν κατὰ μέρος. This definition persisted through the course of the ages down to the time of Leibniz, whose teacher, Jacob Thomasius, still made use of the definition: *individuum est quod constat ex proprietatibus quarum collectio numquam in alio eadem esse potest*.

the other hand, stands higher, the more highly differentiated are its several parts. The fact that all the activities of the separate limbs remain absolutely dependent upon the whole constitutes, however, a rigid limitation. The separate limb ceases to possess any life or useful capacity at all as soon as it becomes detached from the whole, and this organic conception does not tolerate any individual rights as against the whole. When this doctrine is applied to the world as a whole (as was first really consciously done by the Stoics) it appears to be a special design of providence that even the smallest things are not absolutely alike, that no two hairs, two grains of wheat or two leaves are completely identical.*

This organic solution of the problem is closely related to the hierarchic. The latter originated during the latter end of the Greek Period † and attained its fullest development within the Christian Church and during the Middle Ages. It still has immense influence. The whole is here conceived of as a continuous series of ascending steps or grades, drawing nearer and nearer to life; a kind of ladder down which life may be passed from grade to grade; each grade has to receive from the one above and hand on to the one next below. In this scheme each part has its own special value and its own special work so long as it remains within the structure of the whole; it lapses into nothingness as soon as it makes itself separate. This conception of life took historical shape not only in the hierarchy of the Church, but also in the feudal system of the Middle Ages, in which every power vested in any individual was regarded as a loan from the grade above.

Both these systems regard the individual as deriving value solely from his relationship to the whole; it is denied that he has any value in himself. The conception which might be described as the microcosmic was the first to assign such an independent value to the individual. Instead of being a

---

* See Cicero, *Acad. quæst. II.*: *dicis nihil idem quod sit aliud; Stoicum est quidem nec admodum credibile, nullum esse pilum omnibus rebus talem, qualis sit pilus alius, nullum granum, &c.*

† The influence of Plotinus was the most important in this connection.

mere fragment in the world, the individual is now raised to the position of being himself a whole world, a kind of centre where reality is concentrated, a sanctuary in which life is immediately present in all its infinite greatness. The whole thus consists of worlds within worlds and is beyond the reach of all definite comprehension. This point of view also originated towards the end of the Greek Period, and again it is Plotinus who claims chief credit for it: he it was who first fully and clearly enunciated the conception of man as containing within himself a world of his own which, in its own peculiar way, reflects the whole; "each one of us is a spiritual world." Moreover, it was the Neo-Platonic school of philosophy which first brought the term microcosm into common use — though it dates back to Democritus and Aristotle. This tendency of thought was preserved throughout the Middle Ages chiefly by the speculative mystics, and through the medium of various later thinkers (such as Nicholas of Cusa and Giordano Bruno) it came down to modern times to take more precise form in Leibniz's theory of "monads." Closely related to this species of thought is the cult of individuality and personality which prevailed during the classical period of German literature. Here, too, we note a continuous chain of thought stretching from the end of the Greek Period down to the zenith of the New Period.

The organic and hierarchic conceptions of life, on the one hand, and the microcosmic, on the other, are so plainly in complete contrast that a conflict between them is unavoidable: one represents the individual as a mere member, the other as an independent whole; in the one case he can have no share in spiritual things except as one of a body, in the other he can approach them directly and alone. The whole content of life differs according to which of these positions we take up. Is action undertaken for the community or the development of the inner life of the separate individual to be our chief ideal? In the latter case, the community can receive its form and its strength only from the individual, and should never be regarded by him as an end in itself. This liberation results in the life of the individual acquiring an important content—scientific, artistic or religious: this is due first and foremost to the establishment of a direct relationship with infinity, with the sources of creative life. Thus, closely involved with the struggle between society and the individual, is the question whether the chief task of our lives should be sought in human intercourse or in relationship to the whole—whether we should strive, in the first place, towards a social or a cosmic scheme of life. It is not possible at present to trace the historical development of these problems; we must turn our attention, without further digression, to the consideration of present-day thoughts and tendencies.

Our age is subject to the influence of three tendencies of different breadth and strength: these are the general trend of the Modern World towards the individual, the nineteenth-century reaction in favour of society, and the resuscitation of individualism towards the end of the nineteenth century.

The emancipation of the individual is in all probability the most prominent feature of the whole of modern life. The individual sought and won in this emancipation not only a direct relationship to God and the whole, but an independent position with regard to the social whole. Beginning with the Renaissance and the Reformation, this gradually spread over the whole of existence, sinking deeper and deeper in and making it throughout fresher, stronger, and more mobile. Just as the new science was able to ascend through a disintegration of the traditional quantities (such as time, space, mass, and so forth) into discrete elements, so modern life, too, depends upon a growing independence and separation of individuals. From the treatment of the most inward questions to the externals of social custom and intercourse,* such an independence has more and more overcome all resistance. The object is by no means to remove all mutual relationships, but instead of being forced upon individuals

* For example, Ihering (*Der Zweck im Recht*, ii. 439) regards the æsthetical development of the common meal in modern times as indicating a highly important step forward, as compared with the past, since it signifies "an elevation from communism to individualism." Formerly, all who sat at table employed common plates, cups, &c., whereas now each individual uses his own alone.

from without the ties must proceed from their own personal decision and free agreement. Still less does the individualisation of existence mean an abandonment of all inner relationships; on the contrary, on the highest level of spiritual work, in the case of such men as Kant and Luther, the growth of man's independence with regard to man is only one side of the life-process, the other being the absolute, though free, subjection to invisible forces. Those who either praise or blame such men as the advocates of a mere individual freedom are simply demonstrating their own complete ignorance of the real essence of the matter.

In the broader current of the age the matter is less free from doubts and perplexities. In Germany, subsequent to the *Sturm- und Drangzeit*, the movement towards the individual acquired a predominantly artistic and literary character: the individual of that age raised himself above the average through artistic creation and felt himself, as a "genius," to be far superior to all "Philistinism." This self-conscious elevation of the artistic individual is a phenomenon which has been repeated frequently: we see it, to begin with, in Romanticism, which looked upon individuality as man's greatness (Schleiermacher), and through an exaggeration of this type of thought proclaimed the unlimited right of "infinitely free subjectivity"; at the same time art and science tended to take decided precedence over political life.* Similar modes of thought came to the front later in young Germany and in the individualism of to-day. The classical period of German literature set a high value upon the individual, and the chief educators, Pestalozzi and Herbart, carried this mode of thought over into the educational world.† But in this case the individual did not aspire to independence in order to remain in opposition

* Fr. Schlegel's words are characteristic of this tendency: "Scatter not thy faith and love in the world of politics, but in the divine world of science and art, pour thy most inward treasures into the fiery and holy stream of eternal development."

† Pestalozzi, in particular, was an energetic protagonist of the individual as compared with the merely collective; he makes sport of "collective actions," the "collective conscience," and "regimental convictions," and declares: "The collective existence of our race can only *civilise* us; it cannot *cultivate* us" (*Werke*, xii. 154). In this connection, Rousseau's great influence can never be forgotten: he first rendered the contrast between society and the individual clearly evident throughout life as a whole.

to the world and to his social environment and to wrap himself up in a consciousness of proud superiority; he returned joyfully to society, extended his sphere of life further and further, finally growing, in harmony with all environment, to a world-embracing personality. This is more especially to be seen in Goethe's spiritual nature and life-work.

The first resistance to this predominance of the individual came from idealism itself; for the idea of a world-embracing process, driven forward by its own movement, transferred the centre of gravity of human existence from the individual to humanity as a whole. Then came realism with its movement towards the visible world. This gave rise to an immeasurable wealth of tasks, the performance of which demanded a linking up of isolated forces, forced man out of his previous state of separation to a closer union, and compelled him to work with order and system. The desire for political freedom tended in the same direction, also the aspiration towards a social order based upon the power and wish of the citizens themselves, and the building up of national circles which embraced the individuals within a larger whole and united them in the pursuit of great tasks: this movement was still further assisted by the undreamt-of development of technical science, which had the effect of still further correlating work and still more firmly uniting the workmen, and by modern industrial life, with its gigantic businesses, its production of sharp contrasts and its accumulation of huge masses. The modern acceleration of life, the way in which men continually draw nearer to one another, and the manifold inter-ramification of different departments of life, all contribute not a little to the elimination of individual traits and to imparting an overwhelming power to those tendencies which work towards a summation of individual characteristics as mass phenomena. In the age of the press, of railways and telegraphs, public opinion is rapidly formed and acquires great power; it surrounds the individual even in his growth, and causes that which in reality has been communicated to him by the environment to appear as his own work.

Finally theory, too, receiving and reacting, enhances the dependence of the individual: for the more modern social science, "sociology" (Comte, Quetelet, and others), eagerly endeavours to show the complete limitation of man by his social environment, his *milieu*;* from this point of view man seems dominated even in his wishes and dreams by what society communicates to him; even a violent struggle on the part of the individual against society is rooted, ultimately, in the needs of the whole, and therefore lies within the whole. At the same time the concept of the social average, of the normal man, comes to the front; it is shown that the variations of the individual from this norm, so far as they are measurable, fall within much narrower limits than would at first seem probable.† Our attention is therefore drawn rather to the similarity of individuals than to their differences,‡ and the analysis of the psychic

---

* "*Milieu*," as an exact term, was most probably first employed by Lamarck in his *Philos. zoologique*; Comte extended its use from zoology to sociology, while Taine was peculiarly addicted to its employment in the latter sphere. It was due to him that the term became fashionable in Germany.

† In this connection Quetelet's *Anthropométrie* is worthy of particular attention.

‡ The idea of equality, together with that of the equal value and equal right of all men, has older roots, although it did not attain full development until within the last few centuries. It was unknown in the ancient Classical Period, and those factors which worked in its favour during the latter days of the Ancient World failed to produce an impression in face of the actual differences between man and man. The root of the idea of equality lies in religion, and, for our civilisation, in Christianity. It was our relationship to God which caused all human differences to disappear; it was the idea of infinity which caused all finite differences to seem negligible. To begin with, however, exceedingly little attention was paid to the consequences of these religious relationships and ideas for human existence, and in the further history of Christianity the idea of the universal priesthood sank far into the background as compared with that of the hierarchy. That which had come down from isolated secondary tendencies, being laboriously enough preserved by the Middle Ages, attained a fuller manifestation during the Reformation, and consequences for the shaping of the life of the community were energetically drawn from it by the Calvinistic reformers, in particular. It was from this standpoint, too, that the transference to the political sphere occurred, and under Cromwell there was drawn up the first constitution containing a demand for universal suffrage (1647). The Enlightenment, with its appeal to reason, alike in all men, lent still further influence to the idea of equality: thus Descartes, for example, says (at the commencement of the *De methodo*): *Rationem quod attinet, quia per illam solam homines sumus, æqualem in omnibus esse facile credo*. Finally, Rousseau was particularly energetic in bringing the idea of equality into the general life of humanity. The idea of the rights of man probably originated in America. Fichte was responsible for the formula of the " Equality

life of the individual, wherein lay the strength of our great poets, gives place to the study of masses, a form of investigation which, in statistics, has forged for itself a useful instrument.

All this is no mere outward alteration. It carries with it an inner transformation of life. For, from this point of view, the main thing in life becomes the achievement for the community, not what we do and think in our own personal sphere. All power is energetically called into manifestation, while the bonds which link the individual to the whole are brought more into prominence. Moreover, this tendency gives rise to a specific construction of spiritual life. The all-dominating goal of life becomes the betterment of the social condition. Morality becomes altruism, a working for the good of society; art finds no higher task than the sympathetic and accurate representation of social conditions; education endeavours rather to elevate the general level of culture than to develop anything individual. In this case it is more especially work which holds the individuals together, a work which develops vast complexes and fixed methods, thereby becoming strong enough to take up a conflict against the whole of the irrational element in existence, and to produce an essential betterment in the conditions of existence. For the time being it was hardly realised that the affirmation carried with it a negation, that the gain was accompanied by a loss.

This co-operation of closely intertwined forces works against the individual in a more or less concealed fashion. Quite open, however, is the anti-individualistic influence of the tremendous accession of strength which has fallen to the part of the state in the course of the nineteenth century. This accession has been due for the most part to economic complications in the face of which every merely individual effort has seemed hopeless. This is no more than the main feature of a general phenomenon. The increasing complication, the technical development of

---

of everything which bears the human visage"; see, for example, iv. 423 and vii. 573. The eighteenth century brought with it, too, the linking together of freedom and equality, in the first place in the sphere of social life. Thus Montesquieu, in his *Lettres Persanes* (first published in 1721), already has: *A Paris règne la liberté et l'égalité* (Book II.).

civilisation, demands a closer correlation of the separate forces and more organisation of the whole, and therefore calls for a guiding centre. This has had the unavoidable effect, for example, of producing a greater centralisation of education. Moreover, this movement in our civilised life has not lacked the inspiring power of a thought-world. The elevation of the state to be the chief vehicle of civilised work corresponds to the modern conviction of an indwelling absolute reason in our reality; it is no accident that the chief systematisers of pantheistic thought—Spinoza and Hegel—were powerful pioneers of the idea of the state, that Spinoza wished to have men swear not by God but by the welfare of their country, and that Hegel honoured the state as " earthly yet divine." Thus the visible power of the state and the invisible power of society are united against the independence of the individual. Those who escape, or believe themselves to escape, the one, are all the more likely to fall victims to the other.

But a complete victory often brings in its train an exaggeration, and hence a reaction, and in this case the hemming in of man by state and society gave rise, towards the end of the nineteenth century, to a new movement of assertion on the part of the individual. The manner in which this movement manifested itself was frequently far from edifying, as, for example, the self-deification of affected genius and the exaggeration of merely subjective moods to a state of supposed superiority to all the world besides. The matter cannot, however, be settled by merely poking fun at these accretions. At the back of all this problematical element there stands a defensive movement on the part of the individual and the subject against its threatened limitation and stifling. This reaction brings to full consciousness the limitations and negations involved in the movement towards society. An elimination of individual traits, an imperilling of independence, and an impediment of original life and creation seem to be indissolubly connected with the social type of civilisation. Just as history depresses the present, and a depressed present, in its turn, cannot see the greatness of history, it would seem that society, through thus reducing the individual, must itself suffer an unavoidable reduction. Do we not perceive clearly enough how in the midst of all the imposing triumphs of technical science clearly marked personalities are becoming scarcer and scarcer, while at the same time the level of our common life is sinking? Work, the essence of the modern construction of life, was to have strengthened the soul. We are now realising that the gigantic modern developments of work weaken, nay crush, man's soul. This necessarily stimulates the soul to defence, to a resistance of social civilisation and a denial of the value of its results. At the same time the individual tries as far as possible to separate himself from his social ties; it becomes his object to develop himself in complete freedom, to "live himself out" to the fullest extent, to give prominence to his distinctive characteristics, and to mark himself off in some fashion from the average run of humanity.

However much of the foregoing may appear exaggerated and perverted, it nevertheless exerts an influence over the present age. Although it may be poor in positive achievement, in criticism it is powerful; it has severely shaken the belief in the all-sufficiency of a merely social civilisation. In spite of this, however, work, with its direction towards the condition of society, continues, while its pressure upon the individual, and still more our realisation of the pressure, grow greater and greater. We are accordingly drawn in opposite directions: the social type of civilisation dominates our work, while an individual civilisation claims our souls. Must we helplessly surrender to this division or is it possible to resist it and to strive towards some sort of unity of life?

2. The Problems of To-Day

a. *The Inadequacy of a merely Social Civilisation*

It is one thing to recognise the importance of a social civilisation; it is another to look upon it as comprising the whole existence of man. At the present day a crowd of factors work together towards such a recognition. It is obvious that from the very beginning man could only develop his peculiar characteristics in a community; also that during later stages man's whole condition was essentially dependent upon the nature of his social life. It is clear, too, that the effect of social life penetrates far more deeply into the life and soul of the individual than it has in the past been customary to suppose. Our own age has been the first to fully recognise that man is a social being. Our newly acquired insight at once gives rise, however, to tasks of the most fruitful description. Seeing that we are so dependent upon society, and that our happiness is so bound up with its success, it becomes particularly important to raise the level of society and bring all its latent forces into full activity. Closer social relationships have enabled humanity to make continual progress in its fight against the irrational, and have helped it to create a happier state of existence; a stricter organisation of society has raised each individual, and social action has become more effective, because it has attacked general relationships instead of operating in a merely individual and accidental manner. The closer union of humanity in its immediate social life has opened up rich sources of moral feeling, has developed sympathy for others, and has produced a consciousness of complete solidarity. Moreover, the fact of working together, the necessity for mutual support and mutual accommodation, has brought more discipline, manhood, and power into life (which readily weakens when isolated).

Considering these successes, it is not surprising that exaggerated hopes were formed, hopes which went far beyond anything actually accomplished, that what had already accomplished so much believed itself capable of accomplishing anything, and that the social construction of life (*gesellschaftliche Lebensführung*) deemed itself able to supply the whole existence of man with an adequate content and to satisfy all his wishes. In attempting to carry this out it has imparted a characteristic form to each separate department of life. The meaning of ethics is sought in achievement for the benefit of the social environment, in altruism; the training of the individual for the purposes of the community becomes the goal of education; art makes social conditions the chief object of its work and aims at serving the widest circles; science endeavours to study man, not as an isolated individual, but "socio-psychologically," from the point of view of society as a whole; while pragmatism even makes capacity for advancing the welfare of humanity the standard of truth itself. Since, in all the above, our life and conduct is very directly related to the living and feeling man as a whole, it appears to gain in spiritual nearness and takes on a fresher, a more direct, and (it even seems) a more truthful form. All religious and metaphysical difficulties are kept in the background, and the more insecure the modern man becomes with regard to such matters, the more he is inclined to welcome such a riddance.

But although this movement opens up such fruitful prospects and provides us with such important tasks, it can reckon upon a full and joyful acceptance only so long as the negative side which accompanies the positive side remains unnoticed—and this negative side is very important. Life cannot be made simply a question of relationship to environment and of the development of mutual relationships (as this tendency would have it) without the independence of the isolated factor being most seriously reduced. And it must not be forgotten that the individual is the sole source of original spiritual life; corporate social life can do no more than unite and utilise. The maintenance of the strength and freedom of this original life would be less important, and its limitation would be more easily endurable, if human life stood upon a firm foundation and needed only to follow quietly in a naturally appointed direction. In reality, life is not only full of separate problems, but being situated (as it is) between the realm of mere nature and the spiritual world, it must begin by systematically directing itself aright and ascending from the semi-spiritual to the truly spiritual construction of life. It is hence called upon to perform great tasks, which cannot be carried out without serious effort and the mobilisation of all our spiritual forces. This necessarily leads us back to the original sources of strength, and hence to the individual.

The social mode of life, on the other hand, is directed chiefly towards an improvement of outward circumstances. It elevates and advances, alleviates and smooths, but although making life easier and more agreeable, at the bottom its effect is destructive, because it treats the spiritual content of life as a *means* towards human welfare. Every spiritual manifestation inevitably deteriorates unless it be regarded entirely as an end in itself. Utilitarianism, whatever form it may take, is an uncompromising enemy of all genuine spiritual culture. As a mere means, spiritual life can never become an inner necessity of man and can never be essential to self-preservation; hence it will not really possess man's soul and compel him to original creative activity. In spite of all outward development, this path will never lead to any inward elevation of man. In this direction is no original creation, no direct relationship to the whole, no inner independence. Such a life cannot contribute anything essentially new, nor indicate high goals to uplift human existence. It binds man down to his own natural condition, and makes him a slave to himself. It permits man to grace and decorate his existence, but provides no fundamental distinction between higher and lower, and is therefore incapable of stimulating man to rise above the average dead level, or of properly counteracting that confusion of nature with spirit, of the pettily human with the universally valid, which distinguishes ordinary human existence. In spite of its immense activity and immeasurable diligence, this type of life is lacking in true vigour and decision, in the courage to say definitely "Yes" or "No." It possesses no true content and meaning. A merely human culture such as is here placed before us may appear endurable as long as we consider it in detail only and do not look beyond the great variety of separate interests and activities which it undoubtedly offers: but on going into the matter more deeply, and asking what is the final meaning of the whole, the emptiness, the meagre and inadequate character of this type of life must become obvious.

When the disciples of this merely social type of culture believe it possible to escape from such an inner emptiness, they usually do so in the conviction that a union of elements gives rise to something essentially higher than is present in the separate elements; the welfare of society, for example, is looked upon as something far superior to that of the individual, and public opinion seems to constitute a vehicle of truth as compared with the chaos of individual opinions. In reality this appearance of an inner elevation is due to the fact that new matter is added, derived from relationships of a different kind; a new stage of life could never under any circumstances come into being as the result of a mere mingling or juxtaposition. The error in this line of argument is one not uncommon in the present age—the unperceived conversion of the *quantitative* into the *qualitative:* if there is no goal other than that of natural self-preservation, if there is no such thing as the formation of an essential spiritual being, the combination of separate spheres in the social structure cannot give rise to anything essentially new; even when extended to its utmost, the merely useful and agreeable proper to the natural stage of life does not in any way approximate to real good. In the same way the development of certain average opinions, however firmly they may be established and however confidently they may assert themselves, does not bring us the smallest step nearer to the concept of a genuine truth acting as a standard for all human aspiration. Good and true are always presupposed if deduced from a union of elements.

Such a conviction compels us to strong scepticism in respect of the well-known doctrine of the summation of reason in the community, a doctrine of which Aristotle was the first philosophical representative.* Aristotle maintained that the whole, as a body, is better fitted for judgment, either political and artistic, than are the separate individuals of whom it is composed, because one person possesses better judgment in one direction, another in another, and collectively a certain adjustment will take place. He also believed that the community, as a whole, is less subject to anger and other passions than are separate individuals. We must not forget that he had in mind, however, a civic State, limited in scope and held inwardly together by common traditions and fixed customs, not any conceivable mass of people, perhaps uncontrollably large. Thus there remains a wide gap between his democratic opinions and such a belief in the mass of the people as was held by Rousseau. In support

* See *Politics*, 1281 b, 8, 34. For further particulars see my collected essays *Gesammelte Aufsätze*, p. 62 ff.).

of the former we may bring forward, in the first place, the
ancient experience (with which Aristotle was acquainted) that
outstanding literary achievements are usually recognised by the
general public rather than by specialists, not on account of any
moral defect on the part of the latter, but because specialists are
too apt to move within a fixed circle of thought. The unprejudiced attitude of the larger body with regard to such unusual
productions is in this case more valuable than special technical
knowledge. Further, along with this doctrine of the summation of reason goes the conviction that there is an appeal from
the accidental nature of the moment and the individual (in
particular, too, from the narrowness of the party standpoint)
to humanity as a whole, a conviction based upon confidence in
some sort of victory of the good even within the human sphere.
Without such a faith, those who are in the minority must indeed
feel every outward effort to be objectless. The realm of politics,
in particular, has hence been penetrated by this belief. Moreover, historical experience bears abundant witness to the fact
that the truly great has proved victorious in spite of persecution
in the early stages; the stone which the builders rejected has
often proved itself to be the corner-stone. What helped to
bring this about, if it were not the greater whole, the wider
circles, less fixed in their opinions and more open to new
impulses? But it can hardly be said that this penetrating
capacity of the truly great was a result of a mere summation
of human opinion; it was due rather to the compulsion of a
spiritual necessity which made this higher element appear more
and more distinct from the lower until finally it became irresistible. It is, therefore, not belief in the multitude, but in a
spiritual necessity ruling within humanity, which justifies this
hope in the victory of reason even in the human sphere. In
contact with such a spiritual necessity alone, and as its representative, does public opinion obtain a real right and a sure
superiority; otherwise it may easily remain inferior to the
opinions of the separate individuals and may tend towards
unreason rather than reason. There are ages in which the
average level raises the individual, and other ages in which it
tends to drag him down. In any case it is not a question of the
mere multitude.

Since the social type of civilisation places itself entirely within the domain of immediate existence, it will unavoidably make the multitude the chief vehicle of life; for good or for evil it will countenance the fashion in which the great mass of the population deals with the main problems of human culture and civilisation; and the mass is apt to be hasty and excited, to be immoderate alike in affirmation and in negation, to cling to the outward and obvious impression, to seek the greatest possible excitement, to be tossed between contrasts, and to be disinclined for either calm reason or justice. At the same time, the individual will be pushed more and more into the background and even when he accomplishes something indisputably great, he will be reckoned as a mere tool of society * and not credited with any specific value of his own. It may be freely admitted that even the greatest achievement has its historical and social conditions and relationships; all creation takes shape in some particular spiritual atmosphere and hence inevitably bears the impress of its age—Augustine could not have been a contemporary of Kant, nor Kant of Augustine; such a life and work as Goethe's would not have been possible at the time of the Crusades—yet to recognise such limitations need not mean that we admit society as a whole to be the productive force, and the individual, in his own specific nature, an entirely indifferent tool. In spite of all inner connection the truly great has usually been related to the general level of its age in the sense of a contrast; it has generally developed its greatness through knowing how victoriously to assert a necessity of its own being in the face of the age as a whole, the victory being not in the sphere of immediate existence, but in that of spiritual work. Truly great achievement is distinguished, in the first place, by the fact of its being individual, incomparable, and therefore not deducible. With the aid of this independence alone does it become possible to pick out the spiritual element which sprung forth and came into activity in a given age (almost inseparably mingled as it was, in its outward manifestations, with lower and

* See, for example, Comte, *Cours de phil. pos.*, iv. 269: *Les hommes de génie ne se presentaient essentiellement que comme les organes d'un mouvement prédéterminé, qui, à leur défaute, se fût ouvert d'autres issues.*

alien matter) and to bring it to a clearer and more powerful form, to raise it to the level of a moving and elevating force. In the course of this process, the spiritual itself undergoes an *individualisation*, which impels the fate of humanity to take a specific form. We see this with peculiar clearness in the sphere of religion. For there can be no doubt whatever that such men as Augustine and Luther did not merely gather up that which the environment offered them: they solved the problems with which the historical position of humanity had provided their age in a thoroughly individual and characteristic fashion, thereby imposing their own spiritual nature upon whole epochs. Every age of powerful spiritual movement contains different potentialities; which of these potentialities will be translated into actuality, depends, in the first place, upon the leading individuals of the period. This alone is sufficient to prevent history being based upon any formula.

The great once being there, it can attract to itself everything in any way allied to it, assist all that is striving upward, unite all that is scattered and originate a whole movement. The great itself is no mere product of summation; on the contrary, without it the summation is not possible. For a summation, a linking up of scattered elements, easy though it may seem to the exponents of social civilisation, is in reality an exceedingly difficult problem. An age may contain many different and even contradictory elements. A summation may be possible in many directions and upon widely separated levels. The genuine and valuable forces which are making their way upwards at isolated points frequently fail to unite, and are hence as good as lost to the whole. If this linking up of ascending forces will not come to pass, the age may be severely handicapped. Our own age suffers from such a disadvantage. It is the peculiar task of the great men of a period, through the happy moulding of a spiritual character and through a vigorous advance, to prepare the way for a summation in a particular upward direction and to carry this through. Great men have been the masters, not the servants of their age. Do we speak of the age of Goethe because during the second half of the eighteenth century a humanistic and artistic type of thought, after the fashion of Goethe, was widely prevalent, or because his dominating personality created forms and assigned goals which served as rallying-points to attract and elevate that which was less clearly marked?

Social civilisation, on the other hand, places the differences of level in the background and aspires towards the greatest possible equality. Its aim is certainly of the best, namely, to raise the general level, to lead as many as possible, and if possible all, to the highest level, yet without this level being in any way lowered. But in this case, too, the actual nature of the things themselves is stronger than the human intention: imperceptibly, the position of those who are to be raised becomes itself the measure of spiritual movement and the level of the whole unavoidably sinks; work cannot be directed chiefly towards producing an effect upon others without suffering injury in itself. Schopenhauer divided thinkers into such as think for others and such as think for themselves, and would allow the latter only to reckon as true thinkers; if he was right in this, as we believe him to have been, then there can be no doubt as to the danger of a movement chiefly directed towards communication and influence. The resulting diffusion must result in shallowness if it be not accompanied by an original creation to balance the diffusion.

With this is associated the inclination not only to take up responsibility for the weaker, which is undeniably right and noble, but to place ourselves as far as possible in their position and to arrange the whole of life in their interest. " Hard " and " soft " periods are apt to alternate; to-day " softness " is undoubtedly predominant and tends to give rise to the idea that the weak are good and the strong bad, and that it is the duty of the latter to give way to the former the moment there is a conflict of interests. Thus there is a widespread modern tendency to take sides with the child against the parent, with the pupil against the teacher, and in general with those in subordination against those in authority, as if all order and all discipline were a mere demonstration of selfishness and brutality. Kant's saying: " If justice be defeated it is no longer worth while for man's life on this earth to continue," would hardly find acceptance in this quarter. In connection with this tendency we should mention also the feminism with which we are now threatened: this does not aim merely at assisting women to their due rights; it would like to shape education and the whole of civilisation, as far as possible, from the point of view of feminine interests alone—thus co-education, highly problematical though it is, is recommended, in the first place, simply because it will enable women to obtain precisely as much and precisely the same as men. This sort of worship of equality will inevitably cause civilisation to become flaccid and colourless, to avoid everything powerful and all clearly defined individuality, as it would avoid evil or error; and what is still worse, it will cause it to lose that which, according to Goethe's saying, "Nobody brings with him into the world, yet which is all-important if a man is to become a *whole* man"—veneration.*

Movements of this kind, tending towards expansion and superficiality, may be endured for a time, since they are balanced by the traditional construction of life; for a time one may live very well on inherited capital. But the richest hoard cannot last for ever. The question of original production cannot be permanently set aside; and as soon as it comes to the front the limits of social civilisation can no longer be overlooked. Social civilisation cannot base spiritual life upon man without inwardly raising him; it cannot entrust the highest goods to society without making society something greater. But of its own strength it cannot produce such an elevation; on the contrary, it tends, with the weakening and stagnation of spiritual life, to destroy the conditions of true greatness, and therefore it cannot prevent a merely human and mass civilisation overwhelming and extinguishing an essential spiritual civilisation.

Do not such experiences force themselves upon us to-day in the clearest and most painful manner? Could we see our own

---

* The sway which Nietzsche exercises over men's mind is due, in the first place, to a powerful reaction against the dulling and deadening character of this gospel of equalisation: "Life, life itself, struggles to ascend to the heights; by steps and stages it forces itself ever upwards; its desire is to perceive vast horizons and it looks ever outward and forward towards blessed and rapturous beauties—therefore it demands *height*. And because it demands height, it demands stages, and a denial of these stages and of the climbers! Life will ascend—and ascending, overcome itself." (*Thus spake Zarathustra.*)

age from within and as a whole, as great historians have revealed bygone ages to us, we should see a moving picture in the midst of all the glamour of an external civilisation. We should see a humanity seeking to raise and enrich life, through establishing closer relationships and developing an increase of power, a society believing itself strong enough of itself to produce all spiritual life, and endeavouring, with restless activity, to raise a tower as high as heaven: in spite of all outward triumphs, however, modern humanity undergoes an inner defeat; nay, it is no longer able to concentrate itself, to understand itself; it is threatened with an inner collapse. On every hand we see opposition and strife, an increasing passion of conflict, a dissolution into parties, a disappearance of common ideas and goals. We sought to secure unity by ourselves, setting aside all cosmic problems, and hoped for the richest fruits from such unity, but a confusion of speech was the result. If we do not succeed in overcoming this chaos, and in again placing human existence in great relationships and giving it a firmer foundation, we shall more and more become the victims of disintegration.

So far we have been concerned with the problem of social civilisation in general. We will now devote a few words to discussing the position of the state in the spiritual life of the present day. To-day we are all conscious of an increase in the power of the state, and social perplexities in particular are tending to cause a still further increase: hence arises the danger, and it is no insignificant one, of what we may call "politicism"—the whole of spiritual life threatens to fall more and more under the influence of the state, to receive, as it were, an official stamp. The leading idea of the state is and remains the development of power; now power, as we have said, is not by any means a thing evil in itself, but it is morally indifferent; it knows no goal higher than itself. The endeavour to treat all spiritual manifestation as a mere means towards its end is inherent in its nature; it recognises no independence on the part of other spheres of life. When, however, these spheres are valued and judged, in the first place, according to what they accomplish for the life of the state, they lose their self-value, and their original creative activity must at the same time suffer severe injury. Moreover, when the whole of life is dominated by the idea of the state there must be an extreme narrowing down of the specific nature and free movement of the individual. When a man concentrates his mind and thought in the first place upon entering the governmental service and upon securing official promotion, when he is valued according to his official position and accomplishment, the centre of gravity of his life is situated externally and the man's independence and originality must unavoidably be injured. Whether the political system tends towards democracy or aristocracy is of little consequence in this connection. That political greatness may go hand in hand with a lack of spiritual productivity is illustrated in the most striking fashion by Roman history: for it is an exceedingly remarkable fact that notwithstanding their political power, their wisdom, and their discipline, the Roman people never produced of their own capacity so much as a single great philosophical thought or a single great artistic achievement.

In connection with this problem, we Germans, too, must not be unmindful of the dangers which our own development is bringing with it. More particularly in the Prussian state we are confronted by this all-dominating power of the state, this politicism: there was certainly a time when the subordination of every task to the idea of the state was an imperative necessity if the latter was to fulfil its great work in human history; the conception of power was then linked in the closest possible manner to the idea of duty, thus becoming inwardly ennobled. It was the union of these two ideas of power and duty which produced those magnificent achievements which alone made modern Germany possible. But in spite of all this we must not overlook the danger of spiritual unproductivity, of the strangulation of the individual, of a uniform and mechanical moulding of life. *Spiritual creation and genuine personal life-conduct absolutely demand treatment as objects in themselves,* while politicism, no matter how noble the forms which it may adopt, has a utilitarian bias which inevitably makes mere means and tools of the personal and spiritual.

β. *The Inadequacy of a merely Individual Civilisation*

The reaction against social civilisation, which is consummated by the modern individual, arose, in the first place, not so much from any anxiety about the spiritual content of life as from a desire to avoid the injuries with which the progress of this civilisation threatened the individual. At the same time deeper problems stood in the background and helped to make the opposition sharper.

The social type of civilisation treats the individual as a mere cog in its great machine. It values him solely according to his achievements, and finds it necessary for its purposes to impose numerous restrictions upon him. Moreover, with its piecing together of elements, its accumulation of masses, its crude and mechanical methods, it tends overpoweringly towards the suppression and elimination of individual traits; it eliminates the quietude essential to the development of an individual nature: it produces average types who set themselves up as standards of good and evil, of truth and untruth. The individual of a more powerful type ultimately rebels against such a confinement and levelling down and maintains that man is by no means merged in the relationship to social environment, but that, on the contrary, the most valuable element in his nature, the unity and inwardness of life, lies outside this relationship. In this connection he can appeal to the witness of the whole history of humanity, for all predominantly social civilisations and systems of human culture have tended towards a superficial and mechanical life, and it has been no mere self-assertion on the part of the individual which has driven him to resent such a social civilisation; the motive force has been his imperative desire for more inner life. In the sphere of religion, in particular, the social development as a church inevitably brings with it the inclination to place the outward achievement (divine service, pious deeds, orthodox opinions, the so-called religious duties in general) before the inner feelings, the personal life, the independence of the inner man. Hence a struggle against the church has been

continually necessary in the truest interests of religion itself.*
Along with this defence of individual independence is associated a hot protest against the machine-like, "dead-level" construction of civilisation with which society threatens life. Are not the average levels which thus result of a very inferior kind, and do they not readily lead to a fixation of life upon a level of unimportant mediocrity? Is it not true that spiritual force and noble sentiment are rare, and do they not require for their development full freedom and (if they are to influence the whole) a sharp definition and a secure establishment in the narrow sphere of a small band of disciples? Hence there has been no essential progress on the part of human culture and civilisation without a division of humanity; a higher must first be produced in order to be able to attract the rest; a column of fire must go before the host to show it the way through the wilderness. In spite of every objection, precaution, and protest, there has continually resulted a contrast between esoteric and exoteric life-conduct; even the most radical political constitution has not prevented the formation of sharp social distinctions, reaching down even to the outward circumstances of custom and propriety; men being what they are, the ambition to imitate those who stand above is an indispensable incentive to movement. And does not all spiritual activity remain, for each individual, something dead and external if it fails to become bound up with his individual nature and itself to acquire an individual shape, if in struggling for it the individual is not attaining to his own true being? Constructive development means separation, differentiation, individualisation; thus separation has been a universal and indispensable means towards movement and progress.

With such considerations in mind, the individual proceeds from defence to attack, and boldly charges social civilisation with its limitations. Man, as a thinking being, is capable of entering into a direct relationship with reality, he is no mere link in a

---

* On the occasion of the burial of a leader of the German Catholic Party, a prelate of high rank emphasised, as a praiseworthy characteristic, the fact that the deceased left the care of his soul entirely in the hands of the church. Is it not horrible that even to-day such an inner abandonment of life can meet with praise?

chain, he can confront infinity and wrestle with it, he becomes conscious of the narrowness of mere subjectivity and can aspire beyond it to the truth of the things themselves. This endeavour is certainly met by countless difficulties and obstacles, but even as an aspiration it demonstrates the superiority of man to the merely social sphere. Is it not absurd to communicate spiritual life to such a cosmic being through society alone, and hence to try to bind him down to the measure of that spirituality which has been attained by the integration of forces? Shall a being who possesses an infinite value on account of his fundamental relationship to the spiritual world be adjudged his value according to human estimation alone? Shall he exist dependent upon human favour and hence lose all independence of feeling? Must the guarantee of society be obtained before man can enjoy the secure possession of a truth, nay, a spiritual existence? Shall the production of spiritual goods take place, if not in the marketplace, at any rate for the market of life, and shall these goods be thereby degraded to mere marketable commodities?

According to the foregoing arguments, the individual (that is, the spiritually directed individual) appears as the representative of spiritual culture as opposed to a merely human culture, of an inner infinity as compared with all outward limitation. He appears as a force combating superficiality, shaking humanity out of old ruts, holding up necessary aims, ever anew leading the aspirations of humanity back to their true bases. And if this high valuation of the individual acting from spiritual motives necessarily brings with it a separation from the average level of society it will also have no hesitation in proudly rejecting the intolerance of any sort of superiority which is characteristic of this average level. There is a common envy and hatred on the part of the mediocre against the higher, since the latter reflects on the poverty of the former. When the higher conducts itself modestly and humbly, politely apologises for its existence and carefully avoids displaying any consciousness of power, it is barely endured, and then only. Hence modesty is a virtue much honoured of the "Philistines." Nearly related is the practice of employing the same concepts to cover things of quite different types and values, the use of really meaningless labels of praise and blame; this lukewarm and insipid type of thought is alike incapable of powerful love or powerful hate and allows light and shadow to merge into a grey mist. In the face of this sort of thing the individual has a perfect right to work towards an intensification of feeling, a sharpening of judgment, a division of opinion—nay, it is his sacred duty so to do.

In reality, however, the individual can become superior, in the genuine sense of the word, only if he has a spiritual world behind him and is capable of drawing upon its strength. Now, this is far from being the position taken up by modern individualism, in its most usual form; on the contrary, it allows the individual no basis outside his immediate existence and expects him to shape life from this position; it is particularly concerned to loosen all invisible relationships, to abolish not only dependence upon men, but dependence upon a spiritual world. It is therefore left with nothing but the immediate condition of the soul, the subjective state. Hence this becomes the essence of all life and individualism merges into subjectivism. It is obvious that this gives rise to a specific type of reality: this subjective state permits of being fixed and enhanced, that which has a specific character may develop itself without limit, life may spring forth ever anew while its position undergoes continual alteration. Hence we have a great facility, freshness, and fluidity. Life appears to be dependent upon nothing outside itself, and with this freedom it seems to become finer, more delicate, and more intimate than in any other form. The concept of truth, too, loses its customary difficulty and rigidity. For henceforth only that reckons as true which is experienced by the soul of the individual, and experienced, moreover, in the present. Thus the concept of a single truth gives way to that of innumerable truths. Every man has now his own truth. This attitude acquires a peculiar joy and self-consciousness in contrast with society, whose institutions and regulations so often conflict with the life-consciousness of the individual; the subjective attitude, on the other hand, stands for the continual preservation of life in a state of freedom and fluidity and for the greatest possible strengthening and advancement of all that is individual and characteristic.

This could not, however, get beyond a condition of formless excitation and indefinite movement without somehow converting itself into spiritual work, and this conversion takes place in the movement towards art and literature. Art, in its manifold ramifications, now becomes the chief means of grasping and determining in some way the otherwise restlessly heaving and swelling life, of strengthening it through giving it more definite shape, of completely developing it by itself and making it independent of external relationships. The concentration of life in itself and the enhancement of its power hence becomes the main task of art. Art becomes the soul of an individual-aristocratic culture, which, being the more exclusive, feels itself far superior to the practical-social type; art can act this part, in the first place, because it stands itself above all mere utility and causes man to rely for the most part upon his individual capacity; in the second place, because, in the midst of all the confusion and false conceptions of the general life of humanity, it can perceive the simple fundamental characteristics of human existence, can seize the eternally youthful element in it, and rescue this element from becoming petrified in the conventional.

Such a gradation of life is easily transferred, however, to the consciousness of the individuals and in this way very soon finds itself upon a downward path. Not only those who personally participate in the activities of the new type of life, but those who merely express their adhesion to it, fancy themselves superior to the rest of mankind and to social civilisation; this results in an inclination to lay emphasis upon the disparity, to do what is unusual, to take pleasure in detachment and to regard it as greatness. At the same time the claim is more and more being made on the part of the individual to develop his own nature according to his own whim and pleasure, heedless of generally accepted standards, of moral custom and law, to "live himself out" without heed or restraint. The individual culture may not wish to produce these results, but under human conditions they are difficult to avoid. We need hardly point out that subjective movements and moods of this kind play a great part in the most modern construction of life. It is only the name, indeed, which is new; the thing itself is old in the extreme.

For, as if in regular cycles, there again and again come periods when the direct life-consciousness is dissatisfied with the type of human culture it finds around it and the complete emancipation of the individual is proclaimed as the way of salvation, when his immediate feeling, his self-imposed standards, his artistic taste, is looked to to bring about a change for the better. Plato's *Gorgias* illustrates the close relationship between the ancient Sophists and the modern subjectivists. In Germany this species of emancipation of the individual was unheard of until the "Age of Genius," the forerunner of the classical period of German literature; at that time "genius," "force-genius," and "original genius" were fashionable phrases, such as the modern "superman" ("beautiful souls" is also related to this movement).*
Then came a new movement in the shape of Romanticism, which is closely and obviously related to the æsthetical subjectivism of to-day.

It is difficult to pass correct judgment upon the whole because it is clear that we are dealing with a transitional phenomenon,

---

* Hildebrand (in Grimm's *Deutsches Wörterbuch*) treats the origin and development of the expression "genius" (*Genie*) in a manner which is both exemplary and exhaustive. We should like, however, to add a quotation from the recently published correspondence between Goethe and Lavater; this passage is of importance in the task of drawing a sharper distinction between "genius" and "talent." Goethe writes (*Schriften der Goethe-Gesellschaft*, vol. 16, p. 125) on July 24, 1780: "With regard to Wieland's *Oberon* you make use of the word 'talent' as if it stood for the opposite of 'genius' and were (if not quite) at any rate greatly subordinate. We should take into consideration, however, that true talent can be nothing other than the language of genius." To this Lavater replied (August 5, 1780) with a lengthy explanation of the difference between talent and genius (p. 130 ff.), from which we will quote only the following passage: "Just a word with respect to 'talent' and 'genius': two terms which in their meanings and contents are perhaps about as different as 'beautiful' and 'noble.' Talent, so it appears to me, does with facility what a thousand others can do only with extreme slowness and laboriousness, or it does with joy and grace what others can do only with accuracy and correctness. Genius does what no one can do. Works of talent give rise to pleasurable admiration. Genius arouses veneration; it excites a feeling which approximates to worship."

The best information with regard to "*schöne Seele*" (beautiful soul) is to be found in the most recent edition of Büchmann's *Geflügelten Worten* (edited by Ippel).

which becomes more right and reasonable the more it fits itself into wider relationships and points to something beyond itself, and becomes more false the more firmly it consolidates and isolates itself. In addition, we are in this case prevented, by the interdiction of all binding norms, from making any definite separation of higher and lower, of spiritual necessity and human fancy; the most varied elements are mingled together and it is almost impossible to avoid the danger of being indulgent towards the lower while recognising the higher, of being unjust towards the higher while guarding against the lower. Nevertheless, we cannot well avoid the duty of attempting some kind of estimation.

Why must a system of human culture founded upon the mere individual and his subjective condition be unsatisfactory? There are two main reasons:—

1. The individual of immediate existence—and he alone is in question—is neither independent nor self-contained;
2. The life which he develops becomes more and more empty and inadequate the more fully it develops its own consequences.

The empirical individual is, as a matter of fact, anything rather than independent: for heredity, environment, and education not only determine him in innumerable ways, but seem to be entirely responsible for him; they spin such a fine web around him that neither cunning nor force can break through. It is certain that this determination reaches into that inner soul which individualism holds to be completely free of outward influences: at any rate, we cannot regard it as free merely because the immediate impression feels no dependence. For let the individualist assert himself against the world as much as he likes and seem completely to separate himself from it, he still remains overshadowed and overpoweringly influenced by the world and subject to its limitations. His supposed independence is usually another kind of dependence, an indirect dependence. The individualist is inclined to say and do the opposite of what those in his environment say and do; thus it is still the environment which prescribes his course; the connection is not broken. The individualist feels himself superior to the environment, but he cannot measure the height to which he has risen above it, in order to take satisfaction in his elevation, without retaining the environment in mind; here, too, he remains dependent upon it. He delights in the proud consciousness of independence, but at the same time he must continually think of those around him as spectators and admirers of his greatness. Hence this type of life does not attain to firm tranquillity and joyous, independent, creative activity—it does not base itself upon its own necessities. Therefore it cannot give up the relationship to man; it must live upon the contrast and derive its nourishment from thence. Thus it never gets beyond a condition of inner dependence.

Moreover, in the case of such an attitude as this, there is a danger of the consciousness of greatness becoming infected by vanity. It is true that there are sharp differences of life and being, and that the degrees in which spirituality is vivified differ very greatly. The common levelling down which clumsily throws everything together is justly repudiated by the individualists. Far be it from us to obscure or diminish in any way the importance of individuality! It is indispensable to the full truth and development of spiritual creation; if this creation does not attain to the fullness of its peculiar strength at the specific individual point where it completely unfolds its own nature, then it will never overcome its obstacles; but a superior necessity of the life-process must be in control throughout, a spiritual compulsion must drive man forward and guide him; then alone does the movement remain genuine and healthy. It becomes artificial and unhealthy when the individual sets himself as far as possible to demonstrate his greatness and individuality at every opportunity, when he purposely lays emphasis on the difference between himself and the common crowd, and even derives pleasure from its contemplation, while all the while its true carrying out demands pure devotion and selfless love—every withdrawal behind the matter itself, every demonstration of vain self-consciousness, weakens spiritual power and loosens that connection with the inner necessities upon which all success depends: "One must *have* originality, not strive for it" (J. Burckhardt).

There is certainly much work done, apparently under the influence of modern individualism, that is far superior to such reflective subjectivism with its Epicurean self-gratification. In particular, the eagerness and earnestness of modern plastic art, together with the unmistakable greatness of its achievement, can be understood only through the appearance of fresh positive tasks, fresh impulses towards creation, which open up new aspects of reality and lead to a more inward relationship to reality. But the more important the work is, the more it comes under the influence of inner relationships and necessities, the more it subjects creation to a superior truth, the more it liberates from mere subjectivism and individualism. In this case, the individual, as a thing apart from the spiritual world, becomes, unperceived, the individual *with* the spiritual world. To such an one, however, the storm and struggle of to-day can signify only a transition to a higher stage of truth.

In the same way, in the case of the problem of the content of life, pure individualism and subjectivism is preserved from unbearable emptiness only by being continually supplemented. Considered strictly, it must disintegrate the soul into a number of separate processes, finally into mere moods, which pursue and displace one another in rapid succession. Since each moment has just as good a right as another, each would have its own truth. Thus that which may at first have seemed an advantage is finally seen to be a severe loss. Human life does not by any means completely exhaust itself in a number of separate moments. The moments and their experiences are not completely swallowed up; they come back, they present themselves to our souls; hence man must compare them and link them together, measure them and judge them; he thus stands above the mere moments. Occupying this position, he must also experience that what to-day reckons as true becomes untrue; hence he feels the transitory and unreal character of the whole affair, and becomes convinced that a truth for yesterday or to-day is no truth at all, and that his life loses each and every truth when it remains tied down to the mere moment. Is there anything more tiring and more profoundly depressing than the incessant change of opinions and moods, the eager denunciation of that which has just been enthusiastically honoured, the degradation of all spiritual movement to a matter of mere whims and moods?

Individualism would like to assist life to the full development of its power and give it as far as possible the character of greatness. That is an aspiration which can be at once understood and appreciated. If man stands at a critical point of the whole, if a higher stage of reality begins in him, then it becomes our duty to seize this higher and cause it to prevail against all contradiction in everyday life, to live, as Marcus Aurelius puts it, upon a mountain. Thus, from the earliest times, whenever the gap between the demands of spiritual life and the average position of humanity came to clear consciousness, there has arisen, with imperative necessity, the thought of a higher species of life, the idea of man's inner greatness. This thought can be traced from the height of Greek culture through manifold changes down to the present day.* But will modern individualism attain to a true greatness if it abandons all inner relationships and hence all possibility of an enlargement of man to a cosmic being? There could hardly be a more violent contradiction than to desire to lead man to a superior inwardness and at the same time entirely and bitterly to oppose an independent inner world. The present position of religion, which stands in the first place for this independent inner world, may be in many respects unsatisfactory; as free men we should

* It would be an interesting task thus to follow up this problem through the ages. Aristotle's detailed investigations with respect to great natures (μεγαλόψυχος) would form the scientific point of departure for such a study. Here, the concepts are still fluid; the idea of a greatness within the human sphere converts itself, almost imperceptibly, into the idea of a greatness in contrast to all that is human. In the Ancient World the idea of greatness involved more particularly a rest and independence superior to the routine of human activity, while in the Modern World it stands rather for a superior power of achievement and a power of spiritual creation: here, too, we perceive the contrasting ideals of permanence and movement. The exaggerated talk of greatness probably originated more particularly in the time of Louis XIV.; at any rate the writers of that period were peculiarly intoxicated with the concept. Among more recent investigations dealing with historical greatness, the most important is perhaps that by Jakob Burckhardt in his *Weltgeschichtlichen Betrachtungen*.

nevertheless form our concepts and convictions with regard to the highest things, not according to what the environment provides, but according to what the necessity of our own life demands. Without a reversal of the first position, without *metaphysics*, there is no independent inner world, no true greatness of life. Hence whenever any figure towers conspicuously above its fellows in the confusion of modern life, a metaphysical tendency is not far to seek. Consider Nietzsche, for example: in his concepts he emphatically opposes all metaphysics, but in his mental attitudes there is operative a world completely different from that of first appearances, and it is precisely as the artistic creator of this world, as the metaphysician of a particular frame of mind, that he has obtained his sweeping power over men's minds. The same may be said with regard to the whole modern tendency towards Romanticism. The mere frame of mind, however, will never under any circumstances suffice to develop and carry out a greatness in opposition to the depressing and superficialising effects of the environment; it gives only a greatness of opinion, not of reality. Nothing can be built up from nothing, and the mere mental attitude has nothing behind it.

The same is true of the desire for power. To-day, in particular, in the face of difficult complications and great tasks of life as a whole, we need much power, more power than the merely social type of human culture can yield. But through a merely subjective self-elevation, a self-persuasion of power, a placing of oneself above other people, we shall never under any circumstances attain to real power. The actual experiences of modern life illustrate this well enough. It would hardly be possible to talk about power more than we do to-day; but have we become strong, does our literary and political life produce a sufficiency of strong, self-shaped, clearly defined personalities, does it offer us great and elevating creative works?

γ. *The Necessity for an Inner Overcoming of the Antithesis*

When neither the merely social nor the individualistic type of human culture is equal to the tasks which confront it, when neither gives life a real content, and when at the same time it is beyond doubt that only the most deplorable obtuseness can attempt a direct compromise between the two, a division of life into the social and the individual, then it becomes imperatively necessary for us to become superior to the contrast. Society and the individual are necessary aspects and modes of appearance of spiritual life; individuals are essential to its originality, society to its consolidation. Both society and the individual, however, draw their power and truth not from themselves but from the spiritual relationships which surround them. The relationship between society and the individual will take different forms at different historical epochs; when consolidation is above all necessary, after times of upheaval and disintegration (as for example towards the end of the Ancient World), the general trend of life will be towards the social type of civilisation. Augustine enables us to see what it was that at that time imperatively drove even the most powerful individuals to fall back upon society. The movement towards the individual, on the other hand, will be uppermost when fresh upward-striving forces feel the traditional order of life to be too narrow and rigid, and are able to seek new paths only through a liberation from this order. This was the main tendency of the Modern World on into the nineteenth century; then came a reaction, and at the present time society and the individual are both striving for an increase of power, a social-practical and an artistic-individual type of culture struggling for the leadership of humanity. This shows with peculiar clearness the inner division of our age, a division which must at the same time operate as an imperative impulse towards an elevation above the antithesis, towards a transition from a merely human culture to an essential and spiritual culture capable of embracing the contrast. This division can be met and overcome only through an inner forward movement of life, for what is generally true of a real problem is in this case particularly true; namely, that it is not a conflict of opinion with opinion but of specific life-development with specific life-development.

b. The Social-Democratic Movement

In dealing with the spiritual and intellectual tendencies of the age we cannot pass over Social Democracy. This subject has, however, been discussed and written about to the point of satiety, and it will be desirable strictly to confine ourselves to the specifically philosophical aspect of the matter.

From the philosophical point of view, the most characteristic thing about the social-democratic movement is its comprehension of three different movements, all of which it employs to further its ends: the democratic, the economic, and the political movements. It is a question, in the first place, of the transference of the centre of gravity of social life to the masses, then of the elevation of the economic problem to be the dominating soul of this life, and finally of the recognition of the *state* as the sole vehicle of power and intelligence. The central idea is to bring about an economic revolution for the benefit of the masses through the agency of the state, and to maintain this new position; at this point all the separate threads combine. The whole derives strength more particularly from the fact that the separate movements had already aroused men and given rise to much enthusiasm before their union, and that their coalescence seems to be no more than the completion of what would otherwise have remained indefinite and unable to face its own consequences. Let us glance over the history of these movements.

By democracy we do not mean the state alone, but the whole social life of humanity and the whole relationship of individuals to the common goods of life. The Modern World is favourable to this tendency if only for the reason that many severe obstacles, peculiar to previous ages, have been removed. In the Ancient World, the limitation of civilisation to certain special races (so that even the best men saw nothing wrong in slavery) militated against a recognition of the equality of all men. In Christianity there was certainly an element favourable to democracy—the revelation of the direct and equal relationship of all individuals to God; but this was placed very much in the background, partly by the hierarchical system, which reached back to the earliest times, and partly by the transcendental attitude towards life. It attained, for the first time, to a more vigorous development in certain separate branches of the Reformation, soon, however, passing over into the modern movement. The Modern

World directed man more and more exclusively towards the outer world: at the same time, its chief tendency, the Enlightenment, assigned the first place in man's life to something lying outside all individual differences—abstract reason, pure thought; the more this raised itself to full consciousness and the more it penetrated into the convictions of the individuals, the more irresistible it became; therewith humanity increasingly allowed all social differences to pale, and the recognition of the equality of all that bore the human feature became more and more inescapable.

The Modern World is, however, by no means free from counteracting influences tending to favour the aristocratic system of life. We inherit from history great differences in political position, in wealth, and in education. More aristocratic than any of these traditional factors is and remains nature with its differences of physical and mental equipment. A peculiar kind of aristocracy is produced, too, by modern civilisation with its elaborate technical division of work, its increasing ramification: for the more this tendency increases, the more division and gradation results, the more arrangement and governing control society requires and the greater is the trend towards a new aristocratic system. Nevertheless, no such resistance on the part of the actual form of life hinders the progress of the democratic movement in human conviction; now the gradation is opposed as artificial, or at any rate as having become artificial, now it is put aside as being of secondary importance; under any circumstances it is not accepted as a final act of destiny, but reduced as far as possible by human counter-influences. The smaller currents may to a great extent flow backwards, but the main stream still continues to run towards democracy.

Moreover, the independence and predominance of economic questions is a product of the Modern World. The concern for the *mine* and the *thine* has certainly been the commanding problem for the individual in all ages; only by a gross error could it be supposed that the Ancient World was dedicated solely to ideal tasks, because philosophers made a point of strongly stigmatising the too powerful desire for material possessions; but the economic sphere was not valued in principle in antique civilisation. This was due in the first place to the fact that complete satisfaction was awaited from the unrolment of a fixed and limited nature, and such a development as this, demands only a limited employment of outward means; a further cause was that this ethical and artistic ideal of life was carried over without hesitation from the individual to society, and in the latter case, too, the same fixed limit was recognised. Christianity, with its direction of thought towards a super-sensual world, was still more unfavourable to an appreciation of economic goods. In the case of Christianity, the theory still remained entirely subject to influences derived from the Ancient World. The Modern World, on the other hand, with its trend towards a maximum development of power and towards the immediate world, took up quite another attitude from the very beginning. Material goods were now looked upon as an indispensable lever with which to set forces in motion; they seemed both to initiate progress and to advance it. The economic movement was further strengthened and ennobled through the building up of national unities. As economics took on the form of national economy the old doubts faded away. This altered valuation was already visible at the time of the Renaissance, and in seventeenth century France we see its effects in the politics of a great nation. Thus the general circumstances were such as to prepare the world for the new views, when finally the economic theory of Adam Smith made the economic movement the core and standard type of the whole of civilised life, and declared the aspiration towards a better standard of life to be the main motive force of all movement, even in science, art, education, and religion. There was no lack of decisive opposition to this exaltation of the economic factor, but on the other hand the unceasing growth of a technical and elaborate civilisation tended continually to increase the importance of material things; moreover, further support was lent to the economic movement by the swelling tide of realism, which clearly exhibited the dependence of spiritual life upon natural conditions and wished to deduce the inner entirely from the outer. Seeing that recent developments of work have produced serious economic complications (in complete contradiction to Adam Smith's optimism!) it cannot be regarded as very surprising if salvation for the whole of life is awaited from a solution of these complications through the establishment of a new economic order.

The third tendency is political; it represents the valuation and over-valuation of the state. How many important factors worked in this direction during the nineteenth century we have already seen. The inclination to place the state first in all things and to grant it the leadership in the whole work of civilisation and human culture is obviously still on the increase. Here, too, social democracy merely gives full and strong expression to that which dominates most of us, though in a weaker and vaguer form. At any rate it is no accident that in Germany, with its inclination towards the omnipotence of the state, the social-democratic movement has made peculiarly rapid progress, while it has spread much more slowly among the Anglo-Saxon nations.

This union of democracy, economics, and politics is in itself by no means essential. Nay, it may well be said that it involves sharp contradictions. In particular, does not the freedom of the individual, upon which democracy insists, come into irreconcilable conflict with the constraining power of the state? Whatever may be the case, however, with regard to the justifiability of this union, it is, in the first place, a historical fact, and it grips the people of the present day with all the power of a fact. Moreover, in spite of all their differences, these main tendencies possess an inner relationship which is more especially noticeable in their negative characteristics: everything transcendental and metaphysical is consistently rejected—hence no independent spiritual world is tolerated; the whole desires to be entirely *immanent*, to be a culture and civilisation purely and simply for the present world. It hence becomes a merely *human* culture. This fundamental conviction is revealed in the belief in the masses, in the exaltation of economic goods, and in the elevation of the state to be the vehicle of reason. It is hence an error to suppose that a religious conviction can be united to this thought-world, or that the latter may even be transferred into the religious domain. For a secular and merely human character is essential to this movement; it is by no means a mere adjunct given to it by individuals. It is not a case of partial theories which may be applied in this way or that, but of a synthesis of life as a whole, of an all-embracing thought-world which appeals to the whole man and claims his whole soul. To-day, the movement receives its main strength in the first place from the fact that it demands the whole man and subjects his activity, in all its manifoldness, to an all-dominating idea.

Specific developments of life can be met only by specific developments of life; all mere criticism, however ingenious or intelligent, stands in the same relationship to them that a shadow stands in to the solid body which produces it. Thus, in this case, too, criticism will be confined as narrowly as possible to that which specially concerns the philosophy and view of life associated with the movement.

In the first place, it is obvious that our conviction as a whole is sharply and irreconcilably opposed to the life-ideal operative in this movement. We set ourselves in the most resolute possible manner against all merely human culture. This is because we regard man as the meeting-place of two worlds, and because it is only by seizing the higher that a meaning, a value, and a right movement can be imparted to our life. This seizure, however, demands an energetic transformation not only of the first appearance of the world, but still more of man's own being; it cannot be accomplished without powerful disturbances, elevations, and renewals. In this way alone can we attain to a culture which is spiritual and rooted in the essential nature of things, a culture capable of giving man an inner greatness. Resting upon such convictions we resist the democratic system of life (*Demokratismus*) because it is guilty of a false idealisation of the sensuous and merely natural man, and is inclined to subordinate the spiritual world to what is merely human; we resist the economic system of life (*Oekonomismus*) because its construction from without inward involves a denial of the independent problems of the inner life, and because it believes the complete happiness of man to be secured by the establishment of conditions of comfort and freedom from care; and finally we reject the political system of life (*Politismus*) because it represses the independence of personality and hence endangers the originality of spiritual creation, and further because it is ready to sacrifice the self-value of spiritual goods for merely utilitarian considerations. In all these tendencies we see an inner sinking in the midst of all outward progress, a treatment of the chief things as secondary things; we see man becoming spiritually smaller.

We have thus a complete antithesis and a decisive negation. But the mere negation leaves it unexplained how the whole could obtain so much power over man, how it could not merely arouse passion but give rise to great sacrifice and gain the adherence of many noble minds. Behind that which in its more exact form endangers life, there must be operative problems of a more general nature, which we others, too, cannot reject—difficulties which will give us no peace until they have found some kind of solution or, at any rate, alleviation.

A problem of this more universal kind is contained in the idea of democracy. It is the question of an expansion of human culture and civilisation, of a more equal division of its goods, of a more powerful participation of separate individuals in spiritual life. In spite of the work of millenniums, things are still deplorable enough in this respect: notwithstanding all our progress, how small is that portion of the treasures of human development and education which falls to the lot of the vast majority! How narrow is that section of society which participates in the movement towards a higher and more inward culture! Christianity has been operative amongst us for more than a thousand years, yet in this time (so lengthy, according to human standards) how little has it become for us a transforming power, a firm inner possession, a conviction penetrating our whole being! Along with all the talk of progress and spiritual life, our spiritual beliefs have remained far too much a mere cloak cast over an existence dominated by merely natural instincts; the great contrasts and states of tension, and also the great possibilities which our life contains, are far too little worked out for the consciousness of the individual. Now, however, we are beginning—and that is in itself a turn for the better—to feel it as an unreality that a higher kind of life is indeed operative somewhere in humanity, but remains inwardly strange and remote to the majority of individuals; when such a feeling has once become aroused, then it will somehow have to be satisfied; even if in the struggle for such goals the limits of human capacity become ever so noticeable, it makes an immense difference whether the situation we deplore is accepted as a destiny, or the struggle for the larger participation of all is taken up, and hence the guilt removed as far as possible from humanity.

These considerations are strengthened by an observation to which no unprejudiced person can close his eyes. Our age exhibits many signs of senility; a refined Epicureanism conquers more and more ground; many circles chosen to lead show themselves mentally indolent and obtuse, and maintain lofty claims while imparting no worthy content to their life. Is it remarkable that the conviction is continually gaining ground that to-day it is almost more a question of needing new men than new ideas, fresh and unspoiled individuals, upward-striving, mentally and spiritually thirsty sections of society? Those who recognise this need not by any means commit themselves to Social Democracy and regard its methods of reform as the correct ones, but they will understand the desire for a better state of affairs.

Economism, as a system claiming the leadership in life, threatens to guide us along a problematical and descending path. It can obtain an ascendancy over us only if there is no independent inner life and the problems of the soul are neglected. At the same time, the economic elevation would not be greeted as a deliverance from all our necessities if care for the maintenance of life did not press with painful heaviness upon many of us: it would assuredly be no source of happiness if the table of life were ready spread for us and we had only to enjoy ourselves, if all care and struggle disappeared; but it remains profoundly sad that, as is usually the case, this one care for the preservation of life so greatly predominates and so overpoweringly absorbs men's thoughts and feelings. Life thus falls under a heavy yoke, which tends to produce inner littleness and degradation, and to cause a dulling mediocrity inhibiting all fresh and free upward movement. It is true that necessity has often given rise to much that is great; but, as Pestalozzi lastly observes: "There is a poverty which leads to the building up of human powers and serves as the foundation of man's happiness and inner greatness. But there is also a poverty that is the parent of despair" (*Wke.*, viii. 98). The Modern World has done much to remove this pressure and inner degradation. May we not venture to assert that far more still remains to be done, that much might be other and better than it is, not only as regards the attitude and feeling of the individual, but also as regards general conditions?

We have repeatedly referred to the questionable element in the political movement. Not only the freedom of the individual, but the soul of life as a whole, are threatened with danger from this quarter. "If everything should be governed by rule and regulation, then life—difficult already—must become absolutely unbearable": thus spake Plato more than two thousand years ago. Why then does the idea of the state make such immense progress to-day, precisely, too, in the very circles which are more particularly interested in the cause of freedom? It is surely because the individual, on account of the breaking down of traditional relationships and the thorough insecurity of his own position, yearns after some sort of firm hold, because he wishes to see his existence in some way valued and protected by the whole. This reaches far beyond all economic problems into the inner life and life as a whole. At the time of the breaking up of the Ancient World such a desire for more support and more valuation contributed not a little to win men's hearts over to the Christian Church: to-day, the same desire seems to be breaking out again with renewed strength. We must take care not to underestimate these movements because they move quietly and secretly beneath the surface of life; for it is in such movements that psychic conditions are fostered which later break out suddenly with irresistible force and drive the whole of visible life along completely new paths. To-day, inner rearrangements, molecular transformations, if the expression be permitted, are in progress. What shaping of human conditions will result therefrom lies for the time being in profound obscurity.

Moreover, we must not assign too low a value to the unity of the thought-world which is operative in the social-democratic

movement. It is true enough that in view of our rejection of
all merely human culture the specific character of this unity,
with its deification of man, must appear a disastrous error.
But unity is unity. Unity alone makes it possible for the
several departments of work mutually to support one another,
and for the whole man to be active at each separate point.
The only other system which to-day offers an all-embracing
unity is ecclesiastical Catholicism, which, being closely united
to the mediæval mode of thought, is unavoidably placed in an
ever-increasing opposition to the movements of the present age
and the needs of the modern man, nay, to the inner necessities
of spiritual life itself. Within the sphere of the Modern World
itself the Enlightenment possessed a kind of life-unity and at
the same time offered an all-embracing ideal; but since it broke
up we have found ourselves involved in a serious inner division,
which is becoming increasingly intolerable. In particular, it
is customary for those who wish to arrange life upon a basis
of freedom to be guilty of the truly amazing paradox that on
the practical side they are never tired of exalting the greatness,
dignity, and capacity of man, while on the theoretical side they
heatedly oppose that view of life which is alone capable of
supporting such an estimate of man; they fancy themselves
all the more secure in their freedom the more negative and
the more empty is their thought-world (see p. 427). In thus
supporting only negative and superficial views of life, they themselves undermine the very ground upon which their aspirations
rest: such an absence of clarity, or rather such thoughtlessness,
is incapable of producing any deep effect.

It is impossible to avoid recognising that we are face to face
with a severe crisis. It will have to be decided whether the
human culture and society of to-day contains the power to accomplish an *inner synthesis and spiritual elevation of life*, and hence
to offer resistance to the disintegration, or whether it is incapable
of rising to the occasion. In the first case, the attack upon it
can only serve the purpose of bringing the culture into contact
with its own depths and liberating it from the petty human
element; in the second case, the culture and society of to-day
must go under, and it would then deserve no better fate. The

spiritual world itself, together with its effective relationship towards humanity, stands as firm and secure above such changes as do the stars above the trivial turmoil on the surface of the earth. It may even be that a downright negation of all independent spirituality and a dissolution of all invisible relationships will be desirable, in order that humanity, through an indirect proof, should again have the indispensability of the spiritual world emphatically brought to its consciousness, and thus life should be again helped to attain to that content of truth which is to-day so painfully lacking.

4. THE PROBLEMS OF MORALITY

(a) The Present Insecure Position of Morality

TO-DAY, our conception and our valuation of morality are alike extremely unsettled. From one point of view, morality seems to offer a solid foundation in the midst of the upheaval of philosophical and religious convictions, to afford a basis of agreement for all those elements that would otherwise fall apart: for if all else be insecure, there still remains man and his relationship to man; our social life offers us tasks, the reality of which is beyond dispute. Hence there has arisen a movement in the direction of ethical culture, and great interest (extending beyond the limits of this particular sphere) has been taken in all that tends to further the welfare of our fellow-men, and in so doing to give our own lives also a valuable content. Morality is here practically synonymous with altruism. It is interpreted as action for others, the placing of other people's interests before our own. This tendency forms a main element in modern civilisation; great movements to remove pain and necessity, to soften strictness and hardness, to make our existence more humane, have drawn, and are continually drawing, their inspiration from this source.

But in the midst of all these achievements there remains, in principle, much that is doubtful and contradictory. Perhaps men unite so readily on the basis of altruistic morality because it places the deeper moral problems in the background—if not actually denying their existence. After all, is it certain that morality is identical with altruism, with action for others? The expression "altruism" is derived from Comte's philosophy, that is, from a system which entirely surrenders the independence of the soul and reduces the whole of life to a mere matter of relationship to environment. Should this conception of morality be adopted, just as it stands, by those who do not accept this philosophy? As a matter of fact, the identification of morality with altruism means that the former will become narrow in scope and shallow in content. Does social and humanitarian activity exhaust the whole meaning of morality? Have we not to face great tasks within ourselves, in the development of our own souls and in our relationship to the world and external things in general? Throughout our whole lives we are faced by this alternative; shall our conduct serve our own pleasure, or shall it be determined by motives of an objective character? The creative work of an artist, for example, may be guided by all sorts of different motives; he may be seeking fame, recognition, or personal profit; he may aim at satisfying the whims and desires of the public; or, finally, he may be following solely the inner necessities of his creative work, obeying these, if necessary, with heroic courage, in spite of all the opposition which his environment may offer, in spite, possibly, of personal danger : does not such truth to ourselves and our work come under the head of moral conduct? Similarly, spiritual self-preservation may lead the investigator or the man of religious conviction into the sharpest opposition to environment, and may drive him to the complete loss of peace and comfort. In fact, the whole movement towards spirituality, with its demands, troubles, and doubts, may appear as a disturbance of our equilibrium and an enemy to immediate happiness. Nevertheless, do we not recognise in it a moral task? If this be true, then morality is certainly something deeper and better than mere altruism.

Further, it may be brought forward against the altruistic position that it does not understand how to base morality upon the depth of the soul itself, how to make it a matter of spiritual self-preservation : it is favoured to-day, however, by the insecurity which surrounds the more spiritual position; we are influenced by two different thought-worlds from the past, representing more inward types of morality; the world of religion and that of immanent idealism. In the one case it was the relation to a being superior to the world, and in the other man's own reason, which was to give rise to tasks comprehending the whole of life and to provide an ethical valuation for our whole conduct. From the point of view of the spiritual life of to-day, both types are not only shaken to the foundation, but their content has become largely doubtful. The religious world has totally disappeared from the horizon of large masses of people, while immanent idealism has increasingly lost its force and vitality. At the same time, the general tendency of the age regards religious morality as too soft and too passive, while the morality based upon reason appears too abstract and its strict idea of duty makes too stern an impression. Thus social morality, with its altruism, remains the only unchallenged position—and this we have already found to be too shallow and narrow.

It only remains, therefore, to point out the fact that our age possesses no morality at all, corresponding to the present spiritual state of the world's historical development; it is without a characteristic morality capable of satisfying its most inward necessities. Regarded from the point of view of its innermost nature, morality is to-day at least as insecure as is religion.* How greatly the fact that we have no morality of our own reduces the power of morality in the present age, and how very easy it makes it for the opponents of morality to caricature it, to mock at their caricatures, and then to believe morality itself refuted and abolished, is made abundantly clear by numerous observations of modern life. We shall not be able to face these complications if we do not succeed, through a self-recollection and a self-deepening of life, in again obtaining a self-experienced morality of our own. This is perhaps the most urgent of all present-day needs.

* In spite of this fundamental insecurity our age offers an abundance of moral treatises and books for moral instruction. And why not, indeed? Lichtenberg said well when, with regard to Hamlet's saying that there were many things in heaven and on the earth not contained in our philosophies, he remarked: " Good; but on the other hand there are a multitude of things in our philosophies that are not to be found either in heaven or upon the earth." See *Vermischte Schriften* (1801), ii. 356.

(b) Morality and Metaphysics

To-day there is a widespread inclination to separate morality wholly from the problems of cosmic philosophy and to grasp it directly as a thing in itself. Many believe that this will result in a great liberation and simplification of life, while a number of historical examples are brought forward in support of the movement. In particular, an appeal is made to the great name of Kant.

From the earliest times, man has tended to turn away from the perplexities of cosmic philosophy and to seek refuge in a well-ordered life. The individual may be justified in so doing, but can the same be said of humanity as a whole? Does not this action on the part of the individual presuppose the existence, independent of him, of a secure and recognised morality? In particular, only an entire misunderstanding could attribute to Kant the intention of abandoning cosmic problems and taking refuge in the haven of practical work. His thought is concerned, not with the antithesis of theory and practice, but with that of theoretical and practical reason; but where reason enters into the discussion then we have invariably to deal with cosmic relationships; thus Kant does not abandon ultimate convictions with regard to the whole of reality; he merely seeks the point at which these convictions must be decided in a different quarter from that in which it was sought by the old-fashioned speculative philosophy; he does not make morality the centre of his thought-world without announcing it as the appearance of a new order of things, of an intelligible kingdom of reason. Kant is a metaphysician of his own kind; but a metaphysician he is, through and through. The every-day wisdom which places practical work before thought can claim no fellowship with him.

In reality, it is only needful to examine its phenomena a little more closely to perceive that morality comes into the sharpest conflict with the immediate view of the world. However much our conceptions of morality may differ, they always involve a detachment of life and aspiration from the mere ego, a progress beyond mere natural self-preservation:

as soon as it is discovered, with regard to any action that has been praised as moral, that the feeling behind it has been derived (even in a concealed or indirect manner) from mere motives of self-preservation, we regard its moral character as destroyed. Now, even nature shows certain beginnings of a liberation of life from mere self-preservation, but these remain scattered and impure, so that it signifies a change—indeed, a revolution—when the new type of conduct develops in its purity and claims dominion over life. New meanings and new values now reveal themselves. Shall we not need a new world in which to connect and consolidate these?

Further, conduct does not possess a moral character unless it proceeds from free decision and manifests an original life: if, in any way, it comes to light that a presumably moral action proceeds from mere habit, mechanical compulsion, or the pressure of authority, and does not involve personal decision and application, the action at once loses its distinctive character and drops out of the moral sphere. Now, the natural world, with its thoroughgoing causal connection, does not afford the least room for this self-activity and free decision. Its structure resists every attempt to loosen its rigidity. Hence, if there be no domain other than that of nature, and if its order be valid for spiritual life also, then there is no room for any sort of morality which aims at being anything more than a "policing" of social life.

When the moral demand attains to full self-consciousness it makes the claim to be incomparably superior to all other aims. It then rejects all considerations of mere utility and brings an *absolute* directly into human life. It stands or falls with the saying: "For what is a man profited if he gain the whole world and lose his own soul?" But how is this possible if a new type of reality does not stand behind this valuation? And were it possible, would it not then involve an undue strain? For in immediate existence all purposes must fit into one another and be judged by one another; in this sphere there is nothing absolute to raise itself to a position of complete superiority.

Thus, no matter from what side we regard it, morality involves the demand for a new world. It brings with it a reversal of the first appearance of things, and is therefore metaphysical. Hence by having recourse to morality we do not rid ourselves of metaphysics. If we are really earnest in keeping morality free from all metaphysics we unavoidably reduce it to a state of lamentable superficiality. On the other hand, there is certainly good reason for liberating morality from the complicated deductions of the older speculative philosophy and for making it more than a secondary phenomenon dependent upon a cosmic philosophy of totally independent origin.

Our concept of spiritual life as the orientation of reality towards an inner life of its own, again reveals a passage between Scylla and Charybdis. For we look upon spiritual life as the "coming-to-itself" of the world-process, the winning of an essential being and meaning over against the meaningless network of relationships and self-preservative activities which result from the régime of the mere individual. With the recognition of this new world nature necessarily sinks to a second and lower form of being. But just as the higher must be kept up by unceasing self-activity so it must first be awakened at each individual centre, and there appropriated through self-activity. Such a self-active appropriation of the spiritual world is nothing other than morality, which is thus a penetration of life to truthfulness and essential being, a winning of a new, infinite self, a "becoming infinite" from within. For it has been pointed out that the spiritual stage consists essentially in the direct participation of each individual in the life of the whole, the individual no longer receiving such life through the mediation of isolated impressions.

Thus conceived, morality is, in the first place, a movement within the realm of personal life, an endeavour to reach ourselves, a wrestling for our own being. But since this being now exhibits a cosmic character, a cosmic movement is now directly revealed in this labour upon ourselves. It is a consideration of these facts which bids us demand the closest connection between morality and metaphysics and makes us regard a morality without metaphysics as an absurdity. Morality does not demand cosmic concepts merely for its explanation. As a result of its very existence it directly develops a new world which encircles us with an illuminating present. The connection between morality and metaphysics can be rejected only by those whose conception of metaphysics is that of the old school-metaphysics which, from a supposed necessity of thought, devised a new world in addition to the existing one, or by those who would reduce morality to a mere social order, a "policing" of life—the latter assuredly needs no new world, but neither is it morality, except in a merely nominal sense! *It is our conviction that all morality sinks to a mere appearance, if the spiritual life—the appropriation of which is the object of morality—does not form the core of reality.*

Armed with this conception of morality it will be possible for us to confront the problems and difficulties with which morality has to deal, and with which so much error and misunderstanding is associated. Morality, as thus viewed, is primarily the elevation of life, the winning of a true self as opposed to a merely apparent self, the appropriation of the whole infinite universe; but this elevation does not spring from immediate existence through a mere refinement of the natural life; it must be conceived of as opposed to this existence, as a task, a claim, a command. The limitations and negations which are involved in this claim operate ultimately towards the affirmation of life; the idea of duty which originates here springs from our own being and is not imposed from without. Thus we attain to an affirmation of life which, far from asserting any deification of mere nature and selfhood, meets all such pretensions with a decisive "No."

Looked at from this point of view, morality signifies no mere achievement within a given world but the gaining of a new world, no conflict within the world but a struggle for supremacy between different worlds; it is not a question of a new kind of action, but of a new kind of being, though one which must certainly be continually translated into corresponding action. Now man is the meeting-place of different stages of reality, nay of opposed worlds, and his decision must settle which of these worlds is to be dominant. Nay, since henceforth, from his own particular station, he has to maintain the higher stage of reality, since here the new world can come to full realisation only through his action, his conduct reaches out beyond the individual standpoint and wins a meaning that is universal. And with this comes the surest liberation from mere egotism, an expansion of the soul, an elevation above all mere subservience to utility; an incomparable greatness and dignity is added to man.

This greatness is indeed associated with serious perplexities. For the task cannot be magnified in this fashion without bringing to light the widest disparities and the most determined resistances between man and man. Before all else the natural world keeps man bound down to the mere ego; in the face of this resistance the movement towards spirituality makes but little impression, it threatens to remain a mere intention, to sink to a mere appearance; it becomes clearly visible that, as compared with the strength of the mere man, something impossible is being demanded. *Therefore man must become something more than mere man.* How could cosmic life be turned in a new direction except by a cosmic force?—thus a cosmic force must be operative in man from the very outset; there must be a receptivity corresponding to man's activity, a hand from above to draw the climber up; yea, in freedom itself there must shine out some revelation of grace. Truly a transformation of life's first aspect! The original affirmation has become intolerable, but out of the negation has arisen a new affirmation. Here are great demands and great upheavals, gigantic tides of life sweeping men along and transforming them, much incompleteness and insecurity, much stubborn resistance and paralysing constraint; but in the midst of all doubts and resistances, life continues to maintain itself, greater depths are opened up, an inner infinitude becomes increasingly manifest. If anything can show us that our life is not a matter of indifference, that in it something significant takes place, it is morality that can do it.

(c) Morality and Art
(*The Ethical and Æsthetical Views of Life*)

That art and morality have been in frequent conflict from the earliest times and that their relationship to one another has been one of tension and hostility is by no means a mere consequence of human error. There is a reason for it in the very nature of things. The two spheres seem to place life under opposed tasks and valuations: morality demands a subordination to universally valid laws, art on the other hand desires the freest development of individuality; morality speaks with the stern voice of duty, art invites the free play of all our forces; morality has its dwelling-place in the sphere of pure inwardness and is prone to think but little of visible achievement, while art values only that which can be outwardly embodied. In order to arrive at a correct valuation of this contrast and conflict it will be advantageous briefly to review the historical development of the problem, if only as a safeguard against individual prejudice and bias.

1. On the History of the Problem

It is a singular fact that the Greeks, superior as they were to all other peoples in artistic achievement, did not assign an important place to art in their philosophical work. The case against art was maintained by no less a thinker than the greatest artist among the philosophers—Plato: many different tendencies in Plato's work combined to make him find fault with art; his desire for a truly genuine and non-sensuous being forced him to regard art as the mere shadow of a shadow; he was further repelled by the ever-varying nature of its forms, as seen more particularly in the case of dramatic art, by the impurity of the mythological thought-world which dominated art, and, finally, by the feverish excitation of emotional life, which he saw continually increasing. Undisturbed by such accusations, art pursued its way and retained its leading place in the life of the Ancient World. But the more it lapsed into subjective virtuosity — now eccentric exaggeration and now effeminate dilettantism—and the more formal polish replaced real content, the stronger became the reaction in favour of a hard and severe morality, the more Cynicism and Stoicism became the refuge of those proud souls who scorned to render homage to the mere enjoyment of the beautiful.

It was in connection with the rising religious movement that art for the first time secured full recognition of its independent value, as is seen more particularly in the philosophy of Plotinus: the inward deepening which morality thereby experienced had also the effect of deepening the task of art. According to Plotinus the beautiful involved a mastering of the lower by the higher, of the body by the soul, of matter by thought; creative power does not lose itself in the stone, it remains spiritually free and passes from soul to soul; the visible work of art has value only as a medium for the soul's feeling. Art is no longer, as it was with Plato, a mere imitation of nature; it endeavours to depict the highest reason operative in nature, and in so doing it may very well achieve more than nature itself. But the fundamental religious temper here operative did far more to bring the beautiful into sympathy with the interests of mystical contemplation than with those of artistic creation. Hence we find an artistic temper pervading the whole of life, but rather evading than seeking a palpable form of expression.

It was impossible for Christianity to transfer the centre of gravity of life from the artistic to the moral without the reputation and status of art at first suffering the severest injury. Moreover, the type of art which prevailed during the latter days of the Ancient World could only encourage the abandonment of art. But although in the general life of the age art developed in a fashion which was often very unedifying and not infrequently deteriorated into a contempt for all form, its development on the higher levels of culture was of a very different kind: the deepening of spiritual life which had been effected by religion led art into new pathways. This is more particularly to be seen in the case of Jesus Himself. It is true in general of the founders of the historical religions that only the possession of a conspicuously creative imagination enabled them to make an invisible world obviously and overpoweringly present, and indeed to make it man's chief world; it is particularly true of Jesus. In His case this world presentation was marked by a quite peculiar warmth, tenderness, and inwardness. By clearly and plainly holding up the kingdom of God to man as a kingdom of true love and childlike confidence, thereby awakening latent feelings and filling men's minds with a deep yearning, He effected an artistic transfiguration of human existence. This is to be seen with peculiar clearness in the discovery of the purity, innocence, and devotion of child-life and in the wonderful manner in which the simplest processes of nature were employed as illustrations of the condition of the human soul. So that in this case, notwithstanding the setting aside of all sensuous art, a secure pathway was prepared for spiritual art. Later on the Greek idea of beauty became more and more influential. We see this illustrated in Gregory of Nyssa and Augustine. It is true that the latter, to a very large extent, fell under the influence of tendencies hostile to art, and his conversion to Christianity was due in no small measure to his profound dissatisfaction with a formal and literary education and to the desire for a genuine life-content; but in his own sphere of thought he clung firmly to the beautiful, through which the ascent to an all-embracing unity was made, and he taught that all manifoldness was to be understood as a work and witness of this unity. Finally, he came to regard the whole cosmos as an ethical work of art, as an order completely reconciling justice and love. At the same time Augustine was himself a conspicuous master of language; his work reveals the whole power and tenderness of a mind moving to and fro between the contrasts of existence. He imparted a wonderfully musical tone to the Latin language, and as employed by him it became a suitable medium for the expression of the deepest inner life.

The ecclesiastical system of the Middle Ages brought with it a certain far-reaching reconciliation of the main opposing tendencies, and it did not omit to give the beautiful a place within its system. In the general construction of life, this is to be seen in the prominent place assigned to the order and harmony of the whole; in the more detailed arrangement, it appears in the manifold ways in which art is called upon to glorify religion and the Church.

The Modern Period, with its greater vitality and its intensification of all contrasts, destroyed the mediæval equilibrium. During its whole course the struggle and contrast has never ceased. At the very commencement, the Renaissance and the Reformation gave the contrast its most decisive expression. In the Renaissance an æsthetical view of the world and of life in general attained full consciousness for the first time; now the beautiful became the chief instrument in the development of life, the most important means for the expression of every kind of power and for the self-realisation and self-enjoyment of man. Art taught life to find itself, to reach its own highest level. At the same time life rejected as unreal all invisible ties; predominantly devoted to immediate reality, it aspired, through the control of inner and outer nature, to realise a full and boundless happiness. Filled with a powerful desire for life and a proud self-consciousness, it was easy for men to look upon morality as a restriction imposed from without, as a rigid ordinance and a tiresome constraint; the stronger the individuality the more he seemed justified in shaking off all such constraint and following solely his own inclination. Hence arose the immorality of the Renaissance, a chief reason for its collapse as a world-dominating power. At its best, however, there was no lack of personalities who overcame the opposition, grasping art with the whole force of their being and giving it the form of an ethical life-work—we need refer only to Michael Angelo. After the Renaissance the artistic movement pursued the line of the grotesque and rococo. And yet from time to time a wave of the old feeling would draw men back to the Renaissance.

The strength of the Reformation lay in the great importance assigned to morality and in the deepening of personal responsibility. Thus it brought a great earnestness into life, and this exerted an influence reaching far beyond the reformers themselves or even their followers. An inward deepening of this kind was not directly favourable to art: moreover art, with its wealth of sensuous imagery, seemed to render the approach of man to God more difficult; and to gain a direct relationship to God was the all-important object of life. Hence an intense scorn for every species of image and ornament, for did not these obscure the living presence of God in the soul and so tend to make life superficial and effeminate? But, although, in this manner, modes of feeling hostile to art became very influential, art of another kind grew up on a higher creative level—an art comparatively separate from the sphere of sense but more deeply rooted in the soul. In illustration one may mention Luther and Bach.

The rationalistic character of the Enlightenment, with its insistence upon logical clarity, its deliberate and resourceful purposiveness, its unhistorical mode of thought, was but little favourable to art, which was now ranked far below morality. At the same time the latter acquired no particular depth. With the rise of the New Humanism and the dawning of a new epoch the desire for beauty grew proportionately stronger. The humanistic tendency, at its best, as instanced by the leading German poets and thinkers, brought the good and the beautiful into helpful co-operation. Kant made the moral idea the corner-stone of life, but this did not prevent him recognising the independence and self-value of the beautiful, and in fact he was the first clearly to distinguish it from both the good and the agreeable; he founded it in the centre of the soul itself, and securely raised it above all mere utility and enjoyment. Thus Goethe found "the main ideas of the *Critique of Judgment* quite in sympathy with his previous convictions concerning art, thought, and conduct." Goethe himself, however, notwithstanding the greatness of his artistic creation, was far removed from undervaluing morality and from confessing to an æsthetical view of life; his artistic work was far too much an earnest and diligent seeking of his own innermost being, a conscientious labour upon himself. Those who favour a lax view of this problem have no right to appeal to Goethe, if his whole drift be taken into account and not merely isolated expressions. Although it is true enough that he would not hear of art and artistic culture being limited by "conventional moral ideas" or by "pedantry and conceit," yet in demanding that man should seize the order of the world as an order of freedom, and set himself his own limit, he assigned a moral task which embraces the whole of life and puts man into contact with a high and universal duty. Finally, Schiller, half poet and half thinker, was never tired of working towards a reconciliation of the good and the beautiful, for "freedom in the phenomenon." As Kühnemann puts it: "The characteristic, nay the unique quality of Schiller's mode of thought consisted in a high purity of moral standpoint combined with the fullest possible recognition of the independence of artistic life."

Then the two tendencies again became divided. Romanticism gave a peculiarly definite and self-conscious expression to the priority of art and the æsthetical view of life, while Fichte and the other leaders of the national movement exerted a powerful influence in the direction of strengthening morality. The social and industrial type of civilisation, which became more and more powerful during the course of the nineteenth century, was inclined, with its tendency towards social welfare and utility, to assign a subordinate part to art. Modern art rises in protest against this and is ambitious to influence the whole of life: it promises to impart more facility, more joy and more individuality to life; in opposition to morality it holds up an æsthetic view of life as being alone justifiable. Hence at the present time the two spheres again stand wide apart.

Our historical examination shows that this antithesis has existed for thousands of years. It is no temporary state of affairs: again and again morality has reproached art with disintegrating life and rendering it effeminate and inert, and in its turn morality has been charged with being hard, mechanical and soulless. Further, we have convinced ourselves that these same two elements, which become so widely separate on the lower levels of life, tend on the highest level to approach one another; in the case of creative minds, the opposition, if not entirely removed, is at any rate greatly reduced; such minds clearly prove that spiritual life cannot dispense with any of its aspects, and that the blame for this state of division must be attributed to man rather than to the nature of the problem itself. In reality, morality and art cannot take up their own tasks in a really worthy manner without each recognising the other to be not only important but indispensable; they cannot fulfil their respective missions without taking their places in a comprehensive whole of spiritual life, and seeking an understanding in this relationship.

When morality endeavours directly to take over the whole of life, it usually develops into a system of rules and regulations which makes a stern appeal to man while promising him a high reward for its fulfilment. In this manner life has been stirred up and much severe concentration has been attained, but being conceived of predominantly as a command, morality has not here won its way to full inner appropriation, nor has it given rise to love and joy. Man was thus easily tossed to and fro between a consciousness of helpless weakness and a self-conscious Pharisaism. As a matter of fact it was always a certain mediocre type of bourgeois or ecclesiastical life which was satisfied with mere morality; taking their average level, neither the early centuries of Christianity nor the age of the Enlightenment possessed an important spiritual content, in spite of their moral enthusiasm. Morality itself was able to escape the danger of becoming rigid and superficial only by entering into wider relationships. When this movement took place, however, in so far as it led towards the appropriation of a new reality, and in so far as it came to mean not merely the correct fulfilment of command but an inward renewal of man, a progress towards newness of life, it found art absolutely indispensable: for this new matter could not be comprehended as a whole, and become really present and alive, without the assistance of artistic activity; nor could it become really universal in the absence of the constructive labour of art, weaving inward and outward together. When the great object is to attain to a new world and a new life, to rise above the petty aims of the mere man and mere everyday life, then art, with its quiet and sure labour, conditioned by the inner necessities of things, with its inner liberation of the soul, and with its power to bring the whole infinitude of being inwardly near to us, and to make it part of our own life, must be directly reckoned as moral.

On the other hand, a type of art which thinks highly of itself and its task cannot possibly despise morality. There has hardly ever been a creative artist of the first rank who professed the æsthetical view of life, for such an one cannot look upon art as a separate sphere dissociated from the rest of life; he must put his whole soul into his creation, he cannot be satisfied with a mere technique, and he is far too conscious of the difficulties and shortcomings of this creation to make it a mere matter of enjoyment. As a matter of fact the æsthetical view of life is professed not so much by artists themselves as by dilettantists who study art from the outside, and often enough force their theories upon the artists, who, not much disposed to abstract discussion, and indeed defenceless against it, hardly realise that this separation of art from life as a whole does not elevate art but degrades it.

The mutual dependency of art and morality will be more particularly recognised when our world is not looked upon as finished and complete but as being in process of evolution, nay, as being a world in which what already exists has not merely to be continued but *a new stage of reality has to be inaugurated*. For this purpose we need an independent decision, an awakening of the whole being, an energetic *activity* embracing the whole of existence. It is clear that in the first place we are not called to comfortable enjoyment or to contemplation, but to *action and creation*. At the same time a powerful and artistic construction will be essential if the new world is not to remain vague and undefined, and if it is to capture the whole soul. In the construction of a new life art is indispensable.

2. THE PROBLEMS OF THE PRESENT DAY

a. *Modern Æstheticism*

After the preceding remarks it will hardly be necessary to explain our position with regard to æstheticism. But against the æstheticism of the present day, in particular, we have to make a charge of inner untruthfulness: to-day, the world and life in general exhibit far too much that is dark and irrational, and the great contradictions of existence stir us far too profoundly for it to be possible for us, with our whole souls and with complete devotion, to convert our existence predominantly into enjoyment and to experience the harmony of the whole with pure joy. This æstheticism is not so much a true expression of the modern attitude towards life as an attempt to escape from life's difficulty and earnestness. This can only be accomplished by a union with modern subjectivism, a union which gives rise to attitudes of mind, noteworthy as signs of the times, but destitute of all creative capacity and all power to elevate the soul.

A tendency compounded of individualism and æstheticism has evolved the catchword "new ethic," a phrase which has acquired considerable influence, more particularly in feminine circles. Even a movement of this kind must not be straightway depreciated; its root principles must be impartially considered. What society calls morality is nothing more than an order of social life to which custom and use has imparted an appearance of sanctity; hence, in spite of its insufficiency, it is very liable to assert itself with great self-consciousness, just as servants are very apt to be more arrogant than their masters. Now as the progress of history changes the type of social life, alterations may become necessary; the rigid conservation of the traditional type may give rise to painful pressure and may convert right into wrong and wrong into right. The Modern Period has produced such a great alteration in mutual relationships and in the type of work in general that a revision of this social order and hence of conventional morality is necessary in various directions.

But in recognising this we are far from expressing our approval of the hasty and summary manner in which difficult and responsible questions are settled by the representatives (and perhaps more particularly the feminine representatives) of an æsthetical subjectivism. To begin with, morality itself is something other than its visible representative, social order; and moral conduct is not identical with social correctness. On the highest levels of moral creation this correctness has been but little valued. The idea of making the mere means into the dominating aim has been decisively rejected. Nevertheless, in spite of its inadequacy, the means is by no means valueless. It does not follow because certain institutions have become problematical that all social order should be decried as an undue restraint; as human affairs are, it is an indispensable means of raising life to a certain level and offering an adequate resistance to the ceaselessly active disruptive forces. Only an unlimited optimism, so naïve that we are tempted to call it childish, could possibly cherish the delusion that if humanity were granted unlimited freedom the whole of life would become joyful and harmonious. Such optimism might be described as amiable if the superficiality with which it fascinates semi-educated people did not make it dangerous. It may seem regrettable that man should need social order for the disciplining of his desires, but that is not the fault of the order; those who object to it should, if they are logical, reject every medicine which does not taste agreeable. If we were to break down all restraints in the interests of a too idealistic view of life, should we not be only too apt to accomplish the very opposite of that which we desire? "L'homme n'est ni ange ni bête; et le malheur veut que qui veut faire l'ange fait la bête" (Pascal).

In view of the term "new ethic," we must protest against such a misuse of the word ethic. Words are not to be treated lightly. Their misuse may contribute towards the obscuration of genuine problems. We have been accustomed to understand by morality an order removed from mere individual whim or desire and associated with a high respect for duty and conscience. That which æsthetical subjectivism offers us under the catchword of the "new ethic" is in reality a finer form of Epicureanism, a self-indulgence on the part of the individual, who frees himself from every restriction; those who find satisfaction in it should, in consistency, reject both ethics and religion as fundamentally erroneous and remove them from their sphere of thought. They should not, however, make use of these names to gloss over a mode of thought which is essentially different. There is no mistaking the sharp contradiction. Is man nothing more than the sum total of his natural inclinations, and does human wisdom consist solely in bringing these inclinations into a state of the best possible equilibrium, or do we possess a spiritual power capable of converting our existence into free action and of enabling us to become masters of ourselves? Is our relationship to reality predominantly receptive or active? Is our subjective happiness the highest of all good, or is there an inner necessity driving us beyond such a limitation? This opposition has been clear to us since the days of the Stoics and Epicureans, and it admits of no compromise. The old Epicureans, however, thought with greater precision than do their modern followers, for they did not announce themselves as the representatives of a new ethic! *

It is in its treatment of the sensuous, more particularly in the sphere of sex, that modern subjectivism comes most sharply into conflict with other convictions. No one can deny that the subject is a complicated one. In Christianity, more particularly Catholic Christianity, a disparagement, nay, a contempt of the sense element, is still largely in evidence—an attitude of mind which originated in the tendencies of the decadent Classical Period, and the struggle Christianity then fought against a degenerate sensualism. As a matter of fact, we have to deal with a Manichæan element which has forced its way into Christianity, and, in spite of all outward strictness, tends to produce inward shallowness; for shallowness it is when the chief care of life is to carry on a struggle against the sensuous,

* The distinguished Swedish philosopher Vitalis Norström has expressed himself with regard to this problem with singular power and depth in his book *Das Tausendjährige Reich* (Germ. trans. 1907). He says, for example, on p. 31: " How extraordinary is that shallow sentimentality which cherishes the idea of building up a stable psychical equilibrium upon the satisfaction of the senses! What a poverty-stricken soul must dwell in that wisdom which knows no higher aim than that of having a permanent ' good time '—if one may employ the phrase! This world of universal indulgence (in so far as it were possible at all) would not bring out man's best qualities—the elevation above mere satisfaction, the overcoming of self: it would shut out that which, in a condition of affairs which certainly needs betterment, nevertheless involves a certain sacredness and solemnity; that which a countryman of Zola's, the noble Alfred de Vigny, has celebrated as the ' majesty of human suffering.'"

to weaken, degrade, and stultify it as far as possible, and when those who have been peculiarly successful in thus stamping out the sense element are honoured as heroes and selected as patterns, no matter how hard or shallow they may be. For, after all, what inner purification of the soul or development of spiritual life is gained by such a misuse of the senses? Moreover, this repression of the senses, like everything unnatural, must produce greater evils than those which it undertakes to remove. Nature is in the habit of taking a severe revenge for misuse. But the matter does not end with the rejection of this type of asceticism; it is not so simple as it often appears to be from the point of view of æsthetical subjectivism. The sensuous and sexual side of life shows us man associated in the most intimate manner with nature; here, more than anywhere else, nature holds him fast. Yet, at the same time, the development of spiritual life has raised him far above nature, and therefore the simple and unsophisticated attitude is no longer possible. The sensuous has become a problem which from the point of view of spiritual life admits of various solutions. Should it be free to follow its own course in complete freedom, without reference to the higher aims of the spirit, according to the whim and desire of the individual, or should it subordinate itself to the purposes of the spiritual life, here finding its measure? Those who, bearing in mind the indisputable rights of nature, decide in favour of the former course, usually overlook the fact that in our complex and frequently perverted civilisation we have no longer to deal with pure nature; the sense element in modern life is often refined and artificial, nay, degenerate. In order to separate what is genuine in nature from what is not, we need the assistance of spiritual work. A simple capitulation to the so-called sense element in the life of to-day is absolutely out of the question.

β. *The Position of Art in Modern Life*

In the life of to-day art is again pushing victoriously to the front and exerting immense influence upon men's minds; hence we cannot be surprised that it rejects all idea of dependence and insists upon complete independence. This desire finds an expression in the well-known formula, *l'art pour l'art*.* No friend of art will contradict the negative side of this statement. Art should not serve foreign purposes: it should not lend aid to morality, politics, or religion, and thereby sink to the level of "art with a purpose," which may be able to fascinate for a moment, but which cannot promote any real progress. It is not so easy, however, to interpret this saying in a positive sense. To-day it is often asserted that art should be indifferent to all matter and content, concerning itself solely with the perfection of its form; in this way only will it be able to stand entirely alone and be able to go its own way in perfect freedom. But is such a separation from the rest of life conducive to the interests of art itself; can it under these circumstances achieve the highest of which it is capable? There is very great danger that in following this path, art may degenerate into a mere mastery of form, a fascinating and dazzling display of highly technical skill which neither has the whole man behind it nor is able to influence the whole man. Art of this type may make great discoveries in the sphere of sense experience; it may be able to enrich and perfect our sensibilities in undreamt-of fashion; it may revel in the overcoming of difficulties, but it can bring but little benefit to the human soul, and it will not be able perceptibly to elevate spiritual life. Was it not characteristic of the great works of art which have made a permanent appeal to man that in them all opposition between form and content was overcome; in their perfection of form have they not at the same time given full expression to the content of the inner life? Should not art take up the problems of

---

* This expression (see Buchmann's *Geflügelte Worte*, 21st edit., p. 326) had (as first employed by Victor Cousin in lectures at the Sorbonne, 1818) quite a harmless significance: *Il faut de la religion pour la religion, de la morale pour la morale, de l'art pour l'art*. It was not until considerably later that the latter phrase became the creed of a school and an apple of contention between different artistic factions. It may be added that Comte, too, concerned himself at one time with this catchword, employing it, however, in a very external fashion. *Cultiver l'art pour l'art lui-même* signified to him nothing more than *ne se proposer habituellement d'autre bout réel que de divertir le public* (*Cours de phil. posit.*, vi. 167).

humanity and attempt to solve them after its own fashion?*
The inhabitants of the northern countries, in particular, cannot
afford to abandon this inwardness. They do not possess the
natural faculty for sensuous representation which is characteristic of the southern nature; only with difficulty do they
find a path leading from within outwards; hence it is easy for
the centre of the soul to remain unexpressed, its greatest depth
unrevealed. Accordingly, art is to them an indispensable
means of finding themselves, of taking full possession of their
inheritance, of in some way bridging over the division in the
inner being. The most perfect form as mere form will never
be able to satisfy.

Those who reject content as something dangerous and foreign
to art usually have in their minds a product of thought, an
abstract idea. But is spiritual life the same thing as thought;
is there no spiritual content other than a thought element?
The old intellectualism might have answered this question in
the affirmative, but to-day we no longer aim at being intellec-
tualists; how then can we continue to be bound down by
obsolete standards and prevented from aspiring towards a
content for the whole man, a content in the deepest and
widest sense of the word?

In our opinion this setting aside of content constitutes a
danger for that very independence of art in the interests of
which it is demanded. To become independent of material

---

* With regard to this problem, too, Norström has expressed himself in the
most admirable fashion. He remarks, for example, in dealing with the widely
prevalent idea that Greek culture was directed merely towards beauty (*Das
tausendjährige Reich*, p. 73): "It is frequently imagined that the basic force of
Greek life was an irresistible yet spontaneous impulse towards beauty of form;
that is, a need to still more beautify an already beautiful existence. This is far
from being the truth: in reality the productions of Greek art were of essential
value in liberating imprisoned moral energies, illuminating obscure elements
in consciousness and collecting scattered forces to work towards common,
practical ends." And further: "As a matter of fact, it may be said of all
great and true art that it more or less subordinates the form to the content it
seeks to express and maintains an attitude of indifference towards the pleasure
or displeasure which it may arouse—either in the artist or in others—its object
being solely to communicate its content through its images. True art reveals
to us the depths of the creative imagination rather to free us from a merely
pleasurable existence than to confirm us in the same."

does not mean to attain pure independence. An art devoted preponderatingly to form easily becomes a mere matter of professional dexterity, the first concern of which is to display (to itself if not to others) its own skill. This gives rise to a predilection for the eccentric, paradoxical, and exaggerated, and, in seeking after effects of this kind, the promised freedom only too easily becomes merely another kind of dependence, a dependence of the artist upon others and upon his own moods. Genuine independence is to be found only when the creative work proceeds solely from an inner necessity of the artist's own nature. But this cannot take place unless there is something to say, nay, something to reveal. Mere virtuosity knows no such necessity.

We should like to devote a few words to the relationship between modern art and the sex question. Only an inartistic mode of thought can object to art occupying itself thoroughly with this subject rather than withdrawing from it. But that art should often, with such visible predilection, place sex in the foreground and dwell upon it as much as possible; that it should brood over it and refine upon it to the point of absolute disgust, is a sign of moral corruption rather than of technical ability. There is no æsthetical theory capable of defending such a state of affairs.

However much plastic art may be involved in movement and conflict, it has certainly no lack of distinguished personalities and brilliant achievements to represent it. In the realm of literature the outlook is less favourable. The age offers no lack of motives and tasks. Old systems of thought are passing away, and new ones are arising; man has become exceedingly uncertain of his position in the cosmos; the sphere of humanity itself is full of movement and change. But the increasing speed of life gives us no opportunity for adequate self-recollection; hence our existence has become confused, and we have largely ceased to understand ourselves. In the face of such a situation as this literature has an obvious task. It should help to clarify our ideas, to bring to clear expression all that is around us and within us, to point out simple lines of development amidst the chaos of appearances with which we are surrounded. It should as far as possible gather life into a whole and at the same time assist in the work of developing it. For this purpose it has need of an inner superiority to raise it above the oppositions of the age, of *an energetic synthesis* which can reject as well as absorb, of a courageous and powerfully progressive spiritual creation. There is no lack of attempts; but in general it must be said that our German literature—the literature of one of the greatest of civilised nations—does not reach the highest level of the age, and that it offers but little assistance to the modern man in his struggle for spiritual self-preservation and in his endeavour to win a meaning for life. It is our duty to state this in plain terms.

5. PERSONALITY AND CHARACTER

(a) Personality

1. ON THE HISTORY OF THE TERM

To follow the history of the term person, one of the few terms of Latin origin, from its source through its manifold ramifications (apparent even during the Ancient World), and to set forth its significance in Roman law and in Christian theology, would lead us too far away from our present task.* Hence we shall keep to philosophy, at the same time pressing forward as rapidly as possible to the present day.

The newer philosophy took the term from the Scholastics, who in their turn followed the definition of Boethius—a person is a rational individual being.† Serious complications arose

---

* Technical details with regard to the expression will be found in Pauly's *Realenzyklopädie*. In *Good Words* of June, 1866, there is a stimulating article by Max Müller on its origin and development (up to the Middle Ages). Of greater importance is an investigation of Trendelenburg's which I found among his papers and published in the *Kant-Studien*, vol. xiii., nos. 1, 2.

† More exactly it runs (see *De duabus naturis*, edit. R. Peiper, p. 193–4): *persona est rationalis naturæ individua substantia*. In the early Middle Ages "person" was etymologically explained as *per se una*. With regard to the different views of the concept held by the more important mediæval thinkers, see Baumgartner, *Die Philosophie des Alanus de Insulis*, p. 45. Since Thomas, more especially in his investigation of the Trinity (in the first book of the *Summa Theologiæ*), further develops the doctrine of Boethius, he emphasises that persons *non solum aguntur, sed per se agunt*: he defends the application of the term to God, although it is not to be found in the Bible. Like other schoolmen, Thomas, too, has *personalitas*, which had already been given a German form by Eckhardt in *persönlichkeit* (Eckhardt also made frequent use of *persönlich*). In the later scholastic philosophy the most usual definition of "person" was *suppositum intelligens*; *suppositum*, however, meant, in this connection, a *substantia singularis viva*. Zesen rendered *persona* by *Selbstand* (see Paul Piur, *Studien zur sprachlichen Würdigung Christian Wolff's*, p. 58), while Clauberg (*Wke.* (1691), p. 321) translated it by *selbständig verständig Ding*.

from the application of this definition to the doctrine of the Trinity (Roscellin), but they did not prevent its employment in Scholasticism. Philosophical problems of an important description were not taken up in this connection.

Not until the Modern World was the matter dealt with in more active fashion. The concept person now became a chief means of conserving man's distinctive position in the face of the tendency towards a general and uniform order in the world. The concepts person and personality, borrowed from Scholasticism,* were now defined more exactly and more in accordance with psychological knowledge. Leibniz led this movement, since he placed the true essence of personality in self-consciousness, that is, the consciousness of identity during the different periods of an individual's own existence; in support of this view he sharply separated the immortality of man from the indestructibility of the lower beings.† Wolff and the philosophy of the Enlightenment took up this conception, and Herbart carried it forward into the nineteenth century.‡

* In the first half of the eighteenth century the connection with Scholasticism was still very close, and the expressions were looked upon as mere technical Scholastic terms; this is to be seen in Walch's widely employed philosophical dictionary, where it says under "person" (even in Henning's fourth edition of 1775): "Person means, in metaphysics, a specific, complete, and rational substance, which contains in itself its being and its subsistence. The *abstractum* thereof, or the subsistence of such a being, has been called *personalitas*."

† *Theodicée*, i., § 89: *L'immortalité, par laquelle on entend dans l'homme, non seulement que l'âme, mais encore que la personalité subsiste: c'est-à-dire, en disant que l'âme de l'homme est immortelle, on fait subsister ce qui fait que c'est la même personne, laquelle garde ces qualités morales, en conservant la conscience ou le sentiment réflexif interne de ce qu'elle est: ce qui la rend capable de châtiment et de récompense*. Further, in the correspondence with Wagner (*De vi activa corporis et de anima brutorum*), p. 466 b of Erdmann's edit.: *Itaque non tantum vitam et animam, ut bruta, sed et conscientiam sui et memoriam pristini status, et, ut verbo dicam, personam servat.*

‡ Thus Wolff says (*Psych. rationalis*, § 741): *Persona dicitur ens, quod memoriam sui conservat, hoc est, meminit, se esse idem illud ens quod ante in hoc vel isto fuit statu.* Further, in the *Vernünftige Gedanken von Gott, der Welt und der Seele des Menschen*, § 924 (quoted by Trendelenburg): "Now we call 'person' a thing which is conscious of the fact that it is itself that which has previously been in this or that situation: thus animals are not persons. Human beings, on the other hand, are conscious that they it was who were previously in this or that situation: therefore they are persons." Herbart says (*Wke.*, iii. 60): "Personality is self-consciousness, wherein the ego regards itself as being one and the same in all its manifold situations."

So far, the distinctive characteristic of personality had been intelligence. Now, however, begins a new, an ethical phase. After manifold preparation, Kant carried out this alteration in that he placed practical reason in the forefront. Personality is one of the chief ideas affording the new mode of thought an opportunity of definite expression. In the case of Kant, it becomes something far more than mere intelligence; it is made to reveal an essentially higher order founded in freedom. Personality means, namely: "Freedom and independence of the mechanism of the whole of nature"; "that which raises man above himself (as a portion of the sensuous world), that which connects him with an order of things which only reason can think, an order which at the same time has under it the whole sensuous world and with it the empirically-determined existence of man in time and the whole of all purposes" (v. 91, Hart.). As persons, rational beings are ends in themselves (*Zwecke an sich*) and may never be employed as mere means. There may be distinguished in man animality, humanity, and personality. Man is in the first place a living being, then a living and rational being, and finally, as a personality, he is a rational being responsible for his actions (vi. 120).

Later thinkers (such as the elder Schelling and J. H. Fichte) attempted to supplement and deepen this ethical view of the concept of personality on the metaphysical side.* On the whole, however, Kant's position was retained. It has been established (at the least) since his time that the subject standing superior to all separate actions, described as personality, is also to be provided with practical reason; that not merely self-consciousness, but *self-determination*, appertains to its being.

* A history of the concept of personality in the nineteenth century is a task which would well repay the doing. With regard to the manner in which the term is employed by different peoples, Alexander Chamberlain remarks (in *Harper's Monthly* for July, 1903, p. 281): "The word personality is not a native English term, but has been borrowed, ultimately from mediæval Latin, and subsequently rescued from the lawyers. The corresponding French term, *personnalité*, was admitted to the Academy's dictionary so recently as 1762. The German *Persönlichkeit* was once entirely in the possession of the mystics."

2. On the History of the Concept

We now propose to give a short sketch of the history of the concept, understood in the sense which has just been elaborated (as the self-conscious and self-active subject). Greek philosophy did not attain to a clear concept of personality, partly because the question of the unity of psychic life had not at that time come to the front, and partly because the prevailing intellectualism regarded thought as the core and true self of man. Nevertheless, the great investigators of human nature (almost in opposition to their chief doctrines) did not fail to discover a certain concept of personality which was effective in their thought-world: this is to be seen in the case of Plato, and still better in the case of Aristotle (whose ethics clearly enough progresses beyond separate actions to a being experiencing itself in action). The latter days of antiquity placed man more and more upon the basis of his own inner life, and also developed the concept of self-consciousness;* a complete concept of personality was not, however, attained. Prominent thinkers emphatically rejected a view of the Divinity analogous to our concept of personality.†

---

* See Siebeck, *Geschichte der Psychologie*, i. 2, pp. 331–42 : *Die Herausbildung des Bewusstseinsbegriffes*. In the article quoted, Trendelenburg has explained in detail how greatly the Stoics assisted in the development of this concept; he shows how, "In the case of the Stoics, who directed their lives towards self-agreement, towards the consequential development of a character at harmony with itself, we see the πρόσωπον, the *persona*, become the expression of the ethical"; and further, "The right course of action is to live, as was demanded by the first principle of the Stoics, according to nature; that is, to follow reason, which is the basic principle of nature; further, the right course of action individualises the general according to the specific nature of the individual, and bases it upon a rational central point."

† This was first done, as is well known, by the Academician Karneades (213–14 to 129 B.C.), and later by Plotinus with the greatest power and penetration. See Zeller's great work, and also his *Grund. der Gesch. der griech Philosophie*. Karneades sought to demonstrate (see *Grund.*, 6th edit., p. 242 ff.): "that one could not conceive of the Divinity as a living, rational being (ζῷον λογικόν) without attributing to it properties and conditions which contradict its eternity and perfection." In accordance with his whole view of life, Plotinus struggled with peculiar energy against the idea of attributing thought or will, or even self-consciousness, to a fundamental Being, as he conceived it, absolutely infinite and superior to all particularity (see Zeller, as above, p. 293 ff.) "Thus the denial of the personality of God, as led up to by

In ancient Christianity the idea of God acquired a more vital and spiritually intimate meaning, and it now became much easier to speak of a divine personality and a personal relationship between man and God. The danger of anthropomorphism which lay in this view did not pass unnoticed; this is illustrated by the violent conflict which raged round the problem whether a feeling such as anger could be attributed to the Highest Being. The problems involved in the concept of God finally found a solution under the influence of Augustine in the sense that a human and personal conception was superimposed upon the basis of a speculative and mystical one. God is at the same time moral personality and absolute being. The less vital mode of thought of the Middle Ages was conscious of no contradiction in the juxtaposition of these two conceptions. In this case also, however, the Modern World rapidly converted into an "*either—or*" what the Middle Ages had peaceably, nay, willingly, accepted as a "*both—and.*"

Hence the Modern World saw energetic division of opinion with regard to the concept of God. The tendency which moved towards immanence and insisted upon universal cosmic concepts fought against the personal conception as an unbearable anthropomorphism. The movement in opposition to pantheism, on the other hand, relied upon the idea of personality in its desire for a living Divine Being, and laid peculiar emphasis upon the word. Up till then there had been much discussion as to the relationship of the three persons in the Divine Being, but little as to the personality of God.* Now, however, personality became an article of faith and a pet phrase of the anti-pantheists: Jakobi, for example, in his well-known discussion with Lessing, affirms his belief in an "intelligible personal cosmic cause" and finds Spinoza's "substance" lacking in

---

Karneades, here appeared for the first time in definite and decided form" (Zeller). Plotinus' reasons have retained their authority with regard to the speculative rejection of the personality of God; even Spinoza hardly added anything new.

* We may again call upon Walch as witness; in the article "Person" he speaks of the persons of the Trinity but not of the personality of God, and in a detailed discussion of the nature of God makes absolutely no mention of **personality**.

"a specific individual reality of its own" and in "personality and life." From this time onward the conflict continues through the nineteenth century down to the present day. Whenever the life-process takes on a predominantly artistic or intellectual form, then the idea of personality easily seems too narrow and small to be capable of dominating the whole of reality; when on the other hand the ethical tendency is foremost, men are unwilling to dispense with this concept, and aspire towards an interpretation of it which will be comprehensive enough to include the idea of God (Lotze and Ritschl).

In modern times the problem of personality has commanded a great deal of attention; the cultivation of this idea has often appeared to be a safe panacea for all evils. Art, religion, morality, and life in general all desire a more powerful development of personality; it appears as an indispensable help in overcoming the threatened de-spiritualisation of existence, a means towards the rejection of the obsolete and outlived, the only way towards the much desired rejuvenation and simplification of life; men hope to discover, in personality, a secure inner basis in the face of the upheaval of cosmic concepts, to find in it a centre around which humanity can unite in the midst of unbearable division and disintegration.

When so many factors meet together it is only to be expected that there should be great confusion. It would be a very remarkable thing if such a simple development as a mere self-recollection could save us from the immeasurable complications by which we are to-day surrounded. Presumably the help is either merely apparent or the idea of personality involves more and demands more than is customarily attributed to it. Let us see how the matter stands.

3. Investigation of the Problem

Much of the conflict with regard to personality is doubtless merely verbal. An understanding is out of the question so long as some assign the term a narrower and lower, others a wider and higher meaning. But in this case, as in many others, the verbal conflict is only the outward appearance of an actual antithesis. Important thinkers have continued, up to the present day, to set a high value on personality not because they were fascinated by the mere word, but because the term denoted (however incompletely) a thought and asserted a fact which they have regarded as indispensable. Since "person" and "personality" have, from the earliest times, given expression to the supremacy of man, of the spiritual being, it is a fundamental belief in spiritual life and its content and value, which has created, in this term, an instrument, however inadequate. Those who believe in personality as a portion of a view of life as a whole, assert thereby that spiritual life is no mere appendix of nature but a *specific type of being*; they maintain that this life does not consist solely in isolated faculties or manifestations, but contains a unity comprehending these and superior to them, thereby acquiring spiritual freedom and becoming a self-dependent life: they maintain, further, that this self-dependent life is no mere centre of union for elements there brought together, but is itself *active*, exerting a transforming influence upon everything which it receives and raising the whole of existence to a higher level. Only when all the foregoing is understood does personality bring anything essentially new into our existence and thereby justify the enthusiasm with which the idea has been so widely received.

However, these assertions as a whole are right only if thoroughgoing transformations are accomplished in the image of reality as a whole and our position in it. That which is not true as a whole and thoroughly grounded in its relationships cannot be true at any particular point. If this movement towards personality were a merely private affair on the part of man, then it and its view of the world would be mere illusion; it would thus fall into vacuity. It cannot penetrate to the truth itself unless spiritual life constitutes the depth of reality in which it attains to its own being. Only when resting upon a new stage of the world and in connection with this stage can the individual accomplish the movement towards personality, and humanity develop personal life. Nay, this new life must be present in man's soul as a whole and operate in him in order to raise man above the natural order which in the first place surrounds and dominates him. If he does not participate in an inner infinity he will not be equal to the outer infinity. Thus personality is a question of a new fundamental relationship to the world, of a new species of life and being.

If that is the state of affairs, then personality is no ready-made thing for man which can be comfortably and rapidly appropriated, no safe point of departure which can be taken up without effort; its meaning to man is that of a great and difficult task demanding a complete reversal of existing conditions. We are concerned not with the development or adornment of the natural self, but with the gaining of a new self. The movement will not attain to full earnestness and weight unless it also involves a decided negative, a denial of natural self-preservation, an endeavour to rise above the merely human form of spiritual life. And such a negation must form no mere transitory stage of development; it must remain continually present and be energetically retained, if the aspiration towards the new being is not continually to fall back to the natural form of life.

Nay, within the spiritual life, too, personality forms an ascent and a concentration which is reached only through the experiences and decisions of the whole man. Life passes through the three stages of a basal, a struggling, and an overcoming spirituality. The first question is the recognition of a spiritual task at all, an elevation of life above nature, a development of spiritual quantities and goods beyond natural self-preservation. This results in the separation of an idealism from naturalism, which latter looks upon all spiritual life as a continuation of mere nature. This is the first division of opinion. But upon the basis of idealism there at once arises a new problem : in the domain of experiences there exist powerful resistances to the order demanded by idealism. It will be asked, Will this resistance bring the movement to a standstill or will it be overcome? In the first case we are confronted by pessimism, with its abandonment of the task; in the second, we must believe in some kind of strengthening, some kind of further development of spiritual life. This it is, however, which is asserted in the movement towards personal being.

The state of being personal now appears as the highest point of a spiritual movement, and a point of such a nature that it unites the movement together to form a whole, since it retains the earlier stages as permanent factors. For life never ceases to be in a state of flux. The ascent from nature to spirit must be accomplished ever anew; ever anew must we experience the resistance to the spiritualisation of existence, ever anew must we seek an inner overcoming. Thus the whole remains a continuous action, an increasing ascent, and it is only to be expected that the whole field of existence should not enter into this, that personal being should find inner resistance in our own selves, for this being is not so much our whole existence as its motive force, the soul of souls; it is thus obviously not a possession but the highest goal; it is rather a *becoming* personal than a *being* personal. Just as our aspiration has unceasingly to resist an influx of the natural ego, so our concepts have continually to be preserved from sinking back into merely human ideas, a danger to which they are always exposed in the presence of lassitude of thought.

Those who recognise such tasks and complications in the development of personality will also know how to value the struggles which are associated with this problem. In the sphere of religion the idea of personality is often resisted, preference being given to an impersonal spiritual life because personality seems rigidly to fix man's natural ego, while at the same time the highest Being is conceived of in too human a fashion; on the other hand, belief in an impersonal Being, accompanied by the demand for a complete merging of the individual in the ocean of infinity, seems to be a finer, larger, and purer mode of thought; consider, for example, pantheistic speculation and mysticism, the Indian religions at their height, and Spinoza with his saying that the man who truly loves God cannot desire that God should love him in return. This point of view is right in its rejection of the petty human form of existence, but this negation, this submersion in the bottomless ocean of eternity, can satisfy only those who do not recognise new and independent reality in spiritual life, those who perceive in it a liberation from the toil and confusion of human existence, from restless and transitory time, from the narrowness and limitation of the petty ego, but who do not realise that a new life rises up and can be gained. Only a contemplative and predominantly passive method of life, a weak, languid, and invertebrate type of thought, can be content with the negation. Whenever spiritual life develops more power and confidence it will attempt the apparently impossible and will desire to rise above the negation to an affirmation; it will pursue the paths which lead to the idea of personality. This aspiration will, however, be continually accompanied by the dangers of a reversion to the natural form of life; in fact, in the case of religions, a higher and a lower type usually exist mingled together: on the one hand, there is an aspiration towards a new world, a new life and a new domain of thought, for which our human existence does no more than provide symbols; on the other, there is the inclination to make the best of the given existence, to regard the new world as a mere counterpart of the old and to construct the highest concepts anthropomorphically, the whole being far more a fixation of the pettily human than an ascent to new heights. As a rejection of this latter type of thought with its obscuration of the indispensable negation the resistance to the idea of personality is quite justified, and is certainly indispensable to the historical movement as a whole. It falls, however, into error when along with the lower species it rejects the higher and thus abandons all hope of a positive construction of spiritual life. All hope of a thorough overcoming of lower life-instincts depends, finally, upon the gaining of such a construction. For a positive movement cannot ultimately be met by anything except another positive movement. No energy of negation, no yearning towards an absorption in the infinite, will undermine selfishness so completely as will the building up of a new spiritual self charged with great and imperative tasks. Thus we stand face to face with the question whether the positive desire for life and happiness permits of being lifted above mere nature and communicated to the spiritual stage or not. If the answer be given in the negative, all our immeasurable labour will be ultimately wasted.

Civilisation, too, exhibits at this point problems similar to those of religion. Both the artistic and the intellectual views of life agree in their disinclination to assign a leading place to personality. For they perceive in personality a withdrawal of spiritual work to the mere man and an unfortunate interference with its own progress through an admixture of petty human cares. Spiritual life seems to be able to unfold itself purely and completely only when completely detached from man and his purposes; it can then follow its own inherent necessities alone and consolidate itself within its own domain to form an independent construction of life with its own specific laws.

But here, too, lower and higher conceptions of personality are mingled together, and along with that which tends to drag us down, something is surrendered which is necessary to the work of human culture if this work is to reach its full height. Rightly understood, the being and the unity which are the goal of the aspiration towards personality do not lie side by side with work but *within* work; the latter is to be brought to such a point that a self-life comes to light in it, that a spiritual being realises itself in it, converts outward experiences into personal experiences, and for the first time imparts a content to events. For there is absolutely no content without a self which unfolds itself in activity and actual events Only a self thus existing within spiritual life secures for the latter a soul and a basis, guards it from the danger of becoming an empty mechanism or a soulless culture-process, and gives it power to master its own work instead of being mastered and smothered by it. Moreover without such a self, life cannot win a full reality or feel secure of a reality; in the absence of such a core it leads a dreamy and shadowlike existence and reduces everything it receives to this level. India provides us with a classical example of such a dissipation of reality.

Obviously we have here to do not with a more energetic subjective appropriation of a given reality, but with a real elevation and conversion of the whole of reality. It is a question of the ultimate issue of human culture and civilisation, of the possibility of a new, more genuine, and more inspired ideal of culture. The decisive factor in the matter, for individuals and for peoples, is, ultimately, the energy of the life-feeling

(*Lebensaffekt*), the more or less powerful "gripping" of life. The actual decision, however, does not rest with conceptual considerations but with the possibility of the development of a new reality. Never at any time do we draw nearer than we do here to the ultimate axioms of our spiritual existence.

From such a standpoint as this, which demands, on behalf of the development of personality, the building up of a new world and a reversal of natural being, the present-day movement towards personality must seem confused, nay, in many respects false. The customary treatment of the matter does not go beyond the desire for a more powerful concentration and strengthening of the mere subject, for a greater independence with regard to environment. But how is this to take place if man remains a mere fragment of the existing world and does not attain to an inward participation in a new world? If there is no reversal of the first appearance of reality and no winning of a new basis for life, it will be easy for this tendency to do more harm than good, since it must develop into a mere adornment of natural life-instincts, an exaggeration of self-consciousness, a mere enjoyment and pleasant arrangement of life on the part of the subject; moreover, when the movement is regarded as a means of evading the great cosmic problems, when it signifies a retreat within a special circle, it becomes no more than a glorification of a narrow and barren Philistinism. One cannot make anything new out of a man by labelling him a personality! Unless a new world be gained and personal life be itself elevated, this whole movement will remain no more than one of those convenient makeshifts which serve to conceal the deeper problems of humanity and to obscure the seriousness of the present state of affairs.*

It is our belief that personal life must develop a new view of the world; from its own vivification, its own experiences and its own developments, it must produce a domain of basal and life truths. Even if these are not capable of being translated into

* It would be just as well if Goethe's endlessly quoted passage, "The highest happiness granted to the children of this earth is personality itself," were allowed a rest: the pleasing and graceful passage in which it is to be found (in the *Westöstlichen Divan*) was not intended to be taken so seriously.

suitable mental images they remain the truths which ultimately support knowledge as well as all the rest of spiritual life; they are the central truths, compared with which all other opinions are merely peripheral. Now our intellectual attitude and our spiritual position in general acquire a powerful state of tension from the fact that there remains a division between what is central or personal and what is peripheral or impersonal, that there is no direct transition from the former to the latter. Nevertheless we may not divide reality into two finally separated spheres, and rigidly close the domain of personal life to the great world. For that would be to divide life between empty subjectivity and soulless work; it would be an abandonment of its inner unity and at the same time of its full truth. Hence an effort towards unity must be made from both sides. Our task is bravely to retain the goal as a motive and directing force, although we have no prospect of completely attaining to it and thus bringing the two points of departure into full contact.

Looked at from this point of view we see a personal and a subjective construction of work and culture, clearly separate from one another. The subjective type places itself apart from reality, and cannot go beyond itself without carrying its specific nature with it; the personal aims at penetrating to the very life of the things themselves, not as if to something remote and strange but as if to something in which the spiritual being attains to itself, to the truth of its own being. With the conversion of things into a self-life there is here accomplished an overcoming of the contrast between subjective and objective treatment, the result being a treatment which may be called *sovereign* or *eigenständlich*. For here alone the creation attains to full independence, the necessity inherent in the object itself becoming man's direct personal impulse; now for the first time there is attained a complete union with the object itself, upon the basis of which union it can express its own nature in purity and simplicity. This personal or sovereign type alone rises above that which usually stands between man and the object itself. Man cannot directly grasp the object; he needs manifold means to attain to it, such as technical equipment, practice, learning, &c. The danger now arises that what is only a means and a path will become a goal, an end in itself, that it will absorb man's attention, diverting him from what is of real primary importance. There is no people more exposed to this danger than are we Germans, with our thorough but heavy and plodding nature; for us it is particularly difficult completely to overcome technique by creation, to attain to that experiencing of oneself in the things without which our work cannot obtain any purely human greatness and genuine simplicity. Thus, to-day in particular, there exists, in our life, a serious discrepancy between the production of intellectual and artistic work and the origination of creations which appeal to and elevate the whole man. If the desire for a more personal culture means that simple fundamental lines of development are to be selected from the surrounding confusion, thence to operate upon the whole of human being, then the movement is worthy of joyful encouragement. But the question of personality is far from being a matter which can be quickly decided; on the contrary, it is one of the most difficult of problems, needing for its solution not only the greatest possible exertion of strength, but also, in no small degree, the favour of fate. The present age affords ample confirmation of this difficulty: how little has all the subjective affirmation of the value of personality brought us inwardly forward and to what a small extent has it produced strong and original personalities!

(b) Character

1. On the History of the Term and Concept

Among the Greeks the word character was employed to denote not only the instrument employed in making drawings or other impressions but the impression itself, the trace of the tool. The Ancient World already saw the obvious transition to the spiritual and intellectual sphere, which took place in connection with ethics as well as art and literature. The ethical "characters" which bear the name of Theophrastes, the pupil and follower of Aristotle, are indeed, in all probability, a collection made at a later period from the author's larger works, but the in-

PERSONALITY AND CHARACTER

clination towards exact observation and sharp delineation of different human types * goes back to Aristotle, the great student and friend of everything real, and has remained characteristic of his school. The influence of the later comedy and of the rhetoriciaus was exerted in the same direction, so that the later Classical Period acquired a sharpened perception for the various characteristic human types and actions.† At the same time, however, character denoted the specific nature of artistic and literary representation, the individual impression and so forth. In ecclesiastical terminology, it was used, after the period of Augustine, as a technical term for a spiritual sign imprinted upon the soul by certain sacraments (in the Middle Ages—baptism, confirmation, priestly dedication) in such a manner that it could never be obliterated (called later *character sacramentalis*, also *spiritualis*). It occurs occasionally, too, in Middle High German (where it was sometimes employed to signify the written letter—the characters *a, b, c*—as well as in the above technical sense). The literal meaning has persisted down to the present day, and is more or less connected with the official custom of referring to " characters " of rank and title.

In the case of Germany the term, in all probability, came into more general use in the psychological and ethical sense through

---

* *Typus* and *typisch* in their now usual sense, as denoting general forms of life and being, are probably derived from medicine. Dilthey remarks (*Sitzungsberichte der K. Preuss. Akad. der Wissenschaften*, 1896, xiii., p. 18): "In this sense we find the expression employed at first technically when the physician Cœlius (probably in the second century A.D.) speaks of the *typus* of recurring fever, understanding thereby the rule according to which it runs its course. Thus we speak in general of a typical course."

† With regard to the whole matter see Sauppe, *Philodemi de vitiis*, l. X., p. 7: *Peripatetici disciplinæ suæ principis et auctoris exemplum nulla in re magis secuti sunt, quam ut omnia quæ vel in natura rerum existerent vel in vita hominum et publica et privata usu venirent accuratissime observarent et observata sive libris singularibus explicarent sive ad sententias suas firmandas et illustrandas adhiberent.* P. 8: *Neque vita ipsa tantum exempla suppeditabat, sed maximam notationum copiam nova comœdia habebat. Quæ ut eidem sæculi ingenio originem debebat, atque aristoteleum illud studium vitam quotidianam moresque hominum observandi, ita quædam fortasse ex Aristotelis vel Theophrasti libris desumta in usum suum converterat, sed multa plura certe, quam acceperat, deinde philosophis et rhetoribus suppeditavisse censenda est.*

Theophrastes after passing through the French.* In the year 1687 appeared La Bruyère's *Les caractères de Théophraste, avec les caractères ou les mœurs de se siècle*, a book which also attracted great attention and exerted much influence among other nations. Along with other German writings dealing with the depiction of character (works certainly connected with the foregoing) we may mention Gellerts' *Moralische Charaktere*, a supplement to his moral lectures. Here, as elsewhere, character is equivalent to *likeness* (which term sometimes serves to translate it), drawing, or portrait (see Rabener, for example, in his satire *Originalen zu meinen Charakteren*). This meaning is still preserved in the expression "characterise." The expression was later transferred from the representation to the thing itself, and was employed to denote the psychical and more particularly the moral nature of man's fundamental being. In this sense there may exist a wealth of different characters, good and bad; to have no character means, in this case, to possess no sharply defined features. It is not decided whence the character is derived, whether it is the gift of nature or the work of free action.

It was Kant who first raised the concept to a height which made it an important ethical thesis and a difficult problem. He drew a sharp line between physical and moral character: the latter, only, is character pure and simple; the former, comprising natural disposition and temperament, shows what can be made out of the man; true character, on the other hand, signifies that which he is prepared to make out of himself. "A character, in the true sense of the word, means that property of the will according to which the subject binds himself to definite practical principles, which he has unchangeably prescribed for himself through his own reason" (vii. 614). "This is not a question of what nature makes out of man, but of what man makes out of himself." "The foundation of a character is the absolute unity of the inner principle of life-conduct in general"

* On this subject we possess an investigation which reveals both fine understanding and great penetration—R. Hildebrand's *Charakter in der Sprache des Vorigen Jahrhunderts* (*Zeitschrift für d. deutschen Unterricht*, series 6, vol. 7). Upon this work our account of the period is based.

(617). In this sense Kant would not say a man had this or that character, but simply that he had *a* character, "which must be a single one, only, or none at all."

This Kantian conception, with its elevation of life to the level of spiritual self-activity, came rapidly into use;* the high tone in which the following age spoke of character and the value which it assigned to the formation of character are traceable to Kant. But along with the ethical conception the older empirical psychological view has also been maintained; otherwise one could not speak, as one frequently does, of an "inherited character," a character resulting from adaptation and custom, and so forth. Here again we see in a commonplace word the mingled influences of different ages and different views of life.

2. The Present Position

The ethical concept of character is very closely related to the concept of personality; it more particularly emphasises, however, man's self-activity. Until comparatively recently character had not been precisely defined; but the idea of attaining independence and superiority to the world by the exercise of personal will-power is very ancient; it came to the front at times when the breaking up of traditional social systems forced the individual to stand entirely upon his own feet. Its classical expression is seen in the philosophy of the Stoics, who were responsible for a characteristic type of life, the influence of which has made itself felt throughout the whole of history, a type which was again brought into prominence and strengthened by some of the greatest philosophers of the Enlightenment; Kant's teaching with regard to character was in many respects Stoic and he was very fond of making use of thoughts emanating from the Stoic school. The danger of this tendency is that the individual may develop an attitude of harsh isolation and proud self-sufficiency, that he may ignore the dependence of the unit upon invisible, if not upon visible, connections with the whole. Notwithstanding this danger, however, the Stoic attitude re-

* How quickly Kant's ideas spread is to be seen, for example, in an article on character by E. Biester, in the *Abhand. d. K. Pr. Akad. d. Wiss.*, 1803.

mained the only means by which, during certain periods, it was possible for men to ensure their spiritual self-preservation.

The concept of character, however, reaches beyond such a comparatively narrow application. Since it stands for the self-value and independence of the inner life as opposed to all that is merely external, and bears witness to the superiority of the inner over the outer goods, it may receive honour even where this isolation of the individual is rejected. But the concept then approximates so closely to that of personality that it becomes unnecessary to discuss it separately. Therefore we shall do no more than briefly indicate how the problem of character and its development stands when regarded from the point of view of our own age.

The present age, although much occupied with the problem of character, at the same time bitterly complains of the modern lack of strong characters and clearly defined personalities; it appeals to civilisation in general, and to education in particular, for more attention to the training up of men and women of character. But in all this we again notice the lack of clarity and thoroughness which is apt to accompany such popular movements. Frequently it appears to be believed that a moral backsliding has unawares taken place, and that in order to make everything right again an impressive admonition or an ingenious arrangement is all that is needed. But the matter is not so simple. There can be no doubt that the lack of original and independent men, of which we are to-day so painfully conscious, has deeper roots. In the course of the centuries the inner world which man has so laboriously won has been increasingly shaken or obscured; its goods hence exercise a continually diminishing attraction, while man's soul becomes increasingly empty. In addition we must take into account the intense absorption of the modern man in the external world, the petty strife for visible success, the growing struggle for existence, and the appalling "speeding-up" of life, the division of man by a type of work which grows increasingly technical and complicated, and the cheapening influence of a civilisation and culture which has become largely popularised and vulgarised. Can such a bustling civilisation leave any room for the development of independent characters or allow them any meaning?

Those who, trusting in the inner necessity of the thing itself, press forward towards the goal of character will not make the mistake of thinking its attainment too easy: they will sharply differentiate themselves from those modern tendencies, the upholders of which affirm their belief in personality and character with the greatest possible emphasis but at the same time do all they can to destroy the very conditions which can alone secure a place for these factors. In the case of cosmic questions, our advanced social reformers, for example, frequently welcome with peculiar delight everything which causes man to appear small and tends to make him an indifferent and dependent fragment of a soulless nature; yet at the same time in practical matters they wax enthusiastic on behalf of the greatness and dignity of man, warmly espouse the cause of humanity, and are indignant when they perceive a lack of independent characters and an oppressive growth of petty competition. Such an increasing externality as we are to-day conscious of in manifold forms is a serious evil indeed, but how can it be successfully opposed if man possesses no independent inner world, if he is nothing more than a somewhat higher type of animal, and therefore knows no aim other than natural self-preservation?

We shall never achieve solid progress in the formation of character until the problems of the *inner man* again take the central place and unite together to form a view of life as a whole, a view capable of seizing men's minds with an awakening, directing, and elevating force. For the time being we are still far removed from such a position. But although we must utterly reject the idea that the development of personality and character is a matter which can be treated in any offhand fashion,* it is nevertheless possible to do a certain amount of direct work in this direction even under existing conditions. Let us briefly

---

* We may here call attention to Pestalozzi's plain, though not unjustified words (*Wke.*, xii. 217): "Toadstools may easily spring forth from a dunghill when it rains, but human dignity, spiritual depth, and greatness of character do not grow out of routine, even when the sun shines."

consider in what particular directions this work can and must be done.

In the first place, the genuine values in life must be better recognised and more highly honoured. Mere appearance and pretence must be rated at what they are really worth; they must not be allowed to usurp a high position in life.

In attempting to attack these false elements we are hindered more especially by the Epicureanism of a ripe, nay, an over-ripe, civilisation; we are confronted with a society which permits each individual to pursue as far as possible his own individual comfort, while anxiously shunning all conflict and willingly bowing to every social convention. Under these circumstances a man no longer stands upon his own feet and assigns himself his own value; he allows the success of his life to depend upon the recognition of others, thus unavoidably lowering himself to be their servant. In this respect each nation has its own peculiar dangers. With us Germans it is undeniable that artificial distinctions, questions of rank, decorations, and titles—the mere paraphernalia of life—play far too large a part, and thereby interfere with the self-dependence and full manliness of life. It is impossible for secondary things to be treated as primary things without primary things being degraded to a secondary position. Every profession and every man has a right to respect and recognition, a respect which should be fought for if denied; but it will not be obtained by the concession, from outside, of class distinctions or decorations, but by each profession or individual bringing its or his work (with its own inherent strength and independent character) fully to bear upon life as a whole.

This brings us to the second of the requirements for the development of character. That is independence, free decision, and personal responsibility within our sphere of life. We Germans are accustomed to complain of over-government, of the hindrance which bureaucracy offers to free development, and certainly in so far with justice as there is inherent in bureaucracy a tendency to elevate a single central point to full independence, to make everything else depend upon it and to regard all authority as derived from this point. But bureaucracy would never have attained to such power among our people if it did not correspond to an inborn inclination, if there did not exist in us a desire to regulate and mechanically to systematise life, to exercise a police authority over others and obstinately to force others, too, to accept our own mode of thought. We are largely lacking in willingness to tolerate the specific nature of others, to give them the right of free play even when they are in sharp opposition to ourselves; such a *laissez-faire* attitude, we are prone to think, indicates a lukewarmness in our own feelings, an abandonment of our own convictions. The thought of freedom is apt to call to mind in the first place the dangers of a possible abuse. In order to prevent this we prefer to depress the whole level of life, to shape it from the point of view of the exception rather than of the rule, and to confine and limit it as far as possible. Thus we tend to produce conventional figures, typical men, mere specimens of a species, while the development of the individual nature is suppressed and something lost which is in the highest degree necessary to the maintenance of inner independence. In modern life how many forces co-operate to reduce human individuality and shape men according to pattern, and to what a serious extent mass-influence threatens the development of individuality—and not least among the very people who lay particular emphasis upon the right of individuality! For our individualists are often nothing more than the representatives of a particular type exhibiting thoroughly uniform features.

Moreover, the free development of individuality needs more leisure, more inner composure, than the bustle of modern life usually permits. Overpressure of work—which affects not only innumerable individuals but whole sections of society—is becoming a serious danger to inner development, for it hinders all calm self-recollection, all persistent concentration, and all connected construction of life. We Germans possess a magnificent body of teachers, the finest in the world, the born representatives of a true inner culture; but these teachers are heavily overburdened, to some extent with merely mechanical work, of which they could very well be relieved.

It is insufficiently borne in mind that fresh and cheerful men work immeasurably better than men who are tired and jaded—or if it is remembered, no thorough remedy is found. Those who are assisting in this, as in other spheres of life, to create more free room for inner development, for spiritual freedom in life, are, at the same time, helping on the movement towards those high aims with which the problem of character is associated. When so much is at stake, that which in itself may seem a small matter becomes important.

6. THE FREEDOM OF THE WILL

(a) Introduction

"THE problem of freedom gives rise to a discussion which is apparently endless. Each side possesses unlimited resources." Thus wrote the great critic Bayle in his remarks upon the Free Will question.* On the other hand, a distinguished modern German scholar declares that the controversy between determinism and indeterminism is "concluded." † Which of them is right? Thinkers have for long been irreconcilably divided by this problem. Is it true that the last few centuries have brought such a powerful new light to bear upon it that we may now look upon the matter as finally settled? Or do we, perhaps, regard the question as concluded merely because we study it from a special point of view, because we are under the influence of a special kind of thought? Let us examine how the matter really stands, and see if the triumph of determinism is to be accepted as an accomplished fact.

Determinism is in its essence old, though the details of its external form and argumentative support have altered from time to time. The Stoic philosophers may be looked upon as the earliest conscious determinists.‡ They were influenced by the

---

* *Œuv. div.* (La Hague, 1727), iii. 794 a: *On ne finit point quand on s'engage aux questions de la liberté, chaque parti a des ressources infinies.*

† See Meinong, *Psychologisch-ethische Untersuchungen zur Werttheorie*, p. 209: "It is not, however, the deterministic controversy which we are proposing to take up: in my opinion, at any rate, this is a matter which was concluded long ago, for those who believe in the law of causality cannot logically be indeterminists." Höffding quotes this passage (*Ethik*, 2nd German edit., p. 102), and expresses the opinion that a different impression would be received from a study of the Danish literature bearing on the subject.

‡ In a very careful investigation (*Die Zurechnungslehre des Aristoteles*, 1903), R. Löning has shown that Aristotle was by no means an indeterminist, but had not yet brought the problem into a condition of complete clarity.

thought of a causal connection existing throughout the world and making the freedom of any part of it impossible. Stoic determinism was due rather to a view of life as a whole than to psychological analysis. The moral and practical tendency of Christianity, in its earliest stages, again assigned a decidedly predominant position to free will, but without bringing forward any scientific arguments whatever. This was succeeded by Augustine's theocentric conception of reality, which involved complete determinism and conceived of every personal human decision as a suspension of the omnipotence and omniscience of God. The subsequent softening down of this position (completed by the Church and the Middle Ages) was utterly repudiated after the Reformation (especially by the early Reformers), and the most rigid religious determinism was again insisted upon. At the zenith of the Enlightenment cosmic determinism held the field and took classic form in Spinoza's system. Leibniz apparently opposed determinism, but in reality he only gave it a more subtle form. The Kantian rescue of freedom, in an intelligible realm, does not adequately help us in our life and conduct, situated as they are in the flux of time.*

It is thus seen that even prior to the nineteenth century determinism undoubtedly held the leading place in the spiritual and intellectual world. On the highest planes of thought, in particular, it acquired a peculiar clearness and forcefulness, seeming rather to increase life-energy than to diminish it. At the commencement of the Christian era no one stood nearer to determinism than Paul did, and yet no one worked as he worked. Augustine, too, was a man of unceasing activity, with a prodigious capacity for organisation. During the struggles of the Reformation period the conviction that man depended, in all his actions and conditions, solely and alone upon God, and upon no kind of earthly power, was the chief source of a firm confidence and an unbending power of will.

The new determinism, inaugurated in the nineteenth century, is the successor of all these historical phases. Formerly determinism originated in religious or speculative convictions. But

* Strictly understood, this intelligible freedom must condemn our whole life in time to inactivity, depriving it of all possibility of personal action.

now it sprang from a more thorough examination of experience, the results of which seemed, from whatever quarter they came, to make for determinism. Never before had the case for determinism been so obvious and so impressive. The great network of causality closed ever tighter around man. A more exact form of expression had the effect of giving ancient experiences a new and increased weight. It was pointed out that man has obviously inherited the groundwork of his nature, while his further development depends upon his social surroundings and education; by the time he awakens to clear consciousness he is already essentially complete, fate, not his own will, having shaped him. In recent years the study of social science has gone to show that our actions, down to their very roots, are determined by the integral effect of our surrounding influences, while from the historical standpoint it appears that we cannot possibly be anything more than the children of our age—even in taking sides against it. Modern psychology, moreover, gives us a closer view of the intricacies of the inner life, and shows us every action as a link in a chain, conditioned and determined on every side: it allows no scope whatever for indeterminate action. In spite of all this it is hoped to do full justice to the moral side of life. The attempt is made to show that even when freedom has disappeared, the essentials of morality, such as responsibility, still remain; it even appears that morality itself is actually a gainer by the process, on account of the close relationship established between each separate action and our life as a whole and between the latter and social history in general. Hence, when the improvement of these relationships is made the chief object of human action, the latter is placed upon a broader basis, and is, at the same time, provided with definite points of application. There is also a stronger development of the feeling of moral solidarity and a tendency to regard the transgressions of individuals more leniently. Under the influence of determinism a strong humanitarian movement has made itself felt, more especially in the sphere of criminal jurisprudence. When every interest seems to point in the same direction, and when thought thousands of years old acquires a new power through being brought more closely into touch with the life of the day, it appears as if all opposition must cease and determinism be left in a position of final and undisputed triumph. Belief in determinism is by no means confined to scientific circles. In Germany, at any rate, it is looked upon as essential to the education of a really enlightened man, and those who still retain any doubts upon the subject are classed as ignorant old fogies and looked down upon with no little scorn by the apostles of modern wisdom.

Such dogmatism seems, however, somewhat premature when we call to mind that there is still a considerable, and apparently an increasing, number of eminent thinkers opposed to determinism.* Moreover, we notice that among other civilised nations the revolt against determinism has not by any means fallen into such utter discredit as is the case in Germany. France is a particularly good example to the contrary: here the "philosophy of discontinuity" deliberately and energetically rejects determinism, and no less a thinker than Boutroux stands for the "contingency" of the natural laws,† while Bergson, too, in a most living picture of the life of the soul, includes freedom as an essential. This may perhaps be taken as evidence that the matter is not really settled, though it may appear to be when looked at from the point of view of certain special tendencies of German thought.‡

(b) Remarks on the Determinist Position

A problem so full of complication and one which so sharply divides both epochs and thinkers can hardly be dealt with in this somewhat casual manner without exposing ourselves to the charge of being altogether too audacious. But in considering

* Among other recent works we may mention: *Die Willensfreiheit u. ihre Gegner*, Rohland (1905); *Freiheit u. Notwendigkeit*, Froehlich (1908); *Der freie Wille*, Joel (1908).

† E. Boutroux, *Ueber den Begriff des Naturgesetzes in der Wissenschaft u. in der Philosophie der Gegenwart* (German trans., 1907); see also Boelitz, *Die Lehre vom Zufall bei Emile Boutroux* (1907).

‡ Windelband has recently made a very valuable contribution to the clarification of this problem (*Ueber Willensfreiheit*, 2nd edit., 1905) in pointing out the necessity for a separation of different forms "which are usually comprised, without any critical examination, in the phrase 'Freedom of the Will'" (see p. 222).

the tendencies of modern thought it is necessary to pay some attention to the movements which come to the front in connection with the subject of determinism.

The manner in which determinism to-day displays itself as a popular view of life appears to us excessively dogmatic. This ancient problem is looked at much too narrowly, too exclusively in the light of the ideas of our own particular age alone. A historical examination does not produce the impression that determinism was related to its opposing tendency in the manner of a higher plane of thought to lower planes, nor that an increase in human enlightenment brings with it a corresponding decrease of opposition. Determinism has already been before the world some thousands of years, but counter-movements have continually sprung up—not only among the comparatively non-intellectual classes, but in the ranks of the great thinkers—nay, most significant fact of all, among the leading determinists themselves! Moreover, determinism has never been completely and logically carried out at any period. When the Stoic philosophers converted the whole cosmos into a causal structure and placed the destinies of men entirely within its framework, man's power of personal decision still remained; he might recognise the worldwide chain of causes and acquiesce in it, or he might resist and be reluctantly dragged along by the determining factors. The possibility of such decision (the very core of Stoic morality) is obviously in direct opposition to the determinist doctrine.

Augustine was a rigid determinist only so long as his mind was dominated by the theocentric conception of man; the moment he concerned himself with problems of human conduct, and in particular with practical Church affairs, he looked upon men as called to independent co-operation and individual decision. Luther, too, later on in life, considerably modified the original rigidity of his determinism.

And in Spinoza's case, although he so strongly maintained that man is situated entirely within a flawless network of cosmic connections, the fact remains that man has to be won over to a recognition of his position, and this recognition imparts quite a new complexion to the whole of life. It ceases to be a web of human illusion and becomes a domain of unalloyed truth.

Further, speaking of a more empirical form of determinism, such as we have to deal with to-day, does it not finally make an immense difference whether we are conscious of the network of causality and adopt it as a motive of action, or whether we remain entirely unconscious of its influence? It is universally true that the fact of a causal order existing does not carry its own recognition with it; our own affirmative or negative attitude in this connection, however, fundamentally alters the outlook of life. Hence human decision after all does not seem to be a matter of indifference.

The determinists of to-day might have learnt the danger of over-confidence from a consideration of Kant's position with regard to the free will question. They too look upon Kant as a great thinker and his system as the most important philosophical achievement of the modern era: and freedom is an indispensable corner-stone of this system; it cannot be removed without the collapse of the whole structure.* We must not forget that Kant describes the ideality of space and time and the reality of the conception of freedom as the two hinges upon which his criticism of reason hung, and that the idea of freedom formed, from the very commencement, a portion of his theory of knowledge. One may adopt as critical an attitude as one likes towards the particular manner in which Kant solved the problem of freedom; but the fact still remains that this great thinker believed freedom to be absolutely indispensable.

What is it after all which, in spite of an accumulation of apparently unanswerable arguments in its favour, again and again causes men to strive beyond determinism? It is the fact that the logical consequence of determinism can be nothing less than the destruction of everything which is characteristic of the spiritual and intellectual life of man. From the determinist point of view the soul of man and the objects of the external

* We need refer only to Kant's expressions in the preface to the *Critique of Practical Reason:* "The concept of freedom, as far as its reality is proved by an apodictical law of practical reason, constitutes the coping-stone of the whole structure of a system of pure, even of speculative reason" (v. 3, Hart.). Further: "Freedom is, moreover, the only one of all the ideas of speculative reason of which we know the possibility *a priori*, yet without comprehending it, because it is the condition of the moral law, which we already know" (v. 4).

world are simply given quantities; these quantities come together in a certain way and a certain result then follows of absolute necessity. In this case can there, strictly speaking, be any question of personal action? Have we any inner responsibility at all? If we really adhere fully and logically to the determinist position (and do not unconsciously allow our views to be in any way influenced or supplemented by the traditional conception of human life and being), then we can conceive of ourselves only as passive spectators of what is being wrought upon us, upon the soul just as much as upon the body; our entire future development appears to be already completely mapped out and it only remains for us to play the part assigned, to travel patiently further and further along the allotted path, the absolute slaves of fate. This involves the disappearance of the *present*, in any real sense of the word. When there is no demand for decision, no tension and no room for original action, when the future grows out of the past like a flower out of its bud, then there can be only the shadow of a present. At the same time all inner relationship in life and all dominating unity vanishes. Such a unity cannot be handed on passively; it is the product of original personal activity and of nothing else; it must continually be re-created. Hence, when regarded from the determinist point of view, our soul becomes a mere juxtaposition of separate elements, which may look like a whole from outside, but is in reality devoid of all inner solidarity. In short, it is the complete denial of any ultimate spontaneity which in particular stigmatises determinism. When we seriously consider what this renunciation of original action, this condition of being driven and pushed by an obscure fate really means, it is seen to be something so terrible as to be absolutely intolerable. The horror of being bound up with an all-powerful and unavoidable fate which is potent over our entire existence has been realised in a special degree and with overwhelming force by the more profound Indian thinkers, and they made it in consequence their dearest hope and most earnest desire to be delivered from destiny, from the process of incarnation.

It is urged in reply, What is the use of resisting in the face of relentless necessity? The only reasonable attitude open to man under the circumstances is one of surrender and resignation. Is it not true that his nature is an inevitable heritage? Is it not a combination of this with environment (in the broadest sense of the term) which has made him what he now is? Is it not fate which assigns this or that rôle to the men who have been thus shaped, despatching them hither or thither? Moreover, are not definite motives essential to human action, and would not life sink into confusion and chaos if men were perfectly free to choose between these motives, if it were possible (in the absence of any connection with preceding action) for good men to make evil decisions or bad men good ones?

Let us by all means allow these truths their full weight. But that is not the same thing as admitting that they really exhaust the matter, that they do complete justice to the characteristic quality of man as endowed with a spiritual nature. It is an indisputable fact that man (considering in the first place his thought alone) does not, as animals do, remain entirely within the chain-like process of existence. He steps outside this enchainment and is able to confront it and review it as a whole. If he could not do this there would be no search after truth, and the mere fact that there is such a search at all implies an important further development of life. Is it not just the same with regard to action? We do not ascend by a series of disconnected impulses; we raise ourselves to a superior unity and hence acquire a self-activity as a new stage of life. From this position we can survey the region of multiplicity and estimate the true value of each factor. This value is not given to us directly as a ready-made thing. It varies according to the unity upon which it is dependent, and a reorganisation of this unity carries with it a change in the value. If it be asked how such a self-activity, such a breaking forth of primordial spiritual life in man, is possible, and how it can be explained in relation to things as a whole, we must confess with complete frankness our inability to offer any answer. But how poor we should be if we were to deny everything we could not explain! We see around us a prodigious number of conscious and feeling beings, each a characteristic life-unit. These units are continually being renewed. Is there any explanation of this? If this was not an indisputable fact, could it not be rejected as impossible, just as easily as an awakening of self-activity can be thus rejected? For it does not seem as if new life-units could possibly result either from a combination of lifeless matter or from a division of living matter. Therefore new life-units cannot come into being. Yet it is impossible to deny that they are being continually produced! It therefore becomes necessary to subordinate our conception of possibility to the reality of things. We must not force reality until it fits the standard of our narrow intelligence—*at the bottom the chief prop of determinism is intellectualism.*

Moreover, in considering this problem we must not forget the peculiar position of man and the complications attaching to it. On the one side he belongs to nature, and on the other he forms the commencement of a new stage of reality, a realm of spiritual freedom: this converts his whole life into a problem, for the solution of which his own decision is imperatively necessary. His life is thus brought under the influence of opposing impulses; the motives on the one side are utterly incomparable with those on the other; on the one hand we have natural or social existence with its pleasures, on the other a spiritual order with its new and infinite self. Is it possible directly to compare the result of an action in giving rise to selfish pleasure with the effect which the fulfilment of duty and the development of love may have in uplifting our being?* In this case it is obviously not a question of isolated actions, but of the main tendency of life as a whole; it is a matter, not so much of what we do, as of what we are, or rather of what we chiefly set our hearts upon. The soul of man does not simply form an arena, in which two stages of reality meet; it is itself called upon to co-operate: in this sphere spiritual life can attain to full reality only by means of self-active appropriation. The decisions which are involved in this problem cannot be made

---

* We must reject also the idea that our motives are fixed and given quantities which operate within the soul like weights on a pair of scales, thus effecting a decision. Must all conduct result from given motives—cannot new motives arise from inner transformations of life? And, moreover, must not the soul continually assign fresh values to the motives?

at a given moment; they are the product of our whole life. A continual affirmation and strengthening is necessary. Spiritual life, as we have seen, cannot maintain a constant level; it must be perpetually renewed, or it will very rapidly sink. Our life is thus kept in a constant state of tension. We are never allowed quiet and undisturbed possession of its spiritual content. From this point of view free activity is not to be regarded as a matter of mere momentary choice, nor its direction as determined by some sudden whim. Although it is true that a moment may attain to supreme importance, it can only do so in connection with a greater whole, by virtue of its position as the crowning point of continuous effort. It is in the first place a question of the *whole*, of the main tendency of life, and not of isolated points of decision.

The development of a spiritual individuality is a peculiarly good illustration of the way in which freedom and fate work together in the shaping of our lives and are dependent each upon the other. Mere decisions cannot possibly produce such development. Fate precedes and determines the line along which it shall take place: but in so far as the individuality is spiritual it must first be won by our own effort, identified with our own personal activity, separated from what is alien to it, and recognised as central. The core of our strength must first be laid bare and appropriated. The search after one's own self, the soul of our soul, may mean a desperate struggle and cost us many a severe lesson; one may wander far afield before reaching that point. And when it has been found it needs a further struggle and more work to hold it fast and base one's life upon it. Thus the course of our life, from being a dispensation of fate, becomes more and more a personal achievement, more and more uplifted to the level of self-activity.

The same thing is true of whole nations and epochs. What is given to our hand is, from a spiritual point of view, only a possibility which cannot take shape as a concrete reality except by our own act and deed. We can take up a merely passive and receptive attitude and allow ourselves to be driven by our environment, or we can attain to independence of our environment and from this position wring from circumstance its spiritual possibilities. History, as far as its spiritual content is concerned, is not built up in peaceful security upon a given basis; it is continually open, as a whole, to have doubt cast upon it; we find it continually necessary to secure a new foundation; it is continually our duty to grasp history, as a whole, from a new point of view.

With such convictions in our minds we obtain an essentially different picture of reality from that produced by determinism above everything else a different picture of our own inner life. From the point of view of determinism everything appears to lie upon the same dead level, or at any rate to proceed from a given groundwork. In reality our life is not so simple, and its content not so uniform. Different possibilities and different levels of life cross one another, so that we are drawn now in one direction, now in another. During the course of life, one particular point of view comes to dominate the others, and is then easily mistaken for the whole of our life and being. But it is only necessary for a radically new task to present itself, a great upheaval or reversal to take place, and something absolutely new, something totally unexpected, rises up within us, while the old pales and disappears. We are inwardly altered, and all our values are changed. What formerly filled our souls may now appear unspeakably little and insignificant. This is not due to any mechanical process working in us. It takes place as a consequence of our own excitation and activity. After that it becomes clear that what we formerly took for the whole was only a certain stratum, a particular possibility alone; that we have been realising only a portion of our being. The conditions of our social existence and the necessity of earning our daily bread have the effect of forcing us into some such specialisation: a man settles down in the routine of some particular profession; he is expected to devote himself to it as far as possible, and anything not falling within the boundaries that are thus created is put down to his discredit; to become paralysed and ossified is the natural fate which awaits him who is confined within such narrow limits and who does not preserve a wider life, with doors open to new possibilities; he does not so much act himself as allow action to take place through him. He does undoubtedly travel along a path which has already been mapped out, as the determinist would have us believe that we all do. Sorrow, or any great upheaval in life, brings a blessing, in that it has the power of lifting us out of our several ruts and placing us in a new relationship to the sources of life.

In this connection art has a task of the greatest importance to fulfil; it should hold up, in contrast to the customary narrowness of life, the vision of a wider realm filled with new possibilities; in the face of the limitations of circumstance it should strive towards freeing the soul. The crux of the matter is always the same; does our life consist of ready-made data, pieced together, or is it still in a plastic condition?

What has been said of individuals also applies to mankind as a whole. Just as the individual is tied down and limited by the special character of his profession and personal destiny, so humanity falls into established modes of thought, peculiar to special types of human culture, and tends to remain bound down by these. This paralyses, as well as narrows life. It only remains for humanity to follow an appointed path, to become the mere means by which some service is carried out. Those who have attained to the height of some such system of culture believe themselves able to explain with absolute certainty how everything has come to pass, and how it could not have occurred otherwise; from their point of view the whole of history is a chain of inevitable sequences.

But systems of human culture, too, live their lives out, fade, and grow old. It would be a terrible thing, indeed, if humanity, in its cosmic relationship, did not contain, and could not seize and develop, opportunities other than those it has already experienced. Is the new life we see around us capable of being derived in any way from the ancient world? Could Grecian thought by any possibility have predicted the form which civilisation subsequently took through the agency of Christianity and the uprising of the new races? From the point of view of the Middle Ages, was the direction the modern era gave to life at all to be anticipated? And now, as we become increasingly conscious of the inherent limitations of modern culture, of the senility of its inner content, what is it encourages us to continue joyfully working and striving except the hope that humanity has not already exhausted itself along the former lines of effort, and that entirely new possibilities still lie before us? But without our own self-activity such possibilities will hardly become real; we must not be mere passive spectators, we are called to co-operation.

Should not such a mode of thought, with its broadening and vitalising influence over our view of reality, be held to apply to the cosmos as a whole? We moderns are far too apt to regard the world in its present manifestation, as it now surrounds us, as the sole possibility, the sum-total of reality. Is it not, perhaps, only a special form, which can—nay, must—be accompanied by others? The complications and contradictions, the manifold signs of incompleteness which we see in the world about us, and the mixture of reason and unreason which it exhibits, may be taken as indications of this. Looking at the matter thus, to bind the whole development of reality down to the "given facts" must appear to be a stubborn and narrow dogmatism. This conception of "given facts" is in the highest degree unfortunate and misleading. It proclaims as self-evident an assertion which is really most problematical and rejects all self-activity with its accompanying originality. To-day a timid mode of thought is hardly conscious of the degradation of spiritual energy which is involved in this complete adherence to what is "given." "The spirit takes the food that is offered it without a murmur, clinging to the 'given'" (J. Burckhardt).

There is not sufficient space in this short sketch to give an explanation of the problem of freedom and determination as it would appear from our own point of view. We hope soon to go into this subject more in detail in a work upon the foundation of ethics. But we should like to point out at this juncture that determinism is based upon quite definite assumptions as to the nature of reality, and a recognition of what these assumptions really are at once destroys the self-evident character of determinism. The latter regards the world as given and closed, and man as a mere cog in the great machine. If this view is correct, it becomes sheer imbecility to doubt the truth of determinism for a moment. But if the world is still plastic, and if we ourselves can take part in the work of progressive creation, then those who take up a different position can hardly be looked upon as intellectually lost. At the very worst they can console themselves with the society of Plato and Kant.

At the same time we do not wish in any way to belittle the important services which have been rendered by modern determinism in bringing the problem of freedom to the front and throwing light upon it. The whole matter has been essentially deepened and the naïve affirmation of freedom has been made absolutely impossible. It cannot be overlooked that there is much necessity in our lives, that our way is mapped out to a large extent by fate; but it remains doubtful whether this is the whole, whether freedom does not at the same time retain rights of its own, and whether it is not precisely the collision between freedom and necessity which imparts to our life its specific character, which first makes life, in the fullest sense of the word, possible. We agree with Schelling's saying: "If there were no contradiction between freedom and necessity, not only philosophy but every higher spiritual aspiration would decay and perish."

E. ULTIMATE PROBLEMS

1. THE VALUE OF LIFE

(a) Introduction: On the History of the Terms

To give any estimate of the value of life from the point of view of the individual, so uncertain and accidental as this is, must, of course, be impossible: if the problem of optimism and pessimism * has no other meaning it is not worth while to take the matter up at all. At the same time it is impossible entirely to suspend passing any judgment upon life, if only for the reason that life does not carry with it an absolute conviction in the same simple and irresistible manner as does a statement of fact. Life demands either active assent on our part or some other attitude of mind. We may either cheerfully ally ourselves with the stream of life, lending it our best assistance, or we may oppose it and try, in our own case, to bring it as far as possible to a standstill. Great historical developments have taken place illustrative of both these positions. Indian

---

* The expressions "optimism" and "pessimism" are of comparatively modern origin. The former was first employed to denote the Leibnizian doctrine of the best possible world. In this connection Brucker remarks (iv. 2, p. 385): *Non tacendum vero, ipsos Jesuitas Trivaltinos, magnos cetera Leibnizii ad. miratores, cum recensione Theodiceæ facta sententiam dicerent* (as a note adds, 1737, Febr., art. I) *laudata ingenti lectionis et judicii copia, et tractationis ordine, accuratione et concinnitate systematica, fateri tamen, multos errores philosophum summum admisisse, maxime vero optimi mundi assertionem (optimismum vocant) non nisi larvatum materialismum et spiritualem Spinozismum involvere;* see also p. 415. Voltaire in particular helped to spread the use of the term with his *Candide ou l'optimisme.*

In connection with pessimism it is usual to think in the first place of Schopenhauer, though he himself made but little use of the term. Caldwell, in his excellent work upon Schopenhauer, remarks (p. 522): "He rarely uses the word 'pessimism'—perhaps three or four times in all—and then only about the philosophy of others, and generally in the adjective form as opposed to an optimistic view of things."

civilisation at its height was inspired by the conviction that life, with its endless sorrow, struggle, and necessity, is first and foremost suffering, and that the height of human wisdom lies in endeavouring to free ourselves from life, or, at any rate, in trying to reduce its vigour. In opposition to this negation of life stands the attitude of our Western civilisation. According to our valuation, life is a great good. It should be earnestly held fast, augmented, and enriched. Western thinkers have consequently exerted themselves to establish this affirmative position, and to demonstrate the value of reality.

The historical development of the Western tendency may be divided into three chief phases: the Greek thinkers regarded the world as a complete work of art, an all-embracing harmony, and in this manner endeavoured to rise above its obscurities and contradictions; the Christian thinkers, like Augustine, for example, in so far as they were occupied with the problem, saw a moral order in reality which completely obliterated the contrast between justice and love; while, finally, in the opinion of modern thinkers the world is to be looked upon as a progressive current of life, a continual growth of power, and from this point of view even what at first seems to be mere disorder and contradiction appears to justify itself as an incentive and a source of movement.

These attempts to harmonise life have frequently been made the objects of bitter attack and even of mockery. They would have deserved such treatment had they been the fruit of mere idle speculation, if there had been no deep movements behind them. The latter is, as a matter of fact, the case; for these attempts to justify life were rooted in an actual moulding of life, in a self-concentration which separated a kernel from the remainder of existence and endeavoured, with it as a basis, to further develop the whole. The Greek attempts to represent the world as a work of art would have been entirely lacking in content and power had they not been supported and vitalised by that magnificent plastic and artistic construction of life and reality as a whole which rendered Greek civilisation so admirable; this creative artistic work, with all its joy and power, armed the Greek world against the unreasonable element in existence (an element which it by no means underrated) and gave it sufficient confidence to confront sorrow and mystery. There ensued a division of life into a higher and lower grade, into form and absence of form, and man was able to take sides with the higher and work for it in his own sphere.

Christianity took up a similar position. Evil was undoubtedly most keenly realised, but the consciousness of being a member (and one who could not be lost) of a moral order dominating the whole world imparted greatness and confidence to man, provided him with full occupation, and braced him to take up with confidence the hard struggle against rank unreason.

It must be obvious to all of us that the Modern World has not, in the main, departed from this point of view. At the back of our belief in our capacity for development there is an actual increase of life and a restless endeavour towards the betterment of human existence. Without such an experience of progress the belief in development would not have stirred our hearts so deeply.

It was thus thoroughly characteristic constructions of life, independent concentrations of life, syntheses of actions (not mere conceptual structures), vital energies, which bore in upon men the conviction that they were connected with the bases of reality and received power from thence, and raised them out of an attitude in which they merely let life slide by them, to place them in a position of activity, and to fill them with joy and courage. This did not do away with the unreasonable element; it appeared rather to increase it. But man had no longer to face it alone and unarmed, he could now co-operate in the construction of reality; his life had now won a meaning and with it a value. He who bears such syntheses in mind will be the less likely to undervalue the attempts of great thinkers, however unsatisfied he may be with the details of their proofs. Life never drew its strength from proofs.

(b) The Perplexities of the Present Situation

To-day this problem takes up a position similar to that occupied by so many others; from so-called possession we have again passed into a state of enquiry and experiment. Each of the above systems of life has been shaken in the most severe manner, its content and its power being alike affected. With regard to the artistic and ethical systems this is obvious, but the idea of progress, too, has lost its former power and glamour— we are not so sure now where the onward movement is going to take us or who is going to profit by it; moreover, its actuality, in the case of the deeper problems of life, has become extremely uncertain. A hollow phraseology often conceals the real core of the matter and lowers its whole level. The life of to-day is not only altogether lacking in firmness and solidarity and in any central dominating purpose; it is devoid of the strength required to master the ever-increasing body of reality, to inwardly assimilate it, and to find a great and conscious purpose in thus transforming existence into activity. This weakness becomes increasingly apparent in proportion as the development of the Modern World brings with it a prodigious increase in the extent and complication of our environment, and causes it to assume a much greater importance in our eyes, and to penetrate more deeply into our beings than it ever did before. Thus the world conquers us more and more, and increasingly reduces us to a position of the merest subordination. Hence all the expansion of life going on around us only brings with it inner weakness and faintness of heart. There is an increasing tendency to pick out from amidst our manifold experiences more particularly everything which reduces the importance of humanity and deprives it of its distinctive character. On every hand it seems that we are being placed rather in the position of victims of fate than in that of masters of material things, beings capable of attaining to an inner relationship with reality. We are depressed not so much by the increase of the external world as by the fact that we have nothing to set up in opposition to it, and this it is which makes us perceive the negative portion of the content of reality rather than any other.

This tendency becomes apparent in the first place in our relationship to the greatness of nature. We are chiefly impressed by its immeasurability, its infinitude in space and time, and its boundlessness in both great and small. Earlier ages were rejoiced and inwardly elevated by the contemplation of this infinite greatness, they were glad to see the boundless fullness of life made manifest in reality;* moreover, they interpreted it as redounding particularly to the glory of man, since thought could lift him outside all narrowing limitations to share in the infinite and the eternal. To-day we do not think so much about the inward presence of infinity as about its presence around us in space and time and its reduction of our whole existence to a vanishing smallness. Human life appears, in fact, to become a matter of absolute indifference. We are told that nothing which occurs on this tiny little planet can possibly have any importance when we consider the innumerable wonders revealed by the scientific work of modern times. The standard is an external one. We know no other.

At the same time nature (in an inward sense) remains secret and aloof; it withdraws its fundamental verities farther and farther from our gaze the more science penetrates into its territory. Earlier ages possessed definite religious or artistic convictions with regard to nature, but we stand in no sort of inner relationship to it. We have no room for any thought other than that of the limitation of humanity; we seem to be confined to a particular sphere and to know no path leading beyond it. If we are thus isolated from these great relationships, it becomes foolish and baseless conjecture, fanciful anthropomorphism, for us to endeavour in any way to understand or interpret nature and its forms. It remains a profound secret, an absolutely insoluble conundrum. It produces innumerable forms, which we can endeavour to comprehend only by employing the analogy of action directed towards an end. But when it comes to the purposes of nature, these seem to contradict and mutually to stultify one another. With most admirable and elaborate care nature prepares a special sort of creature; then, with equal care, it equips another to destroy the first. It appears to negate in one direction what it affirms in another. It stirs up its creatures one against the other, and drives them into a relentless struggle for existence. Units of life are per-

* The classical period of the Ancient World avoided the infinite because it possessed no limits and was incapable of artistic construction. It was Plotinus who first assigned a positive value to the concept.

fected in immense quantities, often by most elaborate and roundabout methods; but they are sacrificed in equally immense quantities. In the midst of the struggle we cannot avoid perceiving the upward trend of life; the construction of the organisms grows more and more complicated, the differentiation of parts becomes more delicate, the activity of the soul continually increases. But within the sphere of nature itself this upward movement seems to result in no real profit. If the highest stage is still merely a stage of self-preservation in the struggle for existence, then, in all essentials, precisely the same object is being achieved as that aimed at on the lower stages, only it is arrived at in a much less direct manner. This is more like retrogression than progress! What a sharp and terrible contrast there is, in this case, between the immense desire for life on the one hand and the complete emptiness of the laboriously attained life on the other. Each individual creature holds fast to existence, and considers no sacrifice of power and passion too great for its maintenance. Yet what does this existence offer to living creatures, what do they gain by it? What is the meaning of the whole process? We find no answer. And because we find none we feel depressed and confused, as soon as we consider the matter as a whole.* Some sort of reason seems to be in control, but it seems bound and limited; nay, it seems continually to be engaged in thwarting itself. We appear to lose sight of it in an immensity of life devoid of inner connection. Further, the doctrine of evolution shows us this mysterious process much more closely knitted together than the people of earlier ages at all realised to be the case; more and more bonds are continually being discovered to unite us to the stages below us; our souls as well as our bodies seem to be dominated by exactly the same forces that direct lower life. Thus our own lives share in the puzzling obscurity of the world around us; a necessity hems us in and drives us before it, and how far it expresses any reason we cannot understand.

But man still retains the power to turn away from nature

* Hence in considering the whole we may well think of the Aristotelian saying: ἡ φύσις δαιμονία, ἀλλ' οὐ θεία (463 b, 14).

and devote himself to culture. He is able to construct a domain of his own in which he shall find his greatness and discover a value in his life. But to-day even this aspect of life, when regarded as a whole, exhibits more complications than clear profit. At the present time it is no longer doubted that culture does not directly satisfy individuals and make them happy. Hence it must ensure them something which goes beyond happiness, though what this is we do not know. It is undeniable that our power over our environment is being continually increased, and at the same time the conditions of human existence are being unceasingly improved; we are carrying on a successful war against pain and necessity, while we have enormously increased onr opportunities for obtaining pleasure. We have even succeeded in prolonging the length of human life. *But all this put together does not give life, considered as a whole, any meaning and value.* Yet every thinking and observing being must inevitably enquire after some such meaning and value. In spite of all its great achievements our modern culture is lacking in that inward concentration of life which, as we have seen, gave humanity something to lay hold of, and the consciousness of standing in an inner relation to reality as a whole, while imparting to life the form of a great and promising task. Consequently it has become impossible for us resolutely to face our perplexities and rise superior to them—perplexities which are found in every type of human culture, and more particularly in that of the present day.

Great complexes result, forces join together and become intertwined; through this joining-up, work frees itself from individual accidents and chances and attains to an independence which enables it to follow its own paths and achieve splendid triumphs. But at the same time the individual increasingly sinks to the position of a mere tool, and the more this occurs the more his soul loses touch with human culture as a whole, the less able he becomes, in working for the latter, to assert a spiritual self. The greatest outward activity, the most breathless acceleration of life, may be combined with an inner indifference, an absence of true power and joy. As a matter of fact, life is split up into a multitude of isolated phenomena and has almost become a stranger to itself. When culture contains no dominating and directing soul it is difficult to prevent the petty human element (which accompanies every cultural development) from growing in rank profusion and making itself felt with unusual force. When we consider, as a whole, the extent to which small and unworthy purposes are commingled with all our endeavours, the complete untruthfulness of the usual human routine (which proclaims high purposes while teaching those concerned to pursue in the first place their own interests) and the manifold vanity which causes every success to redound to the credit of the petty ego, we are liable to experience a strong feeling of disgust with the whole affair. We feel that we are face to face with forces which we dare not allow to overpower us; yet at the same time we do not seem to be able successfully to confront them. Moreover the idea of progress, which for a time seemed to offer a solution, becomes less and less able to provide us with any effective help, for obviously progress does not affect these elementary circumstances; in this sphere, natural desires and passions seem to set a limit to all upward endeavour, a limit of which we cannot cease to be painfully conscious. Thus it cannot be maintained that the man of to-day finds in human culture a satisfactory meaning and value for his life, and that to work for the sake of culture raises him securely above the doubts and necessities of existence.

But human culture does not form an absolute limit to our endeavour. With a bold upward effort, man can raise himself above its entire sphere and take up a position founded upon his own inner life. With this as a basis and occupying himself with the development of a world-embracing personality, he can rise superior to all this confusion and sham and seek to establish a direct relationship with reality. The Stoic philosophers were the first consciously to attempt this; dating from their time this species of thought may be traced as a constant type through the whole of history; it was especially influential during the period of the Enlightenment. By developing a direct relationship with God, religion seeks another method of raising man above all the perplexities of immediate existence. We will not here discuss whether this separation from the world and withdrawal within the individual soul, which is thus recommended, has not its dangers and limitations (it certainly involves a division of existence); we will only ask if it is possible to tread this path to-day. This separation from the visible world and the activities of humanity demands an inner world as its secure possession if it is not to lapse into vacuity. Such an inner world can result only from a direct relationship to a superior power, which may be conceived of as a divinity or a world-reason. But the modern man is no longer sure of the reality of such a power, so that in his case there is no real foundation for an independent inner world, and in its absence there disappears the possibility of achieving an independent position with regard to the visible world and human affairs in general. With this basis gone, the consciousness of personal value becomes an irrational vanity and the concept an empty phrase. Without a domain of independent and original inner life, what has man to set against a world which continually surrounds him with overwhelming power? The specific nature of modern civilisation further increases the feeling of dependence because it binds the work of humanity more and more down to its environment and increasingly renders work and creation mechanical. When the capacity of the individual appears so small and so limited there must ensue a lessening of impulse towards personal activity; moreover, when we are in a less spiritual condition, we seem, in our own opinion, to be even more dependent than we really are; we incline, on every hand, to seek union with others, to obtain their support rather than rely on our own will; without such union we have no feeling of security; in addition, we expect a great deal from the power of common institutions when the chief thing should be the attitude of the individual. In a word, we reduce the energy of life and that without any imperative necessity. When such a mood preponderates can an appeal for independence be expected to be of much avail? *

* This lack of self-confidence, this continual reliance upon others is pertinently described in an article in the *Spectator*, entitled "English Pessimism" (11 August, 1906), where we read (p. 190): "If we were to suggest the spirit which, when we try to correct our pessimism, would be most efficacious, it

Thus the aspect of the whole is far from cheering. We are surrounded and dominated by an impenetrable natural domain; human culture strives to rise above this, but cannot get rid of the antithesis between soulless work and petty human subjectivity, and consequently fails to satisfy our desire for happiness. An increased application of spiritual power might be able to lift us out of this difficulty and give us a secure foundation in our own being; but our capacity does not correspond to our desire, and the attempt to liberate ourselves only leaves us feeling our tied condition more keenly than ever. The unspeakable effort and labour we have put forth does not return to us as pure profit; it seems, indeed, to have no meaning at all, and this affects us especially painfully in our experience of life. The whole construction of our existence seems to force us into seeing that which is inwardly superior dependent upon the lower. It is true that ascending power makes itself felt in our existence, life presses forward and new aspects open up. But that which is new and ascending does not attain to independence, remaining tied to exactly that which it wished to rise above; it is thus frequently held back and its effectiveness paralysed. Is it anything wonderful that such experiences as these (especially when the state of affairs is looked upon as unalterable) should cause deeper souls, in particular, to lose courage and a gloomy pessimism to spread amongst us? We hear much to-day of the joyful acceptation of life, nay, we sing hymns to life; but this tendency is but one of the many inwardly hollow phases of a superficial and temporary thought. It is an artificial affirmation

would be an increase in individual self-reliance. We are not beaten in public affairs as we imagine we are, and there is no necessity in carrying out our works of philanthropy for relying so entirely upon associations. We establish far too many societies. Everybody seems to feel that before he can do anything he needs the protection of a crowd. He cannot even denounce or defend motorcars unless hundreds will join him to protect him from the consequences of thinking independently. The result is that every one who wants to do something good devotes to it some fraction of his mind, some little chip of his energy, and that the strength which we would derive from the strong will of a leader is seldom or never present. We develop some new and small group, not a Loyola or a Wesley. This, always the danger of democracy, is the *d*anger also of the mental processes of our time, and deprives us first and foremost of all help from individual genius."

of life remote from the real foundation of the soul, a kind of glamour in which we may for a time forget an unsatisfying existence.

But any thorough consideration of pessimism must show that it carries a contradiction within itself and cannot possibly be regarded as final. Real pain cannot be felt unless there is something of value to be lost. If all were actually futile and indifferent, then loss and rejection would have no power to affect us. During the latter days of classical antiquity and during the early Christian period it was maintained that evil was not an independent reality, but simply the absence of good: for example, only a man possessed of sight can suffer the misfortune of going blind! This line of argument was used to support the conviction of the certain predominance of good.* However, the difficulty is certainly not quite so easily overcome, because evil is more than a mere deficiency. But it is true that a feeling (and, moreover, a strong feeling) of evil is simply unthinkable in the absence of any counterbalancing element. "Who can be unhappy at not being a king except a dethroned king?" asks Pascal, very pertinently. For example, would people complain so unceasingly as they do about the evanescence of things and the short duration of life if they were really like the insects that are born and die on the same day, if nothing were operative in them which bore within itself the demand for eternal duration?

Thus in the midst of all the troubles and limitations of the age there stands the deep consciousness of our troubles as a valid witness to the fact that man is not completely absorbed in his present situation, that his being contains something which protests against it. Could we so earnestly desire a liberation from the mere routine of civilisation if there were not something within us superior to it? Could the lack of inner relationships and pure objectivity in our culture cause us so much pain as it does if our nature did not demand them? Could the profound obscurity of the world be felt as such a limitation of

* Augustine defended this doctrine with peculiar vigour, especially in the *Enchiridion ad Laurentium de fide, spe et caritate*. According to his definition evil is not *causa efficiens*, but only *causa deficiens*.

our life if we were not intended to stand in some sort of inner relationship to the world? All this can scarcely be said to offer us anything positive, but it serves to convince us that the matter cannot be concluded by a glib negation, that there are many questions lying beyond.

But when we cast our eyes over modern life as a whole it is possible to go a step further. Just as it lies before us, something more is present than is allowed for in the picture drawn for us by a type of thought dominated by the boundless expansion of modern life. Even that which we already possess (not that which we strive towards) contains more than is taken into account in this view and valuation. A life upheld by world-encompassing personality is more to us than a pious but sterile wish; it certainly cannot be attained at a single bound, but we are diligently working towards it and seeking for assistance in our labour. In particular, we are trying to draw nearer to the great historical personalities and to connect our own lives with theirs. Although all this may be imperfect and incomplete, the fact remains that a movement in this direction is undoubtedly in progress.

The limitations of the pessimistic attitude towards culture are even more obvious. It is not true that to-day nothing holds humanity together save the mechanism of work and that we have thus become no more than cogs in a great machine. In the midst of all our disputes we possess a common thought-world (indeed in its absence we could not even dispute!); a common atmosphere surrounds us with spiritual contents and values, and by more closely examining these we become aware of an inner enlargement and elevation of man through culture. We become convinced that in this culture a new stage of reality is arising, that the world is here acquiring an inner relationship and is not merely a juxtaposition of isolated and sometimes opposed elements, and that what is taking place reaches far beyond the aims of mere humanity. Thus even the achievements of the present day cannot possibly be understood as mere products of man's petty ego. The immense progress of science and the untiring formative activity of art are conceivable only as the work of inner necessities, driving men onward and impelling them to creation. No matter how much the petty human element may appear to be concerned in these movements, their superior nature remains a fact. The same may be said of the practical activities of modern life. An age which far surpasses all previous ones in the exhibition of humane feeling and at the same time readily recognises the right of each individual to the development of his spiritual and intellectual powers and to a share in the possession of the goods of life, an age which grants the social idea so much power over men's minds, is by no means altogether, or even predominantly, dominated by mere egoism. This fact is not clearly perceived because the separate phenomena are not adequately comprehended as a whole; but as soon as the main outlines become apparent through the troubled surface of everyday life we are compelled to recognise its truth.

When once we recognise a spiritual world growing up within humanity our whole view of the cosmos changes, and with it our own task in life. Nature no longer constitutes the whole of reality, and the latter acquires a deeper significance. For there can be no manner of doubt that when such a trend towards inwardness takes place the whole of life must be fundamentally more than it would seem to be at first sight. Evolution, too, assumes a different appearance when spiritual life is recognised as being no mere natural product, but a thing which can only result from nature because the latter has behind it a deeper reality. The closer connection between man and nature will then appear rather to elevate nature than to lower man. With such a fundamental change in point of view our work will find itself confronted with fresh tasks. If man, with his spiritual nature, is no mere limited individual being confined to a sphere of his own, but if a world-life works within him, then his quest of knowledge becomes more hopeful. For it may now be asked, Is it not possible to distinguish the petty human element in man from the genuinely spiritual, and cannot a bridge be found from the latter to connect us more closely with the world and make it more of a home for us?

However, we cannot now pursue this line of thought any further. At present we are concerned solely to establish the fact that the pessimistic view of life does not take in the whole of reality, but offers a perspective corresponding to a special condition only, a condition that by no means finally binds us. Our reality contains far more than the average life of the age allows us to perceive.

It must be admitted freely that this "more" has to be linked-up and properly assimilated before it will be equal to overcoming its resistances. This cannot take place, however, until we have succeeded in again attaining to a self-concentration of life, and therewith to a more definite character and to a more active relationship towards reality.* Making use of Dürer's well-known phrase, we may say: "Reason is contained in reality; he who can pluck it forth may possess it." But we cannot thus pluck it forth until we have ourselves united life into a whole and our own inner organs have thereby undergone development.

The positive element in life and reality cannot possibly become a united whole to us without an analysis of existence, a sharper separation of light and darkness, and a conversion of the whole life of man and of humanity into a thorough-going task. Thus, when this path is taken, irrationality does not by any means cease to exist, but we acquire the possibility of becoming inwardly superior to it and thus escaping its paralysing pressure. Where the resistance comes from; why the higher is dragged down towards the lower; why the cycle of the universe should appear indifferent towards that which it itself seems to produce as a goal—these are questions which we men cannot possibly answer. In attempting solutions, religion and philosophy alike have only made the matter still more complicated. It must suffice, and it does suffice, for us to know that something important is proceeding within us; that we are not called upon to play the rôle of passive spectators while the fate of the world is decided over our heads, but that we are able to place ourselves on the side of reason and to labour in its cause. This imparts a certain

* It has already been indicated that the activism which we advocate does not by any means signify a mere devotion to practical reason or even to moral activity.

justification to Vauvenargue's saying: "The world is full of obstacles, as for an active being it must be!" The nearer we again draw to a complete synthesis of life, the more we can regain living courage, the more the inner structure of life will itself be able to offer us a safe support against the irrationality of existence.

If, thus laying hold of deeper relationships in reality, our age must again return to a positive valuation of existence, this is not in any sense optimism, nor does it involve any minimisation of the obscure element in life. In particular, we must recognise no small difference between this attitude towards life and that which prevailed during the height of the German Classical Period: in the latter case, the world was looked upon as a domain of unclouded reason, and man's chief glory was understood to be the artistic contemplation or intellectual comprehension of the cosmic harmony; humanity's first task was to bring to full consciousness that which surrounded us with unconscious activity on every side. For us moderns the problems of nature and of human life have become so acute that we cannot so quickly venture upon a conclusion and thus withdraw from the conflict. But if these increased difficulties in our existence have caused us to lose much, one thing we have gained, and this more than compensates for all that has been lost. We can *ourselves work towards the advancement of the whole*. We have passed from passive contemplation to active co-operation in the work of the great whole.

2. THE RELIGIOUS PROBLEM

(IMMANENCE—TRANSCENDENCE)

A DISCUSSION of the antithesis between immanence and transcendence might involve us in the entire religious problem. We do not propose, however, to do more than briefly refer to the characteristic modern attitude towards this problem (more especially as we have recently published more than one work upon the subject).* It will again be convenient to commence with a discussion of terms.

(a) On the History of the Terms

The now customary juxtaposition of immanent and transcendent does not go back further than the time of Kant.† Until then *immanens* (also *permanens*) and *transiens* stood in opposition to one another: from the thirteenth century onwards an action or a cause was called *immanent* in so far as it remained within the acting subject; *transeunt* in so far as it went beyond to something else.‡ It is in this sense that

---

* See *The Truth of Religion*, trans Dr. Tudor Jones, pub. Williams and Norgate, 1911, and *Christianity and the New Idealism*, trans. Prof. Boyce Gibson, pub. Harpers.

† See, for example, iii. 245 (Hart.): "We will call *immanent* those principles which apply solely within the limits of possible experience; *transcendent* principles, on the other hand, are those which are intended to reach beyond these limits."

‡ Thus Thomas Aquinas, for example, distinguishes an *actio manens* and an *actio transiens*; see Schütz's *Thomaslexikon* under *actio : duplex est actio, una quæ transit in exteriorem materiam, ut calefacere et secare, alia, quæ manet in agente, ut intelligere, sentire et velle*. This continued on into the Modern World. Clauberg puts the matter as follows (*op. omn.* (1691), p. 322): *si ipsius rei, quæ dicitur agere, status mutetur, est actio immanens, sin alterius, est actio transiens*. This distinction, in common with the whole groundwork of

THE RELIGIOUS PROBLEM

we are to understand Spinoza's famous saying that God is the immanent but not the *transeunt* cause of all things.* It means that God does not go outside Himself when He works upon the things, but that He remains by Himself, thus carrying the world within Himself. From this point of view the world is in God rather than God in the world. This only differs from scholastic philosophy in the exclusiveness of the immanence, for the former was quite prepared to recognise an immanent activity parallel with the *transeunt*.

Transcendent and transcendental have another origin. Transcendent (*transcendentia*) was the term applied in the second half of the Middle Ages to the most general properties of things, which, according to the Neo-Platonic doctrine, lie beyond the reach of the particular categories.† From this standpoint there easily resulted a relationship to God as the Being superior to all human concepts. The term was still employed in this sense in the Modern World.‡ Kant then separated transcendent and transcendental and, reversing their

---

the scholastic terminology, is derived from Aristotle. See, for example, *Met.* 1050 a, 24 : τὴν μὲν ἔσχατον ἡ χρῆσις, οἷον ὄψεως ἡ ὅρασις, καὶ οὐθὲν γίγνεται παρὰ ταύτην ἕτερον ἀπὸ τῆς ὄψεως ἔργον, ἀπ' ἐνίων δὲ γίγνεταί τι, οἷον ἀπὸ τῆς οἰκοδομικῆς οἰκία παρὰ τὴν οἰκοδόμησιν. The definite separation between practical and artistic is founded upon this distinction between an action which is directed towards itself and an action which aims at producing a work. With regard to the expression "immanence," we should like to mention, further, a passage from Augustine (*epist.* 268 ad *Nebr.*) quoted by Heman (*Kantstudien*, viii. ; i. p. 58) : *In se habeat hæc tria et præ se gerat, primo ut sit, deinde ut hoc vel illud sit, tertio, ut in eo quod est maneat, quantum potest. Primum illud causam ipsam naturæ ostentat, ex qua sunt omnia. Alterum speciem, per quam fabricantur et quodammodo formantur omnia. Tertium manentiam quandam, ut ita dicam, in qua omnia sunt.*

* *Ethic. pars. I, prop. xviii*: *deus est omnium rerum causa immanens, non vero transiens.* In the fundamental argument we read : *omnia quæ sunt in deo sunt et per deum concipi debent, adeoque deus rerum, quæ in ipso sunt, est causa.*

† As such, according to the *de causis*, are reckoned, in the first place, the four concepts *ens, unum, verum, bonum* ; later, in addition, *res* and *aliquid*. Thus it was customary to speak of a *unitas* or *veritas transcendentalis*, &c.

‡ Thus, for example, Bayle says (*œuv. div.* (La Hague, 1727), iii. 871 a) : *Si l'Origeniste répond que les vertus de Dieu sont transcendentelles, qu'elles ne peuvent point être dans la même categorie que celles de l'homme*. "Transcendental" in the older sense was still employed by Ch. Wolff and Lessing. Lambert called "transcendental" such concepts as "include what is common to the material and spiritual worlds."

meanings, made them instruments of his characteristic mode of thought.*

(b) The Trend of the Modern World towards Immanence

The general development of the Modern World shows a tendency towards immanence, the specific nature of which becomes particularly clear when a comparison is made with the chief movement of Greek civilisation. The experiences derived from its work drove the Greek world further and further beyond the sensuous world. From the outer world, which was the starting-point of the investigation, the chief centre of interest shifted step by step towards the inner world until the closing religious conception of reality (Plotinus) relegated the external world to the position of a mere symbol of an invisible world. The Modern World pursued exactly the opposite path: the religious conviction of the Middle Ages regarded the other world as the true fatherland, and only in its relationship to the other world did this world acquire value; the Modern World, on the other hand, began with the desire to seek the operation of the Divine more within this world, nay, to understand the latter as an expression and reflection of the Divine Being. This resulted, in the first place, in a panentheism, as professed by the noblest spirits of the Renaissance. Soon, however, this developed further, the world becoming more and more the central thing, and the idea of God was employed not so much to reveal a new reality as to give greater depth to the world; consider, for example, the pantheism of Giordano Bruno and Spinoza. Pantheism proved overwhelmingly attractive to the German Classical Period, since it promised to bridge every antithesis and in particular to combine the broadest and freest treatment of the visible world with the open recognition of an invisible one. Such a pantheistic mode of thought was by no means extinct during

---

* On "transcendent" see the second note on p. 462. On "transcendental" he says (*Krit. d. R.V.*, iii. 49; Hart.): "I call all knowledge transcendental which occupies itself, in any way, not so much with objects as with our knowledge of objects in so far as this may be possible *a priori*."

the nineteenth century; but when it fully unfolded its characteristic nature it inclined far more, if not to atheism, at any rate to agnosticism,* to a rejection of all transcendental questions as absolutely insoluble problems.

In practice, both these views result in a life devoid of religion. At first the divine is brought nearer to our existence, then it is closely associated with it, as an inspiring force, and finally it totally disappears or vanishes to an unapproachable distance. Thus religion, which was once an omnipotent power, has become, for the modern man, a thing of quite secondary importance, nay, a mere illusion, and the world of immediate existence has more and more completely absorbed his whole thought and feeling. There is, and has been, of course, no lack of opposition, if only because each older phase tends to resist the phases replacing it. The newer phases have nevertheless not been checked.

Only a superficial consideration can attribute such profound changes merely to the unbelief and evil disposition of individuals. The matter is certainly more deeply rooted, and its causes, which must be sought in the general conditions, demand an impartial appreciation. The older type of religion came sharply into conflict, in the first place, with an essentially altered feeling towards life on the part of humanity. It corresponded with an age when all courage in facing life and all belief in an earthly future was broken, and when men took refuge in religion in order there to find rest, peace, and security. Meanwhile, in the course of centuries, there had arisen in young and robust peoples a new spirit of life; the cry was now for activity, not rest, for boldness, danger, and struggle, rather than security and shelter; the former rejection of the world gave place to a powerful desire to enter into it, for man to test and increase his strength in contact with the world. To this fundamental change of mood must be added the results

* R. Flint gives an exact account of the origin of the term in his excellent work *Agnosticism* (1903). Huxley was the creator of the word "agnostic," and this soon gave rise to "agnosticism." "According to Mr. R. H. Hutton, this latter word (*i.e.* agnostic) was suggested by Professor Huxley at a party held previous to the now defunct Metaphysical Society, at Mr. James Knowles's house on Clapham Common, one evening in 1869, in my hearing. He took it from St. Paul's mention of the altar to 'the unknown God.'" (See Flint, p. 1 ff.)

of a labour which corresponded to it and tended to strengthen it. In every direction the immediate sensuous world became of greater importance to man; it showed him greater depths and revealed in itself a more connected nature; it increasingly affected his conduct and led him to greater achievements. Science shows nature subject to general laws and arranged in fixed relationships: it removes the miraculous element from history and explains it through its own inter-connections. The social life of humanity takes more spiritual tasks upon itself and endeavours, with an immense output of force, to convert our existence into a realm of reason. All these causes have contributed to make this world, more than ever before, man's spiritual as well as his material home. At the same time, man's unique position was threatened in the severest possible manner. For the larger and more independent the world becomes, the more it exhibits laws of its own running through all its activities, the more man, by comparison, becomes insignificant. But when man is thus reduced in importance his characteristic faculties cannot possibly be thought of as grasping reality and bringing it near to the soul. If the world, while being brought outwardly nearer, becomes, in an inward sense, exceedingly remote, then all inner relationship to its foundations must disappear, while all religion threatens to become a mere anthropomorphism and to degenerate into mythology. Moreover, where religion does assert itself it easily slips from the centre of life to the periphery, and from being a natural, almost matter-of-course, conviction it becomes a bold assertion, not to be maintained without serious difficulty. Hence it is no matter for surprise that those who reject everything outside experience and desire to regard every problem from the point of view of immanence raise their voices more and more loudly and find an increasing response. There is probably more antipathy against religion to-day and a more widespread and popular denial of it than has ever been the case before. One regards it as an obstacle in the way of a clear understanding of life, another as a restriction of active force, a third as a suppression of joyous vital feeling; in each case it appears to be a ruinous delusion demanding our every effort for its removal. Is this the final conclusion of the ancient problem, or is it a mere passing wave affecting the present age, a movement which will perhaps produce an effect the exact opposite of that intended?

(c) The Complications in the Concept of Immanence

The main strength of the movement against religion lies in its attack. As soon as it is called upon to show its own capacity and to attempt a positive construction of life on its own account, it becomes involved in complication after complication. That which is offered us as a substitute for religion is usually miserably inadequate, and even this has been grown for the most part upon foreign soil and subsequently imported. The immanent system of life and view of the world is very far, as a rule, from drawing upon pure experience; unnoticed, it idealises experience and compounds it with elements derived from quite a different tendency of thought, namely, the pantheistic. A diluted form of pantheism has mastered the separate spheres of life and is there taken as a matter of course; this pantheism does not generally venture openly to avow itself as such; it prefers to conceal the fashion in which it places things upon a higher plane. Compared with the convictions of Goethe or Spinoza, this lack of clearness stamps it as a deteriorated and sham pantheism. We see it in this degenerate form in a monistic philosophy of nature which unquestioningly spiritualises nature and treats it as a concept of high value; it is again met with in a philosophy of history which considers the mere movements of men in masses to be productive of reason and expresses belief in an evolution towards reason, although the concept of reason has absolutely no foundation in its thought-world; it appears, too, in socio-political movements which treat man, just as he is in the flesh, as noble and great. In every direction we encounter a concealed idealisation of experience, combined with a smoothing away of contrasts, a decay of characteristic spiritual nature, and a soporification of all self-activity.

Moreover, from a scientific point of view the concept of

immanence is not so simple as it usually claims to be. What is this immediate reality that is to completely absorb us? What is real in ourselves? Is it the immediate condition of juxtaposition, exhibited in its complete purity? In this case man becomes split up into nothing more than a bundle of separate sensations; and this is impossible, if only for the simple reason that there is no such thing as an isolated sensation; we only know of sensations attached to an ego—*my* sensations or *your* sensations—not sensations in themselves. We are thus continually compelled to fall back upon the idea of a unity holding the sensations together; a contrast appears in our own sphere and it becomes a question, What is the essence of life? But if the problem reaches so far back, and if a gradation is apparent in ourselves, it is very obvious that exceedingly little is gained by the catchword " immanent."

In the case of the religious problem, in particular, the general tendency of the period goes against the mediæval transcendence, with its duplication of the immediate world, and it no doubt does so with justice; but it by no means follows that our whole life lies upon a single plane. It may be that gradations are necessary, nay a reversal may be necessary, in the sense that what we at first believe to be the secure basis of our life and activity may itself have first to seek support in a more deeply grounded world. What then is the reality which is to comprise our whole life and effort? If we explain it to be the world of immediate sensuous impression, then we place ourselves in sharp opposition to the great pioneers of immanence, Spinoza and Goethe, then we miss the spiritual depth of the whole modern civilisation. The recognition of a reality based upon spiritual life at once gives rise to the question whether this reality at once draws the whole range of life to itself or whether it does not come upon obstacles, within and without, the overcoming, nay the confronting, of which cannot be undertaken without a further strengthening and assistance derived from wider relationships. This system of exclusively immanent reason, with its pantheism, suffers shipwreck more particularly upon the fact of the manifold unreason in human and natural life. For, from this point of view, there are two alternatives only; either the unreason must be minimised, removed as far as possible from sight or explained away, or it must be recognised as a basic element in reality and hence held to be unassailable. Thus we have either a tendency towards optimism, which involves shallowness, or towards pessimism, which means negation and finally despair. We see that things are not so simple as the tendency towards immanence would represent them to be. We must be on our guard against accepting as true a conception of the world because it appears to us, according to our way of looking at things, to be the smoothest and easiest. For what would this be but a new type of anthropomorphism—an exaltation of human will and desire to be the measure of reality?

(d) The Revival of the Religious Problem

Thus, in attempting a construction of life entirely withou the assistance of religion, we are confronted by very serious complications. This alone, however, would by no means hinder such a movement; it is possible for a great deal of confusion and contradiction to be endured if the trend of life is powerful and self-conscious. Now it is impossible to avoid seeing that, to-day, in ·the midst of all the passionate attacks upon religion, the religious problem is again coming to the front; the denial of religion is becoming more and more popular among the masses, but that does not prevent religion arousing a greatly increased amount of thought and passion on the highest level of spiritual and intellectual life. It is a fact that, at a given period, different movements may cut across or oppose one another, and the tendency of the surface-movement may be directly contrary to that of the under-current. In order to assure ourselves of the re-ascent of religion we need only compare our age with the German Classical Period. Religion was then no more than an agreeable adjunct to life; to-day it stands in the very centre of life, produces differences of opinion to the point of the bitterest conflict, makes its voice heard in the treatment of every circumstance, and exerts an immense power alike in affirmation and negation. For the modern denial is not of the kind which calmly shelves religion as something decayed and obsolete; on the contrary, the violently passionate nature of the attack shows clearly enough that religion is still something very real, powerful, and effective. Perhaps even the denial itself frequently signifies not so much a complete rejection of religion as a desire for another and simpler type of religion, more adapted to the needs of the day. At any rate, religion cannot be regarded as a slowly dying light.

To what are we to attribute this sudden change? It can hardly be the fruit of apologetic work, for this is usually preaching to the converted; it may confirm and consolidate, but it is not in its nature to press forward. In reality, the movement is rooted in a *reaction on the part of modern life itself*. Just because this life with its delight in the world has been able to develop itself freely and put forth all its capacity, its limitations, nay its helplessness, with regard to ultimate questions has become clear. It is another case of that indirect method of proof of which the history of humanity provides us with so many examples, a method according to which the indispensability of an assertion is convincingly demonstrated as the result of a negation, of the unrestricted expansion of the opposite assertion. The direction of life towards immediate existence has dispelled much illusion and superstition, awakened much otherwise latent force and advanced and developed this existence in the most manifold fashion. But that which has been accomplished in this direction is predominantly of a peripheral nature; it has improved the conditions of our life but has not deepened life itself. An inward emptiness is thus the final result of all this immeasurable work, and we cannot but look upon all the labour and endeavour as inadequate. The rejection of each and every invisible relationship reduced culture more and more to a merely human culture. This was able to avoid objection so long as a high ideal value was attached to the concept of human being itself and the latter was viewed in a transfigured form.* This, however, took place under the influence of that very mode of thought which is now rejected as a falsification of reality. With its disappearance the transfigura-

* Herder, for example, made of "humanity" an all-embracing, lofty ideal: "Man has no nobler word for his destiny than that which describes himself."

tion must also cease, man must appear in his natural condition without wrapping or adornment and become the sole standard of all truth and goodness. Now, modern life, in particular, with its liberation of every force, has brought to the surface so much that is impure, unedifying, and unworthy, and has placed so clearly before our eyes the pettiness and unreality of a merely human culture, that it becomes continually more and more hopeless to obtain a satisfying type of life upon this basis and to provide human existence with a meaning and a value. It is being increasingly felt that there is something in man which this immanent type of life does not bring out, and that this undeveloped element is something indispensable, perhaps the best of all!

Thus there grows up a desire for an inner transformation of man, for a liberation from the pettiness which fetters and oppresses him. A new age is at hand. The trend is again from a merely humanistic culture to a *transforming spiritual culture*, elevating man's essential being. This necessarily leads to the demand for a new reality and hence towards religion.

In the first instance this gives rise to a highly complicated situation. There is an inner desire for a new type of life and being, but at the same time our understanding and our work tie us down to immediate existence. We should like something higher but can find no path leading to it; yet we cannot surrender the aim. So we are tossed from the one to the other and unceasingly contradict ourselves. But in spite of all incompleteness and discomfort, one thing at any rate has been attained: from a supposed possession we have again come to a search, a diligent and eager search; the ancient and eternal questions come to the front again with fresh force. What further developments the situation will undergo depends upon all sorts of conditions, appertaining both to man and to destiny. The future alone can decide.

(e) The Demands made by the Present Position of Religion

In reviewing the present position of religion we must be peculiarly struck by the fact that a sharp division exists between the traditional ecclesiastical form of religion and a religious movement of a more universal character arising from the aspiration of the age itself. There are many to-day who wish to be religious but are not in the least attracted by ecclesiasticism; they are as much repelled by the Church as they are attracted by religion. The first cause of the foregoing state of affairs is perhaps to be sought in the existence of a wide gap between the traditional form of Christianity and the civilised life of the present day, a gap which makes a mutual understanding in the highest degree difficult. The whole conception of the world has essentially altered, and in particular it has become larger and less exclusively human; the old-fashioned type of feeling appears to the modern man too soft and too colourless; the age calls him to new practical tasks demanding his whole strength. While ancient Christianity attempted to communicate new power and fresh living courage to a tired and intimidated humanity, religion has now to do with a humanity full of strong desire for life and restless activity. The principal factor in the situation, however, and that which more than anything else gives the contradiction its sharpness, is that the age no longer, out of its own experience, comprises life in one question, the answer to which forms the core of Christianity —the question of moral salvation, of the inner liberation and renewal of humanity. Modern activity and creation in the sense-world and the modern feeling of youthful freshness and strength have driven this question into the background as far as modern humanity is concerned. But when the question is no longer asked with full vigour and spontaneity, the answer must fall upon indifferent ears and the right and necessity of the matter become obscured, while, on the other hand, every imperfection in the historical conception will at once leap into prominence and be very apt to determine the valuation. Finally, in the case of the German nation, the dependence of the Church upon the State and the help afforded it by the State have also greatly contributed to an inner alienation of feeling; for with the other Germanic peoples the alienation is seemingly not so great. The action of the newly uprising religious movement in seeking its own paths is therefore easily understood. When we compare it with the older type of religion (which it regards as too narrow and confined), we see that it is striving in the first place towards a greater width, towards the greatest possible universality, towards a greater receptivity with respect to the environing world; it does not trouble so much about the complications in man's inner life as about his relationship to the whole; it aims at bringing the whole inwardly nearer to him, and permitting him to experience its infinity and enjoy its beauty. In such artistic mood a liberation from everything pettily human seems to be achieved and the soul appears to float in blissful security in the pure ether of the cosmos.

Such a resistance to the absorption of man in the merely human, such a desire for the whole, constitutes an essential aspect of religion, and has had an important influence on its history. But it is another question whether that which here manifests itself is capable of solving the whole task of religion, therewith removing and supplanting the entire historical element. If the new were strictly confined to its own capacity and not silently complemented in all sorts of ways by drawing upon the life presented by historical religion, all its width and freedom could not well conceal a great vagueness and hollowness. This kind of religion does not get beyond fine and delicate moods, it attains no genuine actuality. Instead of revealing a new world to man, it does no more than throw a more amiable light upon the existing world, or it surrounds man's life with agreeable moods suitable enough to the pleasant occupation of his spare time, but miserably impotent in the face of the serious realities of life. It will never be possible in this way to achieve a further development of the soul, to liberate forces capable of overcoming necessity and guilt, to offer life a firm foundation, to draw men together by means of an independent inner world. We have here beautiful pictures and beautiful prospects, but pictures which cannot get beyond the stage of mere designs! This æsthetic-pantheistic mood may provide valuable stimulus and serve a useful preparatory purpose, but it is not equal to the chief task of religion; the truth which it contains must be amalgamated with something else and with something more solid if it is to be of real value in the forward movement.

But however inadequate this new type of religion may be, there remains the fact of its opposition to the ecclesiastical form, there remains a division in the religious life and endeavour of the day. Hence the question becomes inevitable : Can we work towards the overcoming of this division, and if so, how? If there is again to be harmony between the age and religion then the age must put a question to religion, and the latter must answer it in a manner which it is possible for the age to accept ; before this can come to pass, however, there must be important alterations, or at any rate further developments, on both sides. The desire of the age for religion will not again become strong and overwhelming until the age recognises great inner complications in human life, makes these into personal experience, and at the same time finds the centre of these complications in the moral problem. On the other hand, religion, too, must not understand and treat the moral problem from the narrow point of view of the immediate impression, but must look upon it as the summit of an all-embracing movement: it will thus itself win a broader basis and escape the particularity which otherwise unavoidably attaches to it. If religion, at this central point, has gained secure contact with the innermost endeavour of the age, and if at the same time it has become clear and secure with regard to its own fundamental fact, then, without danger, it can subject its traditional content to examination that men may see what is essential and unchangeable, what secondary and subject to temporal mutation. Above everything else religion must be powerfully conscious of its own essential nature and take up a firm stand upon this position. Its ultimate object is not to provide man with intellectual information about the world, merely to arouse new feelings or to set new practical tasks ; it is to reveal a *new life*, nay, a new world, and this it does by means of a direct relation to the deepest foundation of being, to the dominating fundamental life-force. It proves the new life, in the first place, through the actuality of its world-wide historical development, through the re-shaping of reality to which it is continually giving rise. It must insist upon the recognition of the life here offered us as the dominating soul of all life, as the indispensable condition of all spirituality. But although this life is fundamentally super-temporal, its development in the human sphere is subject to the conditions of time and history; it must adjust itself with regard to them, and it can do this without losing itself, only when there is a clear distinction made between the substance of this life and its existing form, for then it will be possible to combine substantial unchangeability with a historical development of the form of existence. In this respect the present day is faced with a particularly important and difficult task, namely that of obtaining *a form of religion in the sphere of human existence to correspond with the historical position of spiritual life* (not with the merely superficial tendencies of the age), without, in the process, losing (or even in any way diluting) the substance of religion.*

The creation of such an understanding between Christianity and the Modern World is, however, a more difficult matter than it is frequently thought to be. It is above everything else necessary that there should be a full recognition and valuation of all the great changes that the ages have produced and of the inner necessities which have thus arisen. The usual type of apology does not do this. It does not grasp the matter as a whole, but treats of isolated points; instead of fully entering into the opposite position, it approaches it entirely from the outside; it operates with mere possibilities, showing that the modern movement still leaves certain paths open, which, granted the will to do so, might lead to an agreement with the faith of the Church. In this way it becomes more and more artificial and even exposes itself to the danger of inner untruthfulness. One is reminded of Hume's saying, that an ocean flood cannot be stopped with wisps of straw! Never in this fashion will religion be able to regain the desired position in life as a whole, never in this way

---

* In my works on the philosophy of religion I have explained more in detail why Christianity, in spite of all those elements which are transitory, seems to contain an imperishable core, rendering a breach with it unnecessary. Here I should like merely to add that I can hardly conceive of anything so absolutely foolish as the attempt to elaborate a religion by conscious reflection: in all other spheres we have happily overcome such a mode of thought, with its superficial enlightenment; it is precisely in the most inward region of life, however, where such thought is peculiarly intolerable, that we still need to be on the defensive against it.

will it attain the directness and simplicity, the spiritual nearness, the secure power of conviction, without which its task cannot be performed. It is undeniable that at the present time religion is becoming insecure, and this fact must not be obscured. To-day, the Christian type of life is far from being present to humanity with such convincing nearness as to powerfully influence the whole construction of life and at the same time to be an actual experience and present reality to every individual. When religion is handicapped by so much that is obsolete and foreign, when the eternal truths are often obscured by the debris of thousands of years, religion cannot develop its full power with confidence of victory, it cannot have any axiomatic certainty; it will itself be disquieted even by the most miserably superficial attacks, attacks which would be totally ineffective in the presence of firm and self-experienced conviction. It is thus seen that religion urgently requires a thoroughgoing revision, an energetic demonstration of its dominating characteristics, a rejection of everything which has become withered and decayed. This is necessary, more particularly in its own interest. Such a task as this, however, cannot be successful except in an atmosphere of perfect freedom.

At the same time the substance of religion must be energetically preserved and summoned to powerful manifestation; it must be employed to distinguish between what is genuine and what is not, between reality and sham, in the content of the age. Religion can accomplish nothing important unless it be independent of the mere position of the age. Christianity, in particular, though not absolutely rejecting the immediate world, rejects the idea that it should be accepted as a final conclusion and is hence uncompromisingly opposed to merely human culture, a culture confined to immediate existence, such as now constitutes the leading tendency of modern life. In this case no adjustment of differences is possible; there is room for nothing but a straightforward conflict. It is true that this conflict must be looked upon as leading finally to peace, but it makes an immense difference to the result whether the contrast is shown up in the first place with full clearness or whether it is weakened from the very beginning. In this respect, there is much weak connivance on

THE RELIGIOUS PROBLEM

the Protestant side and much anxious reverence of modern culture, which is regarded as if it were already a complete truth in its whole being and not itself full of difficult problems; there is a fear of decisive negation, as if an affirmation which did not give rise to a negation could be of any value; people lack confidence in their own position and hence naturally enough make no progress. Modesty may adorn a man, but where a cause is concerned it may lead to injustice. A religion dependent upon mere human culture, a religion trailing at the heels of every superficial and temporary movement, is a miserable and invertebrate thing. The desire for more freedom and spontaneity must unite itself to the desire for greater depth. This is quite possible; it only remains for humanity to accomplish it. Thus we see in this case, too, that although the present situation is full of complications and contradictions we are by no means left helplessly at their mercy; on the contrary, by exerting spiritual force we can rise above them.

CONCLUSION

We have journeyed through the different departments of life and thought which have come within the scope of our work and have considered the problems which they offer. We have thereby become convinced of the overflowing fullness of life which pulses through our time; it can be no decrepit age which exhibits such important problems and accomplishes such remarkable work. But considering its spiritual content and its general trend we perceive it to be an essentially incomplete age. The principal cause of this is that our synthetic power does not correspond to the immeasurable wealth of matter which pours in upon us. The concentration of life is far outpaced by its expansion. We have at the same time seen, however, that we are not compelled to accept this state of affairs as if it were decreed by an inevitable destiny; on the contrary, the life of to-day is full of possibilities which can prepare and facilitate a synthesis. It remains for a progressive creative activity to seize these possibilities and make the most of them. We have, moreover, observed that this cannot take place as a direct result of the " given " situation; what is needed is rather that we should rise above this situation, that we should attain to a new standpoint for life, reversing our immediate existence. *If spiritual life becomes independent, then such a reversal is possible, but not otherwise.* All paths have been seen to lead to this same goal. In the case of each separate investigation we saw how the conviction of such an independence on the part of spiritual life altered the problem and prepared the way for its solution.

Following up this line of thought, the study of our own age is seen to lead beyond its own content into the future. We must endeavour to pass from a scattering of energy in multifarious occupations to a central all-embracing task, from contemplative and analytical reflection to creative synthesis, from a prevailing devotion to the external world to more personal and inner life and more inner independence. Philosophy is called upon to co-operate in this work to the best of its ability.

INDEX OF SUBJECTS

Abstraction, 84
Activism, 79 f., 460
Æsthetical view of life, 393 f.
Æstheticism, Modern, 400 f.
Æsthetics and evolution, 262
Agnosticism and term "Agnostic," 464
Altruism and morality, 385-7
Apperception, Wundt's Theory of, 74
Aristocracy and modern life, 376
Art, 55-6, 371, 404 f., 442, 448
    and civilisation, 304; artistic type of civilisation, 292-4
    and evolution, 249-50
    and idealism, 109
    and individualism, 364, 400 f.
    and morality, 393 f.
    and sex, 407
    and spiritual life, 144
Asceticism, 403-4

B

Body and Soul, Problem of, 216 f.

C

Catholicism, 88, 92, 339, 383, 403
Character and personality, 409 f.
Character, Concept of, 422 f.
Christianity, 96, 108, 170, 275, 277, 292, 448-9, 457, 462 f.
    Core of, 472
    and art, 394-5
    and democracy, 375, 377, 380
    and dogma, 67
    and equality, 348
    and evolution, 244 f.
    and free-will, 432

Christianity and intellectualism, 67
    and modern life, 475 f.
    and sex, 403-4
Church and State in Germany, 472
Classic, Nature of the, 322
Civilisation, 281 f., 453 f.
    and character, 426 f.
    and personality, 419 f.
Content, Concept of, 183-4
Co-education, 360
Culture, Human, 281 f.

D

Democracy, 306-7, 374 f.
Descent, Theory of, 257
Design (see Teleology)
Determinism, 431 f.
Discontinuity, Philosophy of, 187, 434
Dualism and Monism, 215 f.
Dynamical view of life, 293-4, 448

E

Economics—
    and democracy, 374 f.
    and law, 206-7
Ego, Nature of the, 52-3
Empiricism, 119 f., 123, 155 f.
Energetics, 181
Energy, Concept of, 271
Enlightenment, 68, 134, 145, 190, 208, 249, 308-9, 316-17, 329, 341, 348, 376, 383, 397, 432
Entelechy, 271
Epicureanism, 295
Epigenesis, 241
Equality—
    of man, 348, 376
    and Christianity, 348
    and society, 359-60, 364

482 INDEX OF SUBJECTS

"Ethic, The New," 401 f.
Ethical view of life, 393 f.
Ethics, 385 f.
Evolution, 180, 227–8, 240 f.
Experience and Thought, 119 f.

F

Feminism, 360
   and the "New Ethic," 401 f.
Free Trade, 178
Free Will Question, 431 f.
French Revolution, 222

G

Genius, Concept of, 368
Germany, Church and State in, 472
Germans—
   and character, 428–9
   and personality, 422
   and politicism, 362, 378
Good, Idea of the, 53
Greek Thought and Civilisation, 37, 66–7, 86–7, 145, 242–4, 287, 393–4, 406, 412, 422–3, 448, 463

H

Hierarchic view of life, 343–4
"Higher," Concept of the, 110
Histology and Society, 179
Historicism, 316 f.
History, 61, 236–7, 308 f., 441
   of philosophy, 96 f., 467
   and evolution, 267–8
   and law, 207 f.
Humanism, 75, 114
   German, 101, 175, 240, 249, 397, 461, 464, 469

I

Idealism, 139, 163
   Need for a new, 113 f.
   and art, 109
   and realism, 99 f.
   and religion, 102
   and society, 347
Identity, Philosophy of, 52
Immanence, 151, 413
   and transcendence, 462 f.

Indian Thought and Civilisation, 137, 417, 419, 437, 448
Individual, Society and the, 341 f.
Individualism, 400 f., 428–9
Individualistic type of civilisation, 363 f.
Intellectualism, 309
   Criticism of, 81 f.
   and Christianity, 67
   and voluntarism, 64 f.

J

Justice, Idea of, 190

K

Knowledge—
   Problem of, 119 f., 132 f., 149 f.
   Theory of, 93 f.
   and spiritual life, 93 f.

L

Law, 195 f.
Liberalism, Modern, 178
Life—
   Problem of, 185 f.
   Value of, 447 f.
Literature, 91, 407–8
Logic, 87

M

Malthusianism, 264–5
Man—
   Nature of; his place in the universe, &c., 60, 274 f., 288, 327, 392, 439 f., 465–6
   Equality of, 348
   The great, 357–9
   and civilisation, 294 f
Manichæism, 403–4
Materialism, 76, 220 f., 227–8, 232 f.
Mechanical and organic views of life, 165 f.
Metaphysics, 119 f., 145 f., 373
   Tendency towards, 141
   Morality and, 143, 388 f.
Microcosmic view of life, 343–4
Middle Ages, 170, 245, 464
   Concept of the, 333–4
Modern, Concept of the, 330 f.
"Moderns" in Literature, 91

Modern World, Characteristics of the, 38-40
Monism, 467
  of to-day, 230 f., 385 f.
  and civilisation, 292-4
  and dualism, 215 f.
  and law, 205
  and metaphysics, 143, 388 f.
  and religion, 474
Mutation, Doctrine of, 257
Mysticism, 244-5, 247-8, 417

N

Naturalism, 139, 227-8, 232 f.
Nature—
  and spiritual life, 184
  and spirit, 216 f.
Neo-Platonism, 38, 344
Nineteenth Century, The, 44
Nominalism, 331
Noölogical Method, The, 56, 61

O

Objective and Subjective, 35 f.
Ontology, 146-7
Optimism, 447 f.
Organic and mechanical views of life, 165 f.
  view of society, 342 f.

P

Pantheism, 249, 313-14, 413, 417, 464, 467
Permanence, Doctrine of, 242 f.
Person, Concept and Term, 409 f.
Personality, 143
  and character, 409 f.
  The, of God, 412-14
Pessimism, 139, 313, 447 f.
Philosophy—
  History of, 96 f., 467
  Right of an independent, 93 f., 129 f.
  Indian and European, compared, 137
  The task of, 93 f.
  and spiritual life, 136 f.
  philosophia perennis, 336
Politicism, 361-2
  and social democracy, 374 f.

Population Question, The, 264-5
Positivism, 45, 111-12, 179, 187, 269
Poverty, Problem of, 381-2
Practical and Theoretical, 64 f.
Pragmatism, 75 f., 79, 80
Pre-formation Theory, The, 241
Protestantism, 68, 92
Psychologism, 45
Psychology, 216 f.
  and law, 202-3
Psycho-physical Parallelism, 226-7

R

Rationalism, 119 f., 123, 155 f., 328
Realism, 309 f.
  and idealism, 99 f.
  and society, 347
Reality, The Problem of, 110
Reformation, The, 92, 348, 432
Religion, 265, 372-3, 462 f.
  and art, 394
  and civilisation, 289, 292
  and evolution, 244 f.
  and history, 316
  and idealism, 102
  and life, 108
  and modernity, 337
  and monism, 232 f.
  and morality, 474
  and personality, 417-18
  and philosophy, 138
  and socialism, 378-9
  and social life, 363
  and spiritual life, 144, 474 f.
Rights of Man, 348
Ritschlianism, 46-9
Romans, Creative Inactivity of the, 362
Romanticism, 250, 266, 285, 310-11, 346, 398

S

Scholasticism, 86 f., 172, 409, 463
Selection, Theory of, 257 f.
Self-development, Modern Theory of 402 f.
Sex—
  and art, 407
  and modern individualism, 403-4
  and religion, 403-4

Spirit and Nature, 216 f.
Spiritualism, 76, 224 f.
Spiritual Life—
   Nature of the, 57 f., 132 f., 141 f., 149 f., 229, 235 f., 273 f., 298 f, 302 f., 322-3, 479-80
   and civilisation, 298 f., 302 f.
   and evolution, 260 f., 273 f.
   and history, 315 f.
   and human life, 459
   and knowledge 93, f.
   and law, 201
   and the modern world, 193
   and morality, 390-2
   and nature, 184
   and personality, 414 f.
   and the state, 361-2
Social type of civilisation, 351 f.
Social Democracy, 374 f.
Socialism, 222, 341 f., 374 f.
Society—
   Structure of, 189 f.
   and the individual, 341 f.
Sociology, 205-6, 467
Soul—
   Neglect of, in realism, 107
   and body, 216 f.
Sovereign Method, The, 56, 421
State—
   Power of the, 349-50
   in modern life, 361-2
   and democracy, 374 f.
   and church, 472
Stoic Thought and Influence, 38, 49, 66, 119 170, 196, 248, 290, 394, 412, 25, 431-2, 435, 454

Subjective—Objective, 35 f.
Subjectivism, 45 f., 366 f., 401 f.
Summation of Reason, Doctrine of the, 355 f.
Syntheses of Life, 134 f.
Synthesis of Life, Need for a new, 479-80

T

Talent, Concept of, 368
Teleology, 165 f., 175
Theoretical and Practical, 64 f.
Thought and Experience, 119 f.
Transcendence and Immanence, 462 f.
Truth—
   Concept of, 53, 62
   Quest of, 89

U

Utilitarianism, 74, 295

V

Values, Philosophy of, 49 f.
Vitalism, 185 f.
Voluntarism, 70 f.
   and intellectualism, 64 f.

W

Weismannism, 257
Will—
   Freedom of the, 431 f.
   (Voluntarism), 70 f.

INDEX OF NAMES*

A

Abelard, 175
Alanus de Insulis, 245
Alexander the Great, 287
Alexander of Hales, 332
Albert of Saxony, 120
Albertus Magnus, 120, 332
Anaxagoras, 121
Aquinas, Thomas, 65, 71, 102, 146, 241, 332, 409, 463
Aristotle, 37, 65, 66, 84, 120, 121, 146, 147, 165, 167, 168, 169, 171, 188, 191, 192, 196, 218, 242-3, 245, 248, 271, 287, 331, 344, 355-6, 372, 412, 423, 431, 452, 463
Arrhenius, 255
Augustine, 67, 97, 102, 108, 197, 247, 358, 374, 395, 413, 432, 435, 448, 457, 463
Avenarius, 52
Avianensis, Abbot Benedict, 331

B

Bach, 397
Bacon, Francis, 162, 281
Bacon, Roger, 332
Baerwald, R., 330
Barclay, J , 330
Baumgarten, 36, 174
Bayle, P., 36, 69, 215, 233, 282, 431, 462
Bergson, Henri, 185, 186, 188, 258, 434
Berkeley, Bishop, 36, 99, 100, 174
Bernheim, 210, 334
Bichat, 179
Boethius, 341, 409
Bohme, Jakob, 240

Bopp, 203
Bossuet, 282
Boutroux, E., 186-7, 434
Boyle, Robert, 158, 166, 173, 220
Brucker, 447
Bruno, Giordano, 200, 220, 248, 344, 464
Burckhardt, J., 371, 443
Busch, J., 332

C

Caldwell, 447
Cambray, Otto, Bishop of, 331
Carlyle, Thomas, 209
Carneades, 412
Cassiodorus, 331
Cellarius, 334
Chamberlain, Alex., 411
Chauvin, 36
Cicero, 241, 341, 343
Clauberg, B., 146, 197, 251, 409, 463
Coelius, 423
Comte, 119, 187, 199, 205, 208, 269, 348, 357, 385-6, 405
    Criticism of, 111-12
    and intellectualism, 83
    and society, 179
Cousin, Victor, 405
Cromwell, Oliver, 318
Cudworth, 175

D

Dante, 327
Darwin, Charles, 121, 227-8, 251, 257-8
de Maistre, 177
Delbruck, 203
Democritus, 169, 173, 196, 344
Descartes, 36, 99, 121, 166, 173, 203, 217-18, 220, 250, 273, 348

* The more important references are in thick type.

INDEX OF NAMES

Dewey, 75
Dilthey, 127, 330, 423
Dionysius, 247
Dionysius, Pseudo, 241
Duns Scotus, 35, 67, 71
Dürer, A., 460

E

Eckhardt, 409
Empedocles, 253
Eratosthenes, 287
Eucken, Rudolf
  Introduction to his philosophy, 53 f.
  his Activism, 79 f.

F

Fichte, 65, 101, 284, 286, 348, 398, 411
Firmianus, Pater, 330
Flint, R., 464
Frederick the Great, 69
Fries, 49
Froebel, 150

G

Galen, 245
Gellert, 424
Gidionsen, 271
Gierke, 190
Goclen, 36
Goethe, 37, 53, 55, 56, 144, 227, 240, 271, 283, 248, 327, 347, 358–9, 360, 368, 420, 467–8
  and idealism, 101
  and morality, 397–8
Goetze, 36
Gottsched, 36, 121
Goyan, 334
Gregory of Nyssa, 395
Grotenfeldt, A., 312

H

Hagedorn, 240
Harms, 65
Hartmann, Ed. v., 257
Haugwitz, 240
Hegel, 69, 84, 90, 131, 153, 208, 216, 224, 250, 254, 257, 269, 295, 310–11, 326, 350
  his system, 43–4

Herbart, 49, 87, 100, 131, 150, 185, 203, 226, 346, 410
Herder, 168, 240, 283, 470
Herennius, 146
Hildebrand, R., 368, 424
Hirzel, R., 196
Hobbes, 206
Höffding, H., 187, 431
  and problem of values, 49
Hosea, 290
Hume, David, 187, 237–8, 475
Husserl, 46, 157, 204
Huxley, 464
Hyde, T., 215

I

Ihering, 326, 345
Isaiah, 290
Iselin, 282

J

Jacobi, 168, 413
James, William, 127
  and pragmatism, 75 f., 79
Jerusalem, W., 75, 79
Jesus, 394–5 (see Christianity)
John, Saint, Gospel of, 170
John of Salisbury, 170, 332

K

Kant, 49, 50, 55, 84, 87, 110, 114, 119, 130, 134, 146, 147, 158, 167, 168, 169, 175–6, 187, 191, 193, 199, 234, 240, 241, 261, 273, 283, 284, 285, 300, 346, 359, 388, 397, 424–5, 432, 436, 462–3
  and problem of subject and object, 40 f.
  and spiritual life, 59
  and practical reason, 65
  and problem of knowledge, 69
  and voluntarism, 71 f.
  and idealism, 100
  and problem of knowledge, 121 f.
  and the moral law, 205
  and personality, 411
Kepler, 282
Key, Ellen (the "New Ethic"), 401 f.
Klopstock, 285
Kurth, G., 334

INDEX OF NAMES

L

La Bruyère, 424
Lamarck, 252, 258, 348
Lambert, 120, 462
Lamprecht, 210, 330
Lange, F. A., 221
Lavater, 368
Leibniz, 81, 87, 97, 99, 124, 145, 167, 172, 174, 182, 203, 208, 215, 224, 228, 231, 241, 248, 249, 282, 320, 336, 342, 344, 410, 432, 447
  and problem of knowledge, 120
Lessing, 36, 121, 167, 462
Lichtenberg, 387
Locke, 68, 84, 99, 190, 206, 251
Lodge, Sir Oliver, 186, 188, 258
Lorenz, 264–5
Lotze, 49, 178, 182, 191, 271–2, 414
Lucretius, 197
Luther, Martin, 68, 121, 193, 332, 346, 358, 397, 435
  his spiritual power, 92

M

Mach and philosophy of identity, 52-3
Maistre, de, 177
Malthus, 200, 264–5
Marcus Aurelius, 170, 372
Marx, Karl, 207, 255
Meinong, 49, 431
Melancthon, 68
Michael Angelo, 396
Mignot, Archbishop, 253
Montesquieu, 202, 264, 282, 349
Müller, Adam, 177
Müller, A. F., 36
Müller, Max, 409
Munsterberg, 50, 51

N

Newman, Cardinal, 206-7, 253
Newton, Sir Isaac, 199
Nicholas of Cusa, 49, 241, 248, 344
Nietzsche, 360
  incongruity of his works, 91
  and metaphysics, 373

Norström, Vitalis—
  and the "New Ethic," 403
  and art, 406

O

Occam, 332
Ostwald, 181
Otto, Bishop of Cambray, 331

P

Pascal, 69, 200, 402, 457
Paul, 210
Paul, Saint, 432
Paulsen, 64
Perrault, 333
Pestalozzi, 285, 346, 381-2, 427
Petrus Nigri, 100
Pierce, C., 75
Plato, 37, 81, 99, 100, 145, 196, 243, 248, 287, 368, 382, 394, 412
Plattner, 42
Plotinus, 43, 66, 71, 131, 344, 394, 412, 451, 464
Polybius, 248
Porphyry, 342
Pöschmann, 49
Prantl, 35
Priscianus, 331
Pseudo-Dionysius, 241

Q

Quetelet, 206, 348

R

Rabener, 424
Reischle, 253
Renouvier, 187
Rhodius Andronicus, 146
Rickert, 210
Ritschl, 414
Rousseau, J. J., 290, 346, 348, 355
Roux, 181, 186, 189
Rüdiger, 175

S

Saint-Simon, 168
Sauppe, 423
Schelling, 64, 176, 177, 250, 444
  and intellectualism, 83

INDEX OF NAMES

Schiller, 75, 100, 333, 398
Schlegel, F., 203, 346
Schleicher, 203
Schleiermacher, 110, 205, 286, 346
Schopenhauer, 69, 359, 447
Scotus Erigena, 121, 241, 247
Seneca, 341
Sigwart, 200, 204
Simon de Brion, 332
Sleidan, 334
Smith, Adam, 178, 190, 282, 377
Spencer, Herbert, 121, 188, 252-3, 258
Spinoza, 81, 167, 203, 226-7, 350, 412-13, 417, 432, 435, 447, 462, 464, 467-8
   and problem of subject and object, 40 f.
Socrates, 342
Steffensen, B., 141, 209
Steuco, A., 336
Stieler, 240
Strabo, 287
Suarez, 168

T

Taine, 348
Tetens, 240
Theophrastes, 422-4
Thomasius, J., 342
Tönnies, 64

Trendelenburg, 65, 184, 336, 409, 412
Tröltsch, 208
Turgot, 282

V

Vauvenargue, 461
Vico, 208
Volkelt, 262
Voltaire, 447

W

Walch, 330, 410, 413
Weismann, 257
Whitney, 203
Windelband, 50, 157, 204, 210, 434
Wlassak, 52
Wolff, B., 120
Wolff, Ch., 65, 87, 97, 99, 100, 121, 146, 166, 167-8, 174, 203, 215, 216, 241, 248, 410, 462
Wolff, F. A., 101, 285
Wundt, 64
   and apperception, 74

X

Xenophon, 196

Z

Zeller, 205, 413
Zesen, 409

CPSIA information can be obtained
at www.ICGtesting.com
Printed in the USA
FSOW02n2021250417
33565FS